STUDIES IN ANTIQUITY AND CHRISTIANITY

The Roots of Egyptian Christianity
Birger A. Pearson and James E. Goehring, editors

Gnosticism, Judaism, and Egyptian Christianity
Birger A. Pearson

Ascetic Behavior in Greco-Roman Antiquity: A Sourcebook
Vincent L. Wimbush, editor

Elijah in Upper Egypt: "The Apocalypse of Elijah"
and Early Egyptian Christianity
David Frankfurter

The Letters of St. Antony: Monasticism and the Making of a Saint
Samuel Rubenson

Women and Goddess Traditions: In Antiquity and Today
Karen L. King, editor

Ascetics, Society, and the Desert:
Studies in Early Egyptian Monasticism
James E. Goehring

STUDIES IN ANTIQUITY AND CHRISTIANITY

The Institute for Antiquity and Christianity
Claremont Graduate School
Claremont, California

STUDIES IN ANTIQUITY & CHRISTIANITY

Ascetics, Society, and the Desert

*Studies in
Early Egyptian
Monasticism*

James E. Goehring

TRINITY PRESS
INTERNATIONAL
HARRISBURG, PA

Cover art: An etching found in a rock wall in the Wadi Sheikh Ali in Upper Egypt. Photograph by James E. Goehring.

Coin image: The J. Paul Getty Museum, Malibu, California. Hellenistic Greek, Tetradrachm, 323–281 B.C., silver. Used with permission.

Copyright © 1999 by The Institute for Antiquity and Christianity

Trinity Press International, P.O. Box 1321, Harrisburg, PA 17105
Trinity Press International is a division of the Morehouse Group.

Library of Congress Cataloging-in-Publication Data
Goehring, James E., 1950-
    Ascetics, society, and the desert : studies in Egyptian
monasticism / James E. Goehring.
        p.   cm. – (Studies in antiquity and Christianity)
    Includes bibliographical references and index.
    ISBN 1-56338-269-5 (pbk. : alk. paper)
    1. Monasticism and religious orders – Egypt – History. 2. Egypt –
Church history. I. Title. II. Series.
BR190.G64 1999
271′.00962 – dc21   99-20626

Printed in the United States of America

99   00   01   02   03   10   9   8   7   6   5   4   3   2   1

FOR LINDA

Fair, kind, and true have often lived alone,
Which three till now never kept seat in one.
— WILLIAM SHAKESPEARE

Contents

Part Two
ASCETIC ORGANIZATION AND
IDEOLOGICAL BOUNDARIES

Part Three
PACHOMIAN STUDIES: THE LATER YEARS

Foreword

As project director for the Roots of Egyptian Christianity research project of the Institute for Antiquity and Christianity (IAC) in Claremont, California, I am pleased to see the publication of this book on Egyptian monasticism as the sixth volume in the Roots of Egyptian Christianity subseries of the institute's series, Studies in Antiquity and Christianity. This particular volume gives me special pleasure because its author, James E. Goehring, a former student of mine, worked very closely with me in organizing the international conference, "The Roots of Egyptian Christianity," sponsored by the National Endowment for the Humanities and held in Claremont in September 1983. The inaugural volume of our series, containing most of the essays presented at the aforementioned conference (including one by him), was jointly edited by Goehring and myself and published in 1986 as *The Roots of Egyptian Christianity*. So it is fitting, indeed, that the subsequent work that Goehring has done on Egyptian asceticism should appear as a volume in the series that he helped to inaugurate.

The Roots of Egyptian Christianity Project of the institute is devoted to research in the history of Christian Egypt from the beginnings of Christianity in Alexandria in the first century to the Arab conquest in the seventh. The present volume focuses on one of the most important features of early Egyptian Christian history, monasticism and asceticism as practiced and lived not only in the Egyptian desert but also (as the author so convincingly argues) in Egyptian cities and towns.

BIRGER A. PEARSON

Director, Roots of Egyptian Christianity Project, IAC
Professor Emeritus of Religious Studies
University of California, Santa Barbara

Preface

This book is the sixth volume to appear in conjunction with the Roots of Egyptian Christianity Project of the Institute for Antiquity and Christianity of Claremont Graduate School. I wish to thank the members of the institute's research council, Institute Director James M. Robinson, and Roots of Egyptian Christianity Project Director Birger Pearson for consideration and acceptance of the volume in the institute's Studies in Antiquity and Christianity Series. It seems right that these essays should appear in this series. Before I left Claremont in 1985, I was involved in the formative years of the Roots of Egyptian Christianity Project as its associate director. I participated in the organization and success of the project's inaugural conference, selected papers from which, edited by Birger Pearson and myself, became the first volume in the institute's Studies in Antiquity and Christianity series. My participation in the project and conference gave impetus and new direction to my research which has since led down various paths to the articles in this book. On a more personal note, it is also a pleasure for me that this collection of essays will appear as a Roots of Egyptian Christianity Project publication alongside Birger Pearson's 1990 volume of collected essays (*Gnosticism, Judaism, and Egyptian Christianity*). This is not only because I served with him as associate director during the project's formative years, but also because of my respect for him first as my teacher at the University of California at Santa Barbara and since as a colleague and friend.

The publication of this volume would not be possible without the kind permission of the editors or publishers in whose journals and books most of the essays first appeared. I thank them for their willingness to allow me to use previously copyrighted materials: the Yamamoto Shoten Publishing House and Wayne State University Press, publishers of *Eusebius, Christianity, and Judaism* ("Origins of Monasticism"); Polebridge Press, publishers of *Gnosticism and the Early Christian World: In Honor of James M. Robinson* ("The

World Engaged: The Social and Economic Context of Early Egyptian Monasticism"); *Semeia* ("Through a Glass Darkly: Diverse Images of the Ἀποτακτικοί[αί] in Early Egyptian Monasticism"); *Journal of Early Christian Studies* ("The Encroaching Desert: Literary Production and Ascetic Space in Early Christian Egypt" and "Monastic Diversity and Ideological Boundaries in Early Christian Egypt"); *Harvard Theological Review* ("Withdrawing from the Desert: Pachomius and the Development of Village Monasticism in Upper Egypt"); *Le Muséon* ("Pachomius' Vision of Heresy: A Study of the Development of a Pachomian Tradition"); Fortress Press, publishers of *The Roots of Egyptian Christianity* ("New Frontiers in Pachomian Studies"); Peeters Press, publishers of *Studia Patristica* XXV ("Melitian Monastic Organization: A Challenge to Pachomian Originality"); and the Institute for Antiquity and Christianity, publishers of Occasional Papers 15 ("Chalcedonian Power Politics and the Demise of Pachomian Monasticism").

Research requires support. Much of the research and many of the articles contained in this volume were made possible through the financial support of various institutions. I am indebted to them all: the Corpus dei Manoscritti Copti Letterari, for a grant permitting work with Tito Orlandi in Rome in 1980; the National Endowment for the Humanities, for a travel grant (1986) and two summer stipends (1987 and 1993); the Alexander von Humboldt Foundation, for a fellowship allowing me to spend a fruitful year at the Göttingen Academy of Sciences in 1989–90; and Mary Washington College for a series of Faculty Development Grants between 1986 and 1996.

While financial support allows for the time and travel necessary to conduct one's research, it is the support of and discussions with colleagues and friends that nourishes it and makes it grow. For a series of articles spanning some seventeen years, the list is long indeed. Here I can only name a few of the many whose work, support, and friendship have influenced me along the way. Any such list must include at the start Birger Pearson, Ekkehard Mühlenberg, and James Robinson, first as teachers and then as friends and colleagues. I wish especially to acknowledge Ekkehard Mühlenberg, who brought me to the Academy of Sciences in Göttingen in 1979–81 as a research associate to produce a critical edition of the *Letter of Ammon* and again served as my sponsor in 1989–90 when I returned on an Alexander von Humboldt Fellowship. Both occasions allowed my research to flourish. I would also like to acknowledge Tito Orlandi, who supported my work in Rome in 1980 and has remained a good colleague and friend. Since my move to Mary Washington College in Virginia, I have benefited greatly from the friendship and support of Elizabeth Clark. Her work and her kindness are much appreciated. David Johnson has likewise been a very supportive colleague. In the late 1980s and early 1990s, my research was shaped in the context of the Project on Ascetic Behavior in Greco-Roman Antiquity. I wish to thank Vincent Wimbush, who envisioned and directed this project, and the many individuals who participated in it over the years. I have learned much from them. In particular, I want to acknowledge and thank Teresa Shaw and Richard Valantasis, whom I met in the context of the project and who have remained valuable conversation partners and in the process become good friends. More recently, I have enjoyed and benefited from the ideas and friendly challenges of Douglas Burton-Christie. I also wish to thank my colleagues, past and present, in the Department of Classics, Philosophy, and Religion at Mary Washington College. While they do not share my fascination with the late antique world and things ascetic, their friendship and support have created a most pleasant environment in which to accomplish my work. Thanks must also go to Carla Bailey of Mary Washington College's Simpson Library, who tracked down many an obscure text for me through interlibrary loan. I want also to thank those who helped shepherd this volume through the publication process. Jon Asgeirsson, associate director of the Institute for Antiquity and Christianity, served as my liaison with the institute and helped guide the project through the institute's Research Council. Jon also took on the task of identifying Claremont University graduate student Ruben R. Dupertuis to produce the indexes. I am very grateful to Jon for his support and to Ruben for the work on the indexes. I also wish to thank Tim Vivian, who graciously alerted me to a number of mistakes during the final stages of the publication process. His careful eye has certainly improved the final product. Lastly I want to express my deep appreciation to Hal Rast and his fine staff at Trinity Press. They were knowledgeable, sensitive to my concerns, and always easy to work with. Volume editor John Turnbull and typesetter John Eagleson, in particular, did a marvelous job with the details and thereby saved me from numerous errors.

Finally, and most importantly, I wish to thank my family, Linda, Nate, and Matt, in whose love and friendship I am grounded. They have supported me through my bouts with the asceticism of scholarship that produced this book, and their company on walks, canoe trips, mountain hikes, and fly-fishing ventures nourished me along the way. I want, in particular, to thank my wife Linda for her constancy, her kindness, and her humor. Her love is no asceticism at all. It is to her that I dedicate this volume.

Abbreviations

GENERAL

AB	*Analecta Bollandiana*
ACW	Ancient Christian Writers
Aeg	*Aegyptus: Rivista italiana di egittologia e di papirologia*
AegT	Aegyptiaca Treverensia
AmSP	American Studies in Papyrology
AnMG	Annales du Musée Guimet
APVG	*Archiv für Papyrusforschung und verwandte Gebiete*
Aug	*Augustinianum*
BA	*Biblical Archaeologist*
BASP	*Bulletin of the American Society of Papyrologists*
BCNH	Bibliothèque copte de Nag Hammadi
BGAMB	Beiträge zur Geschichte des alten Mönchtums und des Benediktinerordens
BHEL	Bibliotheca historico-ecclesiastica Lundensis
BIAB	*Bulletin de l'institut archéologique bulgare*
BIFAO	*Bulletin de l'institut français d'archéologie orientale*
BMus	Bibliothèque du Muséon
BRHE	Bibliothèque de la revue d'histoire ecclésiastique
BSAC	*Bulletin de la société d'archéologie copte*
ByzA	Byzantina Australiensia
ByzM	*Byzantina Metabyzantina*
ByzZ	*Byzantinische Zeitschrift*
CBM	Chester Beatty Monograph
CCR	*Coptic Church Review*
CistStud	Cistercian Studies

ColCist	*Collectanea Cisterciensia*
COr	Cahiers d'orientalisme
CQ	*Congregational Quarterly*
CRAI	*Comptes rendus des séances de l'Académie des inscriptions et belles-lettres* (Paris)
CSCO	Corpus scriptorum christianorum orientalium
CSEL	Corpus scriptorum ecclesiasticorum latinorum
CWS	Classics of Western Spirituality
EA	*Erbe und Auftrag*
EH	Europäische Hochschulschriften
GCS	Griechischen christlichen Schriftsteller
GöM	*Göttingen Miszellen*
HDR	Harvard Dissertations in Religion
HR	*History of Religions*
HTR	*Harvard Theological Review*
JAC	*Jahrbuch für Antike und Christentum*
JEA	*Journal of Egyptian Archaeology*
JECS	*Journal of Early Christian Studies*
JEH	*Journal of Ecclesiastical History*
JÖB	Jahrbuch der österreichischen Byzantinistik
JRomS	*Journal of Roman Studies*
JSSEA	*Journal of the Society for the Study of Egyptian Antiquities*
JTS	*Journal of Theological Studies*
LCL	Loeb Classical Library
LSJ	*A Greek-English Lexicon,* compiled by Liddell, Scott, and Jones
LTP	*Laval théologique et philosophique*
MC	Miscellanea Coptica
Mémoires	Mémoires publiés par les membres de la mission archéologique française du Caire
MisCath	*Missions catholiques*

MPER	Mitteilungen aus der Sammlung der Papyrus Erzherzog Rainer (new series)
MünSt	Münsterschwarzacher Studien
Mus	*Muséon*
NAPSMS	North American Patristic Society Monograph Series
NARCE	*Newsletter of the American Research Center in Egypt*
NAWG	Nachrichten der Akademie der Wissenschaften in Göttingen (Philologisch-historische Klasse)
NFAQJ	*Numismatic Fine Arts Quarterly Journal*
NHMS	Nag Hammadi and Manichaean Studies
NHS	Nag Hammadi Studies
NovT	*Novum Testamentum*
NumC	*Numismatic Chronicle*
OCM	Oxford Classical Monographs
OECS	Oxford Early Christian Studies
OLP	*Orientalia Lovaniensia periodica*
OP	Occasional Papers
Or	*Orientalia* (Rome)
PatrS	Patristica Sorbonensia
PCol	Papyrologica Coloniensia
PG	J.-P. Migne, *Patrologia graeca*
PL	J.-P. Migne, *Patrologia latina*
PO	Patrologia orientalis
PTS	Patristische Texte und Studien
PW	Pauly-Wissowa, *Real-Encyclopädie der classischen Altertumswissenschaft*
RAC	*Reallexikon für Antike und Christentum*
RAM	*Revue d'ascetique et de mystique*
RE	*Realencyklopädie für protestantische Theologie und Kirche*
REG	*Revue des études grecques*
RevOC	*Revue de l'orient chrétien*

RHE	*Revue d'histoire ecclésiastique*
RHR	*Revue de l'histoire des religions*
RSR	*Religious Studies Review*
SAC	Studies in Antiquity and Christianity
SBT	Studies in Biblical Theology
SC	Sources chrétiennes
SEA	Studia Ephemeridis Augustinianum
SH	Subsidia hagiographica
SP	*Studia Patristica*
SPAW	Sitzungsberichte der preussischen Akademie der Wissenschaften (Philosophisch-historische Klasse)
SpO	Spiritualité orientale
StAns	Studia Anselmiana
STGL	Studien zur Theologie des geistlichen Lebens
SVS	*Supplément de la vie spirituelle*
TAPA	*Transactions of the American Philological Association*
TCH	Transformation of the Classical Heritage
TDSA	Testi e documenti per lo studio dell'antichità
ThLZ	*Theologische Literaturzeitung*
TM	*Travaux et mémoires*
TPL	Textus patristici et liturgici
TU	Texte und Untersuchungen
VC	*Vigiliae christianae*
VetChr	*Vetera Christianorum*
YCS	Yale Classical Studies
ZDMG	*Zeitschrift des deutschen morgenländischen Gesellschaft*
ZKG	*Zeitschrift für Kirchengeschichte*
ZNW	*Zeitschrift für die neutestamentliche Wissenschaft*
ZPE	*Zeitschrift für Papyrologie und Epigraphie*
ZSavR	*Zeitschrift der Savigny-Stiftung für Rechtsgeschichte (kanonistische Abteilung)*

ANCIENT SOURCES

Pachomian Sources

Ag	Arabic *Life of Pachomius* (Göttingen Universitätsbibliothek MS 116)
Am	Arabic *Life of Pachomius,* translated in Amélineau, *Monuments au IVe siècle*
Av	Arabic *Life of Pachomius* (Vatican Library Arabic MS 172)
Bo	Bohairic *Life of Pachomius*
G1	Halkin's *Vita prima.* First Greek *Life of Pachomius*
G3	Halkin's Third Greek *Life of Pachomius*
S1	Lefort's Sahidic Codex 1: *Life of Pachomius*
S2	Lefort's Sahidic Codex 2: *Life of Pachomius*
S3	Lefort's Sahidic Codex 3: *Life of Pachomius*
S3b	Lefort's Sahidic Codex 3b: *Life of Pachomius*
S5	Lefort's Sahidic Codex 5: *Life of Pachomius*
S6	Lefort's Sahidic Codex 6: *Life of Pachomius*
S7	Lefort's Sahidic Codex 7: *Life of Pachomius*
S21	Lefort's Sahidic Codex 21: Letter of Theophilus to Horsiesius
SBo	Veilleux's reconstructed Bohairic *Life of Pachomius* (Veilleux, *Pachomian Koinonia,* 1.1–4)

Papyri

BL Or	British Library, Oriental Manuscripts
CLT	*Ten Coptic Legal Texts* (A. Arthur Schiller)
CPR	*Corpus Papyrorum Raineri*
P. Berl.	*Berlin Papyrus, Staatliche Museen zu Berlin*
P. Berl. Leihg.	*Berliner Leihgabe griechischer Papyri*
P. Cair.	*Greek Papyri. Catalogue général des antiquités égyptiennes du Musée du Caire*
P. Coll. Youtie	*Collectanea papyrologica: Texts Published in Honor of H. C. Youtie*
P. Flor.	*Papiri greco-egizii, Papiri Fiorentini*
P. Giss.	*Griechische Papyri im Museum des oberhessischen Geschichtsvereins zu Giessen*

P. Herm.	*Papyri from Hermopolis and Other Documents of the Byzantine Period*
P. Herm. Land.	*Zwei Landlisten aus dem Hermupolites* (*P. Giss. 117 und P. Flor. 71*)
P. Köln	*Kölner Papyri*
P. Lips.	*Griechische Urkunden der Papyrussammlung zu Leipzig*
P. Lond.	*Greek Papyri in the British Museum*
P. Neph.	*Das Archiv des Nepheros und verwandte Texte* (Kramer and Shelton)
P. Oxy.	*The Oxyrhynchus Papyri*
P. Würzb.	*Mitteilungen aus der Würzburger Papyrussammlung*
SB	*Sammelbuch griechischer Urkunden aus Aegypten*

SHORT TITLES OF FREQUENTLY CITED WORKS

Amélineau, *Monuments au IVe siècle*
  Amélineau, E. *Monuments pour servir à l'histoire de l'Égypte chrétienne au IVe siècle: Histoire de saint Pachôme et de ses communautés.* AnMG 17. Paris: Leroux, 1889.

Amidon, *Panarion*
  Amidon, Philip R. *The Panarion of St. Epiphanius, Bishop of Salamis: Selected Passages.* New York and Oxford: Oxford University Press, 1990.

Atiya, *Coptic Encyclopedia*
  Atiya, Aziz S., ed. *The Coptic Encyclopedia.* 8 vols. New York: Macmillan, 1991.

Bacht, *Vermächtnis*
  Bacht, Heinrich. *Das Vermächtnis des Ursprungs.* STGL 5. Würzburg: Echter, 1972.

Badger, "New Man"
  Badger, Carlton Mills. "The New Man Created in God: Christology, Congregation, and Asceticism in Athanasius of Alexandria." Ph.D. diss., Duke University, 1990.

Bagnall, *Egypt in Late Antiquity*
  Bagnall, Roger S. *Egypt in Late Antiquity.* Princeton: Princeton University Press, 1993.

Barns, "Greek and Coptic Papyri"
Barns, J. W. B. "Greek and Coptic Papyri from the Covers of the Nag Hammadi Texts." In Martin Krause, ed., *Essays on the Nag Hammadi Codices in Honour of Pahor Labib.* NHS 6. Leiden: E. J. Brill, 1975, 9–18.

Barns, Browne, and Shelton, *Cartonnage*
Barns, J. W. B., G. M. Browne, and J. C. Shelton. *Nag Hammadi Codices: Greek and Coptic Papyri from the Cartonnage of the Covers.* NHS 16. Leiden: E. J. Brill, 1981.

Basset, *Synaxaire arabe-jacobite*
Basset, René Marie Josef. *Le synaxaire arabe-jacobite (rédaction copte).* PO 1, 3, 11, 16, 17, 20. Paris: Didot, 1904–29.

Bell, *Jews and Christians in Egypt*
Bell, H. Idris. *Jews and Christians in Egypt: The Jewish Troubles in Alexandria and the Athanasian Controversies.* London: The British Museum, 1924. Reprint, Westport, Conn.: Greenwood Press, 1972. (References in text are to the reprint edition.)

Boon, *Pachomiana latina*
Boon, Amand. *Pachomiana latina: Règle et épîtres de s. Pachôme, épître de s. Théodore et "liber" de s. Orsiesius. Texte latin de s. Jerome.* BRHE 7. Louvain: Bureaux de la revue, 1932.

Brakke, *Athanasius*
Brakke, David. *Athanasius and the Politics of Asceticism.* Oxford Early Christian Studies. Oxford: Clarendon Press, 1995.

Brakke, "Canon Formation"
Brakke, David. "Canon Formation and Social Conflict in Fourth-Century Egypt: Athanasius of Alexandria's Thirty-ninth *Festal Letter.*" HTR 87 (1994) 395–419.

Brock and Harvey, *Holy Women*
Brock, Sebastian, and Susan Ashbrook Harvey. *Holy Women of the Syrian Orient.* TCH 13. Berkeley: University of California Press, 1987.

Brown, *Body and Society*
Brown, Peter. *The Body and Society: Men, Women and Sexual Renunciation in Early Christianity.* New York: Columbia University Press, 1988.

Brown, "Rise and Function"
Brown, Peter. "The Rise and Function of the Holy Man in Late Antiquity." *JRomS* 61 (1971) 80–101.

Butler, *Lausiac History*
Butler, Cuthbert. *The Lausiac History of Palladius I/II.* Cambridge: Cambridge University Press, 1898. Reprint, Hildesheim: Georg Olms, 1967.

Cadell and Rémondon, "Sens et emplois de τὸ ὄρος"
Cadell, H., and R. Rémondon. "Sens et emplois de τὸ ὄρος dans les documents papyrologiques." *REG* 80 (1967) 343–49.

Campagnano, "Monaci egiziani"
Campagnano, Antonella. "Monaci egiziani fra V e VI secolo." *VetChr* 15 (1978) 223–46.

Chadwick, "Domestication of Gnosis"
Chadwick, Henry. "The Domestication of Gnosis." In Bentley Layton, ed., *The Rediscovery of Gnosis: Proceedings of the Conference at Yale, March 1978.* 2 vols. Leiden: E. J. Brill, 1980, 1.3–16.

Chadwick, "Pachomios"
Chadwick, Henry. "Pachomios and the Idea of Sanctity." In S. Hackel, ed., *The Byzantine Saint: University of Birmingham Fourteenth Spring Symposium of Byzantine Studies.* London: Fellowship of St. Alban and St. Sergius, 1981, 11–24.

Chitty, *Desert a City*
Chitty, Derwas J. *The Desert a City: An Introduction to the Study of Egyptian and Palestinian Monasticism under the Christian Empire.* Oxford: Blackwell, 1966.

Clark, *Origenist Controversy*
Clark, Elizabeth A. *The Origenist Controversy: The Cultural Construction of an Early Christian Debate.* Princeton: Princeton University Press, 1992.

Crum, *Coptic Dictionary*
Crum, Walter E. *A Coptic Dictionary.* Oxford: Clarendon Press, 1939.

Crum, *Papyruscodex*
Crum, Walter E. *Der Papyruscodex saec. VI–VII der Phillippsbibliothek in Cheltenham: Koptische theologische Schriften.* Strasbourg: Trübner, 1915.

Debono, "Basilique"
Debono, Fernand. "La basilique et le monastère de St. Pacôme (Fouilles de l'Institut Pontifical d'Archéologie Chrétienne, a Faou-el-Qibli, Haute-Égypte, Janvier 1968)." *BIFAO* 70 (1971) 191–220.

Dechow, *Dogma and Mysticism*
Dechow, Jon F. *Dogma and Mysticism in Early Christianity: Epiphanius of Cyprus and the Legacy of Origen.* NAPSMS 13. Macon, Ga.: Mercer University Press, 1988.

Dörries, "Die Vita Antonii"
Dörries, Hermann. "Die Vita Antonii als Geschichtsquelle." NAWG 14. Göttingen: Vandenhoeck & Ruprecht, 1949, 357–410; reprinted in idem, *Wort und Stunde: Gesammelte Studien zur Kirchengeschichte des vierten Jahrhunderts.* 3 vols. Göttingen: Vandenhoeck & Ruprecht, 1966, 1.145–224.

Eliade, "Quest"
Eliade, Mircea. "The Quest for the 'Origins' of Religion." *HR* 4 (1964) 154–69. Reprinted in idem, *The Quest: History and Meaning in Religion*. Chicago and London: University of Chicago, 1969, 37–53.

Elm, *Virgins of God*
Elm, Susanna. *Virgins of God: The Making of Asceticism in Late Antiquity*. OCM. Oxford: Clarendon Press, 1994.

Emmett, "Female Ascetics"
Emmett, Alanna. "Female Ascetics in the Greek Papyri." In Wolfram Hörander et al., eds., *XVI Internationaler Byzantinistenkongress Wien, 4.–9. Oktober 1981*. JÖB 23, 2. Wien: Der österreichischen Akademie der Wissenschaften, 1982, 507–15.

Festugière, *Historia Monachorum*
Festugière, A.-J. *Historia Monachorum in Aegypto*. SH 53. Brussels: Société des Bollandistes, 1961.

Festugière, *Moines d'orient*
Festugière, A.-J. *Les moines d'orient*. Tome IV/2: *La première vie grecque de saint Pachôme*. Paris: Éditions du Cerf, 1965.

Frank, *ΑΓΓΕΛΙΚΟΣ ΒΙΟΣ*
Frank, K. Suso. *ΑΓΓΕΛΙΚΟΣ ΒΙΟΣ: Begriffsanalytische und begriffsgeschichtliche Untersuchung zum "Engelgleichen Leben" im frühen Mönchtum*. BGAMB 26. Münster: Aschendorff, 1964.

Frazer, "Morphology of Desert Wisdom"
Frazer, Ruth F. "The Morphology of Desert Wisdom in the *Apophthegmata Patrum*." Ph.D. diss., University of Chicago, 1977.

Frend, *Rise of the Monophysite Movement*
Frend, W. H. C. *The Rise of the Monophysite Movement: Chapters in the History of the Church in the Fifth and Sixth Centuries*. Cambridge: Cambridge University Press, 1972.

Ghedini, "Luci nuove"
Ghedini, Giuseppi. "Luci nuove dai papiri sullo scisma meleziano e il monachismo in Egitto." *La Scuola Cattolica* 53 (1925) 261–80.

Ghedini, review of *Jews and Christians in Egypt*
Ghedini, Giuseppi. Review of *Jews and Christians in Egypt*, by H. Idris Bell. *Aeg* 6 (1925) 273–77.

Goehring, "Encroaching Desert"
Goehring, James E. "The Encroaching Desert: Literary Production and Ascetic Space in Early Christian Egypt." *JECS* 1 (1993) 281–96. Appears as chapter 4 in the present volume.

Goehring, *Letter of Ammon*
   Goehring, James E. *The Letter of Ammon and Pachomian Monasticism.* PTS
   27. Berlin: Walter de Gruyter, 1986.

Goehring, "Melitian Monastic Organization"
   Goehring, James E. "Melitian Monastic Organization: A Challenge to Pachomian Originality." In Elizabeth A. Livingstone, ed., *Papers Presented at
   the Eleventh International Conference on Patristic Studies Held in Oxford 1991:
   Biblica et Apocrypha, Orientalia, Ascetica.* Leuven: Peeters Press, 1993. *SP* 25
   (1993) 388–95. Appears as chapter 9 in the present volume.

Goehring, "New Frontiers"
   Goehring, James E. "New Frontiers in Pachomian Studies." In Birger A.
   Pearson and James E. Goehring, eds., *The Roots of Egyptian Christianity.*
   SAC. Philadelphia: Fortress Press, 1986, 236–57. Appears as chapter 8 in
   the present volume.

Goehring, "Origins of Monasticism"
   Goehring, James E. "The Origins of Monasticism." In Harold W. Attridge
   and Gohei Hata, eds., *Eusebius, Christianity, and Judaism.* Detroit: Wayne
   State University Press, 1992, 235–55. Appears as chapter 1 in the present
   volume.

Goehring, "Pachomius' Vision of Heresy"
   Goehring, James E. "Pachomius' Vision of Heresy: The Development of a
   Pachomian Tradition." *Mus* 95 (1982) 241–62. Appears as chapter 7 in the
   present volume.

Goehring, "Theodore's Entry"
   Goehring, James E. "Theodore's Entry into the Pachomian Movement
   (Selections from the *Life of Pachomius*)." In Vincent L. Wimbush, ed., *As-
   cetic Behavior in Greco-Roman Antiquity: A Sourcebook.* SAC. Minneapolis:
   Fortress Press, 1990, 349–56.

Goehring, "Through a Glass Darkly"
   Goehring, James E. "Through a Glass Darkly: Diverse Images of the *Apo-
   taktikoi(ai)* of Early Egyptian Monasticism." In Vincent L. Wimbush, ed.,
   *Discursive Formations, Ascetic Piety, and the Interpretation of Early Christian
   Literature.* Pt. 2. *Semeia* 58 (1992) 25–45. Appears as chapter 3 in the
   present volume.

Goehring, "World Engaged"
   Goehring, James E. "The World Engaged: The Social and Economic World
   of Early Egyptian Monasticism." In James E. Goehring et al., eds., *Gnosticism and the Early Christian World: In Honor of James M. Robinson.* Sonoma,
   Calif.: Polebridge Press, 1990, 134–44. Appears as chapter 2 in the present
   volume.

Gregg, *Life of Antony*
    Gregg, Robert C. *Athanasius: The Life of Antony and the Letter to Marcellinus.*
    CWS. New York: Paulist Press, 1980.

Grossmann, "Basilica"
    Grossmann, Peter. "The Basilica of St. Pachomius." *BA* 42 (1979) 232–36.

Grossmann, "Pbow"
    Grossmann, Peter. "Pbow: Archeology." In Aziz S. Atiya, ed., *The Coptic
    Encyclopedia.* 8 vols. New York: Macmillan, 1991, 6.1927–29.

Grossmann and Lease, "Faw Qibli: 1989 Excavation Report"
    Grossmann, Peter, and Gary Lease. "Faw Qibli: 1989 Excavation Report."
    GöM 114 (1990) 9-12, and figs. 1–6.

Halkin, *Corpus athénien*
    Halkin, François. *Le corpus athénien de saint Pachôme.* COr 2. Geneva:
    Patrick Cramer, 1982.

Halkin, *Sancti Pachomii Vitae Graecae*
    Halkin, François. *Sancti Pachomii Vitae Graecae.* SH 19. Brussels: Société
    des Bollandistes, 1932.

Halkin, "Vie inédite"
    Halkin, François. "Une vie inédite de saint Pachôme: BHG 1401a." *AB* 97
    (1979) 5–55, 241–87.

Hardy, *Christian Egypt*
    Hardy, Edward Rochie. *Christian Egypt: Church and People, Christianity and
    Nationalism in the Patriarchate of Alexandria.* New York: Oxford University
    Press, 1952.

Harvey, "Sense of a Stylite"
    Harvey, Susan Ashbrook. "The Sense of a Stylite: Perspectives on Simeon
    the Elder." *VC* 42 (1988) 376–94.

Hedrick, "Gnostic Proclivities"
    Hedrick, Charles W. "Gnostic Proclivities in the Greek Life of Pachomius
    and the *Sitz im Leben* of the Nag Hammadi Library." *NovT* 22 (1980) 78–
    94.

Hengstenberg, "Bemerkungen"
    Hengstenberg, Wilhelm. "Bemerkungen zur Entwicklungsgeschichte des
    ägyptischen Mönchtums." *BIAB* 9 (1935) 355–62=*Actes du IVe congrès
    international des études byzantines.* Ed. Bogdan D. Filou. Sofia: Imprimerie
    de la Cour, 1935, 355–62.

Hengstenberg, review of *Jews and Christians in Egypt*
    Hengstenberg, Wilhelm. Review of *Jews and Christians in Egypt,* by H. Idris
    Bell. *ByzZ* 27 (1927) 138–45.

Heussi, *Ursprung*
Heussi, Karl. *Der Ursprung des Mönchtums.* Tübingen: J. C. B. Mohr, 1936.
Reprint, Aalen: Scientia, 1981.

Holl, "Bedeutung"
Holl, Karl. "Die Bedeutung der neuveröffentlichten melitianischen Urkunden für die Kirchengeschichte." SPAW (1925) 18–31.

Holl and Dummer, *Epiphanius II*
Holl, Karl, and Jürgen Dummer, eds. *Epiphanius II: Panarion haer. 34–64.*
Jürgen Dummer. 2d rev. ed. GCS. Berlin: Akademie Verlag, 1980.

Holl and Dummer, *Epiphanius III*
Holl, Karl, and Jürgen Dummer, eds. *Epiphanius III: Panarion haer. 65–80, de fide.* Jürgen Dummer. 2d rev. ed. GCS. Berlin: Akademie Verlag, 1985.

Judge, "Earliest Use"
Judge, E. A. "The Earliest Use of Monachos for 'Monk' (*P. Coll. Youtie* 77) and the Origins of Monasticism." *JAC* 10 (1977) 72–89.

Judge, "Fourth-Century Monasticism"
Judge, E. A. "Fourth-Century Monasticism in the Papyri." In Roger S. Bagnall et al., eds., *Proceedings of the Sixteenth International Congress of Papyrology, New York, 24–31 July 1990.* AmSP 23. Chico, Calif.: Scholars Press, 1981, 613–20.

Kahle, *Bala'izah*
Kahle, Paul E. *Bala'izah: Coptic Texts from Deir el-Bala'izah in Upper Egypt.*
2 vols. London: Oxford University Press, 1954.

Koenen, "Manichäische Mission"
Koenen, Ludwig. "Manichäische Mission und Klöster in Ägypten." In Günter Grimm et al., eds., *Das römisch-byzantinische Ägypten: Acten des internationalen Symposions, 26.–30. September 1978 in Trier.* AegT 2. Mainz: Philipp von Zabern, 1983, 93–108.

Kramer and Shelton, *Archiv des Nepheros*
Kramer, Bärbel, and John C. Shelton. *Das Archiv des Nepheros und verwandte Texte.* AegT 4. Mainz: Philipp von Zabern, 1987.

Krause, "Apa-Apollon-Kloster"
Krause, Martin. "Das Apa-Apollon-Kloster zu Bawit: Untersuchungen unveröffentlichter Urkunden als Beitrag zur Geschichte des ägyptischen Mönchtums." Ph.D. diss., Karl-Marx-Universität, 1958.

Krause, "Erlassbrief"
Krause, Martin. "Der Erlassbrief Theodors." In Dwight W. Young, ed., *Studies Presented to Hans Jacob Polotsky.* East Gloucester, Mass.: Pirtle & Polson, 1981, 220–38.

Krause, "Zur Möglichkeit"
Krause, Martin. "Zur Möglichkeit von Besitz im apotaktischen Mönchtums Ägyptens." In Tito Orlandi and Frederik Wisse, eds., *Acts of the Second International Congress of Coptic Studies, Rome, 22–26 September 1980.* Rome: CIM, 1985, 121–33.

Kuhn, *Panegyric on Apollo*
Kuhn, K. H. *A Panegyric on Apollo Archimandrite of the Monastery of Isaac, by Stephen, Bishop of Heracleopolis Magna.* CSCO 394 (text) and 395 (trans.). Louvain: Secrétariat du CSCO, 1978.

Lambert, "Apotactites"
Lambert, A. "Apotactites et Apotaxamènes." In R. P. dom Fernand Cabrol, ed., *Dictionnaire d'archéologie chrétienne et de liturgie.* Vol. 1. Paris: Letouzey et Ané, 1907, cols. 2604–26.

Lease, "Fourth Season"
Lease, Gary. "The Fourth Season of the Nag Hammadi Excavation, 21 December 1979–15 January 1980." *GöM* 41 (1980) 75–85.

Lease, "Traces"
Lease, Gary. "Traces of Early Egyptian Monasticism: The Faw Qibli Excavations." OP 22. Claremont, Calif.: Institute for Antiquity and Christianity, 1991.

Lefort, *Oeuvres*
Lefort, L. Th. *Oeuvres de S. Pachôme et de ses disciples.* CSCO 159 (text) and 160 (trans.). Louvain: L. Durbecq, 1956.

Lefort, "Premiers monastères"
Lefort, L. Th. "Les premiers monastères pachômiens: Exploration topographique." *Mus* 52 (1939) 379–407.

Lefort, *S. Pachomii vita bohairice scripta*
Lefort, L. Th. *S. Pachomii vita bohairice scripta.* CSCO 89. Paris: E typographeo reipublicae, 1925. Reprint, Louvain: Secrétariat du CSCO, 1965.

Lefort, *S. Pachomii vitae sahidice scriptae*
Lefort, L. Th. *S. Pachomii vitae sahidice scriptae.* CSCO 99/100. Paris: E typographeo reipublicae, 1933. Reprint, Louvain: Secrétariat du CSCO, 1965.

Lefort, *Vies coptes*
Lefort, L. Th. *Les vies coptes de saint Pachôme et de ses premiers successeurs.* BMus 16. Louvain: Bureaux du Muséon, 1943.

Leipoldt, *Schenute von Atripe*
Leipoldt, Johannes. *Schenute von Atripe und die Entstehung des national ägyptischen Christentums.* Leipzig: Hinrichs, 1933.

Lewis, *Life in Egypt*
    Lewis, Naphtali. *Life in Egypt under Roman Rule*. Oxford: Clarendon Press, 1983.

McGing, "Melitian Monks"
    McGing, Brian C. "Melitian Monks at Labla." *Tyche* 5 (1990) 67–94.

Meyer, "Wadi Sheikh Ali"
    Meyer, Marvin W. "Wadi Sheikh Ali Survey." *NARCE* 117 (1982) 22–24, and *GöM* 64 (1983) 77–82.

Pearson and Goehring, *Roots*
    Pearson, Birger A., and James E. Goehring, eds. *The Roots of Egyptian Christianity*. SAC. Philadelphia: Fortress Press, 1986.

Peeters, "Dossier copte"
    Peeters, Paul. "Le dossier copte de S. Pachôme et ses rapports avec la tradition grecque." *AB* 64 (1946) 258–77.

Price, *History*
    Price, R. M. *A History of the Monks of Syria by Theodoret of Cyrrhus*. CistStud 88. Kalamazoo, Mich.: Cistercian Publications, 1985.

Quecke, *Briefe Pachoms*
    Quecke, Hans. *Die Briefe Pachoms: Griechischer Text der Handschrift W. 145 der Chester Beatty Library*. TPL 11. Regensburg: Pustet, 1975.

Rapp, "Epiphanius of Salamis"
    Rapp, Claudia. "Epiphanius of Salamis: The Church Father as Saint." In *"The Sweet Land of Cyprus": Papers Given at the Twenty-fifth Jubilee Spring Symposium of Byzantine Studies, Birmingham, England, March 1991*. Birmingham, England: University of Birmingham; Nicosia: Cyprus Research Centre, 1993, 169–87.

Rapp, "The *Vita* of Epiphanius"
    Rapp, Claudia. "The *Vita* of Epiphanius of Salamis: An Historical and Literary Study." D.Phil. diss., Worcester College, 1991.

Robinson, "Discovery"
    Robinson, James M. "The Discovery of the Nag Hammadi Codices." *BA* 42 (1979) 206–24.

Robinson, "Introduction"
    Robinson, James M. "Introduction." In James M. Robinson, ed., *The Nag Hammadi Library in English*. New York: Harper & Row, 1977, 1–25.

Robinson, "Pachomian Monastic Library"
    Robinson, James M. "The Pachomian Monastic Library at the Chester Beatty Library and the Bibliothèque Bodmer." OP 19. Claremont, Calif.: Institute for Antiquity and Christianity, 1990.

Robinson and van Elderen, "First Season"
Robinson, James M., and Bastiaan van Elderen. "The First Season of the Nag Hammadi Excavation, 27 November–19 December 1975." *NARCE* 96 (1976) 18–24, and *GöM* 22 (1976) 71–79.

Robinson and van Elderen, "Second Season"
Robinson, James M., and Bastiaan van Elderen. "The Second Season of the Nag Hammadi Excavation, 22 November–29 December 1976." *NARCE* 99/100 (1977) 36–54, and *GöM* 24 (1977) 57–71.

Rousseau, *Ascetics*
Rousseau, Philip. *Ascetics, Authority, and the Church in the Age of Jerome and Cassian.* Oxford: Oxford University Press, 1978.

Rousseau, *Pachomius*
Rousseau, Philip. *Pachomius: The Making of a Community in Fourth-Century Egypt.* TCH 6. Berkeley: University of California Press, 1985.

Rubenson, *Letters of St. Antony*
Rubenson, Samuel. *The Letters of St. Antony: Origenist Theology, Monastic Tradition, and the Making of a Saint.* BHEL 24. Lund: Lund University Press, 1990. Reprinted with an English translation of the *Letters of Antony* as *The Letters of St. Antony: Monasticism and the Making of a Saint.* SAC. Minneapolis: Fortress Press, 1995.

Ruppert, *Das pachomianische Mönchtum*
Ruppert, Fidelis. *Das pachomianische Mönchtum und die Anfänge klösterlichen Gehorsams.* MünSt 20. Münsterschwarzach: Vier-Türme, 1971.

Russell and Ward, *Lives of the Desert Fathers*
Russell, Norman, and Benedicta Ward. *The Lives of the Desert Fathers: Historia monachorum in Aegypto.* London and Oxford: Mowbray; Kalamazoo, Mich.: Cistercian Publications, 1981.

Säve-Söderbergh, "Holy Scriptures or Apologetic Documentations?"
Säve-Söderbergh, Torgny. "Holy Scriptures or Apologetic Documentations? The 'Sitz im Leben' of the Nag Hammadi Library." In Jacques-E. Ménard, ed., *Les Textes de Nag Hammadi.* NHS 7. Leiden: E. J. Brill, 1975, 3–14.

Sayce, "Deux contrats grecs"
Sayce, A. H. "Deux contrats grecs du fayoum." *REG* 3 (1890) 131–44.

Scholten, "Die Nag-Hammadi-Texte als Buchbesitz"
Scholten, Clemens. "Die Nag-Hammadi-Texte als Buchbesitz der Pachomianer." *JAC* 31 (1988) 144–72.

Shelton, "Introduction"
   Shelton, J. C. "Introduction." In J. W. B. Barns, G. W. Browne, and
   J. C. Shelton, eds., *Nag Hammadi Codices: Greek and Coptic Papyri from the
   Cartonnage of the Covers.* NHS 16. Leiden: E. J. Brill, 1981, 1–11.

Spanel, "Toronto Sahidic Addition"
   Spanel, Donald. "A Toronto Sahidic Addition to the Pakhom Dossier
   (*Fischer A1*, ff. 1–2)." *The Ancient World* 6 (1983) 115–25.

Steidle, "Osterbrief"
   Steidle, Basilius. "Der Osterbrief unseres Vaters Theodor an alle Klöster."
   EA 44 (1968) 104–19.

Steinwenter, "Rechtsstellung"
   Steinwenter, Artur. "Die Rechtsstellung der Kirchen und Klöster nach der
   Papyri." *ZSavR* 19 (1930) 1–50.

Stroumsa, "Manichaean Challenge"
   Stroumsa, Gedaliahu G. "The Manichaean Challenge to Egyptian Chris-
   tianity." In Birger A. Pearson and James E. Goehring, eds., *The Roots of
   Egyptian Christianity.* SAC. Philadelphia: Fortress Press, 1986, 307–19.

Timbie, "Dualism"
   Timbie, Janet Ann. "Dualism and the Concept of Orthodoxy in the
   Thought of the Monks of Upper Egypt." Ph.D. diss., University of Penn-
   sylvania, 1979.

van Cauwenbergh, *Étude*
   van Cauwenbergh, Paul. *Étude sur les moines d'Égypte depuis le Concile de
   Chalcédoine (451) jusqu'à l'invasion arabe (640).* Paris: Imprimerie nationale,
   1914.

van Cranenburgh, *Vie latine*
   van Cranenburgh, H. *La vie latine de S. Pachôme traduite du grec par Denys le
   Petit.* SH 46. Brussels: Société des Bollandistes, 1969.

van Elderen, "Nag Hammadi Excavation"
   van Elderen, Bastiaan. "The Nag Hammadi Excavation." *BA* 42 (1979)
   225–31.

van Lantschoot, "Allocution"
   van Lantschoot, Arn. "Allocution de Timothée d'Alexandrie prononcée à
   l'occasion de la dédicace de l'église de Pachôme à Pboou." *Mus* 47 (1934)
   13–56.

Veilleux, *Liturgie*
   Veilleux, Armand. *La liturgie dans le cénobitisme pachômien au quatrième
   siècle.* StAns 57. Rome: Herder, 1986.

Veilleux, "Monasticism and Gnosis"
Veilleux, Armand. "Monasticism and Gnosis in Egypt." In Birger A. Pearson and James E. Goehring, eds., *The Roots of Egyptian Christianity*. SAC. Philadelphia: Fortress Press, 1986, 271–306.

Veilleux, *Pachomian Koinonia*
Veilleux, Armand. *Pachomian Koinonia*. 3 vols. CistStud 45–47. Kalamazoo, Mich.: Cistercian Press, 1980–82.

Vogüé, "Épîtres"
Vogüé, Adalbert de. "Épîtres inédites d'Horsièse et de Théodore." In J. Gribomont, ed., *Commandements du Seigneur et libération évangelique: Études monastiques proposées et discutés à St. Anselme 15–17 Février 1976*. StAns 70. Rome: Herder, 1977, 244–57.

Weber, *Theory*
Weber, Max. *The Theory of Social and Economic Organization*. Translated by A. M. Henderson and Talcott Parsons. New York and London: Oxford University Press, 1947.

White, *Monasteries of the Wadi 'n Natrun*
White, Hugh G. Evelyn. *The Monasteries of the Wadi 'n Natrun*. Pt. 2: *The History of the Monasteries of Nitria and of Scetis*. New York: Metropolitan Museum of Art, 1932. Reprint, New York: Arno Press, 1973.

Williams, *Panarion I*
Williams, Frank. *The Panarion of Epiphanius of Salamis: Book I (Sects. 1–46)*. NHS 35. Leiden, New York, Copenhagen, and Cologne: E. J. Brill, 1987.

Williams, *Panarion II and III*
Williams, Frank. *The Panarion of Epiphanius of Salamis: Books II and III (Sects. 47–80, de Fide)*. NHMS 35. Leiden, New York, and Cologne: E. J. Brill, 1994.

Winlock and Crum, *Monastery of Epiphanius*
Winlock, H. E., and W. E. Crum. *The Monastery of Epiphanius at Thebes*. 2 vols. New York: Metropolitan Museum of Art, 1926. Reprint, New York: Arno Press, 1973.

Wipszycka, "Monachisme égyptien"
Wipszycka, Ewa. "Le monachisme égyptien et les villes." *Travaux et mémoires* 12 (1994) 1–44. Reprinted in idem, ed., *Études sur le christianisme dans l'Égypte de l'antiquité tardive*. SEA 52. Rome: Institutum Patristicum Augustinianum, 1996, 282–336.

Wipszycka, "Terres"
Wipszycka, Ewa. "Les terres de la congrégation pachômienne dans une liste de payments pour les apora." In J. Bingen et al., eds., *Le monde grec: Pensée, littérature, histoire, documents. Hommages à Claire Préaux*. Brussels: L'Université Bruxelles, 1975, 625–36.

Wisse, "Gnosticism"
    Wisse, Frederik. "Gnosticism and Early Monasticism in Egypt." In Bar-
    bara Aland, ed., *Gnosis: Festschrift für Hans Jonas*. Göttingen: Vandenhoeck
    & Ruprecht, 1978, 431–40.

Wisse, "Language Mysticism"
    Wisse, Frederik. "Language Mysticism in the Nag Hammadi Texts and in
    Early Coptic Monasticism I: Cryptography." *Enchoria* 9 (1979) 101–20.

Introduction

The twelve essays in this volume offer a selective study of early Egyptian monasticism. They supply as well an account of my own journey in the field, a journey that began in 1972 as an undergraduate student at the University of California at Berkeley. It is not a place or time that one immediately associates with asceticism. For me, the interest was ignited in a special undergraduate course on Gnosticism and the Nag Hammadi Codices, taught by a guest professor from the Claremont Graduate School, James M. Robinson. I had been drawn to the course by the esoteric nature of the texts. The opportunity to read early Christian documents that scholars were only then translating for the first time fascinated me, as did what at the time seemed to me like a countercultural Christian movement. The moment I remember most distinctly from the course, however, occurred in an early lecture discussing the site of the original discovery of the codices in Upper Egypt. The details of the story of the discovery are well known, but it was not the account of the fellahin breaking open the storage jar with their mattocks or the dating of the discovery, through its connection with a vivid account of blood vengeance, that caught my attention. Rather, I found myself intrigued by a brief reference to the proximity of the discovery site to the central monastery of the well-known and presumably orthodox Pachomian monastic movement. I found myself wondering whether such monks actually produced and read these texts, and if they did, why they read them and how they understood them. If indeed they did produce the texts, I wondered how it could be that supposedly orthodox monks copied and read such clearly heterodox literature. Why was there no evidence of their use of these texts in the monks' own accounts of their movement? The questions filled my head, but I did not have the training even to begin to find the answers. But the questions alone were enough. Those brief few minutes in a single undergraduate lecture propelled my own intellectual adventure.

1

The papers presented here represent various stopping points along the way.

The essays selected for inclusion in this volume were written over the past seventeen years. They reflect my abiding interest in the relationship between the ascetic world of late antique Egypt and its representation in the surviving sources. Ten of the essays have been published previously as journal articles or as contributions to volumes of collected essays. These articles have been selected, organized, and edited for inclusion in this book. Two essays appear in print here for the first time. They include both the earliest article ("The Fourth Letter of Horsiesius and the Situation in the Pachomian Community following the Death of Theodore"), written originally in 1980 and revised for this publication, and the latest essay ("Hieracas of Leontopolis: The Making of a Desert Ascetic"), which was presented in a much abbreviated form at the 1997 annual meeting of the North American Patristics Society.

Various organizational schemes were considered for the presentation of the articles in this book. The present scheme was chosen as both most reflective of my own current thinking about my work and as most useful in linking articles that address common issues or themes. After an initial article, the more general nature of which allows it to serve as an introductory statement of my work, the essays have been divided under the following section headings: (1) "Ascetics, Society, and the Desert"; (2) "Ascetic Organization and Ideological Boundaries"; and (3) "Pachomian Studies: The Later Years." Within each section, the articles have been placed in chronological order. The first section includes articles that examine the relationships between ascetics and the broader Egyptian society and the way in which these relationships are presented in the literary sources. The later articles in the section carry that interest over to the question of the reality of the desert imagery in the portrayal of early Egyptian monasticism. The issues in these articles flow naturally together, and as a group, they represent the most current focus of my work. The articles in the second section are related by their shared interest in the place of ideology in early monasticism and its portrayal in the literary sources. The articles in this section are somewhat more disparate in their treatment of the subject, with some focusing on questions of organization and others on issues of ideo-

logical boundaries. The final section includes two articles that relate
to my interest in the later years of the Pachomian movement, years
not covered in the narrative history of the movement preserved in
the various editions of the *Life of Pachomius*.

The volume's introductory article, "Origins of Monasticism," was
written for a collection of essays published in 1992 in conjunction
with the first Japanese translation of Eusebius of Caesarea's *Ecclesiastical History*.[1] I was invited to write the article on monastic origins
and agreed to the assignment not because I believed that a particular
origin of the monastic movement could be found, but rather because
I wanted to challenge the very notion of a quest for origins. In the
article, I argue that when one pays attention to the details of monastic development in the late antique Mediterranean basin, any simple
theory of origins falls apart. The quest for such a theory, in fact, re-
lates more to an inherent human need to understand ourselves than
to any historical reality. In making this case, the article includes
sections on "The Life of Antony," "The Village Ascetics," and "Pachomius and the Coenobites," all elements that play a major role in
the subsequent articles and their thematic organization in this volume. In addition, the approach to the material serves to introduce the
reader to the methodological issues that have shaped my thinking
and informed the writings contained in this book.

The articles drawn together in the section on "Ascetics, Society,
and the Desert" explore the concept of ascetic withdrawal (ἀναχώρησις) and its rhetorical use in the literary sources. As one reads
through the articles in sequence, one can note how my thinking focused increasing attention on the literary function of the desert in
the primary narrative sources and how I came to believe that the
common understanding of Egyptian asceticism as primarily a desert
movement is fundamentally flawed. The argument draws heavily
from documentary papyri which supply evidence of Egyptian ascetics residing in villages and towns and interacting in significant
ways with their nonascetic neighbors. The first article in this section,
"The World Engaged: The Social and Economic World of Early Egyptian Monasticism" (1990), gathers evidence from the *Apophthegmata*

---

1. Harold W. Attridge and Gohei Hata, eds., *Eusebius, Christianity, and Judaism*
(Detroit: Wayne State University Press, 1992).

Patrum, the Pachomian dossier, and the papyrological sources to illustrate the social and economic interdependence of Egyptian ascetics with their surrounding world. The impetus for this essay came from the work of E. A. Judge,[2] whose articles introduced the papyrological evidence into the debate. I had met him in 1983 at the International Conference on the Roots of Egyptian Christianity in Claremont and Santa Barbara, California, and became convinced that the documentary sources held the key to understanding the ascetic movement in Egypt.[3]

I was fortunate to be able to continue my research into the papyrological evidence in 1989–90 on an Alexander von Humboldt Fellowship at the Academy of Sciences in Göttingen, Germany. That research led directly to the second article in this section, "Through a Glass Darkly: Diverse Images of the Ἀποτακτικοί(αί) in Early Egyptian Monasticism" (1992). This article offers a detailed analysis of the use of the Greek term ἀποτακτικοί(αί) or "renunciants" as a label for certain ascetics in Egypt. Careful study of the term's use in the papyri led me to challenge the common bipolar division of Egyptian monasticism into anchoritic and coenobitic forms. The use of the term indicates rather the existence of a complex continuum of ascetic practice ranging from the isolated solitary ascetic (anchorite) to the fully communal monk (coenobite). Furthermore, the urban[4] location of most of the ἀποτακτικοί(αί) mentioned in the papyrus sources suggests that the terms ἀποτακτικός (renunciant) and ἀναχωρητής (withdrawer) originally indicated only that the individuals so labeled had renounced or withdrawn from their traditional social obligations and practices. In the beginning, the terms did not locate the ascetic spatially. As the papyrus documents indicate, individuals so labeled could be found within a town or village. It was only in the subsequent development of the monastic movement, real and in the literature, that the meaning of the terms expanded to include the notion of the individual's spatial withdrawal from his or her town or village into the desert.

Continued interest in the papyrological evidence of village or ur-

---

2. Judge, "Earliest Use."

3. For the proceedings of the conference, see Pearson and Goehring, *Roots*.

4. I use "urban" here to refer to a setting within a village, town, or city as opposed to a location in the countryside or desert.

ban ascetics led me to reflect increasingly on the literary nature and function of the desert in the portrayal of early Egyptian monasticism. The third article in this section, "The Encroaching Desert: Literary Production and Ascetic Space in Early Christian Egypt" (1993), serves as a general statement of my views on this matter. I have become increasingly convinced of the formative power of Athanasius's popular and influential *Life of Antony* in defining (and controlling) the ascetic movement as a desert phenomenon. The success of the *Vita* created a dialectical relationship between literary production and ascetic practice. It connected ascetic piety with spatial withdrawal from the village or town and fostered the growth of the movement in that direction by employing the concept of *imitatio*. As the *Life of Antony* became the literary model, subsequent texts furthered the theme, and as these texts became the guidebooks of future monks, the literary model shaped the practice. In the essay, I contend that while the model shaped the movement, both in reality and in the literature, its literary power also finally rewrote history. Egyptian monasticism came to be portrayed and understood as a desert movement. Ascetics, who continued their practices within the towns and villages, were forgotten. They were too vulgar or common to serve as the subjects of a good story. Those whose stories were retained were increasingly portrayed and understood as desert monks. The story of Egyptian monasticism thus underwent a sort of literary "desertification."

The final two essays in this section offer studies of particular ascetic figures and their followings in light of this desertification process. Both articles illustrate the continuing impact of the desert model on the interpretation of the sources and offer alternative readings which challenge the association of the groups with the desert. By relocating these figures within a village or town and stressing these locations, the general portrayal of ascetic development in Egypt as the creation of "a city in the desert" (*Vita Antonii* 14)[5] is significantly qualified. The first of the two articles, "Withdrawing from the Desert: Pachomius and the Development of Village Monasticism in Upper Egypt" (1996), locates Pachomius's coenobitic experiment

---

5. Note, for example, Derwas Chitty's use of this phrase as the title of his 1966 introduction to early Egyptian and Palestinian monasticism. Chitty, *Desert a City*.

wholly within the fertile Nile valley. While he initially experimented with the anchoritic life under the desert ascetic Palamon, his own ascetic innovation occurred through his return to the village. The origin and development of the coenobitic institution should thus be understood as a withdrawal from, rather than to, the desert. As such, it represents a form of village asceticism and should be interpreted in those terms. In the article, I detail the evidence of Pachomius's use of Upper Egyptian towns and villages in the foundation and expansion of his movement. There is little reason to locate any of his communities in the desert, let alone to link him in a general way to Athanasius's emerging city in the desert except insofar as the word *desert* is used symbolically to refer to the ascetic life.

The final article in this section, "Hieracas of Leontopolis: The Making of a Desert Ascetic," published here for the first time, offers a similar reevaluation of the sources on the early Egyptian ascetic Hieracas and their interpretation in twentieth-century scholarship. In the article, I suggest that the continuing pull of the desert imagery is recognizable in the increasing acceptance by scholars of the evidence found in the late and legendary *Life of Epiphanius* that locates Hieracas in a μοναστήριον (cell or monastery) about a mile outside of the city of Leontopolis. Before the *Vita* was introduced into the debate in 1936,[6] scholars had simply accepted the reference in the much earlier *Panarion* of Epiphanius of Salamis that situates Hieracas and his ascetic experiment in the city of Leontopolis. The shift to the evidence of the later *Vita* effectively diminishes the influence of urban asceticism in the formative stages of ascetic development in Egypt. In the article, I contend that the evidence from the *Vita*, unique on this point, should be rejected. It is better understood as a later refashioning of Hieracas as a desert monk under the pressure of the by then strong association of ascetics with the desert. Because of the emphasis in the early sources on Hieracas's ascetic teachings, the later tradition simply came to assume that he lived as a monk outside of the city (in the desert). When one sets the evidence of the *Vita* aside, however, and focuses on the nature of Hieracas's ascetic experiment, he fits more clearly the pattern of a learned urban teacher who drew together an ascetic association in the city of Leontopolis. As such

---

6. Heussi, *Ursprung.*

he represents the early impulse within Christianity toward a separate ascetic community, an impulse located not in the desert, but in
the city.

The four articles joined together in the section on "Ascetic Organization and Ideological Boundaries" do not trace a single theme as
clearly as those in the first section of this book. They do, however,
come together in addressing a broader interest that has remained
influential in my reading and interpretation of the sources, namely,
the manner in which the ecclesiastical desire for ideological conformity influences both how a story is told as well as which stories
survive. The process produces a consistency among the surviving
witnesses, which in turn ignores, and thereby effectively denies,
the existence of the earlier, more diverse situation. The preserved
viewpoints and practices become the assumed pattern. They are
identified with a perpetual orthodoxy, and the rejected ideas are
reinterpreted as errant teachings, wayward exceptions to the rule
(orthodoxy). One result of this process is the assumed orthodoxy of
ascetics met briefly in ancient sources. When there is no evidence of
the ascetic's ideology or practice, he is most often simply numbered
among the orthodox. Thus H. Idris Bell, who published the famous
Melitian papyri (archive of Paieous), concluded that the monk Papnouthios, whose letter archive was purchased by the British Museum
in the same lot with the Melitian texts, was orthodox, simply because there was no direct evidence of his Melitian connection in the
letters.[7] Today, the Papnouthios archive is rightly understood within
the Melitian context.[8]

Evidence of the earlier, more diverse situation is necessarily
sparse. Among the texts that were passed down from antiquity,
evidence is most obviously found in the hostile reports of the proponents of the emerging catholic consensus. More subtle evidence
occurs also in many of the texts that conformed or were made to
conform to the catholic view. Careful study of various editions of
the same work, for example, often reveals the hand of an editor
or scribe working to create conformity, and thus indicates at least
the existence of a more divergent earlier situation. Likewise, within

---

7. Bell, *Jews and Christians in Egypt*, 101–2.
8. Bagnall, *Egypt in Late Antiquity*, 308.

the surviving monastic sources, anachronistic references surface that indicate a more complex situation than appears on the surface. In addition to the texts that have survived within the church, newly discovered documents that had not survived the process of conformity have added a wealth of information through which to test and reevaluate the received tradition. Included among these are the collections of texts discovered in the vicinity of the central monastery of the Pachomian *koinonia* (Nag Hammadi Codices and Dishna Papers) and the wealth of papyrological evidence shedding light on the social world in which the early church arose. The importance of these texts and issues is apparent in most of the articles in this volume. In the four articles in Part Two, however, these issues represent a more central methodological concern.

The first article, "Pachomius's Vision of Heresy: The Development of a Pachomian Tradition" (1982), undertakes a comparative analysis of the various forms of the story of Pachomius's vision that survive in the sources. The methodology employed in this early essay clearly draws from my then recent doctoral study in New Testament. Given the varied versions of the same story, the attempt is made to understand their variations in terms of a developmental trajectory. I concluded that the earliest form of the story concerned a specific unidentified error that had arisen within the Pachomian community itself. Later versions linked the account to subsequent theological issues that vexed all Egypt. The Bohairic Coptic *Life of Pachomius* connected the episode with the debates that swirled in Egypt after the Council of Chalcedon. The Greek tradition, on the other hand, turned the story into a general statement against heresy, designed to underscore the community's close ties with the Alexandrian patriarchy. While the nature of the original error is forever lost, the analysis illustrates the forces at work in the reshaping and generalizing of the tradition. Pachomius, extolled as the founder of the coenobitic institution, becomes thereby an early and powerful advocate of the later positions of the Alexandrian hierarchy.

The article "New Frontiers in Pachomian Studies" (1986) addresses the methodological problems involved in interpreting the Pachomian movement in the periods prior to Pachomius's death (346 C.E.) and after the death of Horsiesius (ca. 400 C.E.). Accounts of the period before Pachomius's death depend heavily on sources composed after his death, and few sources exist relevant to the period after Horsiesius's death. In the article, I suggest that new approaches are needed to identify and separate the issues and concerns of the time of the sources' composition from those of the periods they purport to describe. In the case of the movement's formative stage, I apply a sociological model of institutionalization to the sources in an effort to understand the dynamics involved in the leadership difficulties experienced upon the death of Pachomius and the organizational changes that ensued. The discussion addresses not only the changing organizational structure of the movement, but also raises important questions concerning the impact of these changes on the ideological flexibility allowed within the movement. I argue that the move from an earlier, more charismatic form of authority to a later, more institutional form led, by its very nature, to a more rigorous definition and control of the movement's ideology. The change is, in turn, reflected in the way the sources, composed after the process of institutionalization was complete, portray the earlier period. Since the sources present the early monks as models for the readers to imitate, the portrayal of the early monks must necessarily conform to the more rigorous ideological definitions of the later period. When I turn to the movement's later years after the death of Horsiesius, a period for which few literary sources are available, I suggest that the increasing archaeological evidence offers some hope for improving our understanding of this period of the movement's history. A brief addendum has been added to this article to bring the reader up to date with the most recent archaeological discoveries at the site of the central Pachomian monastery of Pbow.

The brief article, "Melitian Monastic Organization: A Challenge to Pachomian Originality" (1993), resulted from a comprehensive study of the growing number of documentary sources (papyri) that derive from Melitian monasteries and monks in Egypt. While the sources are often difficult to interpret, they have supplied valuable new evidence of the strength and scope of Melitian asceticism in the formative fourth-century period. The present article resulted from the fact that certain of these documents indicate the interconnection of a group of separate Melitian ascetic communities in Upper Egypt. The existence of this community of monasteries in the first half of the fourth century offers an intriguing parallel to the Pachomian *koinonia* or system of affiliated monasteries that arose at approximately the same time. In the first article in this volume, written but a year earlier, I argued that Pachomius's innovation was not communal monasticism per se, but the affiliation of a group of communal monasteries into a single system. While I still believe that it was the affiliated system that led to his fame, here I suggest that he was not alone in that innovation. That the Melitians linked separate monasteries in this same period indicates that the process had more to do with the growing number of ascetic communities than with the spread of a single innovative act. The affiliation of separate monasteries represents a natural organizational advance that increased an individual community's chance of success.

The final article in Part Two, "Monastic Diversity and Ideological Boundaries in Fourth-Century Christian Egypt" (1997), developed originally out of the same research into the sources of Melitian monasticism. The evidence indicated that in spite of the harsh rhetoric against Melitians in the episcopal sources, Melitian and non-Melitian monks interacted within the same monastic communities well into the sixth century. It appears that the ideological boundaries, which are often employed rigorously in the ecclesiastical or theological debate, were used less rigorously in practice in certain ascetic communities. In the paper, the Melitian evidence is supplemented by a section on Origenism, Pachomian monasticism, and the Nag Hammadi Codices in which I argue that, in this case, a more rigorous ideology was imposed on the earlier period by the way in which the later sources were edited and preserved. I contend that an emphasis on ascetic ideals (humility) and practice initially focused attention away from the ideological debate and allowed diverse individuals and different ideas to associate more freely together. A more rigorous, exclusive definition of orthodoxy, which naturally had stronger support in the episcopal realm, took hold in the ascetic movement more slowly on a case-by-case basis over time. As each variant ideology was rejected and subsequently removed from the preserved literary record, the early ascetic movement was remembered as more exclusive and more rigorously orthodox.

The final section in this volume, "Pachomian Studies: The Later Years," includes two articles that explore developments in Pachomian history after Theodore's death, the concluding event in the

Vitae traditions. The first article, "The Fourth Letter of Horsiesius and the Situation in the Pachomian Community following the Death of Theodore," was originally written in 1980 for inclusion in the *editio princeps* of two newly discovered letters of Horsiesius. The edition has not appeared, so the essay is presented here in revised form for the first time. Horsiesius's fourth letter indicates that he experienced difficulties in holding the community together when he assumed the position of general abbot upon Theodore's death. He had experienced the same problem when he first assumed that role shortly after Pachomius's death, but on that occasion, the problem was solved by Theodore's assumption of the leadership position. That the problem occurred a second time confirms both a particular dissatisfaction with Horsiesius among various of the monks and a more general centrifugal force working against the unity of the individual monasteries within the Pachomian *koinonia*. While Horsiesius survived this second attack, there is no way of knowing whether he successfully kept all of the monasteries together in the *koinonia*. In the article, I also note that Horsiesius used scriptural citations as a type of language in and of itself through which he expressed his own views on community matters. He is not alone in this practice in the Pachomian sources, but he uses it most extensively. It serves as a rhetorical device through which scripture and his words merge. To reject him thus becomes tantamount to rejecting scripture. Careful study of his scriptural citations in his fourth letter within the context of the difficulties being addressed allows one to speculate further on the nature of the problems he faced.

The final paper in the volume, "Chalcedonian Power Politics and the Demise of Pachomian Monasticism" (1989), addresses the Pachomian movement in the period after Chalcedon. Evidence contained in the *Life of Abraham of Farshut* indicates that the Emperor Justinian I (527–65 C.E.) sought to compel the Pachomians at their central monastery at Pbow to accept the decisions reached at Chalcedon. His efforts resulted in the departure of Abraham, the abbot, and many other monks. While Justinian was able to install Chalcedonian monks in the monastery, the monastery was, for all practical purposes, no longer Pachomian. In analyzing the sources, I argue that Justinian had seen in the large Pachomian community an ideal base from which to spread the Chalcedonian settlement in Upper

Egypt. He had, however, wrongly assumed its Chalcedonian leanings based on the position of the monks of the so-called Tabennesiote monastery on Canopus in Lower Egypt. They, it seems, were decidedly Chalcedonian. Justinian's efforts in forcing the Chalcedonian settlement on the Pachomian monastery effectively destroyed the future of the Pachomian movement by removing it from the plane of history. Forgotten in the Byzantine empire when Egypt remained non-Chalcedonian, it was ostracized from Coptic history by virtue of its forced adherence to Chalcedon.

All of the previously published articles in this volume have been reedited to bring consistency to the citations and the spelling of Coptic proper names and places. Changes in the content of the previously published articles were made in only a few places to increase clarity. Readers should thus keep in mind that each article still represents my thinking at the time of the article's original publication. Changes in the notes were also kept to a minimum. References to unpublished manuscripts were replaced with references to their subsequently published forms, and in a few cases, additional notes and clarifications have been added. With the exception of the three most important central abbots of the Pachomian *koinonia*, I have used the most common Sahidic spelling for Coptic proper names and place names. I have retained the Latinized forms for Pachomius (Sahidic Pachom), Theodore (Theodoros), and Horsiesius (Horsiese) only because they have become so standard in the literature.

1

The Origins of Monasticism

In an article published twenty-five years ago on "The Quest for
the 'Origins' of Religion," Mircea Eliade began by citing the French
proverb *Il n'y a que les détails qui comptent* (Only the details are really
important). He used the proverb to observe that "there are instances
in the history of culture when details are unexpectedly illuminating."[1] When one narrows the focus from the history of culture to the
history of early Christian monasticism, the validity of Eliade's observation remains. Consideration of the details has, in fact, proven
to be not only illuminating, but essential to a proper understanding of the subject; for when the details are forgotten or ignored, the
origins and development of Christian monasticism are traced down
oversimplified and erroneous paths.

The views of Antony as the first monk and of Egypt as the source
from which his innovation and its developments spread throughout
the rest of Christendom, views still often found in basic accounts of
Christian history,[2] are prime examples of such oversimplified and
erroneous conclusions. Clean and simple as this "big bang" theory
of monastic origins is, the details fail to support it. It is dependent
on the selective use of mainstream Greek and Latin sources and
as such betrays its foundation in and support of a Western "orthodox" view of history. When the net is cast more widely and the
sources read more carefully, the nearsightedness of the theory becomes apparent. The *Life of Antony* itself mentions his predecessors.[3]
Syriac scholars have established the independent origin and devel-

---

First published in Harold W. Attridge and Gohei Hata, *Eusebius, Christianity, and
Judaism* (Detroit: Wayne State University Press, 1992) 235–55.

1. Eliade, "Quest."
2. Roland H. Bainton, *Christendom: A Short History of Christianity and Its Impact on
Western Civilization* (2 vols.; New York: Harper & Row, 1964) 1.104–5; Jaroslav Pelikan,
Jesus through the Centuries: His Place in the History of Culture (New Haven and London:
Yale University Press, 1985) 110–12.
3. *Vita Antonii* 3 (PG 26.843–44); see discussion below.

opment of monasticism in the Syrian province,[4] and recent evidence has called the "orthodox" origin of certain monastic developments into question.[5]

The tendency toward theoretical oversimplification is controlled by remembering the importance of the details. What follows is neither an exhaustive treatment of early Christian monasticism nor yet another quest for its "origins,"[6] but rather an introductory tour through the details of selected sources. It is a tour designed both to reveal the diversity in the "origins and development" of early Christian monasticism and to underscore the impact of Western historiography on its interpretation.

THE EVIDENCE OF EUSEBIUS

Eusebius of Caesarea, in Book 2 of his *Ecclesiastical History*, offers an example of the perfect union of the proclamation of the gospel with the undertaking of an ascetic life. He reports that when Mark preached the gospel in Egypt,[7] "the number of men and women who were there converted at the first attempt was so great, and their asceticism was so extraordinarily philosophic, that Philo thought it right to describe their conduct and assemblies and meals and all the rest of their manner of life."[8] The account of the Therapeutae, a Jewish ascetic community situated above Lake Mareotis in Egypt, which follows, is drawn directly from Philo Judaeus's *On the Con-*

---

4. A. Vööbus, *A History of Asceticism in the Syrian Orient: A Contribution to the History of Culture in the Near East* (2 vols.; CSCO 184, 197; Louvain: Secrétariat du CSCO, 1958–60); S. Brock, "Early Syrian Asceticism," *Numen* 20 (1973) 1–19; Price, *History,* xvii–xxiii.

5. On the relationship between the Pachomian monastic movement and the Nag Hammadi Library, see Goehring, "New Frontiers," 236–52 (chap. 8 in the present volume), and Veilleux, "Monasticism and Gnosis." On the significance of the Manichaean influence, see Timothy D. Barnes, *Constantine and Eusebius* (Cambridge and London: Harvard University Press, 1981) 195, and Koenen, "Manichäische Mission."

6. The quest for "origins" occurred in diverse fields in the nineteenth century and as such has been shown to be a product of Western historiography (Eliade, "Quest").

7. Birger A. Pearson, "Earliest Christianity in Egypt: Some Observations," in Pearson and Goehring, *Roots,* 132–59.

8. *Historia ecclesiastica* 2.16; translation from Kirsopp Lake, J. E. L. Oulton, and H. J. Lawlor, *Eusebius: The Ecclesiastical History* (LCL; 2 vols.; Cambridge: Harvard University Press, 1926) 1.145.

templative Life.[9] Eusebius's identification of this Jewish community as Christian is clearly in error, though his belief that they were Christian betrays his view of the immediacy of the ascetic demand in the Christian call. The evidence should neither be used to support Eusebius's knowledge of "organized monastic communities in Palestine" before 300 C.E.,[10] nor to argue, since he elsewhere mentions no known Christian communities, that such communities did not yet exist.[11] Rather, Christian belief and ascetic practice were so closely connected in Eusebius's theology[12] that the identification of the Therapeutae as Christian seemed only natural to him. The naturalness of the equation is apparent in the fact that some scholars have chosen to discount the Philonic authorship of *On the Contemplative Life* rather than the Christian status of the Therapeutae.[13]

Eusebius's placing of this material near the beginning of his history establishes an origin for the ascetic life very early in the spread of the gospel.[14] The demand of an ascetic life lived in separation from the world is, through this account, made part of the earliest impulse of Christian existence and interestingly linked to Egypt. This treatment reveals in the case of Eusebius not so much a quest for the origins of monasticism nor even evidence of a specific knowledge of it, but rather the impact of his theology on his understanding of history. The elite ascetic life, a life above nature and beyond common human living,[15] is so central to his understanding of Christianity that it pushes itself back into his recovery of Christianity's formative years. If the origins are not understood or known, they are in a sense "mythically" created in the beginning with the gospel.

Beyond this most obvious example of a monastic life in Euse-

---

9. Leopold Cohn and Paul Wendland, eds., *Philonis opera quae supersunt* (7 vols. in 8; Berlin: Georg Reimer, 1896–1930) vol. 4; F. H. Colson, *Philo* (10 vols.; LCL; Cambridge: Harvard University Press, 1967) 9:113–69.

10. Barnes, *Constantine and Eusebius*, 195.

11. Hermann Weingarten, "Der Ursprung des Mönchtums im nachconstantinischen Zeitalter," *ZKG* 1 (1877) 6–10.

12. Eusebius, *Demonstratio evangelica* 1.8; Brown, *Body and Society*, 205.

13. Joseph Juste Scalinger, *De emendatione temporum* (Francofurti: I. Wechelum, 1593); Ernst Lucius, *Die Therapeuten und ihre Stellung in der Geschichte der Askese: Eine kritische Untersuchung der Schrift "De vita contemplativa"* (Strasbourg: Schmidt, 1879).

14. On the order of the material in Eusebius's *Ecclesiastical History*, see Robert M. Grant, *Eusebius as Church Historian* (Oxford: Clarendon Press, 1980). Philo's account of the Therapeutae is examined on pages 72–76 of Grant's work.

15. Eusebius, *Demonstratio evangelica* 1.8.

bius's *Ecclesiastical History,* one finds little evidence for a particular lifestyle defined as ascetic. There are numerous ascetic individuals who lead ascetic lives, but there is no individual or pattern that is established as an archetype that one should follow. Physical withdrawal (ἀναχώρησις) from the world, which became so central to the definition of monasticism through the later *Life of Antony,* is represented in Eusebius, but it is neither a prerequisite for the ascetic life nor is it indicative solely of the ascetic individual. He reports that Narcissus, the bishop of Jerusalem, escaped from the church to practice his "philosophic life" by retiring "secretly in deserts and obscure parts of the country,"[16] and that Clement of Alexandria had to seek Pantaenus out from his concealment in Egypt (ἐν Αἰγύπτῳ θηράσας λεληθότα).[17] Yet Origen, whose ascetic life is recorded in detail by Eusebius, practiced his "most philosophic manner of life" as a teacher, a profession that necessitated his presence in the world rather than his physical withdrawal from it. Eusebius reports that Origen astounded his followers by the severity of his ascetic labors. He disciplined himself in fasting, limited his sleep, which he took on the floor, persevered in cold and nakedness, embraced extreme limits of poverty, walked without shoes, and abstained from wine and all but necessary food. Following the gospel precept, he even made himself a eunuch for the kingdom of God.[18] This ultimate act of ascetic renunciation was undertaken, according to Eusebius, precisely because of Origen's presence within the world, so "that he might prevent all suspicion of shameful slander on the part of unbelievers (for, young as he was, he used to discourse on divine things with women as well as men)."[19]

Likewise Eusebius knows that many fled to the desert and mountains not to practice the ascetic life, but to avoid persecution. Unlike Jerome,[20] he does not link, through the commonality of the desert, the flight of early Christians to avoid persecution with the withdrawal of the later Christians as desert ascetics. He rather saw such

---

16. *Historia ecclesiastica* 6.9.6–6.10.1.
17. *Historia ecclesiastica* 5.11.4.
18. *Historia ecclesiastica* 6.3.9–13; 6.8.1–3.
19. *Historia ecclesiastica* 6.8.2. Translation from Lake, Oulton, and Lawlor, *Eusebius,* 2.29.
20. *Vita Pauli* (PL 23.17–30); Heussi, *Ursprung,* 70; Chitty, *Desert a City,* 6–7.

flight as but another form of persecution that resulted in their death "by hunger and thirst and frost and diseases and robbers and wild beasts."[21] The later understanding of the monk as the latter-day martyr is contradicted in Eusebius in the account of Alcibiades, who, though he had led a very austere life, was dissuaded by fellow Christians in jail from his ascetic practices before his martyrdom.[22] Rather than a picture of asceticism replacing martyrdom, one finds presented here the suggestion that persecution could hinder or even curtail the ascetic life.

Retreat to the desert has its origin for Eusebius not in the enforced flight of the persecuted, but in the voluntary search for solitude of the philosophical elite.[23] In joining together the powers of Christianity and Rome, he presented Christianity as the new philosophy which demanded among its elite practitioners an ascetic life. The life of renunciation is in fact the new "philosophic way of life" (βίος φιλόσοφος).[24] While this life may be perfected by martyrdom, it precedes the martyr's call.[25] While Eusebius might admit that some desert ascetics discovered the value of solitary life in the desert as a result of their flight from persecution, he certainly does not find in them *the* origin of the monastic life.

For Eusebius, the ascetic life cannot be an accidental discovery. Viewed as the elite form of Christian existence, it is the highest demonstration of the gospel. As the pre-Christian philosophers logically led an ascetic life, so the new Christian elite, e.g., Origen and Narcissus, knowingly undertook a philosophic life, by which Eusebius means Christian teaching and ascetic practice. While the dogma shifted from Plato to Christ, the ascetic lifestyle remained the same.

For the historical origins of monasticism proper Eusebius offers little evidence. His linkage of ascetic practice to the philosophic life, while undoubtedly accurate in a broader sense for the intellectual

---

21. *Historia ecclesiastica* 6.42.2.

22. *Historia ecclesiastica* 5.3.1–3.

23. Eusebius posits two ways of life given by the Lord to his church: that of the married Christian and that of the elite, who, in their ascetic life, live beyond or above human nature. *Demonstratio evangelica* 1.8; Brown, *Body and Society*, 205.

24. *Historia ecclesiastica* 6.3.9, 13; 6.9.6; 6.10.1. The same definition of the ascetic life as a practice of philosophy is found throughout Theodoret of Cyrrhus's *Historia religiosa*. P. Canivet and A. Leroy-Molinghen, eds., *Théodoret de Cyr: Histoire des Moines de Syrie* (SC 234, 257; Paris: Éditions du Cerf, 1977–79); Price, *History*.

25. *Historia ecclesiastica* 6.3.13.

elite, does not explain the rapid swelling of the monastic ranks in the late third and early fourth centuries by individuals of lower social and intellectual status both within the geographical boundaries of Greek culture and beyond. His portrayal is that of a Greek intellectual and represents a philosophically elite, Hellenocentric view of monastic development.

THE *LIFE OF ANTONY*

The literary source most often turned to first to explicate the origins of monasticism among the common people is the *Life of Antony*.[26] According to the author of this heroic *Vita*, Antony, after the death of his parents, turned to the ascetic life when he heard in church the call of the gospel, "If you will be perfect, go sell all that you have and give to the poor; and come, follow me and you will have treasures in heaven" (Matt. 19:21). About twenty years old at the time, he gave his inheritance away and began his ascetic career in the vicinity of his village. His subsequent successes in the solitary life led to his ever increasing fame as a holy man, which in turn necessitated his withdrawal to ever more remote desert locations in order to regain his lost solitude. From his first village retreat he soon withdrew to more distant tombs, where he struggled with demons and continued to be visited by old acquaintances.[27] At age thirty-five he withdrew further into the desert of Pispir to a deserted fort where he continued to practice the ascetic life by himself for twenty years. Again his friends came to visit him.[28] In the years that followed, his fame became so great that the many who came to imitate his life eventually broke down the door of his abode to get at him. We are told that when he came forth, he appeared "as one initiated into sacred mysteries and filled with the spirit of God." He had conquered the demands of human life, for his body, in spite of the fastings and struggles, appeared the same as it had been before his withdrawal.[29]

---

26. *PG* 26.823–896; G. J. M. Bartelink, *Athanase d'Alexandrie: Vie d'Antoine* (SC 400; Paris: Éditions du Cerf, 1994); English translations in Robert T. Meyer, *St. Athanasius: The Life of Saint Antony* (ACW; New York: Newman Press, 1950); Gregg, *Life of Antony.*

27. *Vita Antonii* 2–8 (*PG* 26.841–856).

28. *Vita Antonii* 10–13 (*PG* 26.859–864).

29. *Vita Antonii* 14 (*PG* 26.863–866).

Many then came to Antony and were taught by him until once again the pressures became too great. In search of the ever fleeting solitude he desired, he set out on a journey to the Upper Thebaid and established his final abode near the Red Sea at the Inner Mountain (modern Deir Anba Antonius).[30] Here too, of course, his solitude could not be maintained as his fame and influence in matters of ascetic practice and Christian theology continued to grow.

Antony became, through this account, the most famous practitioner of the ascetic life. Much as Paul had become the apostle to the Gentiles par excellence through the fact that he was the most influential if not the first, so too Antony became the monk par excellence. His status as such easily translated into a view of his undertaking as innovative and original. He became not only the monk par excellence, but also the first monk from whom all subsequent developments flowed. From the eremitic life of Antony came the coenobitic innovation of Pachomius, and from these springs in Egypt flowed the monastic rivers that watered Palestine and Syria, Rome and the West.

To base a theory of monastic origins and development on the *Life of Antony* is, however, to base it on a literary model. The image of Antony as the father of Christian monasticism is dependent less on the historical undertaking of Antony than on the literary success of the *Life of Antony*. The rhetorical intent and power of the *Vita* is still evident today in the centrality given to Antony in monastic history. The *Vita* itself, when proper attention is given to the details, rejects the originality of Antony's undertaking.[31] Before embarking himself on an ascetic career, Antony placed his orphaned sister with "known and trusted virgins." He then sought out an individual ascetic whom he might emulate and found one, an old man in a neighboring village, who had lived the ascetic life in solitude from his youth.[32] Precedents thus clearly existed for the young Antony, even according to the *Vita*. In addition in the *Vita*, one hears of monasteries in Egypt at the time, though they are reported to be few in number. While this reference to monasteries may be anachronistic, their mere mention indicates that the author had no intention of claiming Antony as the

---

30. *Vita Antonii* 49–51 (*PG* 26.914–19).
31. Heussi, *Ursprung*, 56–58.
32. *Vita Antonii* 3 (*PG* 26.843–846).

"originator" of the monastic enterprise. He is more concerned with Antony's subsequent fame which, by portraying Antony as staunchly anti-Arian, he uses to garnish monastic support for his own ecclesio-political position.[33] His goal is thus served by portraying Antony as famous and hence more visibly "orthodox."

A comparison of the *Life of Antony* with the letters of Antony and the sayings attributed to him in the *Apophthegmata Patrum* reveals the literary modeling of the Antony of the *Vita*. He bears only an in-direct relationship to the historical Antony.[34] The image of Antony as the father of Christian monasticism is but a product of Antony's subsequent success multiplied in turn by the success of the *Vita*. This success, real and literary, may have added impetus to the mo-nastic enterprise in Egypt and beyond, but it did not originate it. If the *Vita* had not been written, it is questionable whether greater claim would have been given to Antony's influence than to that of Macarios the Great (ca. 300–390 C.E.), Arsenios (ca. 354–412 C.E.), or Poemen (d. ca. 450 C.E.).[35] Athanasius, if indeed he wrote the *Vita*,[36] mentions Antony only once in his other writings. While Athanasius corresponded with various monks, we know of no correspondence with Antony. Antony's fame is the fame of the *Vita*.

THE VILLAGE ASCETICS

When one sets Antony aside and turns instead to the "known and trusted virgins" with whom he left his sister and the old ascetic in the neighboring village whom he sought to emulate, another view of the origins of monastic development in Egypt begins to emerge.

---

33. Robert C. Gregg and Dennis E. Groh, *Early Arianism: A View of Salvation* (Phila-delphia: Fortress Press, 1981) 131–59; but note the anti-Arian stance of the Antony of the letters. Rubenson, *Letters of St. Antony*, 44–45.

34. Dörries, "Die Vita Antonii"; Heussi, *Ursprung*, 78–108.

35. The thirty-eight sayings attributed to Antony in the alphabetical collection of the *Apophthegmata Patrum*, while a fair number, do not set him apart numerically at least from a number of other famous monks in the collection. Forty-four sayings of Arsenios are recorded, 47 of John the Dwarf, 41 of Macarios the Great, 209 of Poemen, 54 of Sisoes, and 27 of Amma Syncletica.

36. Heussi, *Ursprung*, 78–86; Timothy D. Barnes, "Angel of Light or Mystic Initi-ate? The Problem of the *Life of Antony*," *JTS* 37 (1986) 353–68; Charles Kannengiesser, "St. Athanasius of Alexandria Rediscovered: His Political and Pastoral Achievement," *CCR* 9 (1988) 69–70.

Here one finds that withdrawal to the desert is not central; the persons involved remained within the village community. An ascetic life, whether practiced alone or in common with like-minded individuals, involved withdrawal from certain social patterns of human existence (family and sex), but not a physical separation from the community. That persons from his village followed Antony to his desert retreats and sought his presence might be interpreted to mean not that they wished to emulate him but that they felt cheated by his departure. In seeking solitude in the desert away from the village, he was taking with him the power of God made available to the village through his presence. The ascetic had a function in the village, and Antony's innovative departure called this function into question.

The existence of these village ascetics is confirmed from other sources. A party of visitors who traveled between Alexandria and Lycopolis in 394–95 C.E. on an excursion to visit various monks and monastic communities reports that in the Theban city of Oxyrhynchus "the monks were almost the majority over the secular inhabitants."[37] They observed that the old temples were bursting with monks and that no quarter of the city was free from them. They estimated the number within the walls at five thousand. While the details of the account are open to question, the active presence of monks within the city is apparent. These ascetics had not left to make the desert a city, but had remained to turn the city into a virtual monastery.[38]

A documentary papyrus from Egypt dated to June 324 C.E. and supplying the first known technical use of the term μοναχός for a Christian monk uses the term precisely to describe such a "city" or village ascetic.[39] In this brief document submitted to Dioscorus Caeso, the *praepositus pagi* of the region, Aurelius Isidorus, a private citizen of Karanis, filed a claim against Pamounis and Harpalus, whose cow destroyed his farming efforts and who assaulted him when he attempted to remove the animal from his field. In describing the assault, Isidorus claims that the two would have killed him

---

37. *Historia Monachorum in Aegypto* 5; translation from Russell and Ward, *Lives of the Desert Fathers,* 67.

38. Brown, *Body and Society,* 217.

39. Judge, "Earliest Use," 72–89. The term occurs in the *Gospel of Thomas* (36.4; 41.28; 46.12), though not in the later technical sense of "monk."

if not for the intervention of "the deacon Antoninus and the monk Isaac."

This monk, the earliest for whom direct nonliterary evidence is available, is not one who, in a quest for solitude, fled to the desert or mountains where he might avoid the encumbering affairs of the world. Isaac, as a μοναχός, remained an active member of the wider community. The simple inclusion of his title μοναχός in the petition, together with that of the deacon Antoninus, suggests that both the titles and the individuals were recognized in Karanis. The petitioner, Isidorus, undoubtedly hoped to add weight to his claim through his use of the titles.[40]

The monk (or μοναχός) Isaac represents a type of ascetic termed elsewhere an ἀποτακτικός. According to the documentary evidence, the apotactic movement played a significant role in early Christianity.[41] It is, however, summarily dismissed in the surviving literary sources. Jerome, who labeled such monks *remnuoth*,[42] repudiated them as reprobate or "false" monks in his famous letter to Eustochium. He reports that they live together in small groups within the cities, refuse to subordinate themselves to anyone, quarrel frequently, dress ostentatiously and sigh constantly for the effect, visit virgins, and disparage the clergy. He advises Eustochium to avoid them like the plague, while recommending to her the "true" monks who follow the anchoritic or coenobitic life.[43]

Jerome's vitriolic attack against such "city" monks is not unusual, though his vituperative skill is perhaps unmatched. His judgment against them is necessarily suspect. Their numbers were large. Jerome himself admits that they were the most numerous type of monk in his own province of Pannonia. His universal rejection of them undoubtedly has more to do with their unsubordinated power

---

40. Judge, "Earliest Use," 73–74.

41. Judge, "Earliest Use," 79–89.

42. The term *remnuoth* most likely means "a solitary." For a discussion of the meaning of the term and the parallel *Sarabaitae*, see Jürgen Horn, "Tria sunt in Aegypto genera monachorum: Die ägyptischen Bezeichnungen für die 'dritte Art' des Mönchtums bei Hieronymus und Johannes Cassianus," in Heike Behlmer, ed., *Festgabe für Wolfhart Westendorf zu seinem 70. Geburtstag* (Göttingen: Seminar für Ägyptologie und Koptologie, 1994) 63–82.

43. *Ep.* 22.34 (CSEL 54); F. A. Wright, *Select Letters of St. Jerome* (LCL; Cambridge: Harvard University Press, 1933); Judge, "Earliest Use," 78–79.

and perhaps their theology than their corrupt manner of life. The latter is simply part of Jerome's attack against them.[44]

Within the city, monastic and clerical authorities clashed head-on, without the buffer of a desert or monastery wall. In another mainstream literary source, the *Letter of Ammon,* Ammon reports that his priest dismissed as heretical an Alexandrian monk with whom he first considered affiliating himself. The priest sent him instead up the Nile to the Pachomian community.[45] In the literary sources, which represent the successful ecclesiastical party, these "city" monks have lost the struggle for authority and have been dismissed. They are rejected as those who pervert the monastic life for their own gain and are unworthy, in Jerome's view, of even bearing the title of monk. The title is reserved for those who withdraw from the social world of the village and leave the village thereby under the authority of the clergy. The "true" monk lives in isolation or in a community behind a wall. The term μοναχός itself becomes limited in the literary sources to these later anchoritic and coenobitic forms of the ascetic life.[46]

In this literary success of the more easily controllable anchoritic and coenobitic forms of monasticism, the "city" monks or *remnuoth* are not only disparaged, but for the most part they are forgotten or ignored. Their significance for the formative stages of monastic history was thus lost. While the ecclesiastical rhetoric of Jerome and others that carried the day continues to affect the presentation of monastic history, the documentary evidence has begun to challenge their control of that history. The *remnuoth* or ἀποτακτικοί are reclaiming their rightful place. Judge, who wrote the definitive study on the apotactic movement, asserts that

> we must posit an event, or change of fashion, different from and prior to the creation of either eremitism (in its Antonian form) or coeno-bitism, but perhaps close in time to them, and part of a swift series of developments that led to them. The apotactic movement (as later attested) meets this requirement. It represents the point at which the men at last followed the pattern long set for virgins and widows, and

---

44. This is not to suggest that corrupt monks did not exist in the cities, but only that such corruption was not determined by the monk's residence in the city.

45. *Epistula Ammonis* 2; Goehring, *Letter of Ammon,* 124–25, 191.

46. Judge, "Earliest Use," 78–79.

set up houses of their own in town, in which the life of personal renunciation and service in the church would be practiced.[47]

The true significance of the old village ascetic whom Antony encountered before his withdrawal to the desert now becomes clear. The ascetic, like Isaac, while setting himself apart from the normal pattern of human existence, remained within the community where he served as a source of inspiration and as a known conduit to the divine. It was not an accident that Antony turned to him. Given this understanding of the monk, Antony's subsequent innovation of withdrawal from the village broke the pattern. While in the long run the withdrawal pleased the ecclesiastical opponents like Jerome, one suspects that in the short run it was viewed by others as desertion. If all who chose the ascetic life fled to the desert, to whom would the villagers turn in time of need?

Documentary evidence likewise helps to explicate the role of the "known and trusted virgins" to whom Antony entrusted his young orphaned sister before he departed on his own ascetic career. A legal document dated to 400 C.E. records the lease of space on the ground floor and basement of a house owned by two natural sisters, Theodora and Tauris, μοναχαὶ ἀποτακτικαί.[48] While the precise role of these two sisters within the broader community is not given, their status as μοναχαὶ ἀποτακτικαί sets them apart, and their business transactions suggest their social power and prestige. Since the papyrus comes from Oxyrhynchus, it seems likely that Theodora and Tauris should be numbered among the twenty thousand virgins reported living in that city in the *History of the Monks in Egypt*. They outnumbered their male counterparts by two to one.[49]

Two letters from a woman named Didyme of the early fourth century offer tantalizing evidence of an organization of Christian women involved in the daily life of the surrounding community.[50] "Didyme and the sisters" participated in various commercial transactions that include lines of credit and the transfer of goods (grapes,

---

47. Judge, "Earliest Use," 85.

48. *P. Oxy.* 3203; Judge, "Earliest Use," 82; idem, "Fourth-Century Monasticism," 613.

49. *Historia Monachorum in Aegypto* 5.6; Judge, "Earliest Use," 82–83.

50. *P. Berl. Inv.* 13897 and *P. Oxy.* 1774; Alanna Emmett, "The Nuns and the Ostrich Egg" (lecture).

sandals, cakes, a headband, and an ostrich egg). While it is not clear that their organization should be understood as a monastery in the later sense,[51] it does appear to fit an earlier form of Christian ascetic association in which flight from the world was not primary. Like the μοναχός Isaac, Didyme and the sisters mingle openly in the daily life of the wider Christian community. Their embracing of the "solitary" life does not preclude the using of their talents to help in diverse ways their brothers and sisters in the Lord.

The documentary evidence of these early female and male ascetic associations and roles suggests that Antony's innovation lay not in the idea of withdrawal per se, but in its translation from an ethical to a physical plane. Theodora, Tauris, and Isaac withdrew from the traditional ethical patterns of the family, but not from the social and indeed commercial interactions of the Christian community. They chose a solitary life in place of family and children and viewed it as an opportunity to increase their service to the Lord through their service to their fellow Christians. Antony expanded this concept of withdrawal to include a physical separation from one's fellow Christians through flight to ever more remote retreats.[52]

A careful reading of the *Life of Antony* reveals that he took time to develop this idea and put it into effect. Judge notes that the term μοναχός appears for the first time in the *Vita* precisely at the moment Antony terminated his self-imposed solitude. It was only then that he "became the centre of public excitement and began to constitute a social movement."[53] Thus even in this most literary of monastic sources, the term *monk* is linked first to a socially active undertaking rather than to a withdrawal from society. Eventually Antony did outgrow this "social movement" (and with it the original meaning of μοναχός) and withdrew to a distant mountain retreat where he spent the rest of his life, some forty-three years, as a true hermit.

Not all followed Antony in his decision to withdraw further and to abandon his newly created social movement. Some chose to re-

---

51. Emmett, "Nuns," 4–5; P. Barison, "Ricerche sui monasteri dell'Egitto bizantino ed arabo secondo i documenti dei papiri greci," *Aeg* 18 (1938) 138.

52. It is not clear to this author whether this innovation is that of the historical Antony or more likely presented as such by his biographer.

53. *Vita Antonii* 14 (PG 26.863–866); Judge, "Earliest Use," 77. Judge suggests that the monk Isaac may have been influenced by Antony's efforts, since Karanis was but a day's walk from the center of Antony's activities.

main closer to home in and around the villages. To judge from the accounts of papyri from Oxyrhynchus and Jerome's *remnuoth*,[54] their numbers were large. Some eventually found an ordered existence in the coenobitic innovations of monks like Pachomius.[55] Others either filtered into developing ecclesiastical structures under the control of the clergy or came under the opprobrium of church officials like Jerome. In either case, as witnesses to a third form of the monastic life, they disappeared from the scene and were forgotten. While more original historically than either the anchoritic ideal of Antony or the coenobitic innovation of Pachomius, the apotactic movement was supplanted by these later developments and forgotten. The original significance of the term μοναχός was lost. In its new meaning of physical withdrawal, Antony, as portrayed in the *Vita*, became its first exemplar. Having left the apotactic movement behind literarily, it was a short step to see Antony as the first monk and his innovation as the origin of monasticism.

PACHOMIUS AND THE COENOBITES

The story is much the same with respect to the understanding of coenobitic monasticism as an innovation of the Upper Egyptian figure of Pachomius. It has already been suggested that it arose in Egypt as one of two developments from the earlier apotactic movement. When the latter came under disrepute, the successful movement begun by Pachomius in Upper Egypt came to be associated with the origin of coenobitic monasticism much as Antony had come to be associated with the origin of anchoritic monasticism. It was again to a significant degree the success of the Pachomian *Rule* and the *Life of Pachomius*,[56] both of which had gained wide distribu-

---

54. See above discussion.

55. Judge, "Earliest Use," 78.

56. The *Life of Pachomius* survives in various Coptic, Greek, Arabic, and Latin versions, the interrelatedness of which is complex. For an account of the issues see Goehring, *Letter of Ammon*, 3–23, and Rousseau, *Ascetics*, 243–47. The text of the Bohairic version of the *Vita* (*Bo*) is found in Lefort, *S. Pachomii vita bohairice scripta*. The Sahidic versions are found in Lefort, *S. Pachomii vitae sahidice scriptae*. The Greek versions (including the *Vita prima=G1*) are located in Halkin, *Sancti Pachomii Vitae Graecae*. The *Rule*, which survives in Coptic and Greek fragments, was translated into Latin and circulated by Jerome (see Boon, *Pachomiana latina*). English translations of all the major texts within the Pachomian corpus are found in Veilleux, *Pachomian Koinonia*.

tion through their translation into Greek and Latin, that accounted for the assumed preeminence of Pachomius.

The *Vita* reports that Pachomius converted to Christianity at about age twenty. As a conscript into the Roman army, he had been housed in prison to await movement toward the front. It was in prison that he first met Christians, who impressed him by the compassion they showed toward him and his fellow conscripts. He promised to convert if he should be freed, and upon his release, he was baptized and undertook an ascetic life as an anchorite under the tutelage of Palamon, a famous ascetic living near the village of Šeneset (Chenoboskion) in Upper Egypt.[57] The ascetic demands were hard, but Pachomius proved capable.

His coenobitic innovation came as the result of a vision. While gathering wood at the deserted village of Tabennese, he was instructed to remain there and build a monastery. After consulting with Palamon, he undertook the task imposed upon him by the vision. Soon many came to join in his new communal experiment.[58] In time the numbers became too large for the original establishment at Tabennese, and a second monastery was constructed at the deserted village of Pbow. This second monastery soon functioned as the center of a growing system of monastic settlements scattered along the Nile in Upper Egypt. The *koinonia,* as it came to be known, served not only a spiritual need, but invigorated the economy of the area.[59] By the time of Pachomius's death in 346 C.E., his *koinonia* numbered some nine monasteries and two affiliated women's houses. Their organization was governed by a common *Rule,* which soon came to be used by coenobitic establishments beyond his organizational control. This development led to the designation of any monastery that used the Pachomian *Rule* as Tabennesiote, which in turn translated, often incorrectly, into the community's Pachomian origin.[60]

A Greek version of the *Life of Pachomius* was taken to the Alexandrian archbishop Theophilus around 400 C.E., from where we can surmise it spread. Crum, *Papyruscodex,* 12–13; Lefort, *Vies coptes,* 389–90.

57. *Bo* 7–10; *G1* 4–6.
58. *Bo* 17–26; *G1* 12–24.
59. Goehring, "World Engaged" (chap. 2 in the present volume).
60. James E. Goehring, "Chalcedonian Power Politics and the Demise of Pachomian Monasticism" (OP 15; Claremont, Calif.: Institute for Antiquity and Christianity, 1989) 17–18 (see pp. 258–59 in the present volume).

The picture of Pachomius's originality is, however, literary rather than historical. According to the *Life of Pachomius* itself, at least three of the original nine monasteries were not founded by the Pachomians but elected to join the Pachomian system. They clearly had an independent origin. There is no indication how long the monastery at Šeneset existed prior to its decision to affiliate itself with the Pachomian *koinonia*. It is simply reported that it had existed previously under an old ascetic named Ebonh. The monastery of Tmoušons, the fourth to join the Pachomian system, likewise had an earlier independent existence,[61] as did the monastery of Tbewe, which had been founded previously by a certain Petronios. The latter had withdrawn from his parent's home and gathered like-minded individuals around him who wanted to live in Christ. It was only then that he heard of the Pachomian *koinonia* and wrote to Pachomius asking that his monastery be accepted into the system. Tbewe thus became a Pachomian monastery. The *Vita* makes clear through these stories that Pachomius's innovation had little to do with the coenobitic institution itself. It was rather the organizational principle of a *koinonia* or system of affiliated coenobitic monasteries and the development of a monastic rule that are credited to Pachomius.[62]

Furthermore, it is certain that not all coenobitic communities chose to join his *koinonia*. When Theodore, Pachomius's most significant successor as general abbot, joined the movement in its early years, he transferred from an existing monastery further down the Nile.[63] There is no indication that Theodore's original community ever desired to join the Pachomian system. Likewise, while Shenoute appreciated Pachomius's undertaking and borrowed from his rule, his monasteries had an independent origin and followed their own pattern of development.[64] Melitian and Manichaean communities also remained outside the Pachomian fold.[65]

---

61. *Bo* 50–55; *G1* 54.
62. The organizational principle may be dependent in part on the temple hierarchy and organization in Egypt. Ruppert, *Das pachomianische Mönchtum*, 324–26. Manichaean precedents must also be considered (above, n. 5).
63. *Bo* 29–32; *G1* 33–35. Goehring, "Theodore's Entry."
64. Leipoldt, *Schenute von Atripe*, 34–39; Hans Quecke, "Ein Pachomiuszitat bei Schenute," in Peter Nagel, ed., *Probleme der koptischen Literatur* (Halle: Martin Luther Universität, 1968) 155–71.
65. On the Manichaeans see Stroumsa, "Manichaean Challenge," 307–19, and

The theory of a Pachomian origin of coenobitic monasticism must thus be discarded. Attempts to explain his insight through the borrowing of earlier communal experiences or experiments fall into the same trap insofar as they seek to trace the coenobitic development back to a single root. The theory that his efforts to organize disparate monks into a systematic community was a result of his experience in the army, would, if it could be maintained, only account for Pachomius's effort and not those of the surrounding communities that joined his system.[66] While the influence of Egyptian temple organization on his *koinonia* is clearer, once again it helps to explain his particular plans, but hardly the "origin" of coenobitic monasticism.[67]

More recently the early presence of Manichaean missionaries in Egypt has offered a possible source of influence for Pachomius's innovation.[68] While their communities existed earlier, there is no direct evidence of their influence on Pachomius. He might as well have heard of Philo's Therapeutae. Furthermore, even if Pachomius had been directly influenced by the Manichaean movement organizationally, it does not establish a single Manichaean origin of coenobitic monasticism. The vast number of monasteries in Egypt in the late Byzantine era simply cannot be traced to a single point of origin. Archaeological evidence from Deir el-Bala'izah suggests, for example, a monastery structure somewhere between the semi-eremitic communities of the Wadi Natrun and the fully coenobitic establishments of Pachomius. Its unique organizational pattern argues against a Pachomian source of inspiration.[69] Finally, it can be noted that when Justinian forced a Chalcedonian abbot on the Pachomian commu-

---

above, n. 5. On the Melitians, note Bell, *Jews and Christians in Egypt*, 38–99, and chap. 9 in the present volume.

66. Chitty, *Desert a City*, 22; Leonard Lesko, "Monasticism in Egypt," in Florence D. Friedman, ed., *Beyond the Pharaohs: Egypt and the Copts in the 2nd to 7th Centuries A.D.* (Providence: Museum of Art, Rhode Island School of Design, 1989) 46. It seems unlikely that Pachomius's brief sojourn in the army as a conscript, probably against his will, would have influenced him in the positive direction of modeling his community on the experience.

67. Ruppert, *Das pachomianische Mönchtum*, 324–26.

68. See above, nn. 5 and 65.

69. Peter Grossmann, "Die Unterkunftsbauten des Koinobitenklosters 'Dair al-Balayza' im Vergleich mit den Eremitagen der Mönche von Kellia," in *Le site monastique copte des Kellia: Sources historiques et explorations archéologiques. Actes du Colloque de Genève, 13 au 15 août 1984* (Geneva: Mission suisse d'archéologie copte de l'Université de Genève, 1986).

nity at Pbow, many monks fled to other existing monasteries. That such monasteries existed untouched by Justinian's efforts against the Pachomian *koinonia* argues for their independence from it.[70]

The possible influence of the Manichaean movement on Pachomius raises the point of the actual theological nature of the movement. While the surviving literary sources portray it as in close agreement with the mainstream Christian forces exemplified by Athanasius (ca. 296–373 C.E.), increasing evidence suggests that such careful theological concern and definition is anachronistic, a product of the time when the sources were composed and edited rather than of the historical period they purport to describe. Two major manuscript discoveries made near the Pachomian monastery of Pbow raise the question of their origin within the Pachomian system. The Dishna Papers, which include the Bodmer Papyri, include copies of letters from the early Pachomian abbots. This evidence has led James Robinson to claim that the contents of this manuscript hoard represent the remains of a Pachomian library.[71] If true, these contents reveal much about the breadth of Pachomian intellectual activity. As one would expect, biblical texts predominate; but one finds as well apocryphal material, classical texts (including a satyr play), mathematical exercises, tax receipts, and a Greek grammar. While some of this material may have entered the community in the belongings of new members, there appears to have been no effort to weed it out.

The second manuscript collection, the Nag Hammadi Codices, offers an even more startling possibility. This collection preserves a significant number of heterodox texts, many of which are Gnostic in origin and most of which would have been rejected by the Athanasian party. The question of a Pachomian origin and use of these codices has been much debated, and no clear consensus has emerged.[72] That the idea remains a real possibility in itself under-

---

70. Goehring, "Chalcedonian Power Politics" (chap. 12 in the present volume).

71. James M. Robinson, "Reconstructing the First Christian Monastic Library," paper presented at the Smithsonian Institution Libraries, Washington, D.C., September 15, 1986; idem, "The Story of the Bodmer Papyri: The First Christian Monastery Library" (unpublished manuscript).

72. For the basics of the debate and further bibliography on it, see Goehring, "New Frontiers," 247–52 (pp. 173–79 in the present volume), and Veilleux, "Monasticism and Gnosis"; also Robert A. Kraft and Janet A. Timbie, review of *The Nag Hammadi Library in English*, by James M. Robinson, *RSR* 8 (1982) 34–35.

scores a changing view of Pachomian monasticism and its origins. The literary accounts of Pachomian history are no longer assumed to be an accurate reflection of early Pachomian theological concern. They were written to edify future monks and not to record an accurate history for modern scholars. It may well be that the early Pachomians defined their Christianity in terms of their ascetic practice and not in terms of the books they read.[73]

In the case of monastic origins in Egypt, often presumed to be the source of monastic origins in general, the evidence has revealed a complex situation. The image of Antony and Pachomius as respectively the fathers of anchoritic and coenobitic monasticism is a fiction that grows out of and beyond the depiction of these two figures in the literary sources. While both were influential, their insights were at best innovations and not creations. Antony represents an expansion of the monastic concept of withdrawal from its original ethical plane to include a physical dimension. He withdrew not only from the domestic bonds of family and marriage, but from the social bonds of the village in general. Likewise Pachomius's innovation was not the coenobitic lifestyle itself, but the organization of an affiliate group of monasteries under a common rule. His central monastery of Pbow functioned for the affiliate monasteries in Upper Egypt much as Cluny functioned for its affiliate monasteries in medieval Europe. Both were systems that created fame and power. Neither created it *ex nihilo*, but drew on previously existing coenobitic institutions.

The evidence of the apotactic movement certainly expands our understanding of ascetic practice in Egypt before the appearance of Antony and Pachomius. But it would be wrong to conclude that we are now closer to the "origins" of monasticism. The apotactic movement should not serve simply as the "missing link" between early ascetic practices within the home and the later institutionalized forms. Rather it underscores the complexity of the situation, not only in its historical reality, but particularly in the manner in which it has come down to us in the surviving sources. Not only is the available evidence limited, it has been clearly filtered so as to conform with prevailing opinion. The apotactic monk who resided in

---

73. Chadwick, "Pachomios," 17–19; idem, "Domestication of Gnosis," 14–16; Goehring, "New Frontiers," 240–52 (see pp. 166–79 in the present volume).

the village and participated in its social and ecclesiastical affairs was forgotten, or rather repudiated by a later Christianity that had embraced less politically active forms of asceticism. Desert hermits and "imprisoned" coenobites offered a less direct challenge to ecclesiastical and political authority and therefore flourish in the literature that survives, a literature that survives precisely because it represents that ecclesiastical and political authority. The motive behind the silence with respect to the apotactic movement is thus political, and a history of monastic development must take this into account.

EGYPT AND SYRIA

The complexity of the situation in Egypt is repeated throughout the early Christian world. As the biases of the sources and the earlier selective use of them are taken more and more into account, the diverse origins of monastic practice and its meaning become increasingly clear. Thus the old theory that traced the monastic impulse in all corners of the empire back to an original Egyptian inspiration has proven to be a literary fiction. It too was dependent on a Western quest for origins and a Hellenocentric view of the ancient Mediterranean world perpetuated by selective use of the sources and their interpretation.

If one depends chiefly on the *Religious History* of Theodoret of Cyrrhus (ca. 393–458 C.E.) for an understanding of Syriac monasticism, for example, one cannot help but have a view filtered through Theodoret's selection of the evidence and his adopted Hellenism. To begin with, his evidence is limited by the date of his composition, circa mid–fifth century C.E. Theodoret knows of individual monks who flourished in the mid–fourth century and of coenobitic institutions founded at the same time, but the preponderance of his evidence dates nearer his own time in the late fourth and early fifth centuries. This compares to a late-third-century date for Antony (ca. 251–356 C.E.) and an early-fourth-century date for Pachomius (ca. 290–346 C.E.). Given such a database, one might easily conclude that Syriac monasticism was at least later in date if not directly influenced by Egyptian monasticism.[74]

---

74. Price, *History*, xix.

Even should the monastic enterprise in Syria prove temporally later in date than its Egyptian counterpart, however, its distinct practices, spirituality, and organization betray its independent origins. The Semitic roots of Syriac-speaking Christianity are clear, and these roots give Syrian spirituality a distinctive flavor unencumbered by the Hellenistic influences of classical Greece and Rome.[75] The Syrian ascetic embarked on a monastic career not to punish or subdue the flesh but to offer the body as a symbol of the faith. The body was not viewed dualistically in opposition to the spirit but as that portion of the person through which the faith might be acted out and become visible.[76] The Syriac monk simply cannot be understood through recourse to the Hellenistic dualism between the spirit and the flesh. While the latter informed Egyptian monastic practice, it ran counter to the purpose of the Syrian ascete.

If one depends on Theodoret of Cyrrhus, however, one receives just such a Hellenistic image of the Syrian monk. In Theodoret's rendition of the life of Simeon the Stylite (ca. 390–459 C.E.), his ascetic practices are viewed as evidence of his consummate philosophy.[77] His physical discipline has as its purpose the desire to align his body with the higher purpose of his soul. The influence of the Platonic dualism between spirit and flesh is apparent in Theodoret's report that Simeon ascended his pillar in order "to fly heavenward and to leave the earthly life."[78] The description of this ascetic life as philosophic unites Theodoret with Eusebius of Caesarea. In Ashbrook Harvey's words,

> For all their differences, Theodoret's *Life of Simeon* represents a harmonious tradition with the fourth-century *Life of Antony* of Egypt, and indeed with Eusebius of Caesarea's philosopher martyrs. It is Simeon's acquired dispassion that Theodoret is celebrating. Like

---

75. Brock and Harvey, *Holy Women*, 4–12; R. Murray, "The Characteristics of the Earliest Syriac Christianity," in N. Garsoian, T. Mathews, and R. Thomson, eds., *East of Byzantium: Syria and Armenia in the Formative Period* (Washington, D.C.: Dumbarton Oaks, 1982) 3–16.

76. "The religious image and the physical action are inseparable and witness to the making literal of the symbol." Brock and Harvey, *Holy Women*, 9.

77. The following discussion of Simeon and the varied interpretations of his life is dependent on the work of Susan Ashbrook Harvey ("Sense of a Stylite").

78. Theodoret of Cyrrhus, *Historia religiosa* 26.12; Harvey, "Sense of a Stylite," 379.

Antony, Simeon had first to gain that self-control before achieving the spiritual strength necessary to perform God's work.[79]

Given such a source, it is little wonder that a dependent relationship could be found between the Egyptian and Syriac monasticism. But the Hellenistic veneer is apparent as soon as one compares it with the Syriac *Vita*. Here Simeon's actions are understood in the context of the Hebrew prophets, who not only proclaimed God's word, but acted it out.[80] Simeon ascends his pillar not to flee the earthly life, but to serve as a dramatic statement (literal symbol) of the gospel.

> Simeon became a stylite, then, not in penitence, not to deny his body nor to discipline it, but because through it he could fulfill God's purpose. By public witness of his actions — the prophecy of behavior — he could efficaciously proclaim God's word.[81]

The distinctive nature of the Syrian monastic enterprise is clear. The view that it was theoretically akin to its Egyptian counterpart derived from the uncritical use of selected sources, sources that had themselves already translated the Syriac data into a Hellenized form.

If the beginnings of asceticism had a separate origin in Syria, so too did the later forms of Syrian asceticism develop independently. As the Egyptian anchorites can no longer serve as forerunners of the Syrian hermits, neither can Egyptian coenobitism serve to explain the north Syrian monasteries. Archaeology has shown the distinctiveness of the latter with their greater open space and absence of an enclosing wall.[82] Strong Marcionite and Manichaean presences in Syria[83] might have offered precedents, but as in the case of Egypt, the connection is not clear. What is clear is that Syrian monastic origins lay not in Egypt.

The more we learn of early Christian monasticism the more we discover its complexity. While the French proverb, *Il n'y a que les*

---

79. Harvey, "Sense of a Stylite," 380.

80. Harvey, "Sense of a Stylite," 382.

81. Harvey, "Sense of a Stylite," 382–83.

82. Jean Lassus, *Sanctuaires chrétiens de Syrie: Essai sur la genèse, la form et l'usage liturgie des édifices du culte chrétien en Syrie, du IIIe siècle à la conquête musulmane* (Paris: Geuthner, 1947) 272–73; G. Tchalenko, *Villages antiques de la Syrie du Nord: Le massif du Bélus à l'époque romaine* (3 vols.; Paris: Geuthner, 1953–59) 1:19; Price, *History*, xix–xx.

83. Brock and Harvey, *Holy Women*, 7; Walter Bauer, *Orthodoxy and Heresy in Earliest Christianity*, trans. Robert A. Kraft et al. (Philadelphia: Fortress Press, 1971) 1–43.

détails qui comptent (Only the details are really important), may over-state the case, it is fair to say that simplified theories of monastic origins that ignore the details have proven invalid. They were born of that quest for origins with which Western historiography has so long been enamored. But as Eliade points out, "Western man's longing for 'origins' and the 'primordial' forced him finally into an encounter with history";[84] it forced him to consider the details, and the details have dissuaded him from the quest.

The monastic sources themselves almost universally agree in plac-ing the origins of monasticism in divine inspiration. Antony and Simeon responded to hearing the gospel, and Pachomius was given a vision. While one may choose to discredit the supernatural na-ture of this explanation, it shares with the evidence the sense of asceticism as bursting forth simultaneously in myriad places. The "big bang" lies not in one or more historical events, but deep be-neath the historical plane of ancient Mediterranean culture. It was the spirit of the times and the new Christian faith that produced the explosion, and as it welled forth from below, it burst onto the plane of history independently throughout the empire. One may still discover influences on specific forms of asceticism and trace various paths of development, but the quest for the "origins" of Christian monasticism should be let go.

---

84. Eliade, "Quest," 50.

PART ONE

ASCETICS, SOCIETY, AND THE DESERT

2

The World Engaged:
The Social and Economic World
of Early Egyptian Monasticism

The discovery of the Nag Hammadi Codices and their publication gave impetus to the study of the Coptic language in many New Testament departments. While the majority of students produced as a result of this process have centered their research on the Nag Hammadi literature and Gnosticism, a few have moved into the more general field of Coptic studies. James Robinson's own efforts and those of his students reflect this development. His work in New Testament and Gnostic studies is well known. His broader contribution to Coptic studies has been the result of his effort to establish the provenience of the Nag Hammadi Codices and the Dishna Papers (Bodmer papyri). This effort has added considerable fuel to the debate over the relationship of these manuscript collections to the Pachomian monastic movement. While most Robinson students, like Robinson himself, remain close to New Testament and Nag Hammadi in their research, a few have moved more broadly into the study of Egyptian Christianity. The article that follows is offered as an example of such research fostered in part through the influence of James Robinson.

Egyptian monasticism evokes images of the desert. Recluses withdrawn into their desert cells or pharaonic rock-cut tombs, assemblages of anchorites and their disciples far from the city, and coenobitic monks sharing the ascetic life in communities built on the edge of the desert have populated this image in the imagination of Christian authors and artists throughout the centuries. It received its clearest and surely most influential statement early in the *Life of Antony,* in which the author reports that "the desert was made a city

First published in James E. Goehring et al., eds., *Gnosticism and the Early Christian World: In Honor of James M. Robinson* (Sonoma, Calif.: Polebridge Press, 1990) 134–44.

by monks, who left their own people and registered themselves for citizenship in the heavens."[1] In the fifteenth century, the Italian artist Starnina, in his painting of the Egyptian Thebaid, transformed this desert city into a veritable megalopolis.[2] The centrality of the theme in modern scholarship is perhaps best illustrated in the use of the phrase *The Desert a City* as the title of Derwas Chitty's 1966 history of early Egyptian and Palestinian monasticism.[3]

In an environment imbued with the visible separation of the black and red land, it is no mystery that the desert should serve as a symbol of death and distinction from the inhabited realm. As in ancient Egypt, where those who departed this life were entombed in the desert, many early monks fled to the desert to symbolize while yet alive their chosen death to this life and citizenship in heaven. In the major sources of Egyptian monasticism that survive, separation from the *inhabited world* (οἰκουμένη) through *withdrawal* (ἀναχώρησις) into the *desert* (ἔρημος) or behind a monastery wall represents a central, unifying theme.

The symbolic significance of this desert imagery, seared into the mind by the physical geography of the land, is clear. Peter Brown has seen in it a causal factor that sets the practice of monasticism in Egypt apart from the other provinces, where the desert "was never true desert." There the holy man who withdrew to the desert did not "disappear into another unimaginable world," but wandered on the fringe of the οἰκουμένη and interacted with it. In Egypt, on the other hand, with its sharp antithesis between true desert and settled land, "the holy man ... did not impinge on the society around him in the same way."[4]

While Brown's analysis is perceptive, one must be cautious lest the symbolic significance of the separation between ἔρημος and οἰκουμένη in the monastic literature of Egypt be translated into a reality that precludes too drastically the equally real social and economic interaction between the monks and the surrounding world. It is the symbolic importance of the theme of withdrawal or sepa-

---

1. *Vita Antonii* 14; cf. Gregg, *Life of Antony*, 42–43.
2. Geoffrey Barraclough, ed., *The Christian World: A Social and Cultural History* (New York: Abrams, 1981) 36.
3. Chitty, *Desert a City*.
4. Brown, "Rise and Function," 82–83.

ration that makes it so central in the monastic literature of Egypt. While this same literature is replete with references to social and economic interaction with the inhabited world, such references appear only as elements within a larger story, the true purpose of which is to edify the reader in more spiritual matters. As a result, later interpretations of this literature often pass over such peripheral elements and emphasize the more spiritual, otherworldly goals. On occasion, in fact, the social and economic interaction of the monk and the world is not only passed over, but virtually denied as a result of this emphasis on the edificatory spiritual dimension of separation from the world.

The latter error is due to the continuing success of the rhetorical intent of the hagiographical literature. As sources designed for edification, for the encouragement of *imitatio patrum* (imitation of the fathers),[5] they naturally present the life of the monks in idealized form. They are concerned only marginally with the issues of economic and social interaction as facts of everyday existence and stress instead separation from the world as indicative of the truer spiritual life. But that fact does not make the social and economic interaction any less real. Such interaction was not only possible; it was inevitable. The desert in Egypt, while sharply distinct from the inhabited land, was not remote.[6]

The *Life of Antony*, which influenced greatly most subsequent representations of the monastic life, underscores the ideal of withdrawal as Antony moves ever further from the inhabited realm: from home to village boundary, to cemetery, to the near desert, to the distant desert.[7] Without denying such a process of withdrawal by Antony, one may still note that the manner of its formulation in the *Vita* is

---

5. *Epistula Ammonis* 23; cf. Goehring, *Letter of Ammon*, 267–68.

6. Palamon, the anchorite under whom Pachomius began his career, is said to have lived in the inner desert. Lefort was the first to point out that this inner desert was not the remote desert situated far beyond the demarcation of the black land, but a small, barren, desertlike area of land within the confines of the irrigated fields near the village of Šeneset (Chenoboskion). It is still present today and boasts the Coptic Monastery of Palamon, a stone's throw from the village. Lefort, "Premiers monastères," 383–84.

7. The influence of the *Life of Antony* on the presentation of the Pachomian movement in its sources is clear. See Pachomian Greek *Vita prima* (hereafter cited *G1*) 2, 99 (Halkin, *Sancti Pachomii Vitae Graecae*, 2, 66–67; cf. Goehring, *Letter of Ammon*, 188–89).

the product of the propagandistic author.[8] Dörries long ago, through a comparison of the Antony of the *Vita* with the Antony of the *Apophthegmata Patrum*, established the rather weak claim that the *Vita* has to be historical.[9] Nonetheless it is still frequently used as indicative of the anchoritic life in most of its details.[10] It is where many historians begin their presentation of Egyptian monasticism. Withdrawal, central to the image of Antony in the *Vita*, becomes the overriding image of the Egyptian monk.

Dörries's work, however, should caution one from such an uncritical use of the sources. It should raise the question not only in the case of the *Life of Antony*, for which a second source enabled Dörries's analysis, but in the case of all such literature, even when a second source is not available against which to judge an account. The need for such caution is underscored by the fact that in those cases where such sources do exist, Dörries's observation of the precedence of hagiographic concern over historical accuracy seems almost inevitably to hold true. The "mystical alphabet," which is noted in passing in the first Greek *Life of Pachomius* and explained simplistically in Palladius's *Lausiac History*, defies interpretation in the more direct witness of Pachomius's letters.[11] In the Shenoutean corpus, the description in the Bohairic *Vita* of Shenoute's destruction of the idols in the temple at the village of Pneuit, some fifteen miles north of his monastery at Sohag, differs dramatically from the abbot's own account. According to the *Vita*, the non-Christian inhabitants, after failing to hinder Shenoute's arrival through the use of magic, fled their village and left the monk to destroy the images of their gods. That is the end of the incident. But Shenoute himself reports that the villagers brought charges against him to the authorities in Anti-

---

8. The question of the author of the *Life of Antony* is currently under debate. Timothy D. Barnes, "Angel of Light or Mystic Initiate? The Problem of the *Life of Antony*," *JTS* 37 (1986) 353–68; Martin Tetz, "Athanasius und die Vita Antonii: Literarische und theologische Relationen," *ZNW* 73 (1982) 1–30.

9. Dörries, "Die Vita Antonii."

10. I am not suggesting that the *Life of Antony* be discarded as valueless for historical inquiry into early anchoritic monasticism in Egypt. But one must use it with extreme caution. The ἀναχώρησις emphasized in this influential source should not be used indiscriminately as descriptive of Egyptian monasticism in all its forms, but should be seen in large part as hagiographical rhetoric.

11. *G1* 99; Halkin, *Sancti Pachomii Vitae Graecae*, 66; Palladius, *Historia Lausiaca* 32; Butler, *Lausiac History*, 2.90–91; Quecke, *Briefe Pachoms*.

noë.[12] Considerably greater interaction with the surrounding societal order is implied. The *Letter of Ammon*, which describes life in the Pachomian community of Pbow around 351 C.E., clearly goes beyond the facts in its effort to align the Pachomian movement with Alexandrian "orthodoxy."[13] In similar fashion, the archaeological work at Kellia in Lower Egypt has dispelled, at least for the later period, the notion of the monastic cell as small and unpretentious. While one assumes that the first monks at Kellia were not so well furnished, it is indeed remarkable to find that later cells came to include a courtyard, a vestibule, a hallway, an oratory, a bedroom for the ascete with a closet, an attached room, a room with closet for the novice or servant, an office, a kitchen, and a latrine. The cells were, in addition, finely decorated.[14]

A history of Egyptian monasticism needs to be more than a simple recounting of the lives of famous monks written by their faithful disciples. One must examine the texts with an eye to the brief references within them to other, often different, monastic movements, to interaction with secular and ecclesiastical authorities, and to practices that would necessarily lead to such interaction even if it is not expressly stated.[15] In addition one must gather the few shreds of nonmonastic evidence that is accruing. A critical history needs to explore all of these sources and interpret them not only in terms of content, but also in terms of intent. A tax receipt has at best marginal import in terms of the edificatory intent of a monastic *vita*. One cannot expect that the author of a *vita* would find the inclusion of tax information relevant.[16] Likewise, it is no wonder that the Bohairic *Life of Shenoute* ignores the legal charges brought against the abbot in the Pneuit affair. The intent of the *Vita* is to portray the power of

---

12. Bohairic *Vita Sinuthii* 83–84. Johannes Leipoldt, *Sinuthii vita bohairice* (CSCO 41; Paris: E typographeo reipublicae, 1906) 41; cf. Leipoldt, *Schenute von Atripe*, 179.

13. Goehring, *Letter of Ammon*, 103–22.

14. Mission suisse d'archéologie copte de l'Université de Genève sous la direction de Rodolphe Kasser, *Le site monastique des Kellia (Basse-Égypte): Recherches des années 1981–83* (Louvain: Peeters, 1984) 22–23.

15. It is obvious that extreme caution must be used in such interpretation. But the nature of the hagiographic witness must be assumed to have slighted such evidence as unrelated to its intent of religious edification.

16. This fact would hold true for the oral stage of the tradition as well. Stories told for purposes of edification would develop themes that foster the edificatory goal. A list of monastic taxes would hardly be relevant.

Shenoute as man of God, not to detail his struggle with the secular authorities. The fact that it does ignore this struggle, however, leads one to suspect that such material is ignored or played down in most secondary monastic sources.[17]

The very association of Egyptian monasticism with the desert must be kept in perspective. The prevalence of the motif in the literature is due as much, if not more, to its symbolic significance as to its actual predominance in practice. A careful reading of the sources betrays this fact. When Antony, who is often viewed as the father of the anchoritic flight to the desert, began his career, he gained insights into the ascetic life from an old man in a neighboring village who had lived the solitary life from his youth.[18] This ascetic had not found ἀναχώρησις to involve a literal flight to the desert. The centrality of that pattern awaited the hagiographic depiction of his student Antony. The Pachomian monasteries, both those established by Pachomius himself and those which chose to join his expanding community, were situated in the inhabited land. The monastic sources and church fathers know that monks lived in the cities, villages, countryside, and desert, though the fathers favor the last named category.[19] Before Ammon withdrew to the Pachomian monastery in Upper Egypt in 351 C.E., he considered taking up apprenticeship with a monk in Alexandria.[20] The city of Oxyrhynchus was apparently bursting at the seams with the monastic presence, as every quarter was inhabited by monks.[21] A papyrus petition dated to 324 C.E. from the village of Karanis preserves the first known use of the term μοναχός as a title for an ascete, an individual named Isaac, who intervened in a village dispute over a cow. It has been sug-

---

17. The Shenoutean corpus offers great possibilities in this regard, since we possess many writings by Shenoute himself through which we can test the secondary monastic sources about Shenoute and his movement. This is not the case for any other Egyptian monastic movement.

18. *Vita Antonii* 3.

19. Rufinus, in the prologue to the *History of the Monks in Egypt*, reports monks in the cities, countryside, and desert (Festugière, *Historia Monachorum*, 8; *PL* 21.389–90). Jerome, in his *Letter to Eustochium*, dismisses the *remnuoth*, who move about in the cities in small groups with no rule, with contempt (*Ep.* 22.34). Palladius states in the prologue to his *Lausiac History* that he will leave unmentioned no one in the cities, in the villages, or in the desert (Butler, *Lausiac History*, 2.15).

20. *Epistula Ammonis* 2. The local priest steered him clear of this Theban monk, whom he branded a heretic.

21. *Historia Monachorum in Aegypto* 5 (cf. Festugière, *Historia Monachorum*, 41–43).

gested that Isaac represented an early pattern of ascetic practice that preceded the anchoritic and coenobitic developments. E. A. Judge defined it as the apotactic movement, "in which men followed the pattern long set for virgins and widows, and set up houses of their own in town, in which the life of personal renunciation and service in the church would be practiced."[22] Whatever the precise nature of the movement, it is clear that monks such as Isaac chose not to withdraw into the desert and in fact interacted readily with the secular world in which they lived.

The anchorite, who withdrew more dramatically from the inhabited world than his/her apotactic or coenobitic counterpart, had, of necessity, less contact with the secular realm. Άναχώρησις as a term had its origin among those in Egypt who withdrew to the desert to flee their responsibilities, such as taxation.[23] It was difficult for authorities to keep track of such persons, and the anchorite who withdrew to the desert was no exception. Such persons did not impinge upon the arable and hence taxable land, and it remains unclear whether or not they, like the coenobites, were taxed.[24] The necessities of life, however, meager as they may have been to the true anchorite, required contact with the external world, often in the form of trade. While flight from the world may be the predominant sentiment in the *Apophthegmata Patrum*, the collection contains numerous indications of commercial dealings.[25] Esias appears to have been involved in a sharecropping arrangement.[26] John the Dwarf wove ropes and baskets and had an agreement with a camel driver who picked up the merchandise from his cell.[27] He also apparently left Scetis during the harvest season to work for wages.[28] Isidore the Priest went to the market to sell his goods.[29] Lucius plaited ropes to earn the money with which he purchased his food.[30] In the collection of sayings as-

---

22. Judge, "Earliest Use," 85.

23. M. Rostovtzeff, *The Social and Economic History of the Roman Empire* (2d. ed.; Oxford: Clarendon Press, 1957) 2.677.

24. Winlock and Crum, *Monastery of Epiphanius*, 1.177.

25. Chitty, *Desert a City*, 34.

26. *Apophthegmata Patrum*, Esias 5.

27. *Apophthegmata Patrum*, John the Dwarf 5, 30–31.

28. *Apophthegmata Patrum*, John the Dwarf 82.

29. *Apophthegmata Patrum*, Isidore the Priest 7.

30. *Apophthegmata Patrum*, Lucius 1. Megethios obtained sufficient food by weaving three baskets a day (*Apophthegmata Patrum*, Megethios 1).

sociated with Abba Poemen, one reads of meetings with the village
magistrate, of the plaiting and selling of ropes, of monks who went
to the city, took baths, and were careless in their behavior, of a monk
who worked a field, and of one who took his produce to the market.[31]
The flight to the desert was real, but its spiritual significance did not
preclude secular interchange.[32]

The early coenobitic communities in Egypt were in closer proximity to the inhabited world if not directly in its midst and, as a
result, more readily defined in relationship to it by the people and
the authorities. The Pachomian dossier offers numerous examples of
the interaction of the *koinonia*, a system of independent monasteries
answerable to the central monastery at Pbow, with the surrounding society. While the hagiographic accounts do not dwell on this
material, a careful reading reveals much.

According to the tradition, Pachomius received a vision in which
he was instructed to build a monastery at the *deserted village* (κώμην
τινά, ἔρημον οὖσα) of Tabennese on the shore of the Nile. He undertook this task, after which a number of monks joined him. It is then
reported that "when he saw that many people had come to live in the
village, he took the brothers and went to build them a church where
they could assemble."[33] A number of intriguing questions arise from
this account. First it must be noted that the precise meaning of "deserted village" remains unclear. Pachomius's second foundation at
Pbow is likewise described as a deserted village that he took over.[34]
A canal being dug near the site of Pbow in 1976, however, unearthed
evidence of a sizable early Roman presence.[35] The nature of this presence is uncertain, but it clearly calls into question the image of a
deserted village. What can it mean? Wholesale depopulation of villages in Egypt as a result of economic exploitation is not unknown

---

31. *Apophthegmata Patrum*, Poemen 9, 10, 11, 22, 163.

32. One needs to note, as well, the interchange that took place in the opposite direction, namely the secular visitors who went to the cells and monasteries to meet
the monks. This pattern is more frequently stressed in the literature since it corresponds more closely with the edificatory theme of withdrawal expressed in terms of
movement of individuals from the worldly to the spiritual realm.

33. Bohairic *Vita Pachomii* (hereafter cited *Bo*) 17, 24–25 (cf. Lefort, *S. Pachomii vita
bohairice scripta*).

34. *Bo* 49.

35. Goehring, "New Frontiers," 256 (see p. 182 in the present volume).

in this period.[36] Pachomius's deserted villages may indeed represent such a situation. Whatever the case, Pachomius's occupation of the site, besides drawing monks to his monastery, drew the people back to the village. They came in such numbers that his monks built a church in the village for them before constructing one within the monastery for themselves.[37] It is hard to imagine that such a process would not affect the economy of the area and come to the attention of the authorities, if for no other reason than taxation.

The coenobitic monasteries, as they grew in size and number, had not only a significant religious impact on the surrounding communities, but also a considerable economic impact. While the monastery wall represented the separated, spiritual calling of the monks, their physical needs were met by frequent forays outside the monastery wall to gather the materials needed for their livelihood. The plaiting of ropes and baskets required rushes gathered from the Nile.[38] Agricultural production was apparently carried on outside the monastery wall as well. A vegetable garden was situated near the Pachomian monastery of Tabennese alongside the Nile.[39] The monks harvested grain from the islands in the Nile and fruit from orchards beyond the monastery gate.[40] One reads also of herdsmen and the shearing of goats for hair shirts.[41] The somewhat later Pachomian *Regulations of Horsiesius* have an extensive, though unfortunately incomplete, set of rules governing the agricultural enterprise of the monks. These include the existence of a housemaster over the monastic farmers, the regulation of time and leadership beyond the monastery walls, extensive discussion of canals and irrigation methods, and references to the raising of cattle and donkeys.[42] While one must posit stages of growth in such agricultural industry between the founding of Taben-

36. Rostovtzeff, *Social and Economic History*, 2.677.

37. *Bo* 25; *G1* 29 suggests that the church was built in the deserted village for the shepherds of the surrounding region.

38. *G1* 23, 51, 71, 76; *Epistula Ammonis* 19; *Paralipomena* 9 (cf. Halkin, *Sancti Pachomii Vitae Graecae*, 133–34; Veilleux, *Pachomian Koinonia*, 2.30–31).

39. *G1* 24; *Epistula Ammonis* 18.

40. *G1* 106; *Regula Pachomii, Praecepta* 76–77 (cf. Boon, *Pachomiana latina*, 35–36; Veilleux, *Pachomian Koinonia*, 2.158–59); cf. also *Praecepta* 24.

41. *Praecepta* 108; *Epistula Pachomii* 8 (Quecke, *Briefe Pachoms*, 112; Veilleux, *Pachomian Koinonia*, 3.71–72).

42. *Regulations of Horsiesius* 55–64 (cf. Lefort, *Oeuvres*, 98–99; Veilleux, *Pachomian Koinonia*, 2.217–20).

nese in 323 C.E. and the death of Horsiesius (by 400 C.E.), the evidence certainly suggests that the monastery wall did not preclude activity that would involve the monks with the surrounding world. The *Regulations* even mention monks who undertook work in the village as well as in the fields.[43]

In addition to farming for their own needs, the coenobitic monastery also served as a production center for items of commercial value in the outside world. Certainly mats, baskets, and plaited ropes were the early products of the monks, but we also hear of sandals and other articles.[44] Monks were appointed from the beginning of the Pachomian movement to transact sales of the monks' handicrafts and to make the necessary purchases from the proceeds.[45] As the community obtained its own boats, the products were shipped down the Nile as far as Alexandria.[46] A late Pachomian source reports negotiations with a neighboring village for foodstuffs during a time of famine.[47]

The overseeing of such commerce, both within and outside the community, was the responsibility of the steward (οἰκονόμος) of the individual monastery and ultimately of the great steward (μέγας οἰκονόμος) for the *koinonia* as a whole. By the time of Horsiesius, one hears of careful record keeping in the steward's office.[48] Each year, in August (the Egyptian year ended August 28), the monks from the various monasteries in the *koinonia* came together at the central monastery of Pbow for a financial and administrative reckoning.[49] Commercial dealings required careful control.

Shenoute's White Monastery likewise had considerable commercial exchange with the outside world. They sold, among other things,

---

43. *Regulations* 53; *Praecepta* 90.

44. *Paralipomena* 3. It has been suggested that the monasteries served as production centers for papyrus codices, both inscribed and uninscribed. Robinson, "Introduction," 16–17.

45. *Bo* 26; *G1* 28.

46. *G1* 113.

47. *Paralipomena* 21–22.

48. *Regulations* 29; cf. *Praecepta* 27; Ruppert, *Das pachomianische Mönchtum,* 320–23.

49. Early studies of Pachomian monasticism had assumed a fundamentally religious nature to this gathering in parallel with the only other such community-wide gathering during the Easter season. It is now clear that the August meeting was designed as a financial and organizational close of the old year. Veilleux, *Liturgie,* 377–70; Ruppert, *Das pachomianische Mönchtum,* 323–26.

baskets, linen cloth, and books in exchange for money and/or items necessary for the cloister.[50] The trade was carefully controlled by the leadership of the monastery, and detailed records were kept.[51] Leipoldt has argued that Shenoute developed the White Monastery, in part, as a great work cooperative (*Arbeitsgenossenschaft*) that served as a source of relief to the poor Coptic farmers by offering them at reduced prices such necessities as cloth, mats, and baskets.[52]

By Byzantine times, the monasteries had come to dominate the lives of the peasants both economically as well as religiously. They came to parallel in these functions the great Egyptian Byzantine estates. Frend notes that "the peasants were sharecroppers, leasing their seed and equipment from the central monastery stores and paying a perpetual rent."[53] The *Book of the Patriarchs* reports that in the sixth century some six hundred monasteries existed in the vicinity of Alexandria together with "thirty-two farms called Sakatina, where all the people held the true path."[54] While the precise nature of these Sakatina remains unclear, their connection to the monasteries seems apparent.

The interaction of the monasteries with the surrounding world outlined above naturally had ramifications in public places. The monasteries were not above the legal system in Egypt. That one reads little of such interaction in the hagiographic sources is to be expected. Taxes, wills, legal disputes, and the like are hardly edifying. Nonetheless they did form part of the monastic scene in Egypt. A tax list from the Hermopolite nome dated 367–68 C.E. records the payment of land taxes by a certain Anoubion for the monastery of Tabennese, the first Pachomian establishment.[55] One can only expect that the occupation of "deserted villages," the use of agricultural land, and the entry into the commercial life of the community would

---

50. Leipoldt, *Schenute von Atripe*, 136.

51. Leipoldt, *Schenute von Atripe*, 137.

52. Leipoldt, *Schenute von Atripe*, 174.

53. W. H. C. Frend, *The Rise of Christianity* (Philadelphia: Fortress Press, 1984) 844–45.

54. B. Evetts, ed., *History of the Patriarchs of the Coptic Church of Alexandria*, vol. 2: *Peter I to Benjamin I (661)* (PO 1, 4; Paris: Didot, 1948) 472; Frend, *Rise of Christianity*, 845. The number of six hundred monasteries may refer rather to individual cells. Hardy, *Christian Egypt*, 168.

55. Wipszycka, "Terres," 625–36.

lead the authorities to apply the tax laws to the monasteries.[56] In
a physician's will from Antinoë, land is left to a monastery with
instructions to his other heirs to pay taxes on it.[57] Such an arrangement necessarily involved the monastery in the affairs of the outside
world. Ownership and transfer of property by monks was relatively
common. *P. Lips.* 28 (381 C.E.) reveals a woman who left her orphaned
grandson to his uncle Silvanus, an ἀποτακτικός, to be his son and in-
heritor of his property. *P. Oxy.* 3203 (400 C.E.) records the lease of part
of a house to Iose, a Jew, by two sisters, Theodora and Tauris, μοναχαὶ
ἀποτακτικαί.[58] Later wills seem to suggest the transfer of whole monasteries.[59] The laws of Justinian note the sale of monasteries as an
abuse in Egypt, probably because there was little in the law's eyes to
distinguish a monastic cell from a privately owned hut.[60]

As for legal disputes, Shenoute's difficulties with the authorities
in Antinoë as a result of his destruction of the images of the gods
in the village of Pneuit have already been noted. A fascinating example of such difficulties, though without clear evidence of legal
ramification, is seen in the problem of children who entered the monastic life against their parents' will or without their knowledge.
According to the earliest Greek *Life of Pachomius,* Pachomius tested
the person — together with that person's parents — who wished to
join his monastery.[61] This seems, however, to have been a later development based on problems that arose due to young persons who
left their families to join the monastery. Theodore, Pachomius's ultimate successor, left his home to join the system at an early age.
His mother came to the monastery with letters from the local bishop
demanding to see her son. She was refused. There is no indication
that Theodore's parents were informed or tested by the monastic authorities.[62] Ammon left Alexandria at age seventeen and joined the
Pachomian movement in Upper Egypt without informing his par-

---

56. The coenobitic institutions were readily identifiable. Their growing wealth was
also apparent. The anchorite, on the other hand, was less easily controlled by the
authorities. It is still unclear whether anchorites were taxed.

57. *P. Cair.* 67151; cf. Hardy, *Christian Egypt,* 167–68.

58. Judge, "Earliest Use," 82.

59. Winlock and Crum, *Monastery of Epiphanius,* 1.126–27, 2.343–48.

60. Hardy, *Christian Egypt,* 168; *Codex Theodosianus* 12.1.63. I am indebted to David
Hunter for the latter reference.

61. *G1* 24. The Bohairic version (*Bo* 23) does not include this statement.

62. *G1* 33–37; *Bo* 31–37.

ents of his plan. They were greatly grieved and searched throughout the monasteries in the delta for their son. Only by accident did they later learn of his whereabouts in the Thebaid.[63] An apophthegm attributed to Pachomius records the futile efforts of a mother seeking to stop her son from joining the community.[64] The Arabic *Vita* reports that Pachomius, after experiencing difficulties on this issue, relaxed his policy and permitted limited visitation.[65] One can only expect that such problems caused friction between the monasteries and the secular population from time to time. Cases of men deserting their families and of inheritances being given away to the monasteries would naturally add to such friction between monastery and community. Such friction may well lie behind the opposition of certain citizens of Panopolis to Pachomius's construction of a monastery in their community.[66] The practice of Shenoute in requiring a written agreement from prospective monks that confirmed the donation of their property to the monastery surely had a legal basis.[67]

While interaction between the monasteries and the secular world became more complex over time, it seems clear that such interaction was part of the monastic self-understanding in Egypt from the beginning. While the image of separation from the world was definitive of the spiritual stance of the monk toward the world, it functions poorly as a metaphor of the monk's social and economic relationship to the world. Monasticism in Egypt was much more than a "city in the desert," separated from the οἰκουμένη as sharply as the red land is from the black. At times the monastic presence seemed an only too real source of friction as it disrupted traditional patterns of life; but more often it became an integral part of the landscape. Its significance and success in Egypt lay not only in its religious import to the surrounding communities, but also in its social and economic interdependence with them. It enlivened dying villages, increased

---

63. *Epistula Ammonis* 2, 30. It is interesting to note that the first place they seem to have thought to look was the monasteries!

64. Lefort, *Oeuvres*, 28–29.

65. Amélineau, *Monuments au IVe siècle*, 406.

66. *SBo* 54 (cf. Veilleux, *Pachomian Koinonia*, 1:73–74); *G1* 81. There is no reason given for the opposition, which took the form of tearing down at night what the monks had built during the day.

67. Leipoldt, *Schenute von Atripe*, 106–7. A written document was not required in the Pachomian system.

agricultural production and trade, and produced various necessities, e.g., baskets and ropes, for the peasants. Its leaders were the new holy men of antiquity, but its institutions were also among the new purveyors of social and economic power in the hinterland. Its success in Egypt was dependent on both elements.

3

Through a Glass Darkly:
Images of the Ἀποτακτικοί(αί)
in Early Egyptian Monasticism

Increasing numbers of documentary papyri relevant to the study of early Egyptian monasticism have, in recent years, inaugurated new discussions on the precise meaning of the "technical" term ἀποτακτικός and its relationship to the more common "technical" terms ἀναχωρητής and κοινοβιώτης.[1] While basic agreement can be found among scholars, the diverse theories put forward to explain the various usages of the term ἀποτακτικός underscore the complexity of the problem. I intend to argue here that the problem lies not in the Egyptian use of the term, but rather in the influence of non-Egyptian literary models of Egyptian monasticism on our understanding of the Egyptian movement. The impact of the literary ideals of the ἀναχωρητής, understood as the solitary hermit epitomized by Antony, and the κοινοβιώτης, viewed as a fully communal monk of the Pachomian type, has created a simplified bipolar understanding of Egyptian monasticism in which the term ἀποτακτικός does not fit. In the pages that follow, a careful analysis of the evidence of the ἀποτακτικοί in Egypt will be used to challenge this bipolar view of Egyptian monasticism and to argue that the histor-

First published in Vincent L. Wimbush, ed., *Discursive Formations, Ascetic Piety, and the Interpretation of Early Christian Literature*, Part 2=*Semeia* 58 (1992) 25–45. The research for this study was conducted at the Akademie der Wissenschaften in Göttingen, Germany, under the auspices of the Alexander von Humboldt Stiftung in 1989–90.

1. The Greek term κοινόβιον is relatively common, but the use of κοινοβιώτης is rare (G. W. H. Lampe, *A Patristic Greek Lexicon* [Oxford: Clarendon Press, 1961] s.v.). In Coptic, while the loan word ⲕⲟⲓⲛⲱⲛⲓⲁ is again relatively common, particularly in the Pachomian tradition, the term ⲕⲟⲓⲛⲟⲃⲓⲟⲛ occurs much less frequently (Crum, *Coptic Dictionary*, 692a). I have found no use of the form κοινοβιώτης in Coptic. In Latin, the use of both *coenobium* and *coenobita* is more common (Albert Blaise, *Dictionnaire latin-français des auteurs chrétiens* [Turnhout: Éditions Brepols, 1954] s.v.), though judging from the manuscript tradition of Jerome's twenty-second letter, the use of *coenobita* developed here too secondarily (*Ep.* 22.34–35 in CSEL 54.196–97).

ical reality is better served by the notion of a complex continuum from the fully solitary monk to the fully communal monk. As will be shown, the diversity in the use of the term ἀποτακτικός derives precisely from the existence of such a continuum.

Ἀποτακτικός, Ἀναχωρητής, and Κοινοβιώτης: A QUESTION OF COMMUNITY

The scholarly debate over the meaning of ἀποτακτικός illustrates the difficulty presented by the varied use of the term in diverse literary and documentary sources. A. Lambert, writing in 1907 before the publication of the documentary evidence, held that a clear distinction must be maintained between the use of the term ἀποτακτικοί in Egypt and its parallel form, ἀποτακτῖται, in the areas of Asia Minor and Palestine. While the latter term served to label a particular class of Christians who chose an austere life marked by the abandonment of worldly goods, the wearing of clothing (a costume) indicative of poverty, and a practice of rigorous fasting and self-denial, the use of the parallel ἀποτακτικοί in Egypt, where the notion of withdrawal (ἀναχώρησις) predominated, was purely adjectival. It served, according to Lambert, as but one among many qualifiers defining the monastic life.[2]

Seventy years later, E. A. Judge, on the basis of more recently published documentary evidence, set the distinction between Egypt and the more northern provinces aside. He saw in the references to ἀποτακτικοί in the papyri evidence of an early apotactic movement that originated in an urban setting and preceded the subsequent anchoritic and coenobitic developments in Egyptian monasticism.[3] In Judge's view, the ἀποτακτικοί came to represent a class of ascetics in Egypt, men who "at last followed the pattern long set for virgins and widows, and set up houses of their own in town, in which the life of personal renunciation and service in the church would be practiced."[4] According to Judge, the subsequent development of anchoritic monasticism, epitomized by Antony's withdrawal from the

2. Lambert, "Apotactites."
3. Judge, "Earliest Use," 72–89; idem, "Fourth-Century Monasticism."
4. Judge, "Earliest Use," 85.

civic community, and coenobitic monasticism, associated with Pachomius's separate walled ascetic "villages,"[5] rapidly overshadowed the apotactic movement in the middle to latter half of the fourth century. In turn, the literary efforts of such churchmen as Athanasius (*Life of Antony*) and Jerome (*Letter* 22) to capture the monastic movement for their ecclesio-political camp, in part by identifying its "pure" or "true" form with these later anchoritic and coenobitic developments,[6] resulted in the relegation of the apotactic movement to the fringes of the emerging literary history of Egyptian monasticism and the linkage of its later practitioners in that history to the shadowy world of charlatans and heretics.[7]

The shift in the scholarly interpretation of the term ἀποτακτικός in Egyptian sources could hardly be more acute. The documentary evidence, often legal in nature, suggested a more technical meaning of the term; it was more than an adjective. Its use alone seemed to define an individual as a particular type of ascetic, a use that paralleled that of the term ἀποτακτῖται in the northern provinces. Acceptance of this conclusion, however, still left undefined the precise nature of ascesis practiced by the ἀποτακτικοί.

The place of the ἀποτακτικοί in relationship to the "more traditional" categories of ἀναχωρηταί and κοινοβιῶται depends on both the particular source or sources one is considering and the nature of the renunciation (ἀπόταξις) one associates with the name. Judge's definition, which distinguishes the ἀποτακτικοί from the other two categories, has its origin not in the documentary papyri, but in the connection he draws between Jerome's third class of Egyptian ascetics, the *remnuoth*, who lived in small household groups within the cities, and Julian's ἀποτακτῖται, a subgroup of Christians to whom

---

5. Brown, *Body and Society*, 245–46.

6. One can only speculate as to why these "orthodox" church fathers favored the anchoritic and coenobitic forms of monasticism while discrediting so vehemently its urban variety. Perhaps it was precisely because the latter was less remote and hence more active in civil and religio-political issues. Such activity would come into direct conflict with the growing authority of the clergy and the bishops; cf. Rousseau, *Ascetics.*

7. It is clear, however, from these churchmen's opposition to such monks, as well as from the secular criticism of them found in Julian (*Or.* 7.18; *Ep.* 89b) and Libanius (*Or.* 30.8; 2.32), that the more urban form of monasticism continued to exist (Judge, "Earliest Use," 79–80).

Julian likens the Cynics in an attempt to disparage them.[8] With respect to these inner-city ascetics or ἀποτακτικοί, the papyri serve in Judge's analysis simply to add additional elements to a basic definition already derived from these non-Egyptian literary sources.[9] From the papyri, one learns that ἀποτακτικός was a church rank (*P. Würzb.* 16), that the ἀποτακτικός could own land (*P. Flor.* 71, 722), that he might retain family ties (*P. Lips.* 28), that the title later came to include women (*P. Oxy.* XLIV 3203), and that it served to indicate an ascetic's more active position within the civil community in distinction from the less active role of the ἀναχωρητής (*P. Herm.* 9).

Judge's use of Jerome's threefold division of Egyptian monasticism (*coenobium,*[10] *anachoretae,* and *remnuoth* in *Ep.* 22.34–35; cf. Cassian's *coenobiotae, anachoretae,* and *sarabaitae* in his *Conf.* 18.4), suggests a distinction of the ἀποτακτικός, at least originally, from the later ἀναχωρητής and κοινοβιώτης.[11] When one turns to the papyri and Egyptian literary sources alone, however, the situation is less clear. The editor of *P. Oxy.* 3203, a lease agreement dated to 400 C.E. in which the lessors are two sisters titled μοναχαὶ ἀποτακτικαί, linked the label ἀποτακτικός more closely to the anchoritic form of monasticism, since the anchoritic monk, as opposed to the coenobitic monk, could own property.[12] This conclusion is based on the observation that ἀποτακτικαί, according to the papyrus in question, could own

---

8. Jerome, *Ep.* 22.34; Julian, *Or.* 7.18; Judge, "Earliest Use," 78–80.

9. Judge, "Earliest Use," 80–83; cf. idem, "Fourth-Century Monasticism."

10. Jerome employs the term *coenobium* where one might expect *coenobitae.* He refers to *coenobium, quod illi sauhes gentili lingua uocant, nos in commune uiuentes possumus appellare* ("cenobites, called in their Gentile tongue *Sauhes,* or, as we should say, men living in a community"; *Ep.* 22.34) and *quos uocari coenobium diximus* ("[who] are called, as we have said, cenobites"; *Ep.* 22.35). See F. A. Wright, *Select Letters of St. Jerome* (LCL; Cambridge: Harvard University Press, 1933) 137. Some later manuscripts emend the text so that the above citations read *coenobitae* and *coenobitas* respectively (CSEL 54.196–97). I have retained Jerome's use of *coenobium* in this paper when referring to his threefold division of Egyptian monasticism.

11. The use of Jerome's and Cassian's threefold categorization of Egyptian monasticism, while perhaps applicable in a broad sense, drastically oversimplifies the variety of ascetic practice in Egypt. Not only does the presentation stand monastic history on its head by placing the earliest form (*remnuoth* or *sarabaitae*) last (Hengstenberg, "Bemerkungen," 355–62), it tends to foster general definitions for anchoritic and coenobitic monasticism. Such definitions in turn serve to identify all monks under one or the other "descriptive" label and thus blur differentiations within the individual categories.

12. M. W. Haslam, "3203. Lease of Exedra and Cellar," in A. K. Bowman et al., eds., *The Oxyrhynchus Papyri* (vol. 44; London: Egypt Exploration Society, 1976) 183.

property and on the assumption, drawn from the Pachomian model, that coenobitic monks could not own property.[13]

The link between the terms ἀποτακτικός and ἀναχωρητής is further supported in the four letters that form the archive of Apa Johannes (*P. Herm.* 7–10). In this collection, Apa Johannes is twice called ἀναχωρητής and once ἀποτακτικός. While the texts do not offer any specific clarification on the use of the two terms, it seems fair to conclude that in some manner at least they must overlap.[14] If Judge is correct in equating the ἀποτακτικοί with Jerome's *remnuoth*, then in the figure of Apa Johannes we have an ascetic who somehow straddles two of Jerome's three categories.[15]

While the above documents suggest a link between the terms ἀποτακτικός and ἀναχωρητής, other texts seem to equate ἀποτακτικός with κοινοβιώτης. A list of tax payments made in the Hermopolite nome in 367–68 C.E. includes a payment made by the ἀποτακτικός Anoubion for land belonging to the monastery of Tabennese.[16] Since Tabennese was the first community established by Pachomius, whose *koinonia* serves generally to define coenobitic monasticism, the term ἀποτακτικός in this text appears to serve as a virtual synonym for κοινοβιώτης. It is possible, though far from certain, that other documents that record land ownership by an ἀποτακτικός (*P. Herm. Land.*)

---

13. The latter assumption illustrates the impact of the Pachomian model on the current understanding of Egyptian communal monasticism.

14. Judge ("Earliest Use," 83) recognizes the problem of these texts for his thesis and seeks to solve it by suggesting that Apa Johannes, the anchorite, "may not have been so far removed from the position of Jerome's worldly *remnuoth*, and the addressing of him as ἀποτακτικός may be a better index of his position in the civil community." Be that as it may, the overlap of the terms is nonetheless apparent. Emmett ("Female Ascetics") suggests, since Apa Johannes terms himself ἀναχωρητής while he is addressed by another as ἀποτακτικός, that the former term is internal to the monastic society while the latter term, ἀποτακτικός, is used externally. This fits with the use of ἀποτακτικός in other legal documents where, as Emmett shows, it more clearly identified the figure to the outsider than did the label ἀναχωρητής, which had wide currency in Egypt and carried considerable legal meaning in terms of the evasion of one's civic responsibilities. Ἀναχωρητής, in its monastic meaning, occurs most often internally within monastic sources. It should be noted, however, that the other use of the term ἀναχωρητής in the archive of Apa Johannes is in a letter addressed to Johannes, i.e., external.

15. It will be argued below that the ἀποτακτικοί should not be equated with Jerome's *remnuoth*, but rather, at least in some of its manifestations, with the group that Jerome labels *coenobium*. But even when we accept that shift, Apa Johannes overlaps Jerome's categories.

16. *P. Berl.* Inv. 11860 (=*SB* XIV 11972); Wipszycka, "Terres."

or the payment of land tax (*CPR* V 26) by a μοναχή, whose monastic affiliation is not specified, should be understood in this context; i.e., the monk did not own the land himself, but simply paid the taxes for land owned by his monastic community.[17]

At any rate, it is clear from the literary sources that the Pachomian community used the term ἀποτακτικός as a self-designation for its members. The Coptic recensions of the *Life of Pachomius* employ the term ἀποτακτικός (ⲣⲱⲙⲉ ⲛ̅ⲁⲡⲟⲧⲁⲕⲧⲓⲕⲟⲥ) as a label for Pachomian monks,[18] and the Greek *Excerpta* of the Pachomian *Rule* specifically refers to new members as those who come to the monastery to become ἀποτακτικοί (ἐάν τις προσέλθῃ τῇ μονῇ, ἐλθὼν γενέσθαι ἀποτακτικός).[19] In addition, two Coptic sources, a catechesis attributed to Pachomius[20] and a letter attributed to Athanasius,[21] incorporate ἀποτακτικός into a threefold division of Egyptian monasticism. In place of Jerome's three categories of *coenobium, anachoretae,* and *remnuoth,* one finds in these Coptic sources παρθένοι, ἀποτακτικοί, and ἀναχωρηταί. The παρθένοι likely refer to female ascetics, and the ἀναχωρηταί are the solitary hermits. The ἀποτακτικοί, as a result, must, in this Coptic tradition, refer to those ascetics who, in modern scholarly circles, on the basis of Jerome's and Cassian's respective use of *coenobium* and *coenobiotae,* are more commonly termed coenobites.

The blurring of the terminology of ἀποτακτικός and κοινοβιώτης is further suggested by the early-fifth-century diary of Egeria. She distinguishes three types of monks found in the east: *ascites, monazontes,* and *apotaktitai.* However, while the *ascites* remain distinct throughout the diary, the *monazontes* and *apotaktitai* seem at points to blend into one another.[22] It seems likely that the *ascites* represent the ἀναχωρηταί and the *monazontes* some form of the κοινοβιώται. While the diffi-

---

17. Judge, "Fourth-Century Monasticism," 618; Krause, "Zur Möglichkeit," 123.

18. Lefort, *S. Pachomii vita bohairice scripta,* 233 s.v.; idem, *S. Pachomii vitae sahidice scriptae,* 379 s.v.; Krause, "Zur Möglichkeit," 122–23.

19. "If someone comes to the monastery to become an ἀποτακτικός . . . " (my translation). Recension B, sec. 49; Boon, *Pachomiana latina,* 174; Krause, "Zur Möglichkeit," 122; Wipszycka, "Terres," 633.

20. Lefort, *Oeuvres,* 159.16.32–34 (text), 160.17.23–25 (translation).

21. A. van Lantschoot, "Lettre de saint Athanase au sujet de l'amour et de la tempérance," *Mus* 40 (1927) 274 (text), 287 (translation).

22. Pierre Maraval, *Égérie: Journal de voyage (Itinéraire)* (SC 296; Paris: Éditions du Cerf, 1982) 229 n. 3; cf. Judge, "Earliest Use," 80.

culties in understanding the distinction between the *apotaktitai* and the *monazontes* in the diary could be explained by a weak talent for details on Egeria's part, it seems most likely in view of the other evidence cited above that the overlap in the use of the two terms simply reflects the current situation in Egeria's day.

It thus appears from the evidence that the term ἀποτακτικός, at least by the middle of the fourth century,[23] was current in Egypt as a title for ascetic individuals who chose to practice their ascesis within a community of like-minded persons.[24] That it came to be used by the Pachomian monks, who clearly distinguished themselves from the ἀναχωρηταί,[25] as a self-designation suggests that the community element was inherent in the term from an early point in its history.

Alanna Emmett has suggested that the occurrence of the combined form of μοναχαὶ ἀποτακτικαί in *P. Oxy.* 3203 argues for the use of ἀποτακτικός as a word of specification designed to distinguish a particular type of monk.[26] I would suggest that it distinguishes a monk who lives communally from one who chose to practice a more solitary ascesis. The latter form of ascesis is most associated with the term ἀναχωρητής, a connection fostered especially by Athanasius's *Life of Antony*. The hardening of the term ἀναχωρητής as a technical term for a monk who withdrew to a solitary life led likewise to the need, on occasion, to qualify that term. Such qualification was necessary since a solitary lifestyle did not necessarily imply total isolation or lack of some form of community. A letter from the mid–fourth century,[27] for example, is addressed to an ἀναχωρητῇ μονῖς μοναχῶν so as to indicate that the monk in question led an anchoritic lifestyle within a community of monks.[28] In the Pachomian sources, which clearly distinguish their communal practice from the anchoritic lifestyle, Theodore, before he joined the Pachomian community, is likewise said to have entered "a monastery in

---

23. See *P. Berl. Inv.* 11860 (=*SB* XIV 11972).

24. Wipszycka, "Terres," 634. Judge's analysis ("Earliest Use," 85) likewise supports a communal element in the meaning of the term.

25. Bohairic *Vita Pachomii* (*Bo*) 134=Greek *Vita prima* (*G1*) 136; cf. *Bo* 67=*G1* 72.

26. Emmett, "Female Ascetics," 511–12.

27. *P. Lond.* VI 1925; Bell, *Jews and Christians in Egypt*, 106–8.

28. Emmett, "Female Ascetics," 511–12. Another late-fourth-century letter (*SB* VIII.1 9683) also mentions ἀναχωρηταί living in a μονή (Emmett, "Female Ascetics," 512).

the nome of Sne where he led an anchoritic life with some old and pious monks."[29] In all likelihood, it is just such a situation that accounts for the use of both ἀναχωρητής and ἀποτακτικός as titles for Apa Johannes in *P. Herm.* 7–10 (see above). Apa Johannes lived in a community of solitary monks. His solitary nature allows for the title ἀναχωρητής, and his existence in a community of such monks for the title ἀποτακτικός.

It is thus clear that while the term ἀποτακτικός served as a self-designation within the Pachomian community, its linkage to the notion of community did not derive initially from the Pachomian definition of *koinonia*, nor is it likely that it ever became throughout Egypt exclusively a technical term for a Pachomian form of community. It is important to underscore this fact lest the later references to ἀποτακτικοί in the Coptic documentary papyri be read automatically as references to monks who practiced a Pachomian form of communal ascesis.

Ἀποτακτικοί AND THE RENUNCIATION OF PROPERTY

The term ἀποτακτικός, connected in the above discussion with the communal ascetic life in Egypt, derives from the Greek word ἀπο-τάσσω, which meant initially "to set apart" or "to appoint." In the course of time and certainly by the turn of the eras, it came to include the sense of removal or exclusion which, when directed toward the self, translates as renunciation.[30] Its significance in early Christian circles drew from its use in Luke 14:33, in which a disciple is defined as one who is able to give up or renounce all of his possessions (ἀποτάσσεται πᾶσιν τοῖς ἑαυτοῦ ὑπάρχουσιν). Together with the demand to leave behind one's earthly family, which occurs but seven verses earlier (Luke 14:26), this section of the gospel became a *crux interpretationis* for early Christian ascetic practice and later monastic development.

The Lukan passage, especially when read alongside such Gospel accounts as Jesus' call for the rich young man to sell all that he had and give to the poor (Matt. 19:21), is easily interpreted as a call for

---

29. *Bo* 31; cf. Goehring, "Theodore's Entry."
30. M. Rothenhaeusler and P. Oppenheim, "Apotaxis," *RAC* 1 (1950) 558–64; LSJ s.v.; Lampe, *A Patristic Greek Lexicon*, s.v.

the renunciation of ownership of private property. The monk, like the disciple before him, was to renounce all possessions. He was to live like the birds of the air and the beasts of the field, like Adam and Eve before the Fall, and like the angels today,[31] all of whom depend(ed) solely on God for their well-being. The literary accounts of Egyptian monasticism which proclaim this ideal are filled with stories of the renunciation of property and possessions by the movement's elite.[32] The influential *Life of Antony* reports that its hero, following the gospel precept, sold his inheritance and distributed the proceeds to the poor before he embarked on his ascetic career.[33] The anchoritic-oriented sayings of the *Apophthegmata Patrum* indicate that while private property was not forbidden, it was scorned and purposefully kept to a minimum.[34] Monks who received inheritances from relatives in the outside world were informed by their spiritual fathers of the dangers to the ascetic life inherent in them, and rejection of such gifts was strongly advocated.[35] Propertyless poverty became the literary ideal, expressed most beautifully and simply in the account of Apa Serapion, who sold his only possession, a gospel, and gave the proceeds to the poor, precisely because it had daily proclaimed to him the need to "sell all that you have and give to the poor."[36] Poverty remained initially, however, an ideal, since an ascetic life required a minimal amount of property — a cell, clothing, objects to trade for food, etc.[37]

It was the innovation of the Pachomian movement that first appears to offer the individual monk a means to fulfill completely the

---

31. Frank, *ΑΓΓΕΛΙΚΟΣ ΒΙΟΣ*.

32. The literary topos should be seen in part as the expression of a radical norm which functions to maintain group identity. See Petr Pokorny, "Strategies of Social Formation in the Gospel of Luke," in James E. Goehring et al., eds., *Gospel Origins and Christian Beginnings: In Honor of James M. Robinson* (Sonoma, Calif.: Polebridge Press, 1990) 112–18.

33. *Vita Antonii* 1–3.

34. Heussi, *Ursprung*, 251–54.

35. *Apophthegmata Patrum*, Poemen 33 (*PG* 65.329D–332A), Arsenios 29 (*PG* 65.97B–C). Arsenios refused an inheritance from a senator who had died by noting that he himself had died to the world long before the senator's death. Cf. Palladius, *Historia Lausiaca* 14.2 and 61.4.

36. *Apophthegmata Patrum*, anonymous collection, book 3, saying 70 (English translation in Helen Waddell, *The Desert Fathers* [Ann Arbor: University of Michigan Press, 1957] 140); cf. *Apophthegmata Patrum*, Theodore of Pherme 1 (*PG* 65.188A).

37. Goehring, "World Engaged" (chap. 2 in the present volume).

gospel demand to renounce *all* of one's personal property. Such personal renunciation was fulfilled though the act of contributing one's belongings to the monastery. The *Praecepta* of the Pachomian *Rule* require prospective members to renounce their parents and their possessions,[38] and a catechesis attributed to Theodore speaks matter-of-factly of those who renounced their possessions to embark on a monastic career (ⲁⲩⲱ ⲛ̅ⲥⲉⲁⲡⲟⲧⲁⲥⲥⲉ ⲛ̅ⲛⲉⲩⲛ̅ⲕⲁ ⲉⲡⲓⲧⲟⲣ̅ⲙ̅).[39] When Petronios convinced his father to join him in the Pachomian community, the latter brought with him to the monastery "everything he had: cattle, sheep, and all sorts of gear, and he donated it to the community."[40] Shenoute likewise required prospective monks to donate their belongings to the monastery and devised a written document to insure the legal basis of the transfer.[41] The literary evidence of the early Pachomian and Shenoutean systems corresponds well with the demand in the Justinian code that the possessions of a person entering a monastery become *ex lege* the property of the monastery.[42]

Certainly the success of the Pachomian and Shenoutean communities depended in part on this innovation. It permitted the fulfillment of the letter of the gospel through the renunciation of *all* personal property at the same time that it met the ascetic's basic needs of food, clothing, and shelter through the property and wealth of the monastery. The question remains, however, whether such innovation was a universal aspect of communal monasticism in Egypt, or whether it was limited to certain monastic communities. To answer this question, one must return to the evidence of the ἀποτακτικοί, which, as has been shown above, served in Egypt as a label indicating an individual's involvement in communal ascetic practice.

The growing corpus of fourth-century Greek documentary papyri

---

38. *Praecepta* 49; Boon, *Pachomiana latina*, 25–26; Veilleux, *Pachomian Koinonia*, 2.153.

39. Lefort, *Oeuvres*, 49.23; Veilleux, *Pachomian Koinonia*, 3.105.

40. *G1* 80=*Bo* 56; translation from Veilleux, *Pachomian Koinonia*, 1.352.

41. Leipoldt, *Schenute von Atripe*, 106–16; Krause, "Zur Möglichkeit," 123. For an example of an inheritance given to a monk and later disputed by secular relatives, see *P. Oxy.* XLVI 3311.

42. Artur Steinwenter, "Aus dem kirchlichen Vermögensrechte der Papyri," *ZSavR* 44 (1958) 24; Krause, "Zur Möglichkeit," 124; Leslie S. B. MacCoull, *Dioscorus of Aphrodito: His Works and His World* (TCH 16; Berkeley: University of California Press, 1988) 44–45.

that refer to ἀποτακτικοί(αί)[43] offers relatively clear evidence that some monks so titled could own property. As was noted above, in those cases in which an ἀποτακτικός is recorded as paying tax on land,[44] it is possible that the land was owned by the monk's monastery; such was indeed the case in *P. Berl.* Inv. 11860 (=*SB* XIV 11972). In the archive of Apa Johannes (*P. Herm.* 7–10), Johannes, who is called both ἀναχωρητής and ἀποτακτικός, is reported to have taken money (eight *solidi*) for his service of obtaining the letter writer's release from military service.[45] One could also preserve the propertyless state of the ἀναχωρητής-ἀποτακτικός here by assuming that the money taken in by Apa Johannes belonged to the larger community of which he was a part, but that goes beyond the evidence of the letters.

Other documents supply more conclusive evidence. A text dated to 381 C.E. (*P. Lips.* 28) records that a woman at Hermopolis entrusts her grandson to his uncle Silvanus, an ἀποτακτικός, who promises in turn to hold the child's inheritance until the child comes of age and to make the child heir to his own estate. Here there seems to be little doubt that an ἀποτακτικός did own property.[46] A second document, a lease agreement of 400 C.E. (*P. Oxy.* XLIV 3203), records the lease of a portion of a house in Oxyrhynchus to a Jew by two natural sisters, Theodora and Tauris, μοναχαὶ ἀποτακτικαί. The personal ownership of the house by these two female ἀποτακτικαί seems clear.

A final text (*P. Oxy.* XLVI 3311; 373–74 C.E.) is particularly illuminating. It is a legal document in which two sisters petition to regain control of property that their paternal cousin willed to his natural uncle, Ammonios, an ἀποτακτικός. Ammonios has subsequently died, and the property is being held by a certain Ammon, whom the sisters claim is neither a son nor an heir.[47] While the Ammon

---

43. Judge, "Fourth-Century Monasticism"; Wipszycka, "Terres"; Emmett, "Female Ascetics," 510–13.

44. *P. Berl.* Inv. 11860 (=*SB* XIV 11972); *P. Herm. Land.* (=*P. Giss.* 117 and *P. Flor.* 71).

45. Johannes fits well the pattern of the patron noted by Peter Brown ("Rise and Function"). It is interesting to note that the author writes to Johannes to get his money back, since Johannes was apparently unsuccessful in obtaining the writer's release from military service.

46. This text raises the further question of the extent to which the monastic ideal of renunciation of one's earthly family was actually carried out in practice.

47. The editor of the text, J. R. Rea (*The Oxyrhynchus Papyri* [vol. 46; London: Egypt Exploration Society, 1978] 96–98), suggests that Ammon was indeed next of kin and

in question may be a fellow ἀποτακτικός who has retained Ammonios's inheritance for the community,[48] there is no question but that the cousin had willed it originally to the individual ἀποτακτικός Ammonios. As such, the sisters' legal claim is that the title to the inheritance, in view of the absence of a will, should revert to them, i.e., it should remain in the natural family.

It must therefore be concluded that in the fourth century the term ἀποτακτικός did not, in and of itself, indicate the status of the person so labeled as propertied or propertyless.[49] While the Pachomians, self-styled ἀποτακτικοί, did not own property as individuals, the papyri discussed above indicate that other ἀποτακτικοί did, as individuals, retain ownership of personal property. If we assume that such ἀποτακτικοί lived in some form of community, then we must conclude that not all ascetic communities required their members to renounce their personal property. The Pachomian innovation of donating personal property to the monastery was not universal among communal ascetics in fourth-century Egypt.

This view is confirmed in the growing documentary evidence of Melitian monastic communities in Egypt. The sources include two sales contracts dated to 512–13 C.E.,[50] an archive of texts from the 330s connected with the Melitian monastery of Hathor (P. Lond. 1913–22),[51] and the archive of Nepheros, dated slightly later in the fourth century and also deriving from a monastery of Hathor, presumably to be equated with the monastery of Hathor in P. Lond. 1913–22.[52] While the term ἀποτακτικός does not appear with certainty in any of these texts,[53] the monasteries' communal organization and the fact that individual members could retain personal property seems clear.

heir to Ammonios and that the sisters were simply arguing that the latter was never really the full legal owner of the estate.

48. Judge, "Fourth-Century Monasticism," 618–19.

49. Cf. Krause, "Zur Möglichkeit," 122; Elm, Virgins of God, 238.

50. SB I 5174–75; Sayce, "Deux contrats grecs."

51. Bell, Jews and Christian in Egypt, 38–99.

52. Kramer and Shelton, Archiv des Nepheros. It must be noted that the monastery of Hathor in the P. Lond. 1913–22 archive is situated in the Upper Kynopolite nome, while that of the Nepheros archive is said to be in the Hermopolite nome. Kramer and Shelton (11–15) argue convincingly nonetheless for the equation of the two sites.

53. The one possible use of the term appears only as a result of textual emendation. It is certainly not clear that the lacuna should be so reconstructed (Kramer and Shelton, Archiv des Nepheros, 44, note to line 12–13).

The two sales contracts (*SB* I 5174–75) record the sale of two groups of monastic cells that exist within the Melitian monastery of Labla in the vicinity of Arsinoë. The cells belonged to a certain Eulogius who apparently came into their possession when he was a Melitian monk in the Labla monastery. He is selling the cells because he has since left the Melitian community and joined the orthodox monastery of Mikrou Phyon in the same vicinity.[54] When one turns to the earlier documents contained in the archive of Nepheros, the individual ownership of property is again underlined. The texts include references to a monk who owns a small piece of land, to one who sold a house and inherited a weaving workshop, and to one who made loans at interest.[55] Finally, the earliest materials (*P. Lond.* 1913–22), while they do not contain any clear references to private ownership, do indicate considerable economic activity. Furthermore, it is possible that the main figure in this archive, Apa Paieous, not only headed, but owned the community under his control.[56]

Other documents offer evidence for the continuing practice of private-property ownership within various Egyptian monasteries. A Greek text of 589 C.E. from Apollonos Polis (*P. Köln* 157)[57] records the emancipation of a slave by the monk Victor of the monastery of Apa Macrobius. Since emancipation requires previous ownership, the text once again affirms private ownership within a monastery setting. Among the papers of the sixth-century lawyer from Aphrodito, Dioscoros, one finds documents that make arrangements for certain monks entering a monastery to inherit property from their mother.[58] An eighth-century document from Jeme, which preserves

---

54. It is interesting to note that the *postophoroi* of the Egyptian temples of the Greco-Roman period lived in rooms or *postophoria* within the temple, which they purchased and owned. An individual *postophoros* could, moreover, own more than one *postophorion*. While the *postophorion* could be willed to an heir, proceeds from its sale apparently went to the state (J. A. S. Evans, *A Social and Economic History of an Egyptian Temple in the Greco-Roman Period* [YCS 17; New Haven: Yale University Press, 1961] 194–95, 205).

55. Kramer and Shelton, *Archiv des Nepheros*, 18.

56. Hengstenberg, review of *Jews and Christians in Egypt*, 140–41; cf. Steinwenter, "Rechtsstellung."

57. Dieter Hagedorn, "Sklavenfreilassung," in Bärbel Kramer et al., eds., *Kölner Papyri (P. Köln)* (PCol 7; Opladen: Westdeutscher Verlag, 1980); Krause, "Zur Möglichkeit," 124.

58. Leslie S. B. MacCoull, "A Coptic Session of Land by Dioscorus of Aphrodito: Alexandria Meets Cairo," in Tito Orlandi and Frederik Wisse, eds., *Acts of the Second*

the only surviving application for admission to a monastery, makes no mention of the applicant's renunciation of his property or its donation to the monastery, in obvious distinction to the Pachomian and Shenoutean practices.[59] Finally, 'five documents (*BL Or* 6201–4, 6206) edited by Martin Krause[60] record the purchase and sale of specific cell groups within a larger monastery by individual monks, three of whom are distinctly identified as ἀποτακτικοί (ⲀⲠⲞⲦⲀⲔⲦⲒⲔⲞⲤ ⲘⲘⲞⲚⲀⲬⲞⲤ). These texts date from the ninth century (833–50 C.E.) and derive from the non-Pachomian monastery of Apollo at Bawit.[61] They clearly illustrate that in the ninth century in certain communities individual ἀποτακτικοί could possess their own money with which to purchase their own cell(s).[62] The situation is complicated in these later texts by the fact that in certain monasteries individual monks could turn money over to the central authority of the community to be held by the community until the individual monk had need of it.[63]

While additional late documents could be noted, the evidence for a continuity in the practice of private-property ownership within certain monastic communities in Egypt seems clear. The question about the classification of these various monasteries naturally arises. The traditional answer is that those monasteries in which pri-

---

International Congress of Coptic Studies, Rome, 22–26 September 1980 (Rome: CIM, 1985); idem, *Dioscorus*, 36–47.

59. Walter E. Crum, *Varia Coptica: Texts, Translations, Indexes* (Aberdeen: University Press, 1939) 9–10; Krause, "Zur Möglichkeit," 124.

60. Krause, "Apa-Apollon-Kloster,"; idem, "Zur Möglichkeit," 126–28.

61. Krause, "Apa-Apollon-Kloster"; idem, "Bawit," in Klaus Wessel, ed., *Reallexikon zur byzantinischen Kunst* (vol. 1; Stuttgart: Hiersemann, 1966) 568–83; idem, "Zur Möglichkeit," 126; René-Georges Coquin and Maurice Martin, "Bawit: History," in Atiya, *Coptic Encyclopedia*, 2.362–63; Hjalmar Torp, "Le monastère copte de Baouit: Quelques notes d'introduction," in Hjalmar Torp et al., eds., *Acta ad archaeologiam et artium historiam pertinentia* (MC 9; Rome: Giorgio Bretschneider, 1981).

62. According to a clause in the documents, a cell could not be left to relatives or others outside of the monastery, but reverted on the death of the individual to the *diakonia* of the monastery (Krause, "Zur Möglichkeit," 127). This was, however, not always the case. *P. Oxy.* XVI 1891 records that a certain Serena inherited a milling bakery from the monk Copreous, which she in turn leased to a baker and his son. The bakery was located in the monastery of Apa Copreous in the western desert of the city.

63. Krause, "Apa-Apollon-Kloster," 213–24. Wipszycka ("Terres," 634) considered this theory "très fragile," but the Coptic evidence is certainly there to support the existence of the practice (for example *CLT* 1 and 2; Krause, "Zur Möglichkeit," 132–33 n. 81; A. Arthur Schiller, *Ten Coptic Legal Texts* [New York: Metropolitan Museum of Art, 1932] 16–33).

vate property was permitted represent anchoritic communities[64] and should be carefully distinguished from full coenobitic communities such as those of Pachomius and Shenoute. Martin Krause rightly questioned the rigidity of this division with respect to the monastery of Apollo at Bawit, observing "dass wir das nach den Regeln Pachoms und Schenutes organisierte Klosterwesen nur aus den zwar reichen literarischen Quellen des 4. und 5. Jahrhunderts kennen."[65] I would go further and argue that any sharp division between anchoritic and coenobitic communities in Egypt in general is best eliminated as a product of the impact of the literary sources. This is not to deny the significance of the Pachomian communal organization, but to recognize that in making it the defining model of communal monasticism on the basis of its literary success, we force all other models of communal asceticism into the anchoritic camp and lose thereby any sense of a continuum between the two.[66]

It is better to accept a fluidity in the practice of communal ascetic organization in Egypt, a fluidity confirmed in the sources' own use of the term ἀποτακτικός. As we have seen, it was used from the beginning both of monks who owned personal property and those, like the Pachomians, who did not. It is not necessary to account for the later uses of the term with reference to communal monks who owned property by positing a shift in meaning brought on by changing times and the imposition of the poll tax on the monasteries.[67] While in those communities that originally required their members to surrender all personal property such a shift in meaning may have occurred in later years through necessity, the evidence argues against any notion of a more general shift in the meaning of the term throughout Egypt. There were after all various ascetic communities, e.g., those of the Melitians, where private-property ownership had always been accepted. In such communities the notion of a shift

64. The anchoritic community is best represented by the communities in the Wadi Natrun. They are seen to parallel to an extent the *lavra* pattern in Palestine. Note that the Melitian texts, *SB* I 5174–75, refer to a monastery of Labla, which Hengstenberg ("Bemerkungen," 357) already connected with the term *lavra*.

65. "...that we know the monastic system organized according to the rules of Pachomius and Shenoute only through the abundant literary sources of the fourth and fifth centuries" (Krause, "Zur Möglichkeit," 128).

66. Cf. Kramer and Shelton, *Archiv des Nepheros*, 18–20.

67. Krause, "Zur Möglichkeit," 127–29; H. Idris Bell, "Two Official Letters of the Arab Period," *JEA* 12 (1926) 265–75.

in the meaning of ἀποτακτικός to include the ownership of personal property is meaningless. In the case of the monastery of Apollo at Bawit, where the documentary evidence indicates private-property ownership in the ninth century, it is just as likely that the monks of this monastery had always been able to own property as it is that their original rule shifted in later years to allow it.

Ἀποτακτικός: MEANING AND HISTORY

In her recent study on "Female Ascetics in the Greek Papyri," Alanna Emmett held in her conclusion that "as monasticism developed, ἀποτακτικός accumulated more usage but remained a term which drew a line between those who remained more or less in conformity with regular ways of handling family, property and other social ties and those who renounced customary patterns."[68] While the ideal of ἀπόταξις might include total renunciation of family, possessions, and social ties, practical reality surely led to diverse degrees and patterns of implementation. The use of the term ἀποτακτικός thus indicated a person within the church who, on the basis of his or her Christian belief, renounced the traditional social patterns of Roman Egypt; it did not necessarily specify which patterns were renounced nor the degree to which they were renounced.

One suspects that the term ἀναχωρητής had originally a similar meaning within the church, namely, a person who withdrew, on the basis of Christian belief, from the traditional social responsibilities of Roman Egypt. Over time the term ἀναχωρητής came to indicate one who withdrew spatially from the community, a definition fostered in particular by Athanasius's *Life of Antony,* whose hero fled to the desert. It is possible that as this spatial element was emphasized in the definition of ἀναχωρητής, it propelled the meaning of the term more toward the idea of solitary withdrawal and its customary equation with the anchorite or hermit monk. Ἀποτακτικός, on the other hand, perhaps in part to compensate for the void left by the newer meaning of ἀναχωρητής, came to refer to those ascetic individuals who chose to live together in some form of community. It thus became the communal life that defined the ἀποτακτικός in

---

68. Emmett, "Female Ascetics," 513.

Egypt, though the organizational principles of that communal life could vary widely. The Coptic literary sources and late documentary evidence clearly indicate that this communal dimension to the term's definition remained in force at least through the ninth century. Thus, Emmett's final stage in her history of the meaning of ἀποτακτικός, namely that "with the hardening of institutional forms and the spread of the terms μοναχός and then μονάζων, ἀποτακτικός reasserted itself in a more specialized sense, with something of the original eremitic overtones emphasized," appears incorrect.[69]

It seems more likely that the apparent shift in the meaning of ἀποτακτικός in an anchoritic or eremitic direction detected by Emmett is a result of the redefinition of Egyptian ascetic terminology for a non-Egyptian audience. In the more northern provinces, the term ἀποτακτῖται came to be associated with certain "heretical" groups. Basil of Caesarea, for example, in his second canonical letter (374–75 C.E.), calls for the rebaptism of ἐγκρατῖται, σακκοθόροι, and ἀποτακτῖται.[70] Epiphanius, writing about 376 C.E., refers to a heretical sect in Phrygia, Cilicia, and Pamphylia who term themselves ἀποστολικοί or ἀποτακτῖται.[71] Given such developments outside of Egypt, it is no surprise that the general Egyptian use of the term ἀποτακτικός for individuals practicing a communal ascetic life required careful translation in the literary presentation of Egyptian monasticism to the outside world. The importance of the issue is apparent in the transmission of the *Life of Pachomius*, in which, while the term ἀποτακτικός occurs with relative frequency in the Coptic recensions of the *Vita*, it has disappeared from the Greek and Latin versions.[72] The latter, meant at least ultimately for a non-Egyptian audience,[73] deleted the term as incompatible with the literary orthodoxy of the Pachomian movement.

---

69. Emmett, "Female Ascetics," 513. Emmett's conclusions are based on the earlier Greek documentary evidence.

70. *Ep.* 199; *PG* 32.729–32; cf. Lambert, "Apotactites," 2615–16.

71. *Panarion* 1.2.1; *PG* 41.1040–52; Lambert, "Apotactites," 2616; Judge, "Earliest Use," 80.

72. Compare the Bohairic text wherein Apa Psahref informs the investigating duke Artemios that "we are apotaktikoi" (ⲁⲛⲟⲛ ⲅⲁⲛⲣⲱⲙⲓ ⲛⲁⲡⲟⲧⲁⲕⲧⲓⲕⲟⲥ; Lefort, *S. Pachomii vita bohairice scripta*, 166.10–11) with the Greek *Vita prima* version in which the line drops out (Halkin, *Sancti Pachomii Vitae Graecae*, 87).

73. While early Greek forms of the *vita* may have originated in Egypt, they survive today in later non-Egyptian manuscripts.

Perhaps the clearest and most influential example of this development occurs in the relabeling of the threefold division of ascetic practice current in Egypt. In two separate Coptic sources attributed to Athanasius and Pachomius respectively, the three types of ascetics noted in Egypt are the παρθένοι, the ἀποτακτικοί, and the ἀναχωρηταί. For the Egyptian audience, the terms denoted simply the various forms of ascetic life; they appear to have offered no information on the practitioner's position relative to theological issues. When Jerome reports the three forms of Egyptian ascetic practice to the Roman lady Eustochium, however, the terms become *coenobium, anachoretae,* and *remnuoth.* Not only has the Egyptian term for the communal ascetic, ἀποτακτικοί, been replaced by *coenobium* (or *coenobiotae* in Cassian, *Conf.* 18.4), but now the terms carry a theological dimension. The *anachoretae* and the *coenobium* represent the politically correct forms of the ascetic life, and the *remnuoth* are dismissed as heretics.

What is important to note is that the term by which we today most often describe an Egyptian communal ascetic, the term *coenobite,* was not the common term used to describe a communal monk in Egypt.[74] In its modern usage, the term connects too readily with the literarily well-documented Pachomian community or self-styled *koinonia* and comes thereby to equate too simplistically Egyptian communal monasticism with its Pachomian form. The more diverse use of ἀποτακτικός in the Egyptian sources argues for more diversity in the organizational forms of communal ascetic practice in Egypt.[75]

The continuing impact of Jerome's terminological shift is seen in the tendency to equate forms of Egyptian monastic life that do not at first glance fit the usual definitions of anchoritic and coenobitic monasticism (which are in fact Jerome's definitions) with Jerome's *remnuoth.* Judge made this move when he connected the papyrolog-

---

74. Jerome notes (*Ep.* 22.34) that the *coenobium* are called *sauhes* in Egypt. *Sauhes* is the Coptic and is used of monastic communities or monks residing in them, though not exclusively of those of the Pachomian variety (Crum, *Coptic Dictionary,* s.v.). The Coptic recensions of the *Vita Pachomii* refer to the ⲕⲟⲓⲛⲱⲛⲓⲁ and employ the verb ⲕⲟⲓⲛⲱⲛⲉⲓ; they refer to the monks, however, as ⲁⲡⲟⲧⲁⲕⲧⲓⲕⲟⲥ and ⲙⲟⲛⲁⲭⲟⲥ.

75. The archaeology of various monastic sites suggests a similar diversity. Cf. Peter Grossmann, "Die Unterkunftsbauten des Koinobitenklosters 'Dair al-Balayza' im Vergleich mit dem Eremitagen der Mönche von Kellia," in *Le site monastique copte des Kellia: Sources historiques et explorations archéologiques. Actes du Colloque de Genève, 13 au 15 août 1984* (Geneva: Mission suisse d'archéologie copte de l'Université de Genève, 1986); Krause, "Bawit"; Coquin and Martin, "Bawit"; Torp, "Le monastère copte."

ical evidence of the ἀποτακτικοί with the *remnuoth*.[76] Kramer and Shelton, in similar fashion, suggest that Melitian monasticism, as evidenced in the papyri, also fits Jerome's third category.[77] While not denying the existence of monks who lived a life as Jerome describes that of the *remnuoth*, we must be careful not to allow his threefold division to become a sine qua non for our understanding of Egyptian monasticism. It is probably not an accident that the ἀποτακτικοί and the Melitian monks do not fit easily into the usual picture of Egyptian monasticism defined in anchoritic (Antonian) and coenobitic (Pachomian) terms. That is not sufficient reason, however, to equate them with the *remnuoth*. Evidence for both derives from non-literary papyrological sources which, as such, do not participate fully in the literary definitions of the monastic life. Rather than force them into the literary models by linking these "odd" monks with Jerome's *remnuoth*, we should question the literary models.

In his identification of the ἀποτακτικοί of the papyri with the *remnuoth*, for example, Judge accepted Jerome's terminological shift from ἀποτακτικοί to *coenobium* as the label for communal ascetics in Egypt. As a result, the use of the term ἀποτακτικοί, which in the Egyptian sources is most likely a simple reference to communal ascetics, with no specification of the organizational form of their community, becomes evidence of a third form of the ascetic life (the apotactic movement), a form probably not recognized, as such, in Egypt.[78] The theologically motivated imposition of a non-Egyptian terminology on the literary presentation of Egyptian monasticism outside of Egypt has come, not only here, but in general, to define the Egyptian movement. It is a false step. To understand Egyptian monasticism, we must listen to the Egyptians.

In terms of the impact of the literary models on our understanding of asceticism, it must be recognized that ascetic practice in Egypt was more diverse than the literary models indicate. This is true not only with reference to doctrine, but also with reference to practice.

---

76. Judge, "Earliest Use."

77. Kramer and Shelton, *Archiv des Nepheros*, 18–20; cf. Hengstenberg, review of *Jews and Christians in Egypt*, 141–42.

78. This is not to deny some form of urban monasticism as posited by Judge, but rather to question the identification of the term ἀποτακτικοί with individuals who practiced that form. One doubts that the term had any connection with the geographic location of one's ascetic enterprise.

As the literary models of asceticism took hold in the minds of the early Christians, their rhetoric of *imitatio* not only forced the future into a prescribed mold, it also reshaped the past. Historically, the ascetic practice represented by the literary source is most at home in the later age that the source itself helped to shape. Documentary sources, on the other hand, do not present models of ascetic practice designed to shape the future or the past, but simply record examples of such practice. While their interpretation has its own methodological difficulties, they offer direct access to specific cases in specific ages and thus serve as a check against the ascetic models of the literary sources. They can never replace the literary sources, but they can help put them in perspective. The study of the technical terminology of asceticism offered above is but an attempt, through the use of such documentary evidence, to lift ever so slightly the literary veil.

4

The Encroaching Desert: Literary Production and Ascetic Space in Early Christian Egypt

A fable depicting the absence of truth in human society appears among those collected and put to verse by Babrius toward the end of the first century C.E.

> A man journeying into the desert found Truth standing alone and said to her, "Why, revered lady, have you left the city and dwell now in the desert?" To which with profound wisdom she straightway replied, "Falsehood found a place with few among those of old, but now it has spread to all humankind." [Moral:] If I may say and you wish to hear, the life of humans today is evil.[1]

In this fable, the author makes symbolic use of the visual distinction between desert and city to more vividly express the ethical division between truth (or good) and falsehood (or evil) in human society. It is a literary device, a metaphor clear in its simplicity and powerful in its impact. It works so powerfully because it divides so sharply. There are no suburbs here, no grey zones where one finds the polar opposites of truth and falsehood mixed and difficult to distinguish. No. The city, the product of human achievement and the locus of human habitation, has become symbolically the center of evil. Truth has left the city, and presumably only falsehood remains. Truth now resides alone in the desert.

In fourth-century Egypt, the metaphor was translated into radical reality as ascetic Christians embraced a life which demanded spatial withdrawal (ἀναχώρησις) from the social world of the villages and towns to the isolation of the desert. The sources suggest that the initial trickle of ascetics into the desert rapidly turned into a flood.

First published in *JECS* 1 (1993) 281–96.

1. Fable 126. Ben Edwin Perry, ed., *Babrius and Phaedrus* (LCL; Cambridge: Harvard University Press, 1975) 162–63; my translation.

By 357 C.E., their numbers had become so extensive that Athanasius could claim in his *Life of Antony* that "the desert has been made a city by monks who left their own people [in the towns and cities] and registered themselves for citizenship in the heavens."[2] In fact, he made ἀναχώρησις a fundamental message of this *Vita*, whose hero Antony is perfected through his ever further withdrawal from humanity into the desert. The widespread success of this work simply continued the process. Those who now would imitate the most famous ascetic hero in Egypt must likewise withdraw from the towns and cities. Many did. They, like the wanderer in Babrius's fable, found "truth" in the desert.

While few would argue that the division between the desert and the city in Babrius's tale is anything more than a metaphor, when the same division occurs in early monastic literature it is understood as a fairly accurate depiction of historical events. The latter conclusion, however, fails to address seriously enough the literary nature of our sources. While the division between the city and the desert is certainly more nuanced in monastic literature than in Babrius's fable and its relationship to historical events more complex, the widespread literary use of the dichotomy in antiquity raises the question as to the degree of influence the metaphor exerted on the literary portrayal of early Egyptian monasticism.

The sharp division drawn in Babrius's fable between the geographical and ethical categories of city/falsehood and desert/truth was not meant to be taken literally. Its author does not claim to offer historically accurate statistics on the number of ethical individuals in the city versus those in the desert. Rather, he offers in mythic form a radical version of the more common dichotomy that separates the complexities of city life from the simplicity of the pastoral setting. The fable's moral is not stated in terms of geography, but in terms of the human predicament. "The life of humans today is evil." The author is not denying that good persons live in the city nor that evil ones reside in the desert, but rather affirming (teaching) the real difficulty of living an ethical life in an increasingly complex society. Truth is more easily found in the simplicity of the desert than in the

---

2. Athanasius, *Vita Antonii* 14 (PG 26.865); my translation. Cf. Gregg, *Life of Antony*, 42–43.

city with its complex variables and constant pressures. While there were undoubtedly those in antiquity who left the cities for a quieter abode, the author of the fable did not intend to incite an exodus from the cities. The moral was meant simply to warn of the snares and pitfalls of urban life.

The literary accounts of the early Christian ascetics who embraced the desert have a more complex understanding of the truth of the desert than is found in Babrius's fable.[3] Alongside the metaphorical connection of the city with falsehood and the desert with truth appears the earlier and seemingly opposite view that associates the areas of human habitation with life and the desert with death.[4] The importance of this latter image in early monastic literature indicates that its authors did not simply equate the truth of the desert with the absence of evil. Its truth lay rather in the clarity it offered the monk on the reality and nature of evil. The battle against evil was a battle against the demonic, and in the desert the demons had fewer places to hide. If ascetic life in the desert made the struggle with evil easier, it did so only in the sense that it made it more direct. In the desert, there was less to distract the monk from the fight and fewer ways for the enemy to confuse him.

When this image of the desert as the home of demons comes to the fore in the literary portrayal, the flood of ascetics to the desert can be understood as an effort by the monks to expand divine civilization into the uncivilized realms of Satan.[5] The author of the *Life of Antony* thus portrays the desert as the natural home of the demons[6]

---

3. For an excellent account of the varied conceptions of the desert in early Christian monasticism, refer to Antoine Guillaumont, "La conception du désert chez les moines d'Égyptes," *RHR* 188 (1975) 3–21; reprinted in idem, *Aux origines du monachisme chrétien: Pour une phénoménologie du monachisme* (SpO 30; Bégrolles en Mauges, France: Abbaye de Bellefontaine, 1979) 69–87.

4. The two versions of the desert/city dichotomy (desert/truth versus city/falsehood and desert/demonic versus city/divine) were both present in Egypt before the rise of Christian monasticism. The desert/demonic–city/divine dichotomy finds expression in the ancient Egyptian division between the fertile Nile-watered valley as symbolic of life and the desert as symbolic of death. The desert/truth–city/falsehood pattern participates in the ancient Israelite belief in the nearness of God in the desert. For the latter see Ulrich Mauser, *Christ in the Wilderness: The Wilderness Theme in the Second Gospel and Its Basis in the Biblical Tradition* (SBT 39; Chatham, Great Britain: W. & J. Mackay, 1963).

5. The image of the monks as the carriers of divine civilization connects with the understanding of their life as angelic. Frank, *ΑΓΓΕΛΙΚΟΣ ΒΙΟΣ*.

6. *Vita Antonii* 13 (*PG* 26.861C); 8 (*PG* 26.856A).

and views the desert monks as those who are turning it into a city of God.[7] While in this image the city serves a positive role that appears to counter the association of the city with evil (falsehood), the positive role is defined narrowly by the "spiritual" nature of the new city. The city in the desert is as distinct from the real cities of Egypt as the heavenly Jerusalem is from its earthly counterpart. The real, earthly city remains fundamentally a negative image in early monastic literature.[8]

Keeping this more complex definition of the truth of the desert in mind, the *Life of Antony*, with its emphasis on ἀναχώρησις, appears to build on the more positive half of the desert/city metaphor in Babrius's fable. Antony flees to the desert because truth resides in the desert. The negative half of the equation, namely that falsehood resides in the city (earthly city), is replaced by the author's positive use of the city (spiritual city) to describe the success of the desert experiment.[9] The negative image of the earthly city does, however, find clear expression in other examples of early Egyptian monastic literature. In the prologue to the *History of the Monks in Egypt*, the author connects the positive image of the monk as a citizen of heaven (ἐν οὐρανοῖς πολιτεύονται) with the negative image of the human city as evil through the added assertion that "some of them [the monks in the desert] do not even know that another world exists on earth, or that evil is a citizen of the cities (ὅτι κακία ἐν πόλεσιν ἐμπολιτεύεται)." Here the city/falsehood–desert/truth dichotomy is more complete. The visible distinction between the desert and the city serves to express the ethical distinction between good and evil. While in the *Life of Antony* the true monk fled to the desert to confront the demonic, in the *History of the Monks of Egypt* he also flees from the earthly city to escape its evil and to become a citizen of heaven. The negative evaluation of the earthly city is clear. At the same time, the reference to the monk's heavenly citizenship suggests the presence of the other image of the city as the spiritual city of the

---

7. *Vita Antonii* 14 (*PG* 26.865).

8. The case of Oxyrhynchus (*Historia Monachorum in Aegypto* 5) offers a notable exception. The lack of other examples to support it, however, suggests that as an exception it only proves the rule.

9. Athanasius, the bishop of Alexandria, would have had vested interests in avoiding the negative view of the city.

desert. The two forms of the desert/city metaphor thus coalesce in the literature in such a way that whichever image one chooses to apply, the result with respect to the monastic enterprise is always the same. Like Truth in Babrius's fable, the true monk is forced to reside in the desert.[10] The only city which he may call home is the spiritual city of the desert.

The impact of this view of the desert on Egyptian monastic literature cannot be underestimated. It not only forms the fabric of the story, but offers, I would suggest, the very basis for the telling of the story in the first place. By connecting the common metaphorical use of the desert/city dichotomy[11] with earlier monastic views of withdrawal, the image necessary for literary production was forged. In the accounts of early Egyptian monasticism, for example, the metaphorical use of city and desert has interacted with the concepts of withdrawal (ἀναχώρησις) and renunciation (ἀπόταξις) in such a way as to impart to these terms a distinct spatial dimension alongside their more original legal or ethical meaning.[12] Christian renunciation of or withdrawal from traditional societal expectations (family, sex, property, business, etc.), which initially could occur within the home, the village, or the city, became in the literary sources of early Egyptian monasticism demands for physical separation from the society at large. Withdrawal to the desert or enclosure behind monastery walls became, in this literature, the visible expression of the ethical, ascetical stance.

Intriguing questions arise when one ponders the interaction between this literary depiction and the developing practice of asceticism in Egypt. Careful study of the varied sources underscores the diversity of possible relationships between the ascetic and society in Egypt. While the remote hermit may be the figure that most often comes to mind when one thinks of Egyptian monasticism, in real-

---

10. John of Lycopolis advises one to "flee to the furthest parts of the desert if one realizes that one is becoming proud. For living near villages has often harmed even the perfect." *Historia Monachorum in Aegypto* 1.31 (cf. prologue 11; 1.36; 8.20; 10.12, 30); translation from Russell and Ward, *Lives of the Desert Fathers*, 56.

11. Note, for example, Philo Judaeus, *De decalogo* 2; Tacitus, *Annales* 15.44; Augustine, *Confessiones* 3.1.

12. Ἀναχώρησις was the official legal term for illegal absence from civic duties and for tax evasion. While it is traditionally translated by the word "flight," it is not clear that those evading their responsibilities actually fled. Rubenson, *Letters of St. Antony*, 93.

ity his physical location represents but one end in a continuum of spatial location between city and remote desert throughout which asceticism was practiced in Egypt. Even the *History of the Monks in Egypt*, with its view that evil resides in and near the city, reports that "there is no village or city in Egypt and the Thebaid that has not been surrounded by monasteries as if by walls."[13] In the case of Oxyrhynchus, the city itself becomes a monastic city of God. It was, the author says, "so full of monasteries that the walls were made to resound with [the voices of] the monks themselves." Five thousand monks, almost a majority of the population, lived within the city, and another five thousand made their homes beyond the walls. The city's temples and public buildings became monasteries overfilled with monks who worshiped God every hour of the night and day. Their presence was felt in every quarter, and the city became so pure that not a single heretic or pagan called it home![14] While considerable literary license is clear in the pious exaggerations of this account, it does indicate the existence of monks within the city toward the end of the fourth century. These urban monks represent the opposite end from the remote desert hermit in the continuum of the spatial or physical location of ascetics in Egypt.

Other sources suggest, in fact, that the urban location of ascetic practice may have been the more original. Judge, in a well-known article, argued on the basis of the Oxyrhynchus evidence that "far from abandoning the city, the [monastic] retreat seems to have swallowed it up."[15] Drawing from the papyrological evidence, he suggests that monasticism has its origins in what he labels the apotactic movement, which "represents the point at which the men at last followed the pattern long set for virgins and widows, and set up houses of their own in town, in which the life of personal renunciation and service in the church would be practiced."[16] The presence of as-

---

13. *Historia Monachorum in Aegypto*, prologue 10; my translation.

14. *Historia Monachorum in Aegypto* 5.1–7. On the exaggerated numbers, see Julien Krüger, *Oxyrhynchus in der Kaizerzeit: Studien zur Topographie und Literaturrezeption* (EH 441; Frankfurt: Peter Lang, 1990) 60–73; cf. Russell and Ward, *Lives of the Desert Fathers*, 20.

15. Judge, "Earliest Use," 80; cf. idem, "Fourth-Century Monasticism"; Emmett, "Female Ascetics."

16. Judge, "Earliest Use," 85. Judge's use of *P. Coll. Youtie* 77, the text in which the monk Isaac intervenes in a village dispute, as a basis for his argument seems over-

cetics within the towns and villages continues to be hinted at in the later sources, though such ascetics remain an exception in the literature.[17] The Bohairic *Life of Pachomius* reports Pachomius's interest in "brothers who lived as anchorites in Alexandria" (ⲚⲚⲒⲤⲚⲎⲞⲨ ⲈⲦⲈⲢⲀⲚⲀⲬⲰⲢⲒⲚ ϩⲈⲚⲢⲀⲔⲞϯ),[18] and the *Letter of Ammon* indicates that when Ammon converted to Christianity in 351 C.E., he sought first to apprentice himself under a monk in Alexandria before his priest steered him to the Pachomians in Upper Egypt.[19] Papyrological evidence establishes the presence of Melitian monks in the village of Hipponon,[20] and although the village of Tabennese was deserted when Pachomius founded his first monastery there around 323 C.E., the *Life of Pachomius* reports that his presence in the village quickly led to a nonmonastic resurgence in the town.[21] In the end, village and monastery seem to have existed together.[22]

If the two ends of the continuum of ascetic spatial location in Egypt are represented by the city and the remote desert, it is important to understand that monks occupied locations everywhere along the continuum between the two poles. The *Life of Antony* indicates this fact through the stages of Antony's own withdrawal. He began his ascetic life by imitating the common pattern of the day and

---

drawn. It is not clear from the text that Isaac lived in the village. Ascetics did often visit nearby villages.

17. A good study of the evidence of urban ascetic practice in Egypt appears in the Duke University dissertation of Carlton Mills Badger ("New Man," chap. 4). He contends that Athanasius's interest in ascetic Christians began and centered on those who remained within the church communities in the towns. See also Brakke, *Athanasius;* Goehring, "Through a Glass Darkly" (chap. 3 in the present volume); idem, "World Engaged" (chap. 2); idem, "Origins of Monasticism" (chap. 1).

18. Bohairic *Vita Pachomii* (*Bo*) 89; Lefort, *S. Pachomii vita bohairice scripta*, 104.

19. *Epistula Ammonis* 2; Goehring, *Letter of Ammon*, 124–25, 191.

20. *P. Lond.* 1913–22. Bell, *Jews and Christians in Egypt*, 38–99; Goehring, "Melitian Monastic Organization" (chap. 9 in the present volume); Judge, "Earliest Use," 84–85.

21. *Bo* 17, 24–25; Lefort, *S. Pachomii vita bohairice scripta*, 18–25; Veilleux, *Pachomian Koinonia*, 1.39–48; cf. Goehring, "World Engaged," 139–40.

22. With the exception of Tabennese, where Pachomius founded a monastery in a deserted village, the urban monks mentioned above are all seen as heretical. The Alexandrian anchorites turn out to be of evil repute, and Ammon is steered to the Pachomians because the Alexandrian hermit is considered heretical. The Melitians, of course, were opponents of Athanasius. Cf. also Sozomen, *Historia ecclesiastica* 8.9. One suspects that the orthodoxy-heresy dichotomy is here being superimposed on the desert-city dichotomy. The cause for such a literary overlay may lie, at least in part, in the simple fact that the more remote ascetics caused fewer problems for the ecclesiastical authorities. Cf. Goehring, "Origins of Monasticism," 241–42 (see p. 23 in the present volume).

remaining in close proximity to his native village (καὶ πρῶτον μὲν ἤρξατο καὶ αὐτὸς μένειν ἐν τοῖς πρὸ τῆς κώμης τόποις).[23] From there he eventually withdrew further to tombs located some distance from the village (ἀπήρχετο εἰς τὰ μακρὰν τῆς κώμης τυγχάνοντα μνήματα),[24] and then to a deserted fortress beyond the river. Eventually he set out to withdraw further into the Upper Thebaid, but was steered by a voice to the even more remote location of the inner mountain along the Red Sea.[25] While the model of Antony suggests a relationship between the distance of physical withdrawal and the status of the saint,[26] the various stages in his withdrawal process represent in fact the full range of sites occupied by ascetics in Egypt, a continuum between the village and the remote desert.

The *History of the Monks in Egypt* reports that monks of all ages could be found in the desert and in the inhabitable land (ἐν ταῖς ἐρήμοις καὶ ἐν ταῖς χώραις).[27] The latter category, the inhabitable land, bridges the space between the desert and the city. The desert itself is furthermore differentiated between the nearer desert (ἡ πλησίον ἔρημος) and the more remote or further desert (ἡ μακροτέρα ἔρημος and ἡ πορρωτέρω ἔρημος), both of which were occupied by monks.[28] As precise as the terminology appears, however, one must still use

23. "And he first began by remaining in places near the village" (my translation; *Vita Antonii* 3 [*PG* 26.844B]).

24. "He left for the tombs that were located some distance from the village" (my translation; *Vita Antonii* 8 [*PG* 26.854C]).

25. *Vita Antonii* 12 (*PG* 26.861); 49 (*PG* 26.913–16). Theodore of Tabennese follows a similar path of increased spatial separation, but one measured in terms of spatial distance from his biological family. Goehring, "Theodore's Entry."

26. The connection between the distance of the saint's withdrawal and the degree of his sanctity becomes a hagiographic topos and results, as authors seek to heighten their particular hero's sanctity, in an increasing literary exaggeration of the distance of withdrawal. In the late *Life of Onnophrius,* the reported author Papnouthios is said to have journeyed at least twenty-one days into the desert, aided repeatedly in the process with special food and water delivered by an angel, before he reached the solitary (!) place where Onnophrius lived. By means of this topos, the text suggests that Onnophrius was so holy that one could not reach his withdrawn desert abode by human means alone. A new English translation of this text has been published by Tim Vivian, *Histories of the Monks of Upper Egypt and the Life of Onnophrius by Paphnutius* (CistStud 140; Kalamazoo, Mich.: Cistercian Publications, 1993); idem, "The Life of Onnophrius: A New Translation," *CCR* 12 (1991) 99–111.

27. *Historia Monachorum in Aegypto,* prologue 10; Festugière, *Historia Monachorum,* 8.

28. *Historia Monachorum in Aegypto* 1.32, 45, 46. Festugière, *Historia Monachorum,* 20, 26; cf. Cadell and Rémondon, "Sens et emplois de τὸ ὄρος," 343–49; Russell and Ward, *Lives of the Desert Fathers,* 125.

caution. The *Life of Pachomius* reports that Pachomius began his monastic career as an apprentice of the anchorite Palamon, who had settled a little way from the village (ⲉϥⲥⲁⲃⲟⲗ ⲙ̄ⲡⲓϯⲙⲓ ⲛⲟⲩⲕⲟⲩϫⲓ) of Šeneset. There he practiced his asceticism "in those deserts, in the acacia forest that surrounded them, and in the far desert" (ϧⲉⲛ-ⲛⲓϣⲁϥⲉⲩ ⲉⲧⲉⲙⲙⲁⲩ ϧⲉⲛⲡⲓⲛⲓϣϯ ⲛ̄ϣⲟⲛϯ ⲉⲧⲕⲱϯ ⲉⲣⲱⲟⲩ ⲛⲉⲙⲡⲓϣⲁϥⲉ ⲉⲑⲟⲩⲏⲟⲩ).[29] The geography seems confused since Palamon is said both to reside near a village situated in the fertile valley and in the desert. The latter is furthermore surrounded by an acacia forest that must be traversed to reach the further desert. The confusion clears as soon as one realizes that a small inhospitable outcropping of rock occurs within the fertile zone in close proximity to the village of Šeneset (Chenoboskion). This was the "desert" of Palamon, a small inarable space surrounded by the fertile soil of the Nile valley and within a stone's throw of the village of Šeneset.[30] The further desert, which here refers simply to the desert beyond the fertile zone, corresponds at least in part to the "nearer desert" of the *History of the Monks in Egypt!* The term *desert* itself thus represents a continuum of possible ascetic locations defined in terms of distance from the settled social world of Egyptian society; while it is always inarable land, it need not be land beyond the fertile zone. Its meaning in monastic literature has as much or more to do with the concept of withdrawal from the space traditionally occupied by civilization as it does with any precise definition based on annual precipitation.

The presence of monks along the entirety of the continuum of spatial location between city and remote desert seems clear. The *History of the Monks in Egypt* refers to monks in the cities, in the inhabitable land (ἡ χώρα), and in the desert.[31] Ammon's first choice for a monastic master resided in Alexandria, and Melitian monks lived in the village of Hipponon.[32] Antony first imitated an old man in a nearby village who had practiced the solitary life from his youth,[33] and Palamon lived in an "inner" desert a stone's throw from the vil-

---

29. *Bo* 10, 15; Lefort, *S. Pachomii vita bohairice scripta*, 8.1–2 and 16.23–25; Veilleux, *Pachomian Koinonia*, 1.30, 38.

30. Lefort, "Premiers monastères," 383–84.

31. The *Historia Lausiaca* (prologue 16), which does not limit itself to Egyptian monasticism, refers to monks in the cities, in the villages, and in the desert.

32. *P. Lond.* 1913–22; see above, note 20.

33. *Vita Antonii* 3 (*PG* 844B).

lage of Šeneset. Pachomius's communities existed in the fertile valley (Tabennese was located near the Nile),[34] and Shenoute's White Monastery was situated at its edge.[35] John of Lycopolis made his home in the desert escarpment some five miles from the city of Lycopolis (modern Asyut),[36] and it took Abba Helle a day's journey on an ass to reach his cave.[37] The Wadi Natrun was forty miles from Alexandria, and Kellia some ten miles beyond it.[38] Antony eventually settled in the desert near the Red Sea about eighty-five miles from the Nile.[39] Monks clearly occupied the entire physical landscape in Egypt, from the largest city to the furthest desert. While it can be said with Athanasius that "the desert was made a city by monks," if Judge is correct in placing monastic beginnings in an urban setting, it is perhaps more accurate to assert that geographically all Egypt became an ascetic metropolis as a result of monastic sprawl.

The emphasis on the desert in the literary production of early Egyptian monasticism can readily foster, for later readers who know the movement only through these sources, the idea that earlier ascetic locations in and near the villages were abandoned as additional, more distant ground was broken by monastic pioneers.[40] While there is little question that the literary portrayal impacted later developments, it is doubtful that it led to the wholesale desertion of the towns and cities by the monks for increasingly remote desert spaces. Later papyrus sources, when they do mention an ascetic in connection with a town, do not often supply specific evidence on the relationship of the monk to the town. In such cases, it remains unclear whether the ascetic resided within the town, near it, or at a further distance from it. Where the evidence is available, the

34. René-Georges Coquin, "Tabennese," in Atiya, *Coptic Encyclopedia*, 7.2197; Goehring, "World Engaged," 139 (see p. 46 in the present volume).

35. René-Georges Coquin and Maurice Martin, S.J., "Dayr Anba Shinudah: History," in Atiya, *Coptic Encyclopedia*, 3.761–66.

36. *Historia Monachorum in Aegypto* 1.6; Festugière, *Historia Monachorum*, 11.

37. *Historia Monachorum in Aegypto* 12.5; Festugière, *Historia Monachorum*, 93–94.

38. White, *Monasteries of the Wadi 'n Natrun*, 17–39.

39. Otto Meinardus, "Dayr Anba Antuniyus: History," in Atiya, *Coptic Encyclopedia*, 3.719–21.

40. While the literary sources clearly indicate a close economic connection with the outside world (Goehring, "World Engaged"), the monks themselves almost always reside spatially separated from the society, either in the desert or within a walled community.

proximity of the ascetic community to a town or village is often underscored. Papyrus evidence from sixth-century Aphrodito, for example, reveals a close interconnection between the town and its nearby monasteries,[41] and archaeological efforts at Djeme in western Thebes located numerous monastic sites from the sixth and later centuries in the nearby cliffs within easy walking distance (500 to 3,000 meters) of the town.[42] The evidence indicates that the number of monasteries in close proximity to the towns continued to grow in the fifth and sixth centuries. At the same time, while economic connections came to favor these nearby monasteries,[43] there can be little doubt that the remote desert continued to beckon the few. The continuum of ascetic spatial location thus appears to remain intact in Coptic Egypt.

Given the geographical expansion of ascetic practice within Egypt and its enduring continuity, it is interesting to reflect on the significance given to the desert in the early literary sources of Egyptian monasticism. The three major early sources of anchoritic practice, the *Life of Antony*, the *Apophthegmata Patrum*, and the *History of the Monks in Egypt*, all connect true monastic withdrawal to the desert.[44] While exceptions are certainly noted, they remain exceptions.[45] The pattern set in place by the *Life of Antony*, namely that ascetic power and prestige increases in direct proportion to the depth of the withdrawal into the desert, carries the day.[46] One is forced to wonder, however, what happened to the monks in the city and on the out-

41. Leslie S. B. MacCoull, *Dioscorus of Aphrodito: His Work and His World* (TCH 16; Berkeley: University of California Press, 1988).

42. Winlock and Crum, *Monastery of Epiphanius*, 1.3–24, plate 1; cf. Cadell and Rémondon, "Sens et emplois de τὸ ὄρος."

43. Goehring, "World Engaged," 141–42 (see p. 49 in the present volume).

44. The following discussion is limited to anchoritic monasticism. The place of the desert in descriptions of anchoritic monasticism is paralleled in coenobitic monasticism by the gated monastic wall.

45. Those accounts which report the humbling of a desert hermit when he learns of a person in the city who leads a more austere ascetic life than he, should not be seen as offering a positive image of the earthly city. While such examples offer evidence of ascetic practice in the city, their literary function still draws on the standard desert-city dichotomy. The story's rhetorical power depends on the fact that one would not expect to find such an ascetic in the city.

46. According to the *Vita*, Antony does return to the city during the Arian crisis. Withdrawal to the desert does not preclude subsequent interaction with the world, but it does become a process of empowerment which allows for effective interaction in the world.

skirts of the villages in the literary production of early Egyptian monasticism. Why were they not the subject of monastic treatises? Why did they produce none? Why do we learn of them only in passing? Why is there no life of Palamon, no collection of apophthegms of city and village ascetics? The answer is perhaps suggested by the *Life of Antony* itself. Its hero began by imitating a village ascetic, but he became famous by withdrawing to the desert. Did his fame result in a collection of his sayings and the writing of his *vita*? Or was it rather his withdrawal to the desert that fostered the literary production that made him famous?

The answer to this question is complex and depends in part on the nature of the source in question. Differences in authorship and intended audience must necessarily impact our interpretation of the forces that led to the creation of the literary product. The *Apophthegmata Patrum*, for example, insofar as it records the sayings of actual monks, differs from the *Life of Antony* and the *History of the Monks in Egypt*, both of which were produced by outside observers. The forces that compelled the monks to gather and preserve the sayings of their masters[47] were surely different from those that led to the composition of the *Life of Antony* and the *History of the Monks in Egypt*. In both cases, however, it is the reality of the desert that somehow seems to create an incentive for literary production.

In the case of the *Life of Antony* and the *History of the Monks in Egypt*, the incentive for the literary production may be explained by returning for a moment to Babrius's fable. There the division between city and desert is employed metaphorically to sharpen the distinction between truth and falsehood. The ethical decline of human society is portrayed in mythic terms; personified Truth departs to the desert. The power of myth functions to make the point more powerfully. The problem could have been presented in detailed analytical fashion. One might have noted that increases in the percentage of falsehood in the city had, over the years, raised it to the majority position, and therefore truth was harder to find. But in making the point statistically, the power would be lost. Statistics may be more accurate, but they are also more boring. The fabler knew that people are moved more by myth than by history.

---

47. Frazer, "Morphology of Desert Wisdom," 82–114.

I would suggest that the nonmonastic production of literary descriptions of Egyptian monasticism conforms to this pattern. The historical reality of early ascetic developments in Egypt, when told in its full complexity, can be tedious.[48] Of interest to the modern historian, historical reality is not the version of Egyptian monasticism which forms the movement's ascetic heroes. The latter are rather the product of a monastic literature which captures the reader's interest through the simplicity and power of its myth. Before that literature could appear, however, ascetic practice had to develop historically to the point where it supplied the basic metaphor on which the "myth" could be built. In its beginnings, ascetic practice in Egypt had simply "[drawn] a line between those who remained more or less in conformity with regular ways of handling family, property and other social ties and those who renounced customary patterns."[49] Such practices occurred initially within the general framework of society. Sons or daughters could renounce their customary role within the family and still reside in their parents' home.[50] A house of virgins could still serve the church and village.[51] In such cases, the ascetic was too common, too well known, too much a part of everyday village life to become the subject of story and myth.[52] The break with social cus-

---

48. This is not to deny the existence of considerable detail, which may seem tedious at times, in various monastic sources. The issue is not the detail within individual episodes or even within the presentation of desert monasticism in general. So long as the details exist against the background of the overarching (and simple) theme of the desert, they serve merely to fill the mythic landscape.

49. Emmett, "Female Ascetics," 513.

50. Goehring, "Theodore's Entry."

51. Judge, "Earliest Use," 85; Badger, "New Man," 176–77, 225–33; Susanna K. Elm, "The Organization and Institutions of Female Asceticism in Fourth-Century Cappadocia and Egypt" (Ph.D. diss., Oxford University, 1986) 116–139; idem, *Virgins of God,* 331–72.

52. A large body of literature was produced around the figure of the female virgin who remained within the traditional space of civilization (Brakke, *Athanasius,* chap. 1). While it has not been the purpose of this essay to examine this literature, it is undoubtedly true that both the nature of ascetic practice and its literary portrayal was influenced by issues of gender. If Judge is correct in his argument that male ascetics copied patterns first begun by females ("Earliest Use," 85), it may be that male emulation of the female ascetic life not only led to a new terminology, but eventually to a new literature as male monks embarked on a more male form of withdrawal, namely, physical withdrawal to the desert. While female ascetics of note appear in the desert literature, they are a definite minority. They furthermore often appear in male disguise. John Anson, "The Female Transvestite in Early Monasticism: The Origins and Development of a Motif," *Viator* 5 (1974) 1–32; Teresa M. Shaw, *The Burden of the Flesh: Fasting and Sexuality in Early Christianity* (Minneapolis: Fortress Press, 1998) 220–53.

tom alone was not decisive enough to generate literary production. Only when ascetic practice began to express renunciation spatially did literary production ensue, because only then was the necessary "literary metaphor" at hand. The act of individuals withdrawing to the desert found harmonic response in the city-desert metaphor already established in the literary world. The metaphor became the literary vehicle used by Athanasius in the *Life of Antony* and to a lesser degree by the author of the *History of the Monks in Egypt* to present the Egyptian movement to the outside world.

The case of the *Apophthegmata Patrum,* which preserves sayings of desert monks, is necessarily different.[53] While it may be difficult to determine the specific forces that shaped the various collections that have survived,[54] it does seem apparent that the sayings themselves had their origin in the process of ascetic formation practiced in anchoritic desert communities. They represent a form of ascetic formation built around an anchoritic guide-disciple relationship.[55] Although a guide-disciple relationship could of course exist within the city, it is striking that no collection of sayings from such city monks exists.[56] One is led to conclude that it was the desert location itself that gave impetus to the particular form of the guide-disciple ascetic formation represented in the sayings collections,[57] namely, an ascetic formation built around the spoken, and eventually around the written, words of the guides. Although the forces that led to the liter-

---

53. The difference lies in part in the authors' different experience of the desert. Guillaumont ("La conception du désert") notes that the desert monk knew the desert and was, as a result, less likely to idealize it.

54. Frazer, "Morphology of Desert Wisdom"; Jean-Claude Guy, *Recherches sur la tradition grecque des Apophthegmata Patrum* (SH 36; Brussels: Société des Bollandistes, 1962); Wilhelm Bousset, *Apophthegmata: Textüberlieferung und Charakter der Apophthegmata Patrum. Zur Überlieferung der Vita Pachomii. Euagrios-Studien* (Tübingen: Mohr, 1923) 1–203.

55. I have benefited here from exchanges with Douglas Burton-Christie. See his *The Word in the Desert: Scripture and the Quest for Holiness in Early Christian Monasticism* (Oxford: Oxford University Press, 1993).

56. The *Apophthegmata Patrum* does include certain figures who lived in closer proximity to Alexandria (Frazer, "Morphology of Desert Wisdom," 106–7). They did not, however, reside in the city. Furthermore, not only is the proximity not emphasized, the very nature of the source with its preponderance of sayings attributed to more remote ascetics works to deemphasize it.

57. One can well imagine that the solitude of the desert gave greater power to the spoken word. The austerity of the desert is reflected in the simplicity and brevity of the spoken words of the desert monks.

ary production of the *Apophthegmata Patrum* thus differed from those that led to the writing of the *Life of Antony*, in both cases it was the reality of the desert that supplied an initial impetus toward literary production. The three major literary sources of anchoritic monasticism in Egypt can thus all be said to depend ultimately on the spatial expression of ascetic renunciation.

Given the dominant influence of the *Life of Antony* in subsequent presentations of Egyptian monasticism, the later dominance of the desert imagery is perhaps no accident. The success of the *Life of Antony* is due in part, however, to the reality of the desert's influence in ascetic literary production in general. The desert's influence on literary production meant that the other major literary sources all fit to a degree the Antonian model. The *Life of Antony* was such a successful model in part because it was a literary model, and those who wrote about monasticism wrote about or in the desert. As a result, to read monastic literature, both the literature produced by monks and that produced about monks, was to read about desert monks. And as access to the early monks came to depend on the literature, the only monks that were remembered were those in the desert.

It is thus fair to assert that when monasticism emerged onto the literary plane, it did so as a desert movement. Of course the desert, a symbolic metaphor in Babrius's fable, was a physical reality in the lives of desert monks. In the case of the nonmonastic narrative descriptions of Egyptian monasticism, it was the linkage of that reality with the symbolic power of the metaphor that generated the literary product. As the power of the metaphor in the fable depended upon the decisiveness of the break between city and desert, the production of this monastic literature in Egypt depended upon the clarity supplied by the physical withdrawal of monks to the desert. The spatial expression of the ascetic's decisive break with society made the story. It dramatized ascetic renunciation in a marginally flamboyant manner conducive to literary expression.[58] As a result, the desert monk

---

58. Geoffrey Galt Harpham, "Old Water in New Bottles: The Contemporary Prospects for the Study of Asceticism," in Vincent L. Wimbush, ed., *Discursive Formations, Ascetic Piety, and the Interpretation of Early Christian Literature*, Part 2=*Semeia* 58 (1992) 141–43; idem, *The Ascetic Imperative in Culture and Criticism* (Chicago: University of Chicago Press, 1987). I have benefited greatly from the discussion of such matters facilitated by the Ascetic Behavior and Greco-Roman Antiquity Group (Vincent L. Wimbush, director) of the Society of Biblical Literature.

became the icon of renunciation in Egypt.[59] The literary products of the desert monks themselves, dependent in part on their withdrawal to the desert, simply confirmed the literary model.

The pattern, once established literarily, of course, fed upon itself. The desert monk, the source of the literary impulse, became through the literary product the figure to imitate.[60] Imitation, in turn, created new subjects for literary production. The process was self-perpetuating, and as a result the desert monk came, in the end, to represent a sizable portion of the Egyptian ascetic population. The city and village ascetics continued in their role, but their place in history was lost. Their form of renunciation was not the "stuff" of story, and hence they never emerged in a significant way in the literature of early Egyptian monasticism.

It has been argued here that ascetic practice had its beginnings in the cities. From there it encroached on the surrounding lands and then expanded into the deserts. It was in fact this final expansion into the desert that brought it literary fame, since the desert supplied the metaphor (the spatial image of renunciation) necessary for literary production. The literature's dependence on the desert, however, caused a "literary" reversal of sorts in the expansion process. Whereas the location of ascetic practice had expanded to include the desert, in the literary model, the desert encroached more and more on the portrayal of ascetic space. A literary "desertification" of Egyptian monasticism occurred. While monks in and near the cities and villages continued to thrive, they all but disappeared from the plane of history. The desert hermit became the symbolic center of Egyptian monasticism. The literary icon conquered history.[61]

---

59. Compare the function of stylite asceticism discussed by Harvey in "Sense of a Stylite," 376–94; idem, *Asceticism and Society in Crisis: John of Ephesus and the "Lives of the Eastern Saints"* (TCH 18; Berkeley: University of California Press, 1990).

60. On the book as spiritual guide, see the fascinating study by Richard Valantasis, *Spiritual Guides of the Third Century: A Semiotic Study of the Guide-Disciple Relationship in Christianity, Neoplatonism, Hermetism, and Gnosticism* (HDR 27; Minneapolis: Fortress Press, 1991), especially chap. 3.

61. On the myth of the desert, see Brown, *Body and Society,* 215–16, 256–57.

5

Withdrawing from the Desert: Pachomius and the Development of Village Monasticism in Upper Egypt

In a recent article entitled "Le monachisme égyptien et les villes,"[1] Ewa Wipszycka cataloged for the later Byzantine period the abundant evidence of monastic habitation in or adjacent to the towns and villages of Egypt as well as in or on the margins of the cultivated land. Her analysis, which begins after the late third- to fourth-century formative period of Antony, Pachomius, and the Lower Egyptian semi-anchoritic centers in Nitria, Scetis, and Kellia, supplies convincing evidence of the rhetorical selectivity employed in the portrayal of Egyptian monasticism by the authors of the literary sources. In the literary texts, the dominance of monastic sites located in places of solitude generates a monastic geography of physical isolation. While acknowledging this dominance in the literature, Wipszycka draws together the infrequent literary references and the more numerous documentary examples of less physically isolated and more socially integrated monastic centers.[2] The resulting picture of Egyptian monasticism is spatially and socially more complex than that derived from the literary sources alone.

The significant presence of monastic centers within the inhabited zones (fertile valley, villages, and cities) of Egypt dispels the idea of Egyptian monasticism as a predominantly desert phenomenon. While isolated monasteries flourished in Egypt as a result of the discovery of the desert, Egyptian monasticism was neither in its origins a product of that discovery nor in its subsequent expansion a re-

---

First published in *HTR* 89 (1996) 267–85. A shortened form of this paper was first delivered at the Twelfth International Conference on Patristic Studies, Oxford, August 21–26, 1995. I wish to thank Richard Valantasis, whose comments on the final form of the paper were most helpful.

1. Wipszycka, "Monachisme égyptien."
2. Wipszycka, "Monachisme égyptien," 3.

sult of an ensuing flight from the inhabited world (οἰκουμένη) to the
newly found isolation of the desert (ἔρημος).[3] The growth of monasticism in Egypt did not follow a simple linear path from an ill-defined
urban ascetic movement in the later third and early fourth centuries
to the withdrawn desert monks of the fourth-century classical period, to the large well-defined urban and suburban[4] monasteries of
the later Byzantine era. While the discovery of the desert and the
growth of desert monasticism intervenes temporally between the
early urban ascetics and the later Byzantine monasteries, there is
no reason to assume that it formed the necessary link between the
two. Ascetic formation within the οἰκουμένη developed continuously
within the οἰκουμένη. While the urban ascetics were not unaffected
by the emergence of the desert ascetic movement, neither were they
necessarily remade through it. The widespread presence of ascetic
communities within the οἰκουμένη in the Byzantine period represents, rather, a continuity in urban asceticism that reaches back to
the formative apotactic movement identified by E. A. Judge.[5] I do
not suggest a simple, direct path of development from the apotactic
movement to the Byzantine monasteries, but argue that the practice of ascetic formation never left the οἰκουμένη. While it expanded
into the desert in the fourth century, it continued to grow and develop as well within the inhabited regions of the Nile valley where
it first began.

The rhetorical power of the desert image, however, still casts its
shadow over the "history" of Egyptian monasticism. The portrayal
of the Pachomian monastic movement, which began with the founding of the monastery of Tabennese in 323 C.E., offers a case in point.
The Pachomian movement, which postdates Antony's withdrawal
to the desert, is often enrolled without reflection in the desert city
formulated by Athanasius in his *Life of Antony*.[6] The equation is

---

3. Goehring, "World Engaged" (chap. 2 in the present volume); idem, "Encroaching Desert" (chap. 4).

4. I use the term "urban" loosely to indicate monasteries situated in or adjacent
to towns and villages as distinct from true desert cells or communities. In reality,
ascetic habitation existed across the full range of geographical possibilities in Egypt.
Goehring, "Encroaching Desert" (chap. 4 in the present volume).

5. Judge, "Earliest Use."

6. Note that the literary portrayals of the Pachomian movement also postdate
Athanasius's idealization of Antony's withdrawal in his *Life of Antony*. Text: *PG*

simple. The seminal *Life of Antony* defined Egyptian monasticism as a desert movement. Pachomian monasticism is an Egyptian monastic movement. Therefore, Pachomian monasticism is part of the desert movement. For example, in his article on "The Rise and Function of the Holy Man in Late Antiquity," Peter Brown distinguished the less remote desert in Syria from the "true desert" of Egypt. In speaking of Egyptian monasticism, he asserted that

> to survive at all in the hostile environment of such a desert, the Egyptian had to transplant into it the tenacious and all-absorbing routines of the villages of the *oikoumene*. . . . Groups had to reproduce exactly, on the fringe of the desert, the closed-in, embattled aspect of the fortified villages of Upper Egypt. The monastery of Pachomius was called quite simply The Village.[7]

Pachomius's monastery of Tabennese, situated on the shore of the Nile River in a village in which the monks built a church for the local inhabitants, has thus become a fortified desert community.[8]

I shall argue here that the emergence of Pachomian monasticism and the subsequent expansion and development of the movement is better understood within the context of urban asceticism. Pachomius founded his first two ascetic communities in deserted villages, and a careful review of the evidence suggests that the subsequent seven monasteries added to the *koinonia*, or community, in his lifetime were also situated in the fertile valley in or near villages whose names they bore. The Pachomians, who called themselves ἀποτακτικοί ("renouncers"), supply an important link from the classical period of Egyptian monasticism between the early apotactic movement of the towns and villages and the later urban monasteries of the Byzantine era. They illustrate the continuing draw of the οἰκουμένη as a location for ascetic formation and ascetic community. Properly understood, Pachomian monasticism is not a product of the desert, but a form of village asceticism.

26.825–924; G. J. M. Bartelink, *Athanase d'Alexandrie: Vie d'Antoine* (SC 400; Paris: Éditions du Cerf, 1994). English translations: Gregg, *Life of Antony*; Robert T. Meyer, *St. Athanasius: The Life of Saint Antony* (ACW; New York: Newman, 1950).

7. Brown, "Rise and Function," 83; compare his later assessment in his *Body and Society*, 217.

8. The same process is seen at work in Derwas Chitty's use of Athanasius's phrase "the desert a city" as the title for his general history of Egyptian and Palestinian monasticism (Chitty, *Desert a City*). See also the reference to "desert monasteries" in Brakke, "Canon Formation," 398.

Tradition has bestowed on Antony and Pachomius the status of founders of early Egyptian monasticism. They serve as the movement's primary icons. Antony represents the anchoritic model of the ascetic life, Pachomius its coenobitic form.[9] Antony's earlier date has fashioned him as the individual representative of monastic origins. His discovery of the "ascetic" desert marks the beginning of the movement, and the withdrawn anchoritic life becomes its initial form of ascesis. This understanding of the origins of Egyptian monasticism is dependent in large part, however, on the widespread success of the purposeful biography of Antony published by the Alexandrian archbishop Athanasius. It is Athanasius who links ascetic practice so intimately with the discovery of the desert. In the *Life of Antony*, he fashions the desert as the *telos,* or final (locational) goal, of male ascetic formation.[10] From his family home within his village, to the outskirts of the village, to nearby tombs, to a deserted fortress in the nearer desert, to the further desert along the Red Sea, Antony's ascetic progress is marked by a directional movement away from his village, away from the οἰκουμένη, into the desert. The desert is the location of Antony's ascetic perfection and the source of this ascetic power.[11] His subsequent returns to the οἰκουμένη simply offer the occasion for using his ascetic power on behalf of an ecclesiastical polity defined by Athanasius. The success of Athanasius's *Life of Antony* made the desert the sine qua non of Egyptian asceticism.[12] True ascetics were desert ascetics. The power of the equation is seen in the enrolling of later ascetics, regardless of the location of their cells or monasteries, as citizens of Athanasius's new ascetic city rising in the desert.[13]

---

9. Heussi, *Ursprung,* 69–131; Chitty, *Desert a City,* 1–11 and 20–29.

10. Athanasius's portrait of Antony was the most successful, though certainly not the only portrait of the saint. Brakke, *Athanasius;* Rubenson, *Letters of St. Antony;* Dörries, "Die Vita Antonii."

11. *Vita Antonii* 14.

12. The process also has much to do with the modern study of early Egyptian monasticism. In the aftermath of Chalcedon and the eventual Arabic domination, knowledge of Coptic developments mostly vanished outside of Egypt. Egyptian monasticism was defined through the monastic texts that had appeared in Greek and Latin: the *Life of Antony,* the *Life of Pachomius,* the *Apophthegmata Patrum,* the *Lausiac History,* and the *History of the Monks in Egypt.*

13. *Vita Antonii* 14; Wipszycka, "Monachisme égyptien," 9.

Pachomius too became an inhabitant of this city.[14] Later authors interpret his coenobitic experiment as a secondary development born out of the original anchoritic model. Its origins too were understood to lie ultimately with Antony and the desert.[15] While it is true that Pachomius began his ascetic career as an anchorite under the desert ascetic Palamon, it is seldom acknowledged that his coenobitic innovation occurred through his withdrawal from the desert. In fact, his orientation to the οἰκουμένη and its villages was quite distinct from that of Antony. Rather than moving in a direction that led ever further away from the village into the desert, Pachomius, in his ascetic career, never left the fertile Nile valley. He always moved within the sphere of the village, and his innovations occurred precisely through his return to and use of the village.

The Pachomian dossier suggests that Pachomius first came into contact with Christians as an imprisoned military conscript in Thebes around 312 C.E.[16] He was amazed at the kindness of strangers who came to the prison to encourage the conscripts and to give them food. He struck a deal with God that night in prayer promising to serve him and humankind all the days of his life should he be freed from prison. Released after Licinius's defeat of Maximinus Daia in 313,[17] he proceeded to the village of Šeneset (Chenoboskion) where

---

14. The main Coptic and Greek texts of the *Life of Pachomius* have been edited by Lefort and Halkin respectively. Lefort, *S. Pachomii vita bohairice scripta*; idem, *S. Pachomii vitae sahidice scriptae*; Halkin, *Sancti Pachomii Vitae Graecae*. Translations: Lefort, *Vies coptes*; Veilleux, *Pachomian Koinonia*. Citations from the first Greek *Life* are cited as *G1*. Citations from the Coptic *Lives* are cited as *Bo* (Bohairic) and *S* (Sahidic). The numeral immediately following the *S* identifies the specific Sahidic version (*S7*=Sahidic *Life* number 7). *SBo* indicates the "complete" version fashioned by Veilleux by filling in lacunae in the Bohairic version from the Sahidic and Arabic texts. Following section numbers are those found in Veilleux's *Pachomian Koinonia*. Veilleux follows the sectional divisions for *G1* found in Halkin's *Sancti Pachomii Vitae Graecae*, and for *Bo*, those found in Lefort's *Les vies coptes*. The *vita* traditions are complex. A history of the debate can be found in Goehring, *Letter of Ammon*, 3–23; for a discussion of the issues, refer to Rousseau, *Pachomius*, 37–48.

15. Such is already the case in the *Life of Pachomius*; *Bo* 2; *G1* 2.

16. *Bo* 7–8. His parents are portrayed as non-Christian (*Bo* 4; *G1* 3). Note, however, that Pachomius's sister's name is given as Mary (*Bo* 27; not named in *G1* 32). A recent study of the chronology of Pachomius (Christoph Joest, "Ein Versuch zur Chronologie Pachoms and Theodoros," *ZNW* 85 [1994] 132–44) argues for a date of 308 C.E. for Pachomius's conversion.

17. The traditions do not, for the most part, correctly identify the emperor as Maximinus Daia. Chitty, *Desert a City*, 7, 17 n. 39; Veilleux, *Pachomian Koinonia*, 1.267. Joest's revised chronology ("Versuch," 144) calls this entire episode into question.

he was baptized.[18] He remained in the village and served the people, in part by gathering wood for them from the nearby acacia forests.[19] Eventually, he decided to embrace more fully the ascetic life and apprenticed himself under the old anchorite Palamon, who lived on the outskirts of the village of Šeneset in a small patch of "interior" desert surrounded by fertile land.[20] Palamon was not a withdrawn desert anchorite of the type represented by the perfected Antony of Athanasius's *Life of Antony*, but an ascetic who lived on the edge of the village within the fertile valley. He is more akin to the old village ascetic whom Antony first emulated or to Antony himself in his initial ascetic withdrawal to places close to the village (ἐν τοῖς πρὸ τῆς κώμης τόποις).[21] The fact that Palamon lived in a desert has little bearing on his social connection with the village, since his desert was simply a barren patch of land in the fertile valley adjacent to the village.[22]

Pachomius remained with Palamon for seven years and continued his trips through the acacia forests. The *Life of Pachomius* reports that on one such trip he wandered ten miles south to the shore of the Nile River, where he discovered the "deserted village" (Coptic: ογϯⲙⲓ ⲛⲏⲣⲏⲙⲟⲥ; Greek: κώμη τις, ἔρημος οὖσα) of Tabennese.[23] It was the opportunity offered by his chance discovery of the deserted village that led to his decision to remain and build a monastery. Unlike Antony, Pachomius's ascetic vocation was not fulfilled by withdrawing further into the desert. He did not move from his initial location near his village deeper into the desert to distance himself further from society. His ascetic career moved him in exactly the opposite direction. Pachomius finds ascetic perfection in his return to the village, albeit a deserted village on the shore of the Nile.

The religious tradition naturally understands both the discovery of the village of Tabennese and the decision to remain and build a

---

18. *Bo* 8; *G1* 5.
19. *Bo* 9.
20. *Bo* 10; *G1* 6; cf. *Bo* 15.
21. *Vita Antonii* 3.3–4.
22. Lefort, "Premiers monastères," 383–87; Goehring, "Encroaching Desert," 288–89 (see pp. 80–81 in the present volume).
23. *Bo* 17; *G1* 12; on its location, see Lefort, "Premiers monastères," 293–97. Tabennese is the Sahidic spelling for the Bohairic Tabennesi. The Sahidic spellings are used for place names throughout this essay.

monastery there as directed by God. The Spirit led Pachomius to the village and once there, a voice from heaven instructed him to build a monastery. After confirming the vision with his ascetic father Palamon, Pachomius began the construction of the monastery.[24] Shorn of the religious interpretation, however, Pachomius's decision to relocate and fashion an ascetic community appears as an innovative idea triggered by the opportunity perceived in the "deserted" village. Ascetics were masters in the reuse of deserted space,[25] and Tabennese, if indeed it was deserted,[26] offered ready space and housing for an emerging ascetic community. Its location on the shore of the Nile made it particularly attractive in terms of the projected needs of such a community. Fertile land for vegetable gardens and the water necessary for their irrigation were immediately available,[27] as were the materials required for the traditional monastic work of basket and mat weaving.[28] Commercial markets for the monks' handiwork were nearby,[29] and the Nile offered a ready means of transportation.[30] In fact, the subsequent expansion of the Pachomian *koinonia* into a system of affiliated monasteries spread over 175 kilometers between the towns of Šmin (Panopolis) and Sne (Latopolis) is difficult to imagine apart from the ease of transportation offered by the river. In the later periods of the movement, agricultural holdings outside of the monasteries proper were added,[31] and farming and irrigation regulations became an essential part of the community's rule.[32] As

---

24. *Bo* 17; *G1* 12.

25. Deserted tombs (*Vita Antonii* 8), fortresses (*Vita Antonii* 12), and temples (*Historia Monachorum in Aegypto* 5; Festugière, *Historia Monachorum*, 41–43) were all put to use by ascetics. Open spaces within towns and villages likewise offered locations for monastic habitation. Wipszycka, "Monachisme égyptien," 3.

26. See below, pp. 97–100.

27. *Bo* 23; *G1* 24; cf. *G1* 106.

28. See, for example, *Bo* 22; *G1* 23; *Paralipomena* 9 (Halkin, *Sancti Pachomii Vitae Graecae*, 133–34); *Epistula Ammonis* 19 (Goehring, *Letter of Ammon*, 139–40).

29. *Bo* 26; *G1* 28; cf. *Paralipomena* 21–22.

30. Travel often took place by ferry or boat (*Bo* 30), and boats were soon given to the Pachomian communities (*Bo* 53, 56). Communication with Alexandria likewise took place via travel up and down the Nile (*Bo* 28; *G1* 30).

31. In 367–68 C.E., a monk (ἀποτακτικός) named Anoubion made payment for taxes on good agricultural land (ἄπορα) in the Hermopolite nome that belonged to the monastery of Tabennese (*P. Berl.* Inv. 11860 [=*SB* XIV 11972]). Wipszycka, "Terres"; cf. *G1* 106.

32. *Regulations of Horsiesius* 55–64; Lefort, *Oeuvres*, 98–99; Veilleux, *Pachomian Koinonia*, 2.217–18.

the community grew in size and wealth, its markets expanded,[33] and its use of the Nile increased. Eventually, shipbuilding occurred within the monasteries,[34] and monks sailed not only between the communities in Upper Egypt, but also to and from Alexandria, and possibly to Constantinople.[35] The subsequent growth of the *koinonia*'s agricultural and commercial dealings was a natural result of the original village orientation of the movement.[36] A truly desert movement could not have been so active in the common affairs of the society.

Pachomius's success of establishing a monastic community in the deserted village of Tabennese led him to seek out a second deserted village when the time for expansion arose. He built his second monastery at Pbow, a village located approximately three kilometers downriver or west of Tabennese in the direction of Šeneset.[37] One may assume that Pachomius knew the area well, since he had discovered Tabennese while walking from his earlier ascetic abode adjacent to Šeneset. He could have passed by Pbow on such a trip. Pbow is the only Pachomian community whose actual location is still identifiable today. The remains of its great fifth-century basilica can still be seen on the edge of the modern village of Faw Qibli, which, while not located on the shore of the Nile, lies close to it in the heart of the greenbelt.[38] There is no inner desert surrounding Pbow, only fertile agricultural fields.[39] Moreover, the Pachomian dossier itself suggests that Pbow was located near the river. The first

---

33. Note *G1* 113, which mentions two boats returning from a commercial trip to Alexandria where the monks had sold mats to procure foodstuffs and tunics.

34. *G1* 146; cf. *Bo* 204.

35. *SBo* 96, 124, 132; *G1* 113. Cf. Roger Rémondon ("Le monastère alexandrin de la metanoia était-il beneficiaire du fisc ou à son service?" in *Studi in Onore di Edoardo Volterra* [vol. 5; Milan: Giuffre, 1971] 769–81) for a discussion of the involvement of the later Egyptian monasteries in the transportation of the grain tax, not only on the Nile River, but also between Alexandria and Constantinople.

36. Goehring, "World Engaged," 139–41 (see pp. 46–48 in the present volume).

37. *Bo* 49 (Lefort, *S. Pachomii vita bohairice scripta*, 51; Veilleux, *Pachomian Koinonia*, 1.71); *G1* 54 (Halkin, *Sancti Pachomii Vitae Graecae*, 36–37; Veilleux, *Pachomian Koinonia*, 1.334); on its location, see Lefort, "Premiers monastères," 387–93.

38. Grossmann, "Basilica"; note the map of the site on p. 234. A color photograph of the remains of the basilica (p. 203) offers a good illustration of its location at the edge of the village well within the fertile valley.

39. Egyptian villages were normally surrounded by fertile land (Bagnall, *Egypt in Late Antiquity*, 114).

Greek *Life of Pachomius* reports that when Theodore died at Pbow, the weeping of the brothers could be heard on the far side of the river,[40] and the *Letter of Ammon* refers to monks from Pbow arriving at an island in the river by boat.[41] Like Tabennese, Pbow was not a desert monastery. It was not even located on the fringe of the fertile valley, but in a "deserted" village in the heart of the greenbelt. Pachomius's use of a second deserted village to expand his community further underscores his commitment to the village rather than the desert. Both his initial innovative idea to create a communal form of the ascetic life and his later development of a system of affiliated monasteries occurred through his discovery and use of deserted villages.

Although the "deserted village" becomes something of a literary topos in the Pachomian tradition,[42] there is little reason to doubt the deserted nature of the villages of Tabennese and Pbow when Pachomius first stumbled upon them. It is clear from later sources that vacant buildings and open land both within and adjacent to the towns and villages of Egypt were being occupied by the growing ascetic population.[43] Although the question still remains as to the precise meaning of the term *deserted* (ἔρημος) as it is applied to the villages, the Pachomian accounts of Tabennese and Pbow likely fit this pattern. While the Pachomian accounts suggest a completely vacant village akin to the ghost towns of the old American West, it is possible that the label indicates nothing more than that a sufficient degree of vacancy and open space existed within the villages to enable Pachomius to establish ascetic communities there.[44] Any population loss rendered portions of a village vacant and thus made

---

40. *G1* 149.

41. *Epistula Ammonis* 28; cf. *Bo* 59–60; *G1* 55, 60, 109, 113. The point of embarkation for the monks from Pbow may have been Šeneset (*G1* 107).

42. Note that the author of the Bohairic *Vita* asserts that Šeneset too was deserted when Pachomius first arrived (*Bo* 8). The fact that it contained some inhabitants and that Pachomius was baptized in its church and cared for many of its people during the subsequent plague gives the author no pause. Pachomius's initial efforts were linked with deserted villages; since he began his ascetic career in Šeneset, it too became deserted for the author.

43. Note the description of Oxyrhynchus in the *Historia Monachorum in Aegypto* 5; Wipszycka, "Monachisme égyptien," 3.

44. This may result from the use of *deserted* to refer to less than complete depopulation, or it may arise as the result of exaggeration in the *Vita* tradition.

available living space for ascetics. One need not press the deserted nature of the village too far to imagine Pachomius's decision to establish his new community there.

While village populations and house occupancy remained relatively stable in Egypt,[45] tax and census records preserved among papyrus documents demonstrate that village populations could fluctuate for various reasons and that, on occasion, the complete desertion of a village did occur. Not all of the reasons are relevant to the cases of Tabennese and Pbow. The evidence of village growth and decline in the Fayyum, for example, where the changing reach of the irrigation system and disputes over water determined village viability, has little application to the cases of Tabennese or Pbow which were situated on or near the shore of the Nile.[46] On the other hand, the effect of Roman taxation in all its forms[47] may well apply to the situation of Tabennese and Pbow. Individual flight to avoid taxes and service was common throughout the history of Roman Egypt,[48] and, on occasion, it accounted for a sizable loss in a village's population. Records from the mid-first-century Arsinoite village of Philadelphia illustrate the possible severity of such tax desertion. At the height of the problem in 57 C.E., one in every seven or eight men from the village of Philadelphia was a tax fugitive. The situation was so severe that those responsible for the collection of the taxes, which were set

---

45. Peter van Minnen, "House-to-House Enquiries: An Interdisciplinary Approach to Roman Karanis," *ZPE* 100 (1994) 230–31; cf. Lewis, *Life in Egypt*, 65–67.

46. Neglect of the irrigation system, disputes over water, and the burden of Roman taxation (including liturgies) all affected village economies and population. J. A. S. Evans, *A Social and Economic History of an Egyptian Temple in the Greco-Roman Period* (YCS 17; New Haven: Yale University Press, 1961) 276–77, 282–83; Deborah Hobson, "Agricultural Land and Economic Life in Soknopaiou Nesos," *BASP* 21 (1984) 108; Peter van Minnen, "Deserted Villages: Two Late Antique Town Sites in Egypt," *BASP* 32 (1995) 41–55; Arthur E. R. Boak, "An Egyptian Farmer of the Age of Diocletian and Constantine," *ByzM* 1 (1946) 53; cf. Bagnall, *Egypt in Late Antiquity*, 138–39.

47. Lewis, *Life in Egypt*, 159–84; Bagnall, *Egypt in Late Antiquity*, 153–60, 172–74; Boak, "An Egyptian Farmer," 39–53.

48. Lewis, *Life in Egypt*, 163–65, 183–84; Bagnall, *Egypt in Late Antiquity*, 144; Arthur E. R. Boak and Herbert C. Youtie, "Flight and Oppression in Fourth-Century Egypt," in Edoardo Arslan, ed., *Studi in onore di Aristide Calderini e Roberto Paribeni* (2 vols.; Milan: Casa editrice Ceschina, 1956–57) 2.325–37; Allan Chester Johnson, *Roman Egypt to the Reign of Diocletian*, vol. 2 of Tenney Frank, ed., *An Economic Survey of Ancient Rome* (Paterson, N.J.: Pageant Books, 1959) 114–15 (*P. Berl. Leihg.* 7), 482–83, 546; Rousseau, *Pachomius*, 9–10.

for the village regardless of its population, pleaded with the prefect for an adjustment.[49]

While the case of Philadelphia stems from a much earlier period, we know that the problem persisted in the period of Roman rule.[50] As such, it suggests a sequence of events that could account for the vacated property discovered and used by Pachomius in both Tabennese and Pbow. If this were the case, however, it would suggest that the term *deserted*, as applied to Tabennese and Pbow in the Pachomian texts, refers to a population loss rather than to the total abandonment of the village. While tax desertion was a significant problem in Egypt, it does not appear that it often led to the complete desertion of a village. On the other hand, the problems encountered by a village that had experienced considerable desertion in meeting its tax obligations may well explain the local acceptance of the Pachomians' occupation of vacant village property and land. If the Pachomians occupied deserted land and paid taxes on it, their entry into the village would have been a boon to the village economy.[51]

A second cause of village decline was plague. While tax desertion had a more limited effect on village population, the outbreak of plague could and did result in village abandonment. Documents from the reign of Marcus Aurelius (161–80 C.E.) supply an example of the rapid population decline experienced in certain villages as their inhabitants fled an outbreak of plague. In one case, surviving records report a fall in the number of village males from twenty-seven to three to zero.[52] The reality of plague is also apparent in the Pachomian dossier. The Bohairic *Vita* reports that a plague ravaged the village of Šeneset during Pachomius's initial sojourn there prior to his apprenticeship under Palamon.[53] Pachomius himself died in

---

49. Lewis, *Life in Egypt*, 164–65; Alan K. Bowman, *Egypt after the Pharaohs* (Berkeley: University of California Press, 1986) 77.

50. Boak and Youtie, "Flight and Oppression," 325–37; Lewis, *Life in Egypt*, 163–65, 183–84; Bowman, *Egypt*, 77; Bagnall, *Egypt in Late Antiquity*, 144; Rousseau, *Pachomius*, 9–10.

51. Goehring, "World Engaged," 139–40 (see pp. 46–47 in the present volume); Wipszycka, "Terres." This may have been the case in particular for Pbow, since the evidence for the Pachomians' revitalization of Tabennese would probably have been known by that time.

52. Lewis, *Life in Egypt*, 68 (only males are recorded); van Minnen, "Deserted Villages," 43.

53. *Bo* 9.

346 C.E. in a plague that decimated the *koinonia*.[54] Another outbreak occurred during Theodore's leadership of the community.[55] Such an outbreak, perhaps even the specific one experienced by Pachomius in Šeneset, might well account for the deserted nature of the villages of Tabennese and Pbow. Plague may have created the opportunity for Pachomius's innovative translation of deserted villages into ascetic villages. This explanation of the term *deserted*, which corresponds most closely with the accounts in the Pachomian literary tradition, supports the interpretation of *deserted* as a more extensive population loss in the villages prior to their use by Pachomius.

While we can never know with certainty the degree to which the villages were deserted when first inhabited by the Pachomians, it is clear that they did not remain deserted for long after the Pachomians' arrival. According to the Bohairic *Vita*, the lay population of Tabennese grew so rapidly after the Pachomians entered the village that the monks built a church for the villagers even before they constructed one for themselves. They attended the village church to partake of the eucharist.[56] While less is said of Pbow, one suspects a similar situation.

Archaeological efforts place the monastery on the edge of the modern village of Faw Qibli, and dredge work some 750 meters beyond the monastery in the farmland has revealed the remains of sizable Roman structures.[57] While it may have been the deserted nature of the village that initially drew the Pachomians to it, they did not understand their occupation of the village as exclusive. While they did establish an ascetic village within the village, they also brought the village, as village, back to life. Ascetic withdrawal for the Pachomians was accomplished within the village, eventually behind a gated wall. It was never accomplished by spatial separation from the village in the near or distant desert. While undoubtedly controlled to some degree, social interaction between the Pachomians and the nonascetic village population was part of the Pachomian ascetic life from its inception.

---

54. *S7* (Lefort, *S. Pachomii vitae sahidice scriptae*, 87–96; *SBo* 117–23 (Veilleux, *Pachomian Koinonia*, 1.171–79); *G1* 114–17.

55. *Bo* 180; *G1* 139.

56. *Bo* 25; *G1* 29.

57. Goehring, "New Frontiers," 252–57 (see pp. 179–84 in the present volume).

The village pattern inaugurated by the use of Tabennese and Pbow was continued in the later Pachomian establishments. While the precise locations of the subsequent seven monasteries added to the *koinonia* in Pachomius's lifetime[58] are not known with any degree of certainty,[59] the evidence suggests that like Tabennese and Pbow, they are best understood as village communities. Like Tabennese and Pbow, two of the later establishments, the monasteries of Šeneset (Chenoboskion)[60] and Šmin (Panopolis),[61] were clearly named after the village or town with which they were associated. There is every reason to assume that they were located in or near the villages whose names they bore. One may argue that the monastery of Šeneset was situated in Palamon's "interior desert,"[62] but the location of the "interior desert" adjacent to the village argues for the close association of the monastery with the village. Šeneset itself, with its "interior desert," was located near the Nile in the greenbelt at a considerable distance from the desert proper.[63]

The Pachomian monastery of Šmin was built on land donated by the bishop of Šmin.[64] The bishop's additional gift of a boat supports

---

58. A female monastery was established in the village of Tabennese, although it is never included in the number of monasteries listed in the sources. It is viewed as a sister monastery of Tabennese. *Bo* 27; *G1* 32 (Greek text in Halkin, *Corpus athénien*, 21–22).

59. Although Lefort's efforts to connect the Pachomian monasteries to specific sites are intriguing, they remain speculative ("Premiers monastères"). Cf. M. Jullien, "A la recherche de Tabenne et des autres monastères fondés par saint Pachôme," *Études* 89 (1901) 238–58; Henri Gauthier, "Notes géographiques sur le nome Panopolite," *BIFAO* 4 (1904) 63–64, 86–87, 94–95; idem, "Nouvelles notes géographiques sur le nome Panopolite," *BIFAO* 10 (1912): 93–94, 103, 121–27; René-Georges Coquin, "Akhmim," in Atiya, *Coptic Encyclopedia*, 1.78.

60. *Bo* 50; *G1* 54. The monastery of Šeneset was the third community in the *koinonia*. It had existed independently under the leadership of an old ascetic named Ebonh prior to joining the Pachomian system, and was already known as the monastery of Šeneset when Pachomius accepted it into the *koinonia*.

61. The monastery of Šmin, the sixth community in the *koinonia*, is not named as such in the main published editions of the *Life of Pachomius* (see above, n. 14). Pages preserved in Toronto, however, include Šmin in a list of Pachomian establishments. Spanel, "Toronto Sahidic Addition."

62. This is the site of the current monastery of Palamon (René-Georges Coquin and Maurice Martin, "Anba Palaemon," in Atiya, *Coptic Encyclopedia*, 3.757); for a photograph that shows the relationship of the monastery to the village, see *BA* 42 (1979) 208.

63. Lefort, "Premiers monastères," 383–87.

64. *S5* (Lefort, *S. Pachomii vitae sahidice scriptae*, 146–47; *SBo* 54 [Veilleux, *Pachomian Koinonia*, 1.73–74]); cf. *G1* 81.

the placement of this monastery near the Nile rather than in the desert. Furthermore, the opposition of townspeople to the construction of the monastery makes more sense if the proposed monastery was being built on land valuable to the community. Šmin, a nome (or district) capital, was not a deserted village where land and housing were more readily available. In the nome capitals, land and housing were more valuable and in greater demand.[65] The building of a monastery in such a location was likely seen by some of the inhabitants as adding unnecessary pressure on the town's limited resources.[66]

The locations of the Pachomian monasteries whose names do not correspond to known village names remain more speculative. If the pattern of village monasteries established above is correct, however, there is little reason to place the other monasteries in the desert. The Pachomian sources report that the monastery of Tse was located in the land of Šmin (ϩⲛ ⲧⲕⲁϩϣⲙⲓⲛ)[67] and the monastery of Tsmine in vicinity of Šmin (ⲡⲓⲕⲱϯ ⲛϣⲙⲓⲛ).[68] While these designations could indicate a desert location, they could equally identify communities situated in or near villages of the same names in the Panopolite nome. The latter alternative follows the pattern established by Tabennese, Pbow, Šeneset, and Šmin. Unless proof exists to the contrary, it seems most appropriate to assume that the pattern held. While inconclusive, evidence from the *Life of Pachomius* can easily support the village theory for the location of these communities.[69]

---

65. Deborah W. Hobson, "House and Household in Roman Egypt," in Naphtali Lewis, ed., *Papyrology* (YCS 28; Cambridge and New York: Cambridge University Press, 1985) 225; Bagnall, *Egypt in Late Antiquity,* 111 n. 11.

66. While the cause of the townspeople's opposition to the Pachomians is not given, there is no reason to assume that they opposed them on religious grounds alone.

67. S5 (Lefort, *S. Pachomii vitae sahidice scriptae,* 145); SBo 52 (Veilleux, *Pachomian Koinonia,* 1.72–73); cf. G1 83; on its location, see Lefort, "Premiers monastères," 403–4. The monastery of Tse was the fifth community in the *koinonia.*

68. Bo 57 (Lefort, *S. Pachomii vita bohairice scripta,* 56); Veilleux, *Pachomian Koinonia,* 1.77–78); G1 83; on its location, see Lefort, "Premiers monastères," 403–4. The monastery of Tsmine was the eighth community in the *koinonia.*

69. The author of the Sahidic account of the founding of Tse follows it immediately with the story of a gift of a boat to the Pachomians by a city councillor from Kos (Apollinopolis; modern Kous) (S5 [Lefort, *S. Pachomii vitae sahidice scriptae,* 145–

There is little evidence for the location of the Pachomian monastery of Tmoušons,[70] though once again there is an indication of travel to and from the monastery by boat[71] which suggests its location near the Nile. Lefort's calculation of distances between this community and the others in the Pachomian *koinonia* likewise supports its location in the fertile valley.[72] There is certainly no reason to situate it in the desert. The monastery of Tbewe, founded by Petronius, was located on lands belonging to his wealthy parents.[73] This alone suggests land within the fertile valley, a conclusion further supported by Petronius's father's donation of livestock, carts, and boats to the Pachomians.[74]

Phnoum is the final monastery to enter the system in Pachomius's lifetime and is the only one for which a desert location is even suggested. It was located in the vicinity of the nome capital of Sne (Latopolis). The Greek *Life of Pachomius* locates it simply near the town of Sne (ἄνω περὶ Λατῶν),[75] the Sahidic *Vita* in the district or

46]; *SBo* 53 [Veilleux, *Pachomian Koinonia,* 1.73]). The boat is offered so that Pachomius might receive cargo for the monks' use. While the gift of the boat is not linked directly to the monastery of Tse, the placement of the story immediately after the account of the founding of Tse suggests an association between the two in the mind of the author. While the distance between Šmin and Kos (over 150 kilometers along the Nile) militates against an actual connection between the two stories, the very nature of the gift, a boat to be used to deliver cargo to the monasteries of the *koinonia,* underscores the author's understanding of the *koinonia* as a group of affiliated monasteries connected by the river. The gift of a boat was easily understood and fit readily into the account of monasteries established in the fertile Nile valley; it is hard to imagine an author's use of such a story in an account of desert communities.

70. *SBo* 51 (equals *Bo* 51 plus missing pages from *S5* [Lefort, *S. Pachomii vita bohairice scripta,* 52; idem, *S. Pachomii vitae sahidice scriptae,* 145; Veilleux, *Pachomian Koinonia,* 1.72]); *G1* 54. The monastery of Tmoušons was the fourth community in the *koinonia.*

71. *Bo* 59; *G1* 55; but note *Bo* 81, 95.

72. Lefort, "Premiers monastères," 400; René-Georges Coquin and Maurice Martin, "Dayr Anba Bidaba," in Atiya, *Coptic Encyclopedia,* 3.731–32. Lefort suggested Tmoušons's possible identification with Dayr Anba Bidaba, a monastery-village located beside a pond in the midst of the cultivated zone some two kilometers west of Nag Hammadi.

73. *Bo* 56; *G1* 80; on its location, see Lefort, "Premiers monastères," 399–403. The monastery of Tbewe was the seventh community in the *koinonia.* Petronius, its founder, came from the town of Pdjodj, located in the diocese of Hiw (Diospolis parva). Pdjodj has been identified with the modern village of Abu-Chouche, located on the western shore of the Nile.

74. While it is not specifically stated that the donation went to his son's community, there is no reason to think otherwise.

75. *G1* 83 (Halkin, *Sancti Pachomii Vitae Graecae,* 56–57).

nome of Sne (ⲡⲧⲟϣ ⲛ̄ⲥⲛⲏ),[76] and the Bohairic *Vita* in the mountain of Sne (ⲡⲧⲱⲟⲩ ⲛ̄ⲥⲛⲏ).[77] If one accepts the Greek and Sahidic reading as correct, then like the other Pachomian establishments, the monastery of Phnoum can easily be located in the fertile valley. It is only if one gives the Bohairic reading primacy that one might place the monastery in the desert of Sne, since the term *mountain* (Coptic: ⲧⲟⲟⲩ; Greek: ὄρος) is commonly translated as desert.[78] Given the fact that the Bohairic version was translated from Sahidic,[79] it seems more likely that the use of the term *mountain* (ⲧⲟⲟⲩ) reflects a scribal shift from the term *district* (ⲧⲟϣ), perhaps under the influence of the growing association of monasticism with the desert. The monastery's proximity to the town of Sne is further suggested by the local opposition that its construction aroused. The bishop himself led the crowd that sought to drive the Pachomians away. It thus seems most appropriate to assume that Phnoum, like the other Pachomian monasteries, was located in the fertile valley near the village of Phnoum in the Latopolite nome.

None of the nine monasteries in the Pachomian system was named after an individual, as was often the case with later singular establishments.[80] In the first half of the fourth century, ascetics had not yet garnered the fame that resulted in monasteries bearing their names. When Ebonh, Jonas, and Petronius joined their ascetic

---

76. *S4* 58 (Lefort, *S. Pachomii vitae sahidice scriptae,* 230; idem, *Vies coptes,* 303). Lefort chooses to translate ⲉⲡⲧⲟϣ ⲛ̄ⲥⲛⲏ as "à la montagne de Snê."

77. *Bo* 58 (Lefort, *S. Pachomii vita bohairice scripta,* 56–57); on its location, see Lefort, "Premiers monastères," 404–7.

78. Crum, "ⲧⲟⲟⲩ," *Coptic Dictionary,* 440–41; Lefort, "Premiers monastères," 404–7. Even if one accepts the term *mountain,* however, the precise location of the monastery remains unclear. The term occurs in papyrus documents in reference to the further or proper desert, to the nearer desert or escarpment at the edge of the fertile zone, as well as to raised arable land that borders the desert (Cadell and Rémondon, "Sens et emplois de τὸ ὄρος"). Thus even if one accepts the Bohairic reading, there is no assurance that the monastery of Phnoum was located in the desert. A lease contract dated 616 C.E. (*P. Lond.* 483), for example, refers to a monastery, hamlet, and fields located in the mountain of the village of Tanaithis (ἐν τῷ ὄρει κώμης Ταναίθεως). The text refers to livestock and pasturage, and even fish in the waters around the monastery (πιάσαι ὀψάρια ἐκ τῶ παντοίων ὑδάτων τῶν περικύκλωθεν τοῦ αὐτοῦ μοναστηρίου). The monastery of Phnoum may well have existed in a similar location in or near a village of the same name in the Latopolite nome.

79. Lefort, *Vies coptes,* LXXVIII; Veilleux, *Pachomian Koinonia,* 1.2.

80. Peter van Minnen, "The Roots of Egyptian Christianity," *APVG* 40 (1994) 71–85.

communities to the Pachomian *koinonia,* they were already known as the monasteries of Šeneset, Tmoušons, and Tbewe, respectively.[81] In those cases in which the origin of the name of a Pachomian monastery is known, namely, Tabennese, Pbow, Šeneset, and Šmin, it derives directly from the name of the village or town with which the monastery is associated. Furthermore, in the two cases in which the precise spatial relationship between the monastery and the village or town is clear, namely, Tabennese and Pbow, the monastery was located in or beside the village in the fertile valley. The monastery of Tabennese was the ascetic community located in and thus connected with the village of Tabennese. One suspects that the remaining Pachomian establishments, the precise locations of which are unclear, were similarly called after the villages whose names they bore. The monasteries of Tse and Tsmine, for example, located in the land or vicinity of Šmin (Panopolis), were likely situated in or beside villages of the same names in the Panopolite nome. The social, commercial, and agricultural efforts of the Pachomian monasteries support such a close and intimate relationship with their neighboring village communities.

A careful reading of the Pachomian sources supports this contention.[82] It has already been noted above that the foundation of Tabennese led to such an increase in the village population that the monks built a church for the villagers before they constructed one for themselves.[83] At least in the beginning, they continued to receive the eucharist in the village church. When Theodore's mother came to Tabennese with letters from the local bishop demanding to see her son, she was only permitted to catch sight of him by climbing up on the roof of a nearby house.[84] The monastery of Tabennese was clearly situated in the village.

The monastery of Pbow was likewise situated in the fertile valley, where it was affected by the flooding of the Nile. During a plague that ravished the community, the brothers were distressed because the rising waters cut off their path to the mountain or ceme-

---

81. *Bo* 50–51, 56; *G1* 54, 80.
82. Goehring, "World Engaged" (chap. 2 in the present volume).
83. See above, p. 100; *Bo* 25; *G1* 29.
84. *Bo* 37; cf. *G1* 37. Goehring, "Theodore's Entry."

tery in the desert.[85] The Greek *Vita* indicates that the flood normally reached such a height around the monastery that the monks traveled by boat during the flood season.[86] Elsewhere in the sources, one reads of monks working fields on an island in the Nile[87] and gathering fruit from orchards outside the monastery walls.[88] Monks unload a wealthy councillor's gift of wheat from his boat anchored nearby,[89] and in time of famine, they purchase wheat on the local market.[90] Specific monks were appointed to sell the *koinonia*'s handicrafts and to make the necessary purchases for the community, practices that underscore the community's contact with the outside world.[91] In the Pachomian *Rule*, while permission is required to leave the monastery,[92] monks may walk about the village at certain times and even visit their families.[93] Permission was also required to go to the monastery's shops or stables and to launch a boat or skiff from the harbor.[94] The stables were essential given the gifts of sheep, goats, cattle, camels, and donkeys to the *koinonia*.[95] Extensive pasturage for the livestock would have also been required. The necessary involvement of the Pachomians in agricultural life is underscored by the detailed agricultural and irrigation legislation in the later *Regulations of Horsiesius*.[96] While the ascetic nature of the movement necessitated its regulation of contact between the monks and the wider society, the location and needs of the *koinonia* made such contact not only unavoidable, but essential. The *Regulations of Horsiesius* simply assert that conversation with seculars whom monks meet on the road be done for the glory of God.[97]

---

85. *Bo* 180.
86. *G1* 139.
87. *G1* 106.
88. *Regula Pachomii, Praecepta* 76–77.
89. *Bo* 39; *G1* 39.
90. *Paralipomena* 21–22.
91. *Bo* 26; *G1* 28.
92. *Regula Pachomii, Praecepta* 84.
93. *Regula Pachomii, Praecepta* 90, 102, 54. In the two cases that refer to monks walking about in the village, Jerome changes the text in his Latin translation to *in monasterio*. Veilleux, *Pachomian Koinonia*, 2.189.
94. *Regula Pachomii, Praecepta* 108, 111, 118.
95. *Bo* 56; *G1* 80.
96. *Regulations of Horsiesius* 55–64.
97. *Regulations of Horsiesius* 52.

While the ascetic enterprise emphasized withdrawal, for the Pachomians it meant withdrawal practiced within the normal sphere of village life. The village monasteries of the Pachomians continue the urban ascetic presence of the earlier apotactic movement, albeit with considerably greater planning and organization. It was not by accident that the Pachomians called themselves ἀποτακτικοί rather than monks or coenobites.[98] As the papyrus evidence of the urban ἀποτακτκοί(αί) illustrates their legal and social connection with the wider community,[99] so too the Pachomian evidence reveals their legal and social integration within Roman Egypt.[100] A list of tax receipts from 367–68 C.E. for agricultural land (ἄπορα) in the Hermopolite nome includes a payment by the ἀποτακτικός Anoubion, son of Horion, for the monastery of Tabennese.[101] Twenty-one years after Pachomius's death, the monastery of Tabennese, located in the Tentyrite nome, was responsible for taxes on land located at a considerable distance in the Hermopolite nome. In the time since his death, his successor Theodore had expanded the *koinonia* by founding two additional monasteries near the town of Hermopolis, the capital of the Hermopolite nome.[102] It may be that the older community at Tabennese was legally responsible for land possessed and worked by the younger communities in the Hermopolite nome. Whatever the case, the location of the Pachomian *koinonia* within the legal structures of fourth-century Roman Egypt is clear. There is no reason to doubt that the connection began with Pachomius's innovative move into the deserted village of Tabennese. While the land he occupied may have been deserted, as possessable land his occupation of it would undoubtedly have been noted.[103] Agricul-

---

98. Goehring, "Through a Glass Darkly," 28 (see p. 58 in the present volume).

99. Judge, "Earliest Use"; idem, "Fourth-Century Monasticism"; Goehring, "Through a Glass Darkly" (see chap. 3 in the present volume).

100. Goehring, "World Engaged," 139–41 (see pp. 46–48 in the present volume).

101. *P. Berl.* Inv. 11860 (=*SB* XIV 11972); Wipszycka, "Terres." Judge ("Earliest Use," 73–74) makes the same point with respect to the *monachos* that appears in a Karanis petition.

102. *G1* 134.

103. The question of the legal availability of vacant land and buildings for occupancy by individuals like Pachomius lies beyond the scope of the present essay. In the period in question, the *praescriptio longi temporis* awarded uncontested possession of property to an individual who had been in possession of it for forty years, regardless of how the person actually came into possession (Casper J. Kraemer and Naphtali Lewis, "A Referee's Hearing on Ownership," *TAPA* 68 [1937] 357–87; Roger S. Bag-

tural land would have been taxable from the start of his communal efforts.[104] As his community expanded through the occupation of additional village property and agricultural land, the koinonia's legal and social responsibilities would have increased proportionately. One suspects that the appointment of a steward (ΟΙΚΟΝΟΜΟC) at each individual monastery and a great steward (ΠΙΝΙϢϮ ΝΟΙΚΟΝΟΜΟC) for the koinonia as a whole, as well as the annual financial reckoning in August, for which the leaders of all the individual monasteries came together at the central monastery of Pbow, were necessitated in part by the legal demands of Roman Egypt.[105] Like the ἀποτακτικοί(αί) before them, the Pachomians possessed their land and paid their taxes. They too developed and practiced their asceticism within the social and legal framework of the towns and villages of Egypt.

In a similar fashion, the village monasteries of the Pachomian koinonia presage the later forms of urban monasticism recognized by Wipszycka in the Byzantine period. The Pachomian monasteries were not located in the distant desert or even on the marginal land where the desert begins,[106] but in or in close proximity to the towns and villages whose names they bore. They were not part of the desert city whose praises Athanasius sang, but rather an expansive development of ascetic practice within the towns and villages of Upper Egypt. Their communities indicate a developmental path from the earlier, less organized forms of urban asceticism represented in the apotactic movement to the later, more structured forms of as-

nall and Naphtali Lewis, Columbia Papyri VII: Fourth-Century Documents from Karanis [AmSP 20; Missoula, Mont.: Scholars Press, 1979] 173–85; J. A. Crook, Legal Advocacy in the Roman World [Ithaca, N.Y.: Cornell University Press, 1995] 104–7). The cultivation of land in this period was often unprofitable (Kraemer and Lewis, "A Referee's Hearing," 366–67). This may account for the lack of opposition to Pachomius's occupation of it. On the other hand, the opposition of local townspeople to his founding of a monastery near the nome capital of Šmin (G1 81) may have been occasioned in part by legal concerns over the land in question. Documents do record disputes over vacant property (SB 5232; Johnson, Roman Egypt, 158–59) and complaints about others encroaching on one's land (van Minnen, "House-to-House Enquiries," 244–45).

104. Urban property was not taxed. Bagnall, Egypt in Late Antiquity, 153.

105. Goehring, "World Engaged," 141 (see p. 48 in the present volume); Ruppert, Das pachomianische Mönchtum, 320–24.

106. Compare the White Monastery of Shenoute. René-Georges Coquin and Maurice Martin, S.J., "Dayr Anba Shinudah: History," in Atiya, Coptic Encyclopedia, 1.761–66.

cetic practice seen in the urban and suburban monasteries of the Byzantine period. The Pachomian monasteries illustrate the steady and innovative growth of asceticism within the towns and villages of Egypt. They were not a product of the desert movement, but rather serve to challenge the common portrayal of Egyptian monasticism as a predominantly desert phenomenon.[107]

---

107. Melitian ascetic communities also appear to have been closely connected with villages. *P. Lond.* 1913 refers to a community in the village of Hipponon in communication with the monastery of Hathor in the eastern desert of the Upper Kynopolite nome. Goehring, "Melitian Monastic Organization" (chap. 9 in the present volume).

6

Hieracas of Leontopolis:
The Making of a Desert Ascetic

Twentieth-century accounts of Hieracas (late third to early fourth centuries C.E.) and his followers have increasingly fashioned him as a desert ascetic.[1] This development has occurred in spite of the fact that Epiphanius, whose account in his *Panarion* represents the best and most contemporary description of Hieracas, locates him *in* Leontopolis (ἐν τῇ Λεοντῷ τῇ κατ᾽ Αἴγυπτον).[2] He gives no indication that Hieracas lived in a monastic cell or monastery, nor that he resided outside of the city. The basis for these claims derives from the fifth- or sixth-century legendary *Life of Epiphanius*, which relocates Hieracas about a mile outside of Leontopolis (ἔξω Λεοντοπόλις ὡς ἀπὸ σημείον ἑνός),[3] where Epiphanius reportedly found him teaching great crowds of people in his monastery (ἐν τῷ μοναστηρίῳ αὐτοῦ).[4] Once the evidence from the *Life of Epiphanius* entered into the scholarly debate, Hieracas and his movement were increasingly envisioned by some in terms of the desert ascetic movement. In the

This paper was first presented at the North American Patristics Conference at Loyola University in Chicago, May 29–31, 1997. It is published here in expanded form for the first time.

1. I use the phrase "desert ascetic" to indicate the standard formulation of the Egyptian anchorite established by Athanasius's *Life of Antony*. The focus is on the withdrawal of the individual from the town or village setting, rather than on the specific eventual location of the ascetic in the desert.

2. Epiphanius, *Panarion* 67.1.2; Holl and Dummer, *Epiphanius III*, 133; Amidon, *Panarion*, 244; Williams, *Panarion II and III*, 308. In addition to the account in *Panarion* 67, Epiphanius refers to Hieracas elsewhere in the *Panarion* in his accounts of the Melchizedekians (55.5.2–3), Origen (64.67), and the Arians (in a letter of Arius; 69.7.6). He also mentions him in his *Anachoretus* (82). There are two sites in the Delta which bear the name Leontopolis. One, Tell al-Yahudiya, is located some nineteen kilometers north of Heliopolis. The second, Tell al-Muqdam, is approximately sixty-five kilometers north of Heliopolis. See Hermann Kees, "Leontopolis," *PW* 13.2053–57; Stefan Timm, *Das christlich-koptische Ägypten in arabischer Zeit* (Beihefte zum Tübinger Atlas des vorderen Orients, ser. B, no. 41/3; Wiesbaden: Ludwig Reichert, 1985) 3.1490–93.

3. Since Leontopolis is located in the interior of the Delta, Hieracas's withdrawal would not have placed him in the desert proper.

4. *Vita Epiphanii* 27; *PG* 41.57C.

following essay, I will trace the path of this interpretive development in the twentieth century, challenge the basis for the interpretation, and explore the ramifications of its rejection for our understanding of Hieracas and the emerging monastic movement.

When Adolf Harnack composed his account of "Hierakas und die Hierakiten" for the *Realencyklopädie für protestantische Theologie und Kirche* in 1900,[5] he drew his evidence from the best contemporary ancient source on the movement, namely, chapter 67 of Epiphanius's *Panarion*. His account follows Epiphanius closely. He locates Hieracas *in* the Egyptian town of Leontopolis, where he made his living as a calligrapher, a skill which he practiced into his old age. He was a man of great learning, equally skilled in Greek and Egyptian literature, in medicine, and the other sciences, including astronomy and magic. He knew the Old and New Testaments by heart and composed commentaries in Greek and Coptic. His writings included an exposition on the Hexaemeron and his own psalms. Among his teachings were the rejection of marriage in the age inaugurated by Christ, belief in spiritual resurrection, an understanding of the relationship between the Father and the Son that involved a mild modalism, and the contention that the Holy Spirit is Melchizedek. In terms of practice, he remained unmarried, leading a strict ascetic life in which be abstained from wine and other foods. Through his teaching and practice, he exerted a strong influence over the ascetically inclined Christians in Leontopolis and gathered them together to form an ascetic association (*Asketenverein*).

After presenting the facts found in Epiphanius's report, Harnack, not surprisingly in view of his own interests, focuses the discussion on Hieracas's place in the history of doctrine. In his analysis, Hieracas was a devout and learned Christian scholar of the Alexandrian persuasion who built on the impulses of Origen's thought. His major innovative step was the founding of an academic ascetic association (*ein wissenschaftlich gerichteten Asketenverein*) composed of and limited to virgins, monks, continent persons, and widows. Harnack's portrayal of the Leontopolitan movement, dependent as it is on Epiphanius's account in the *Panarion*, thus suggests a type of inner-city ascetic school centered around the Origenist philoso-

---

5. Adolf Harnack, "Hierakas und die Hierakiten," *RE* 8.38–39.

phy of a famous teacher named Hieracas. His encyclopedia article remained the major descriptive account of Hieracas for the next thirty-six years.

In 1936, Karl Heussi published his important *Der Ursprung des Mönchtums*.[6] Setting out to trace the origins and development of early Christian monasticism, he naturally found in Hieracas a forerunner of the later monastic movement. Necessarily dependent on Epiphanius's report, Heussi's account outlines the now well-known facts of Hieracas's learned abilities, his ascetic practices, and his theoretical teachings. Heussi, however, incorporates into his account the additional evidence found in the later *Life of Epiphanius*. This results in his relocation of Hieracas from a setting within the town of Leontopolis to an anchorite's cell (μοναστήριον) situated about a mile outside of town. In a note, he even suggests that Hieracas may have begun his ascetic career nearer the town (*vor der Stadt*), but that by about 335, when Epiphanius visited him, he had moved to an anchorite's cell further outside of the city (*ausserhalb der Stadt*).[7] Heussi does not offer any support for this idea, but by suggesting it, he fits Hieracas nicely into the pattern of ascetic withdrawal employed by Athanasius in his portrayal of Antony. While Heussi does not specifically place Hieracas's cell in the desert, his account refashions Hieracas as a typical ascetic of monastic origins, one who, modeled after Antony, moved out of the city to a withdrawn location ("desert") in his quest for *anachoresis*.

Heussi does not, however, posit a withdrawn community built up around the anchorite's cell, in spite of the fact that the *Life of Epiphanius* reports that many were being taught by Hieracas in his monastery (ἐν τῷ μοναστηρίῳ αὐτοῦ ηὑράμεθα πλήθη πολλὰ διδασκόμενα ὑπ' αὐτοῦ).[8] He concludes rather that many or most of Hieracas's ascetic adherents lived in Leontopolis or in other villages or towns.[9] He notes that Hieracas encouraged his male followers to acquire ascetic women with whom to live,[10] and he interprets

---

6. Heussi, *Ursprung*.

7. Heussi, *Ursprung*, 64 n. 1.

8. *Vita Epiphanii* 27 (PG 41.57C).

9. Heussi, *Ursprung*, 64. His claim implies that some may have lived outside of the town.

10. It is unclear why Harnack left this reference out of his article. As we will see, it plays an important role in more recent research.

Epiphanius's reference to the gathering of virgins, monks, continent persons, and widows as a reference to a worship service. He thus seems to assume a situation in which individual Hieracite men and women, who lived in the town and often cohabited as ascetic couples, gathered together on occasion as a community for common worship services.[11] By locating the ascetic community in Leontopolis and its leader in an anchoritic cell a mile outside of town, Heussi's reconstruction effectively fashions a connective link between urban ascetic practice and the origins of "desert" monasticism. His detailed analysis of the sources rapidly became the most widely used descriptive account of Hieracas and his movement.

More recently, interest in the social world of early Christianity has led to new appraisals of Hieracas's influence and the nature of his community. Two works in particular, Susanna Elm's *Virgins of God*[12] and David Brakke's *Athanasius and the Politics of Asceticism*,[13] have advanced our understanding of the Hieracite movement in terms of its social formation and influence. Both, however, build on Heussi's analysis and thereby further the portrayal of Hieracas as an anchorite who had withdrawn from the city. Elm's work focuses on the cohabitation of Hieracite male and female ascetics as evidence of an earlier form of asceticism marked by the more equal participation of men and women. She argues that the ascetic movement "originated primarily in urban centers or their direct vicinity, and was characterized by a symbiosis of men and women."[14] In her view, the move to the desert and to separate ascetic institutions for men and women represents a later development. In support of this thesis, she emphasizes Epiphanius's report that Hieracite monks lived with like-minded ascetic women whom they had brought into their cells (συνεισάκτους γυναῖκας). With Heussi she locates Hieracas about a mile outside of Leontopolis, but whereas he left the connection with the desert movement implicit, she makes it explicit. Elm writes that "Hieracas, like most of the desert anchorites, had removed himself

---

11. He does not indicate whether these gatherings took place in town or in or around Hieracas's *monasterion* outside of the city.

12. Elm, *Virgins of God*.

13. Brakke, *Athanasius*.

14. Elm, *Virgins of God*, 376.

from the village and its community, that is from the direct influence of the Church and its clergy."[15]

She further rejects Heussi's interpretation of Epiphanius's assertion that "no one assembles (συνάγεται) with them except one who is a virgin, monk, continent person or widow" as a reference to a communal worship service, preferring to see the term συνάγεται as a reference to a more permanent community or συναγωγή.[16] Although she does not further explain the nature of these συναγωγαί, her line of argument certainly suggests some form of permanent ascetic community. She also does not identify the location of these communities, either in Leontopolis or outside of the town, though once again her overall reconstruction of the Leontopolitan Hieracite movement suggests a community more akin to the semi-anchoritic desert communities of lower Egypt than to an inner-city ascetic association or school.[17] At least implicitly, the Hieracite community has become a more direct forerunner of later communal monastic developments. The major difference lay in the latter's organizational separation of men and women. The connection is furthered by the suggestion that "Hieracas and his followers, rather than being an aberration, in fact represent a strand of asceticism prevalent in all of Egypt."[18] This claim is supported by reference to later sources that connect Macarios the Great, the famous ascetic from Scetis, with efforts against certain followers of Hieracas.[19]

David Brakke, in his *Athanasius and the Politics of Asceticism*, focuses on the conflicting social and organizational visions of the church evidenced in the Hieracite controversy. Brakke perceptively notes that in Hieracas's day, his teachings on the resurrection, the relationship between the Father and the Son, and the moral superiority of virginity would not have appeared as radical as one might at first think. Rather

---

15. Elm, *Virgins of God*, 342.

16. Elm, *Virgins of God*, 340–41; esp. n. 20. "Heussi concludes that these *synagogai* were occasional gatherings for divine service; but a permanent community seems more likely. Hieracas wrote ψαλμούς and νεωτερικούς (psalms and hymns) for these *synagogai*, used in liturgical practices."

17. Elm does not mention the reference in the *Life of Epiphanius* to Epiphanius finding Hieracas instructing large crowds in his monastery, nor does she address Heussi's contention that most of Hieracas's followers lived in Leontopolis or other similar towns.

18. Elm, *Virgins of God*, 341.

19. Elm, *Virgins of God*, 341–42.

it was his vision of a separatist ascetic church that ran most directly afoul of the emerging "institutional, episcopally centered Christianity that Athanasius was forming."[20] He finds support for this view in Athanasius's *First Letter to Virgins,* a text in which the bishop directly attacks Hieracite influence among Alexandrian ascetics. While Hieracas was attracting male and female ascetics with his rejection of marriage and his creation of an ascetically pure community, Athanasius was striving to define the church more broadly and to place it more fully under episcopal control. While Hieracas's theoretical teachings supported his social practices,[21] it was in fact the social practices that first generated the conflict over theory. Brakke's important discussion reveals the gold that can be found when one applies new methods to old sources. When one separates the evidence from the analysis, however, the basic description of Hieracas and his followers, dependent as it is on the same sources used by Harnack, Heussi, and Elm, remains much the same. In terms of Hieracas's specific location, Brakke follows Heussi and Elm in accepting the evidence of the *Life of Epiphanius.* He places the ascetic about a mile outside of Leontopolis,[22] but whereas Elm had only implicitly suggested that his followers had joined him in an ascetic community outside of the town, Brakke makes the move explicit. He concludes that Hieracas "formed a Christian community of celibate men and women outside Leontopolis."[23] The transformation of Hieracas and his following is thus complete. Based on information in the late *Life of Epiphanius,* Hieracas, whom Epiphanius describes as gathering ascetics around him *in* Leontopolis, has become the leader of a withdrawn ascetic community located outside of the town.[24]

A problem with this depiction of Hieracas immediately arises,

---

20. Brakke, *Athanasius,* 48.

21. Drawing from Athanasius's *First Letter to Virgins,* Brakke reveals that the issue of human nature and free will lay at the heart of the different ascetic interpretations of Hieracas and Athanasius. Brakke, *Athanasius,* 49ff.

22. Brakke, *Athanasius,* 45.

23. Brakke, *Athanasius,* 268.

24. Not all scholars followed this interpretation. Guillaumont, for example, does not believe that Hieracas and his followers lived in a monastery, but "according to the way of life of the ascetics of the premonastic period." Antoine Guillaumont, "Hieracas of Leontopolis," in Atiya, *Coptic Encyclopedia,* 4.1229. Brown (*Body and Society,* 244–45) likewise identifies Hieracas as "a spiritual guide in a provincial town of the Nile Delta."

however, if one challenges the use of the evidence in the *Life of Epiphanius*. The *Vita*, dated to the fifth or sixth century, is a legendary text designed "to depict Epiphanius as a great holy man endowed with astounding miraculous powers that made him popular through-out the world."[25] It is replete with hagiographic commonplaces and, as such, it has been mostly neglected and treated with contempt by scholars.[26] Recently, however, Claudia Rapp has undertaken a fasci-nating study of the *Life of Epiphanius*, tracing the complex nature of its composition and exploring the function it played in the devel-oping traditions concerning Epiphanius.[27] The text is composed of four parts, the first two of which are represented internally as the work of two different eyewitnesses. The first part, which includes the account of Epiphanius's meeting with Hieracas, is attributed to a certain John, Epiphanius's first disciple. The second part claims to have been written by Polybios, to whom John entrusted the project on his deathbed. The final two parts of the text are a letter by Poly-bios to Sabinus concerning Epiphanius's death and Sabinus's reply.[28] After a careful analysis of the language of the first two parts of the text, Rapp concludes that they do indeed reflect two distinct sets of notes used by the final compiler in his creation of the *Vita*. She fur-ther believes that the compiler "preserved the original character of his material," which, in the case of the first part, "probably went little beyond a record of the history of Epiphanius's monastery in Spanhydrion."[29]

While the existence of a set of early notes used by the com-piler supplies a plausible source for the additional details concerning Hieracas with which the present essay is concerned, caution is war-ranted. Rapp notes that the "*Vita* lacks originality and historical accuracy. To a large extent, the narrative depends on other sources and employs a whole array of hagiographical topoi."[30] In fact, in ad-

---

25. Rapp, "Epiphanius of Salamis," 182.
26. Rapp, "Epiphanius of Salamis," 181.
27. Rapp, "The *Vita* of Epiphanius"; idem, "Der heilige Epiphanius im Kampf mit dem Dämon des Origenes: Kritische Erstausgabe des Wunders BHG 601i," in Fred-erike Berger et al., eds., *Symbolae Berlinensis für Dieter Harlfinger* (Amsterdam: Adolf M. Hakkert, 1993) 249–69; idem, "Epiphanius of Salamis."
28. Rapp, "The *Vita* of Epiphanius," 44–52.
29. Rapp, "The *Vita* of Epiphanius," 49, 59.
30. Rapp, "The *Vita* of Epiphanius," 48.

dition to the two sets of notes, she identifies fourteen other certain or possible sources used by the compiler. Included among these are Athanasius's *Life of Antony* and Epiphanius's *Panarion*. It is certain that the compiler knew and used the *Life of Antony*, since he actually weaves quotations from it into his own text.[31] He does not, however, use the source for its information on Antony, but rather as inspiration for the fashioning of his own creative account of Epiphanius's youth. The *Life of Antony* serves as the archetype or mold from which the compiler extracts a model hagiographic version of Epiphanius's early life.[32] This use of the *Life of Antony* underscores the author's interest in creative hagiography rather than history. He readily mines and reshapes his source materials to create the perfect wonder-working ascetic saint.

In the case of the *Panarion*, however, his use of the source is less clear. There are no direct quotations of the *Panarion* in the *Life of Epiphanius*. In fact, Rapp observes that while "the correspondence in content between the two texts is undeniable, . . . the expressions used by the compiler bear no resemblance to those in the *Panarion*." As a result, she concludes that it cannot be proven that the parallel accounts found in the *Life of Epiphanius* are dependent on the *Panarion*.[33] Once again this leaves open the possibility that the additional material on Hieracas found in the *Vita* derived from John's notes and thus may represent additional accurate information. When one sets the account of Hieracas contained in the *Vita* into the larger context of the literary work, however, one remains suspicious of the evidence. The account in the *Vita* agrees with the *Panarion* in portraying Hieracas as an intelligent individual who practiced a strict asceticism and held a controversial teaching on the resurrection.[34] The compiler, however, sets this description into a story of his saint's miraculous intervention and conversion of Hieracas. The *Vita* reports that Epiphanius appeared at Hieracas's monastery about a mile outside of Leontopolis, where he found him teaching great crowds of people. After miraculously striking the heretic dumb, Epiphanius preaches the true doctrine of the resurrection to the people. His ex-

---

31. Rapp, "The *Vita* of Epiphanius," 63–66; idem, "Epiphanius of Salamis," 179.
32. Rapp, "The *Vita* of Epiphanius," 66.
33. Rapp, "The *Vita* of Epiphanius," 89–93, 137.
34. *Vita Epiphanii* 27; *PG* 41.57–60. A summary is given in Brakke, *Athanasius*, 45.

planations are so persuasive that in the end even Hieracas repents and thus regains his speech.

The legendary nature of the account is clear. The basic material, most likely drawn from the *Panarion*, is simply fit into a creative story designed to further the compiler's aim of presenting Epiphanius as "a great ascetic with extraordinary miraculous powers."[35] The goal requires direct contact between Epiphanius and Hieracas; how else could the glories of the saint be revealed? The fact that Epiphanius does not mention a meeting with Hieracas[36] does not interfere with the compiler's creative storytelling. Likewise, there is no indication that Hieracas ever altered his teaching in the face of opposition from the emerging episcopally centered Christianity represented by Athanasius and Epiphanius. While one might still argue that the particular facts concerning the location of Hieracas's monastery outside of Leontopolis were taken from another source and are accurate, the compiler's ready shaping of the source to his own ends makes it difficult to build much history upon such claims. One can as readily imagine that the compiler relocated Hieracas outside of the city in a μοναστήριον both to separate him further from the sphere of the episcopacy and to fashion him, as an ascetic, in terms of the then current image of Egyptian monasticism. He was familiar with the *Life of Antony*, which by the time of his writing had become the archetype for imaging Egyptian ascetics. He used it to fashion his own ascetic hero, Epiphanius, as a model ascetic. It is thus very possible that the literary success of Athanasius in spatially locating male ascetic withdrawal outside of the city in the desert led the compiler, or the author of one of his sources, to posit that Hieracas, described so forcefully as an ascetic, must have lived as an ascetic outside of the town.[37] The fact that he, as an ascetic, gathered followers around him naturally suggests some form of monastic community.

While one cannot prove with certainty that evidence placing Hieracas outside of Leontopolis in a μοναστήριον was created out of whole cloth, the creative nature of the *Vita* as a whole, and the account of Hieracas in particular, raises serious doubts about it. When one turns

---

35. Rapp, "Epiphanius of Salamis," 180.

36. Williams (*Panarion II and III*, 308 n. 1) rejects this possibility. Note that Epiphanius does refer to his contact with the Gnostics.

37. Goehring, "Encroaching Desert" (chap. 4 in the present volume).

to the other sources that preserve information on Hieracas, no clear supporting evidence is found for such a location. In fact, the evidence is more readily interpreted in support of Hieracas's location in the town of Leontopolis. Epiphanius himself locates Hieracas in Leontopolis (ἐν τῇ Λεοντῷ), and he does not identify him as an anchorite or a monk. While it is possible to interpret the preposition ἐν to mean "at" or "near," there is no reason to think that Epiphanius meant to convey anything other than that Hieracas dwelt in Leontopolis. In fact, elsewhere in the *Panarion*, when he wishes to identify opponents as monastics and to locate them in withdrawn places, he does so explicitly. He traces the origin of the Archontics, for example, to an elderly man named Peter who lived as an anchorite (ἀναχωρητής γὰρ ἐδόκει εἶναι) in a cave three miles beyond Hebron, apparently near the village of Capharbaricha.[38] He further reports that some members of the sect deceive simple people by pretending to fast and appearing in the guise of monks (προσχήματι μοναζόντων).[39] He likewise complains that Origenist teachings are now found "among the very persons who are the most eminent and appear to have adopted the monastic life (δοκοῦσι τὸν μονήρη βίον) — who have really retired to the deserts (κατὰ τὰς ἐρημίας ἀναχωροῦσι) and elected voluntary poverty."[40] Epiphanius recognized that the spatial withdrawal of these figures from the ancient polis served as a basis for their authority, and he purposefully countered it. For Epiphanius, Christian anchorites and desert monks whose teachings did not correspond to his understanding of the faith are but apparent or "docetic" ascetics. They have no value or authority as the real thing.[41] It is thus surprising that Epiphanius, should he have met Hieracas in a withdrawn μοναστήριον or cell some distance from the town, did not mention this fact and discredit Hieracas as a false anchorite or monk.

In fact, the descriptions of Hieracas's training, his work, and his

---

38. *Panarion* 40.1.3–4; Holl and Dummer, *Epiphanius II*, 81; Williams, *Panarion I*, 262. Epiphanius actually seems to place Peter in a village called Capharbaricha some three miles beyond Hebron, but he also describes him as a hermit dwelling in a certain cave.

39. *Panarion* 40.2.4; Holl and Dummer, *Epiphanius II*, 82; Williams, *Panarion I*, 236.

40. *Panarion* 64.4.1; Holl and Dummer, *Epiphanius II*, 409–10; Williams, *Panarion II and III*, 134.

41. James E. Goehring, "Monastic Diversity and Ideological Boundaries in Fourth-Century Christian Egypt," *JECS* 5 (1997) 84 (see p. 218 in the present volume).

following best correspond with an inner-city ascetic teacher who developed a separatist movement within the Leontopolitan Christian community. He was recognized as a calligrapher, and if indeed he earned his living through this trade, the most likely location for his work would have been within the city. This is not to deny that withdrawn monks, both anchorites and those living in communities, could and did produce books and other written materials, but apart from any direct statement placing Hieracas outside of the town, Epiphanius's reference is best understood as a simple description of Hieracas's occupation.[42] As an occupation, it fits well the description of a man with the intelligence and learning that Epiphanius attributes to Hieracas. An Egyptian, he was fluent in both Coptic and Greek, and he composed works in both languages. He had received a fine education and was well versed in all of the Greek subjects (λόγοι), having also mastered medicine and the other Greek and Egyptian sciences (μαθήματα), including astronomy and magic. While none of this, of course, precludes Hieracas from having moved at some point in his career to a location outside of the town, there is no evidence for such a move other than the report in the later *Life of Epiphanius*. Given Hieracas's relatively early date, the description of him as a learned teacher and author more easily corresponds to that of a leader of an inner-city ascetic study group. Since Epiphanius himself never mentions a move outside of Leontopolis, his account is most readily read in these terms.

Epiphanius's brief references to Hieracas's ascetic followers are likewise best interpreted in terms of an inner-city Christian separatist ascetic movement. He reports that Hieracas won over many souls through his ascetic practice and his learned teaching. His influence seems not to have been limited to Leontopolis, since Epiphanius reports that many Egyptian ascetics were drawn to him.[43] When he does get specific about Hieracas's followers in Leontopolis, however, he reports that "no one worships with them except one who is a virgin, a monk, a continent person, or a widow" (οὐδεὶς δὲ μετ' αὐτῶν συνάγεται, ἀλλὰ εἰ εἴη παρθένος ἢ μονάζων ἢ ἐγκρατὴς ἢ χήρα).[44]

---

42. Heussi (*Ursprung,* 59–60) reports that he earned his living by copying books.
43. One need not assume that these ascetics lived in the desert.
44. *Panarion* 67.2.9; Holl and Dummer, *Epiphanius III,* 135; translation from Amidon, *Panarion,* 246.

As was noted above, Heussi already interpreted this passage as a reference to a Hieracite worship service held in Leontopolis, and the recent translators of Epiphanius's *Panarion* have taken the verb συνάγεται in this sense.[45] Elm's suggestion that the passage refers to a more permanent community or συναγωγή moves the interpretation beyond the evidence at hand. As Elm uses it, it suggests a more permanent ascetic community similar in some ways to later, spatially separated monastic developments. The noun ⲥⲩⲛⲁⲅⲱⲅⲏ was used in Coptic, for example, by Shenoute to refer to his monastic communities.[46] Epiphanius, however, never uses the noun in that sense. He employs the noun twelve times in the *Panarion*.[47] Eight of those occurrences, some of them dependent on biblical passages, refer specifically to Jewish synagogues.[48] One use reports that the Ebionites called their churches synagogues,[49] and two uses of the term refer to a gathering other than people ("a gathering of different types of wood," and "a gathering of wealth and property").[50] The two remaining references to συναγωγαί appear in accounts of certain so-called Gnostic groups. In his attack on the Gnostics, Epiphanius mentions their "blasphemous assembly" (βλάσφημος συναγωγή) in the context of his description of their peculiar worship practices,[51] and in his report on the Heracleonites, he reports that Heracleon won for himself a following of deceived persons (ἵνα καὶ ἑαυτῷ συναγωγήν ποιήσηται τῶν ἡπατημένων).[52] Neither of these uses suggests a permanently separated ascetic group. The first, in fact, locates the term συναγωγή in the context of a worship service, and the second simply refers to the following of a particular teacher. The group's social location within the broader community is not defined. While both

---

45. Heussi, *Ursprung*, 62; Williams, *Panarion II and III*, 310; Amidon, *Panarion*, 246.

46. See, for example, text 5 (Vienna K 924 and 925) in Dwight Wayne Young, *Coptic Manuscripts from the White Monastery: Works of Shenoute* (MPER 22; Wien: Brüder Hollinek, 1993) 32–37.

47. The noun also appears in the compound ἀρχισυνάγωγος seven times (*Panarion* 30.11.4, 18.1; 31.25.3; 42.11.15; 42.12; 46.3.4; 69.59.2). This evidence was generated through the use of the Thesaurus Linguae Graecae CD-ROM.

48. *Panarion* 29.9.2; 30.1.4, 11.5; 50.3.7; 55.4.3; 69.81.4–5 (three times).

49. *Panarion* 30.18.1.

50. *Panarion* 61.3.4; 75.2.2–3.

51. *Panarion* 26.3.5.

52. *Panarion* 36.1.1.

groups may represent "permanent communities," they do so only in the sense of any ideologically distinct group or sect.

Epiphanius does, however, refer to a more distinctly separate ascetic community in the *Panarion* in the context of his account of the Audians. He is, in this case, explicit in his description. He reports that when Audius separated from the church, many followed him. They formed "a party [of lay people] who withdraw (ἀναχωροῦντες) and reside in monasteries (ἐν μοναστηρίοις) in the deserts (ἐν ἐρημίαις) and also in cities and suburbs and wherever they have their cells (τὰς ἑαυτῶν μονάς) or 'folds.'"[53] It is interesting to note here that the Audians withdrew to monasteries or cells not only in the desert, but also in the cities and suburbs.[54] In terms of the current discussion of Hieracas, however, the point is that Epiphanius was clearly capable of using precise language to locate individuals spatially in relationship to the city and to situate them, when appropriate, in permanent ascetic communities outside of the city in the desert. The terms that he employs in the case of the Audians are the terms most associated with the developing monastic movement: ἀναχωρέω, μοναστήριον, and μονή. He does not employ these terms when referring to Hieracas and his followers, and he does not use the noun συναγωγή in his discussion of the Audians. Once again, while Hieracas and his followers certainly represent a permanent sect with a separatist ideology, it does not follow that they lived in permanent separate ascetic communities.

Finally, Epiphanius reports that male Hieracite ascetics brought ascetic women (συνεισάκτους γυναῖκας), whom they had at their service, into their abodes. While such ascetic living arrangements were not uncommon in the early church, the practice, to the best of my knowledge, occurred for the most part in urban settings. A parallel example from Egypt might be seen in the continent marriage of Amoun of Nitria. Forced by his uncle to marry at age twenty-two, he convinced his bride to share a continent life with him. They lived together in the same house for eighteen years, during which time he labored on a balsam plantation. When he finally left for the Nitrian desert, he left alone. The practice of continent marriage was a

---

53. *Panarion* 70.1.1; Holl and Dummer, *Epiphanius III,* 232; translation from Amidon, *Panarion,* 271.

54. Goehring, "Encroaching Desert" (chap. 4 in the present volume).

practice of the city.[55] Thus once again, Epiphanius's description of Hieracite social practices suggests a community of urban ascetics. One suspects that those who practiced this form of continent marriage lived in separate houses in Leontopolis, carried on their lives as Amoun had done, and gathered together with like-minded individuals to hear and discuss Hieracas's teachings and to participate together in ascetically restricted worship services.

The association of Hieracas and his followers with the city, suggested by Epiphanius's account, is further supported by the only contemporary account of a struggle over the expanding influence of his teachings. Athanasius's writings to virgins on virginity[56] supply valuable evidence of the lives and practices of Alexandrian virgins and of the bishop's efforts to define and limit their calling in terms of his own developing ecclesiastical ideology.[57] What is of importance to the present argument is that Athanasius, in his efforts to control and define the practices of the Alexandrian virgins, confronts the problem of Hieracite influence directly in two of his letters to virgins.[58] The *Second Letter to Virgins*,[59] while it does not specifically mention Hieracas, contains a lengthy argument against spiritual marriage.[60] Athanasius condemns this ascetic living arrangement as equivalent to adultery for the virgin, who is a bride of Christ. He rejects the contention that monks who seek a virgin with whom to live are doing a noble thing for God's sake and calls on them to live up to

---

55. Palladius, *Historia Lausiaca* 8; Butler, *Lausiac History*, 2.26–29; Robert T. Meyer, *Palladius: The Lausiac History* (ACW; New York: Newman Press, 1964) 41–43. *Historia Monachorum in Aegypto* 22.1–2 plays down the continent marriage by asserting that the couple remained together for only a few days, at which point Amoun departed for Nitria. His wife continued her celibate life by converting her house into a monastery. Festugière, *Historia Monachorum*, 128–29; Russell and Ward, *Lives of the Desert Fathers*, 111.

56. Brakke (*Athanasius*, 19) recognizes "at least four letters to virgins as well as a treatise *On Virginity*." See also his "The Authenticity of the Ascetic Athanasiana," *Or* 63 (1994) 17–56; idem, "St. Athanasius and Ascetic Christians in Egypt" (Ph.D. diss., Yale University, 1992) 15–64.

57. For discussions see Brakke, *Athanasius*, 17–79; Elm, *Virgins of God*, 331–72; Badger, "New Man," 176–82.

58. Athanasius elsewhere refers to Hieracas's understanding of the relationship of the Son to the Father (*De synodis* 16).

59. J. Lebon, "Athanasiana Syriaca II: Une lettre attribuée à saint Athanase d'Alexandrie," *Mus* 41 (1928) 169–216. Brakke (*Athanasius*, 292–302) supplies an English translation.

60. Secs. 20–29; Brakke, *Athanasius*, 298–301.

their title as solitaries. Likewise he calls on virgins to remain faithful to Christ and to guard their virginity in a pure and solitary life. Virgins who live in a spiritual marriage with a monk lose the honor of their calling, and the solitary or secluded virgins whom Athanasius extols should be ashamed of them.

While this letter does not mention Hieracas directly, the description of solitary ascetics who live in a spiritual marriage certainly corresponds well with the practice of Hieracite ascetics who brought ascetic women in to live with them. In fact, as Epiphanius asserts that it was the Hieracite male ascetics who initiated the relationship, so Athanasius suggests that it was the male solitaries in Alexandria who sought out virgins as "cell mates." The connection that is only suggested by Athanasius in his *Second Letter to Virgins*, however, is made explicit in his *First Letter to Virgins*.[61] In this letter, the bishop attacks Hieracas and his followers as wolves in the vineyard of virginity, who sow evil thoughts and snare simple-minded ascetics with their rejection of marriage as evil. He calls on the Alexandrian virgins to sweep their bridal chambers clean of every evil thought of the heretics. They should ignore alien teachings and avoid the confusion caused by thinking thoughts other than those generated through their daily conversation with the bridegroom Christ as mediated through the Word of God. There is no doubt from this letter that certain ascetics in Alexandria were embracing Hieracite teachings and practices. Their success offered a direct challenge to Athanasius's understanding of the role and social location of male and female ascetics within the church.

It is not necessary here to detail further the nature and import of this struggle. That task has been thoroughly and admirably done by David Brakke in his book *Athanasius and the Politics of Asceticism*. What is of importance to the current argument is that the most current evidence of Hieracite influence that survives locates the influence in the city of Alexandria and sets it within a conflict over the definition and practice of virginity. While this does not, of course, preclude Hieracite influence among solitaries outside of the urban setting, it does suggest that the practice of spiritual marriage

61. L. Th. Lefort, *S. Athanase: Lettres festales et pastorales en copte* (CSCO 150–51; Louvain: L. Dubercq, 1955). Brakke (*Athanasius,* 274–91) supplies an English translation.

supported by the Hieracites was particularly appealing in an urban environment where virgins abounded. Athanasius's arguments against the practice also suggest that those ascetics who practiced spiritual marriage still lived as solitaries rather than in larger communities. While this could suggest a semi-anchoritic colony, in the Alexandrian context, it is best understood in terms of ascetic couples who lived together in their own houses. The social setting of the Alexandrian Hieracite ascetics depicted in Athanasius's letters in turn supplies the most plausible framework for understanding the social location of Hieracas and his followers in Leontopolis.

In addition to the above sources, an additional account exists of a conflict between a Hieracite ascetic and Macarios the Great of Scetis. The story, which survives in varied form, reports that a local bishop enlisted Macarios's help to defeat a Hieracite ascetic whose influence was spreading in his diocese. Macarios refutes the Hieracite teachings and reveals the truth of the resurrection of the body by raising a man, who had died before the Christian era, back to life. He then baptizes the man and leads him away to the desert to become an anchorite. This account, together with a few scattered references to a debate about Melchizedek in Scetis involving the same Macarios, has been used to support the existence of Hieracite influence in Scetis during the reign of the archbishop Theophilus. Elm, in her analysis, cites this evidence to support her contention that "Hieracas and his followers, rather than being an aberration, in fact represent a strand of asceticism prevalent in all of Egypt."[62]

While the initial source does indeed link a Hieracite ascetic and Macarios the Great, the other texts in fact make no mention of Hieracas. The relationship of the other texts to the Hieracite movement is asserted on the assumed connection between Hieracas's teaching that Melchizedek is the Holy Spirit and the conflict over Melchizedek that occurred in Scetis. It is Epiphanius who reports that Hieracas believed that Melchizedek is the Holy Spirit.[63] He does so first in his refutation of another sect that he labels the Melchizedekians, but he nowhere equates the Hieracites with the Melchizedekians. In fact, he includes the reference to Hieracas in a paragraph that begins

---

62. Elm, *Virgins of God*, 341.
63. *Panarion* 55.5.2; 67.7.1.

by noting that "others in their turn imagine and say [other things] about this Melchizedek."[64] This suggests that he was citing Hieracas's teaching as but one of a number of fanciful teachings about the figure of Melchizedek.[65] It is certainly clear that Hieracas was not the only person speculating about Melchizedek.[66] Jerome, for example, attributes the same teaching to Origen and his follower Didymus.[67] Given the known Origenist influence among the desert monks of Lower Egypt and the eventual controversies that it unleashed in the ascetic communities there,[68] it seems safer to set the debate over Melchizedek within an Origenist context than to posit a specific Hieracite influence in Scetis. Harnack, who refers to these sources in his account of Hieracas, seems to have recognized this fact. He believed that any agreement between Hieracas and the Theodotians or Melchizedekians was accidental.

Nonetheless, Hugh G. Evelyn White, in his monumental *History of the Monasteries of Nitria and Scetis* (1932), seems simply to assume the connection.[69] He interprets the reference in the *Apophthegmata Patrum*[70] to an assembly called in Scetis to discuss Melchizedek as an indication of Hieracite influence. Macarios the Great is brought into the equation through later sources which report that the archbishop Theophilus called upon him to settle a controversy over Melchizedek.[71] The Hieracite connection is then furthered by reference to the only source that actually mentions the Hieracites, namely, the story of Macarios's conflict with a Hieracite ascetic in which he raised a

---

64. *Panarion* 55.5.1; translation from Williams, *Panarion II and III*, 81.

65. Immediately after the reference to Hieracas, he notes the example of the Samaritans who believe that Melchizedek is Noah's son Shem (*Panarion* 55.6.1).

66. Note, for example, the Nag Hammadi codex entitled *Melchizedek* (Codex IX,1). Birger A. Pearson, "The Figure of Melchizedek in Gnostic Literature," in idem, ed., *Gnosticism, Judaism, and Egyptian Christianity* (SAC; Minneapolis: Fortress Press, 1990) 108–23.

67. Jerome, *Ep.* 73.1.1–2; cited by Williams, *Panarion II and III*, 81.

68. Clark, *Origenist Controversy*; Dechow, *Dogma and Mysticism*, 139–81. If Antony himself was influenced by Origenist thought as Rubenson (*Letters of St. Antony*) suggests, this would further underscore the impact of Origenism among the monks in Lower Egypt.

69. White, *Monasteries of the Wadi 'n Natrun*, 115–17.

70. *Apophthegmata patrum*, Copres 3; *PG* 65.252.

71. White cites a reference by Thomas of Marga (840 C.E.) and a passage from another Syrian source. E. A. Wallis Budge, *The Book of Governors: The Historia Monastica of Thomas Bishop of Marga, A.D. 840* (London: Kegan Paul, Trench, Trübner, 1893) 2.94–95; R. Payne Smith, *Thesaurus Syriacus* (Oxford: Clarendon Press, 1901) vol. 2, col. 2146.

corpse. This story, however, is not set in Scetis. Later scholars, dependent on White, eventually assert that "the patriarch of Alexandria ordered an anti-Hieracian purge of the monastery of Macarios."[72] While it is possible that Hieracite teachings influenced ascetics in Scetis, one cannot conclude with any degree of certainty that it was Hieracite influence that led to the debate over Melchizedek in Scetis toward the end of the fourth century.

In terms of specific evidence of the Hieracite movement among these sources, this leaves only the legendary account of Macarios's conflict with the Hieracite monk over the resurrection of the dead. The story, which was rejected as spurious by Butler in his edition of Palladius's *Lausiac History*,[73] is preserved in various Greek manuscripts of the *Lausiac History* and collections of *Apophthegmata*,[74] in a shortened form in the Latin text of the *History of the Monks of Egypt*,[75] in a Bohairic Coptic version of the *Life of Macarios*[76] that has been recently interpreted as preserving a lateral tradition composed by Palladius,[77] and in the Ethiopic synaxarium.[78] A version of the story also appears in Cassian's *Conferences*, in which the heretic in question is portrayed as a disciple of Eunomius rather than of Hieracas.[79] The history of the tradition is thus very complex and lies beyond the

72. Wisse, "Gnosticism," 438–39; Elm, *Virgins of God*, 341. The sources do not appear to locate the controversy specifically in the monastery of Macarios.

73. Butler, *Lausiac History*, 2.194–95.

74. Butler, *Lausiac History*, 2.194–95. A critical edition based on three manuscripts is found in Erwin Preuschen, *Palladius und Rufinus: Ein Beitrag zur Quellenkunde des ältesten Mönchtums* (Giessen: J. Rickershe Buchhandlung, 1897) 124–30; see also *PG* 34.200–16. For a French translation based on MS Coslin 126 see Lucien Regnault, *Les sentences des pères du désert: Troisième recueil & tables* (Sablé-sur-Sarthe: Abbaye Saint-Pierre de Solesmes, 1976) 27–30.

75. Eva Schulz-Flügel, *Tyrannius Rufinus: Historia Monachorum sive De Vita Sanctorum Patrum* (PTS 34; Berlin and New York: Walter de Gruyter, 1990) 367–68; Russell and Ward, *Lives of the Desert Fathers*, 152.

76. Georg Zoega, *Catalogus codicum copticorum manuscriptorum qui in Museo Borgiano Velitris adservantur* (Rome, 1810; reprint, Leipzig: Hinrichs, 1903) 127–29; M. Chaîne, "La double recension de l'Histoire Lausiaque dans la version copte," *RevOC* 3–4 (1925–26) 245–55; for a French translation, see Gabriel Bunge and Adalbert de Vogüé, *Quatre eremites égyptiens d'après les fragments coptes de l'Histoire Lausiaque* (Spiritualité orientale 60; Bégrolles-en-Mauges: Abbaye de Bellefontaine, 1994) 108–16.

77. Bunge and Vogüé, *Quatre eremites*, 17–80; cf. the detailed review of this work by Mark Sheridan in *ColCist* 57 (1995) 548–52.

78. E. A. Wallis Budge, *The Book of the Saints of the Ethiopian Church: A Translation of the Ethiopic Synaxarium Made from the Manuscripts Oriental 660 and 661 in the British Museum* (Cambridge: Cambridge University Press, 1928) 4.742–43.

79. *Conlationes* 15.3.

scope of the present essay. There are nonetheless some important factors to note in the interpretation of this story that bear on the present argument. Apart from the question of the story's historical accuracy, its literary formulation suggests a particular understanding of the nature and location of Hieracite influence in the church.

To begin with, the tradition varies in its location of the Hieracite ascetic. The Coptic account locates him in the desert regions of the village of Boushem (ϩⲉⲛ ⲛⲓϣⲁⲫⲉⲩ ⲛⲧⲉ ⲃⲟⲩϣⲏⲙ). The Latin version also refers to the heretic disturbing brothers who lived in the desert (*fratrum, qui habitabant in eremo*). The Ethiopic synaxarium, on the other hand, places the erring monk *in* the city of Wesim, and the Greek account simply sets the story in the Arsenoite nome (περὶ τὸν ἀρσενοίτην). Thus already there is some conflict as to whether the Hieracite ascetic was operating in the desert or in a village or town. In terms of the identity of the Hieracite, at least two of the Greek manuscripts describe him as a monk (μοναχός τις or τις μονάζων). The Coptic version agrees with this identification (ⲟⲩⲙⲟⲛⲁⲭⲟⲥ), as does the Ethiopic account. On the other hand, one Greek text refers to him as a "a certain one" (τις), and the Latin version simply calls him a heretic. While the preponderance of the evidence suggests the monastic identity of the figure in the author's mind, one must keep in mind that that identity alone does not establish his location in the desert.[80]

More significant, the Latin version stands alone in claiming that the heretic came to Macarios the Great, presumably in his desert abode in Scetis. The other versions all report that the local bishop (Greek, Coptic, and Ethiopic texts) and his clergy (Greek and Coptic texts) sought out Macarios and enlisted his help in freeing their neighborhood or land (χώρα, 1 MS; or γειτονία, neighborhood, 2 MSS; Coptic ⲑⲟϣ, district or nome) of the Hieracite error. According to the story, the problem emerges not within an external ascetic community, but rather because the Hieracite ascetic, whether located within a village or in its immediate environs, has disturbed the local episcopally centered Christianity controlled by the bishop. Given the

---

80. Judge, "Earliest Use"; Goehring, "Through a Glass Darkly" (chap. 3 in the present volume); idem, "Encroaching Desert"; idem, "Withdrawing from the Desert: Pachomius and the Development of Village Monasticism in Upper Egypt," *HTR* 89 (1996) 267–85 (chap. 5 in the present volume).

evidence from Athanasius's letters to virgins, one suspects that this story is best understood as depicting a similar situation, namely, Hieracite ascetic practices and teachings infiltrating the bishop's churches and challenging his religious ideology and his construction of Christian asceticism.

The literary construction of the story suggests, in fact, the author's careful distinction between the institutional authority of the bishop within the inhabited regions (city) and the more charismatic authority of the desert ascetic.[81] With the exception of the Latin version, all of the traditions have the bishop bring Macarios in from the desert to solve the problem of a powerful ascetic wielding his influence in the bishop's realm. If Macarios is to be located in Scetis, he must have traveled some distance to reach the village of Boushem (Coptic) or the Arsenoite nome (Greek). Boushem has been identified with the modern village of Ausim located just north of Cairo,[82] about forty-six miles from the monastery of Macarios in the Wadi Natrun. The Arsenoite nome in the Fayyum is even more distant. In the story, therefore, the bishop's appeal to the desert monk Macarios represents an appeal to the greater authority of the desert to control an ascetic problem in the bishop's own sphere, namely, in his churches and their immediate environs. The bishop's concern is occasioned by the Hieracite's challenge to the clerical authority which he held in his community. Unable to meet the challenge, the bishop summons a desert monk to enter his territory (the church), to defeat the enemy (the Hieracite), and then to return to the desert (presumably Scetis). In the story, it is Macarios who represents the desert, not the Hieracite monk. Even should the latter be imagined to have lived outside of the bishop's city in a nearby village or adjacent desert, he appears in the story as an intimate part of the city's social fabric. The true desert anchorite, on the other hand — Macarios — comes from outside. He is other. He does not belong in the bishop's sphere, but represents an alternate form of authority more capable of confounding the Hieracite. While he can enter the bishop's sphere and fight on behalf of the bishop's cause, he cannot remain there. As the story

---

81. Rousseau, *Ascetics*.

82. E. Amélineau, *La géographie de l'égypte à l'epoche copte* (Paris: Imprimerie nationale, 1893; reprint, Osnabrück: Otto Zeller, 1973) 51–54. The Ethiopic Wesim likely also refers to Ausim.

ends, in fact, Macarios leaves the bishop and returns to the desert (εἰς τὴν ἔρημον), taking the man whom he raised from the dead with him. The latter, whom Macarios baptized, remained with Macarios in the desert for three years before he died. In the context of the story, the Hieracite and his following belong more to the sphere of the city than to that of the desert.

Once again a text used to support the Hieracite influence in the desert proves itself, on closer examination, to be capable of an alternative reading. In fact, with the exception of the later *Life of Epiphanius,* the sources that refer specifically to Hieracas and his followers seem to situate the movement and its influence in a more urban setting where, because of its alternative ideology and social construction of the church, it came into conflict with the local bishops. The evidence from the more contemporary sources indicates that Hieracas was a learned ascetic teacher (Harnack) who drew a considerable following from the growing Christian community in Leontopolis, whose ideology supported creative ascetic living arrangements (Elm), and whose separatist beliefs and practices eventually led him into conflict with the emerging episcopally centered Christianity represented by Athanasius (Brakke). That his teachings, like those of his intellectual ancestor Origen, influenced later Christian ascetics, including some who lived in the desert, need not be doubted. The contention that he himself lived outside of Leontopolis with his followers, however, seems to depend more on the ongoing association of asceticism with the notion of withdrawal to the desert than with the evidence of the sources.

The relocation of Hieracas back into the city necessitates a reexamination of his influence on the developing monastic traditions in Egypt.[83] His significance as an urban ascetic lies in the fact that he was creating in the city what would eventually emerge more fully in the withdrawn setting of the desert, namely, a separatist ascetic community in which ascetics, who practiced their ascesis in their individual abodes, came together for occasional communal meetings. Harnack had, in fact, already credited Hieracas with taking the innovative step that linked the intellectual impulses of Origen's thought

---

83. Recall that not everyone followed Heussi's lead in moving Hieracas out of Leontopolis. See above, n. 24

with the creation of an academic ascetic association (*ein Mönchverein; ein wissenschaftlich gerichteten Asketenverein*) or school (*seine Mönche zugleich seine Schüler waren*) composed of and limited to virgins, monks, continent persons, and widows.[84] While he did not explore the significance of this development further, his fundamental thesis remains sound. As an outstanding teacher of an inner-city ascetic school, Hieracas's intellectual speculation and innovative ideas, as well as the episcopal reaction to them, make perfect sense in the context of the then current conflict between the episcopal and academic models of Christianity. The tension between these two models is well described by David Brakke in his recent study, "Canon Formation and Social Conflict in Fourth-Century Egypt." Referring to the Arian conflict, he observes that it

> was the most spectacular example of this tension between what scholars have called episcopal and academic Christianities. Two forms of Christian life clashed. On the one hand, the episcopate was centered around the practices of worship and dealt with conflicts juridically as questions of admission to the cult; on the other hand, the school was centered around the personalities of outstanding teachers and dealt with conflicts scholastically as questions of intellectual speculation and debate.[85]

The accounts of Hieracas and his opponents preserved in the sources correspond very well indeed with these two forms of Christianity. Epiphanius, in fact, associates Hieracas with Origen, a primary figure in the academic model, and his description of Hieracas's speculative teaching and scriptural exegesis clearly situates him as a Christian teacher within this model. The opposition that Hieracas and his followers arouse likewise comes from figures (Epiphanius, Athanasius, an unidentified bishop) representing the episcopal model.

While Epiphanius's account of Hieracas focuses primarily on his theoretical teachings, it was in fact the formation and practices of his innovative separatist ascetic association that sharpened the conflict between him and the episcopacy.[86] Through the creation of his ascetic association, he moved the academic model directly into the sphere of activity that the episcopal model had, in particular, defined

---

84. Harnack, "Hierakas," 38–39.

85. Brakke, "Canon Formation," 399; see also Rowan Williams, *Arius: Heresy and Tradition* (London: Darton, Longman, & Todd, 1987) 82–91.

86. Brakke, *Athanasius*, 48.

as its own. The issue was not simply that Hieracas advocated the co-habitation of male and female ascetics, though that was bad enough, but at a more fundamental level, he had challenged the episcopacy's control of worship and the requirements for admission to the cult. In Leontopolis, Hieracas not only created an academic school devoted to intellectual speculation and debate, but he fashioned the school as a separate worship community with its own psalms and its own requirements for admission.[87]

Hieracas was thus forming a separate ascetic community within the broader Christian community in the city of Leontopolis. The ascetic impulse, present from the beginnings of the Christian move-ment, became in Leontopolis an issue of Christian community and thus of church polity. Hieracas's creative steps[88] forced those rep-resenting the episcopal model to define more clearly their own understanding of ascetic practice within the church. Athanasius de-fended definitions that supported an inclusive church in which both married and ascetic Christians had their valued place. Virgins, as brides of Christ, should not enter into ascetic marriages, but remain secluded in their homes or monasteries as much as possible.[89] Male ascetics, as he fashioned them in his creative *Life of Antony*, should shun "academic models of ascetic authority and instead [use] Antony [as] a pattern for moral imitation."[90] Perhaps even more significant, he uses the *Life of Antony* to locate the sphere of male ascetic practice outside of the city. Antony finds ascetic perfection through spatial withdrawal from the sphere that Athanasius would have understood as the domain of the episcopacy. While Antony can of course later return to support the episcopacy, the source of his own authority as an ascetic lies in the desert. Athanasius, through his *Life of Antony*, effectively took control of the impulse to form separate ascetic com-munities by shifting its focus away from the academic setting, where

---

87. Sexual abstinence was a requirement for admission. Attendance was thus lim-ited to virgins, monks, continent persons, and widows. The fact that Epiphanius credits Hieracas with composing his own psalms further suggests that their worship services had their own unique elements.

88. I do not mean to suggest here that Hieracas alone was responsible for the con-nection of an ascetic community with the academic model of Christianity. The sources do not allow such a conclusion. He does serve, however, as a prime example of the connection.

89. Brakke, *Athanasius*, 21–44.

90. Brakke, *Athanasius*, 270.

it had developed in terms of an ideological separation within the broader Christian community, and redirecting it to the more benign issue of the spatial separation of ascetic Christians from their less ascetically oriented counterparts.[91] The separation of ascetic communities in the desert or within walled complexes had the further advantage of withdrawing them from the immediate sphere of the episcopacy. While the image of withdrawal is most often portrayed and understood in terms of the ascetic's flight from the world, it also represents for the episcopacy the removal of a competing form of authority from the episcopacy's immediate sphere of influence. The ascetic impulse for community is thus honored, while its threat as an ideologically destructive force within the episcopal sphere is removed.

Hieracas and his followers, located within the city of Leontopolis, represent an important early step in the development of Egyptian monasticism. They most clearly represent the impulse toward a separate ascetic community that emerged in the Christian *urban* environment in the late third and early fourth centuries. The impulse likely came from within the academic model of Christianity, and its ideological basis and threat to the emerging episcopal model of the church quickly aroused a response. The growth of spatially separated monastic communities, which may well have originated simultaneously, was quickly recognized and supported by the episcopacy as the acceptable alternative. The impulse toward ascetic community could not be denied, but the episcopacy could use its own power and literary talents to support and foster a withdrawn form of community less challenging to its authority. The success of the episcopacy in fostering the spatially withdrawn or separated model of ascetic community resulted finally in the general association of ascetics and their communities with the desert, an association that in the end led ironically to the literary re-creation of Hieracas as a withdrawn "desert" ascetic.

---

91. Goehring, "Encroaching Desert."

PART TWO

ASCETIC ORGANIZATION
AND IDEOLOGICAL BOUNDARIES

7

Pachomius's Vision of Heresy: The Development of a Pachomian Tradition

Pachomian traditions are complex. Various lives (*Vitae*), letters, rules, regulations, sermons, instructions, apophthegms, and fragmentary accounts survive from the Pachomian community.[1] These are supplemented by the description of non-Pachomian monastic tourists,[2] ecclesiastical authors,[3] and minimal archaeological evidence.[4] Only certain letters have a sure claim of going back to Pachomius himself,[5] and while the letters, instructions, and regulations of Horsiesius appear to be authentic, they derive from the post-Pachomius period in which the life of the founder had already been glorified for edification at the expense of history.[6] The remaining evidence, including the *Vitae*, represents the tradition, at best, through the eyes of latter-day Pachomian monks. The Pachomian *Rule* likewise has gone through

First published in *Mus* 95 (1982) 241–62.

1. The sources are extensive. Lefort's efforts form the basis for work on the Coptic sources. Lefort, *S. Pachomii vita bohairice scripta*; idem, *S. Pachomii vitae sahidice scriptae*; idem, *Oeuvres*; idem, *Vies coptes*. The standard reference work for the Greek *Vitae* is that of Halkin, *Sancti Pachomii Vitae Graecae*. The Latin material is found in Boon, *Pachomiana latina*, and Van Cranenburgh, *Vie latine*. The Arabic *Vita* (*Am*) is found in Amélineau, *Monuments au IVe siècle*. The entire Pachomian corpus in English translation is available in a convenient edition published by Veilleux, *Pachomian Koinonia*. The bibliography in these volumes lists the sources not noted above.

2. Palladius, *Historia Lausiaca* 32–34; *Historia Monachorum in Aegypto* 3; Cassian, *Institutiones* 4; Veilleux, *Liturgie*, 138–54.

3. Sozomen, *Historia ecclesiastica* 3.14; Jerome, *Praefatio Hieronymi*, in Boon, *Pachomiana latina*, 3–9.

4. Debono, "Basilique"; Robinson and van Elderen, "First Season"; idem, "Second Season"; van Elderen, "Nag Hammadi Excavation"; Grossmann, "Basilica"; Lease, "Fourth Season."

5. Quecke, *Briefe Pachoms*; Veilleux, *Liturgie*, 135.

6. The problems experienced by Horsiesius in leading the community after Pachomius's death naturally led to a reminiscence of the way things were. The current difficulties were judged against the "golden age" under Pachomius. *G1* 127–28; Horsiesius, *Liber Horsiesii* 47 (Veilleux, *Pachomian Koinonia*, 3.206–7); idem, Letter 4 (Chester Beatty MS Ac 1495; Veilleux, *Pachomian Koinonia*, 3.161–65).

various stages,[7] and the question of pseudepigraphical authorship must hang heavy over the various sermons and instructions.[8] The *Vitae* are hagiography. In them, history serves only as a guise through which to tell the real story, the glorious and successful way of life of "our father, Apa Pachomius." The *Vitae* function as guidebooks, in which the lives of the monks who have gone before serve as a type and model (*imitatio patrum*) for the life in accordance with Christ.[9]

In such material, one has not only to deal with the development of the oral and written traditions within the Pachomian communities, but also with the use of these traditions by non-Pachomian groups both inside and outside Egypt.[10] The vast majority of the surviving Sahidic texts, for example, come from the closely related, but non-Pachomian,[11] White Monastery of Shenoute. A late library inventory from that monastery lists among its holdings twenty copies of the *Life of Pachomius*.[12] From the fragments of these *Lives* that survive, it is clear that they were not simply multiple copies of a single version, but various redactions or editions of the material.[13] Furthermore, the most complete form of the Coptic *Vita* that survives is in Bohairic, the dialect of Lower Egypt. Non-Pachomian influences from this region are to be expected.[14] Already in the Coptic tradition alone, the complexity is very great.

The *Vita* also survives in various Greek, Arabic, and Latin editions.[15] Although the Greek tradition originated within the Pachomian community,[16] it was destined to become a vehicle through which the non-Egyptian, Eastern church presented its view of Pa-

---

7. Veilleux, *Liturgie*, 116–32.

8. Tito Orlandi, "Commento letterario," chap. 6 in Orlandi et al., "Pachomiana Coptica," manuscript. Cf. idem, "Coptic Literature," in Pearson and Goehring, *Roots*, 60–63.

9. *Epistula Ammonis* 23. Frank, *ΑΓΓΕΛΙΚΟΣ ΒΙΟΣ*, 4.

10. Thus Lefort established that the shorter form of the *Rule* was produced for Italian monasteries. L. Th. Lefort, "Un texte original de la Règle de saint Pachôme," *CRAI* (1919) 341–48; James E. Goehring, "The Letter of Ammon and Pachomian Monasticism" (Ph.D. diss., Claremont Graduate School, 1981) 4.

11. Leipoldt, *Schenute von Atripe*, 36.

12. W. E. Crum, "Inscriptions from Shenoute's Monastery," *JTS* 5 (1904) 566.

13. Veilleux, *Liturgie*, 37–107; Lefort, *Vies coptes*, LXII–LXX.

14. Veilleux (*Liturgie*, 21–24 and 108–11) notes the Lower Egyptian influence on the Greek *Paralipomena* and *Letter of Ammon*; cf. Goehring, *Letter of Ammon*, 114–15.

15. See above, n. 1.

16. *G1* 98–99.

chomian monasticism. The earliest Greek form of the *Vita* survives in an eleventh-century manuscript from the Calabrian monastery of St. John of Apiro in southern Italy.[17] Even before the material left Egypt, however, it was molded under the influence of non-Pachomian monasteries and the Alexandrian church hierarchy. The *Paralipomena*, a collection of episodes about Pachomius that have not yet "jelled" into a *vita*, reveals Lower Egyptian influences.[18] The important *Letter of Ammon* likewise imposes Nitriote practices on the Pachomians.[19] It is the best example of the presentation of the Pachomian tradition through the eyes of the ecclesiastical hierarchy.[20]

The recognition of the problem of non-Pachomian influences on the tradition is heightened by the division of the Pachomian community during the reign of Justinian I (527–65 C.E.). Justinian attempted to force the Chalcedonian position upon the Pachomian monks. A large number chose instead to leave the monasteries, including the abbot of the central monastery of Pbow, Apa Abraham.[21] While it is assumed that the Chalcedonian elements remained in the monasteries, there is virtually no evidence of the history of the community after these events. The non-Chalcedonian Copts did not support this new Chalcedonian brand of Pachomian monasticism, at least not in Upper Egypt.[22] They had no reason to record its history.

The efforts of the church hierarchy to control the movement eventually destroyed it in its original form. In the process, it identified the earlier traditions as its own.[23] One has only to compare the renown of Antony and Pachomius in non-Egyptian Greek- and Latin-

---

17. Halkin, *Sancti Pachomii Vitae Graecae*, 10; Goehring, *Letter of Ammon*, 34–35.

18. Veilleux, *Liturgie*, 21–24.

19. Veilleux, *Liturgie*, 108–11, 298–305.

20. Goehring, *Letter of Ammon*, 103–22.

21. Van Cauwenbergh, *Étude*, 153–59; Campagnano, "Monaci egiziani"; Kuhn, *Panegyric on Apollo*, xiii–xvi; James E. Goehring, "Chalcedonian Power Politics and the Demise of Pachomian Monasticism" (OP 15; Claremont, Calif.: Institute for Antiquity and Christianity, 1989). The latter appears as chapter 12 in the present volume.

22. The Chalcedonian brand of Pachomian monasticism appears to be linked originally to the Lower Egyptian monastery on Canopus. Three Chalcedonian archbishops were supplied by that monastery in the fifth to sixth centuries. Frend, *Rise of the Monophysite Movement*, 163, 274.

23. The attempt to force the Chalcedonian position upon the Egyptian church drove the already existing wedge between the Greek Melchite elements and the native Egyptians much deeper. The Greek Chalcedonian elements eventually disappeared from Egypt. While the Coptic *Life of Pachomius* survived in Egypt, the Greek version owes its continued existence to the fact that it was taken out of Egypt.

speaking areas to the ignorance about Shenoute outside of Egypt to recognize this fact.[24] The *Life of Pachomius*, like the *Life of Antony*, became a paradigm for monastic life in support of the church.

These factors force many negative conclusions with respect to the historical value of the sources. The historical Pachomius, to a large extent, lies beyond the grasp of modern historians. Scholars have become increasingly aware that literary forms take precedent over historical fact.[25] The literature tells us more about the attitudes at the moment of its composition than about the figures it portrays.[26] Pressing the positive aspect of hagiographic literature, Brown asserts that "there was more to this than validating by a standard literary device propaganda that put a strain on the reader's credulity. For the hagiographer was recording the moments when the seemingly extinct past and the unimaginably distant future had pressed into the present."[27] In pressing into the present, however, the past and future are necessarily molded by it. If this is the case, how can the historian hope to arrive at the formative period of Pachomian history?

For the most part, early Pachomian history is dependent upon the *Lives of Pachomius*. Working with the various forms of the *Vita*, scholars have attempted to understand their interrelationship and through this understanding to get back to the earliest tradition. The *Life of Pachomius* survives in various forms in Coptic (Sahidic and Bohairic), Greek, Arabic, and Latin. While the relationship of the various versions of the *Vita* within a single language tradition may be fairly clear,[28] the precise interrelationship of the language groups is difficult to surmise.[29] This has been particularly true for the rela-

---

24. Shenoute, whose renown arose later, had no Greek life to pass out of Egypt. He was a Copt known to the Copts alone. This factor has endured well into modern times. General studies seldom ignore Pachomius, while frequently failing to even mention Shenoute. Derwas Chitty, in his *The Desert a City*, never mentions Shenoute.

25. Edward N. O'Neil, "The Chreia and History," paper delivered at the 1981 annual meeting of the Society of Biblical Literature in San Francisco.

26. The isolation of the "moment" of composition remains a problem, particularly in the compiled Pachomian traditions.

27. Peter Brown, *The Cult of the Saints: Its Rise and Function in Latin Christianity* (Chicago: University of Chicago Press, 1981) 81.

28. G1 is widely accepted as the most primitive form of the Greek *Vita*. Halkin, *Sancti Pachomii Vitae Graecae*, 90; Veilleux, *Liturgie*, 34–35.

29. The complexity of Veilleux's analysis (*Liturgie*, 103–7) is telling. Cf. François Halkin, review of *La liturgie dans le cénobitisme pachômien*, by Armand Veilleux, *AB* 88 (1970) 337; Goehring, *Letter of Ammon*, 3–23.

tionship between the Coptic and the Greek versions. The quest for the earliest tradition, which in scholarly circles often carries the connotation of the best,[30] led to a division among scholars and to charges of "coptomania" and "grecomanie."[31]

Today, that division has been quieted. Halkin has firmly established the *Vita prima (G1)*, together with the *Letter of Ammon* and the *Paralipomena*, as the primary Greek sources.[32] While the importance of the Coptic traditions established by Lefort has been generally accepted,[33] they have not so much replaced as supplemented the Greek material. It is clear that the earliest form of the Coptic tradition no longer survives in anything like a complete form. The history of the Pachomian community reaches us only through the primary compilations and translations of earlier material. Shared oral traditions lie behind all of the surviving versions of the *Vita*,[34] be they Coptic *(Bo)*, Greek *(G1)*, or Arabic *(Ag)*.[35] No single source has a clear claim to absolute authority. All drew from earlier material which is no longer extant.

The simple solution of a single surviving primary *Life of Pachomius* from which to reconstruct Pachomian history does not exist. The historian must sift and weigh the material from the various *Vitae* to determine, in each case, which account deserves to be followed. Actually, behind the highly visible debate over Coptic versus Greek priority, Pachomian scholars have always recognized this fact. Achelis had put it well already in 1896 when he stated with respect to the *Vita* traditions that "in jeder findet sich soviel Gutes und soviel Sekundares, dass man bald einen, bald der andern Recht geben

---

30. While the equation of earliest with best has its merits, the Pachomian traditions are too complex to allow for such a simple solution. This is particularly the case for the larger units of the tradition, e.g., the Coptic tradition versus the Greek tradition.

31. Derwas J. Chitty, "Pachomian Sources Reconsidered," *JEH* 5 (1954) 38–77; L. Th. Lefort, "Les sources coptes pachômiennes, *Mus* 67 (1954) 217–29.

32. Halkin, *Sancti Pachomii Vitae Graecae*, 56.

33. Lefort, *Vies coptes*, XIII–XCI.

34. Chadwick, "Pachomios," 15–17.

35. Veilleux, *Liturgie*, 17–107; idem, "Le problème des Vies de saint Pachôme," *RAM* 42 (1966) 287–305. Veilleux's claims about the Arabic *Life of Pachomius* in Göttingen *(Ag)* have not received universal acceptance. Chadwick, "Pachomios," 15; Adalbert de Vogüé, "La vie arabe de saint Pachôme et ses deux sources présumées," *AB* 91 (1973) 379–90; idem, "Saint Pachôme et son oeuvre d'après plusieurs études récentes," *RHE* 69 (1974) 425–53.

muss."[36] Of course, when all the sources agree, the historian's task is simplified.[37] Nonetheless, even then, each story or pericope must be explored in all its forms. The historian must determine the forces that led to these various forms. Only after this has been done can he begin to reconstruct the earliest layer.

Festugière and Veilleux have done considerable work along these lines. Festugière studied the relationship of the individual stories in G1 with their parallels in the Coptic tradition.[38] Veilleux explored the nature of the various sources as he had reconstructed them.[39] Although his reconstructed sources have not received universal acceptance,[40] his detailed efforts have added to our understanding of the development of the Pachomian traditions.

In such reconstruction, however, a methodological roadblock is encountered as soon as one has completed this initial sifting. Even at the earliest recoverable stage of the tradition, hagiographic concerns are fully present. It may be that this is as far as the historian can go in recovering the formative period of Pachomian history. After all, the historian has already removed the later layers of the tradition that could serve as a comparison. To move behind the remaining, single, earliest tradition involves speculation.

It is the aim of the current essay to suggest a methodological innovation and to employ it in an effort to reach back into the formative Pachomian period. The innovation involves the recognition of the limitation of the search for the most primitive written tradition. In comparing the various forms of the tradition, the aim of earlier research has been to filter out the later developments and thus to arrive at the earliest form of the story. Once one has that "earliest form," the process is at an end. If, however, as a concomitant task with the recovery of the earliest form of the story, the historian seeks to understand the trajectory of the story's hagiographic development, he may be able to trace that trajectory, at least in a general way, back

---

36. "... so much that is good and so much that is secondary is found in each, that one must give preference sometimes to one, sometimes to the other" (Hans Achelis, review of *Pachomius und das älteste Klosterleben*, by Georg Grützmacher, *ThLZ* 9 [1896] 240–44).

37. Rousseau, *Ascetics*, 18.

38. Festugière, *Moines d'orient*.

39. Veilleux, *Liturgie*, 69–107.

40. See above, n. 35.

behind the earliest surviving account. Although the method cannot create new hard facts, it can detect the developing and changing hagiographic concerns present in the sources. With these changes in the open, a clearer picture of the original Pachomian concerns is allowed to emerge.

The present essay seeks to employ these ideas in a new look at a single Pachomian pericope, Pachomius's vision of heresy. Both the fluidity of the sources in which this tradition is embedded and its hagiographical development within those sources will be examined. The purpose is not to reconstruct the original "historical" vision. Rather, by tracing the vision's hagiographical development, the factors involved in the formation of the various stages of the tradition will be clarified. By noting the trajectory of these factors, one can separate the more original Pachomian understanding of the account from the later, more developed use of the material to support a new, later Pachomian, and/or non-Pachomian cause.

Pachomius's vision of heresy survives in one Coptic (*Bo*) and two Greek (*G1* and *Letter of Ammon*) sources.[41] A fourth account from the *Paralipomena*, though not a precise parallel, is close enough in content to be included in the discussion.[42] The four accounts are printed below (my translations).[43]

BOHAIRIC LIFE OF PACHOMIUS 103

(INTRODUCTION) Again one day it happened that the Lord revealed a vision to our father Pachomius.

(VISION) And when he looked he saw the likeness of Amenti, dark and oppressive, in the middle of which stood an upright pillar. And there were voices on every side of it crying out and saying, "Behold, the light is here with us." The men in that place were groping

---

41. It is present in the Arabic *Vita* (Amélineau, *Monuments au IVe siècle*, 498f.), in which it seems to be a translation of the Coptic account. Hence, I have not dealt with this version in the present study.

42. Parallels exist to this vision in *Bo* 66 and *G1* 71.

43. The translations are based on the following texts. *Bo*: Lefort, *S. Pachomii vita bohairice scripta*, 130–32; *G1*: Halkin, *Sancti Pachomii Vitae Graecae*, 67–68; *Epistula Ammonis*: Halkin, *Sancti Pachomii Vitae Graecae*, 103; *Paralipomena*: Halkin, *Sancti Pachomii Vitae Graecae*, 140–41. A short portion of the account was omitted in *Bo*. It is supplied from its Coptic and Arabic parallels using Veilleux's translation (*Pachomian Koinonia*, 1.144). Veilleux's translations were consulted throughout.

about because the darkness of that oppressive [place] was great. And it was very frightening. And again when they would hear, "Behold, the light is with us," they would run there searching for the light, hoping to see it. But as they ran ahead, they would hear another voice behind them, "Behold, the light is here." And they would turn back immediately because of the voices that they heard, searching for the light. And he also saw in the vision some in the darkness who were circling around a pillar, thinking that they were making progress and approaching the light, without realizing that they were circling around a pillar.

And he looked again and saw the entire congregation of the community there, proceeding in single file and holding on to one another lest they become lost because of that great darkness. And those who led them had a small light to illumine their way, like the light of a lamp. And only four of the brothers could see the light, while all the others saw no light at all. Our father Pachomius watched how they proceeded. If one let go of the one in front of him, he would get lost in the darkness together with all those who were following him. And he saw one called Paniski, who was great among the brothers, together with some others cease from following the one who preceded them and led them. And the man of God Pachomius cried out in ecstasy to each one who had not yet let go by name, saying, "Hold on to the one ahead of you lest you become lost." And the small light that went before the brothers, went before them until they reached a great opening, above which was a great light. They proceeded up to the opening, but it had a large knot [in it], so that the light could not descend past it, nor those in the darkness ascend through it.

(INTERPRETATION) And after our father Pachomius had seen these things, he was also informed of the interpretation of the vision by the one who had shown him these things. "The image of Amenti that you saw is this world. And the oppressive darkness there is all the futile errors and vain anxieties. And the men who were in it are the souls of the ignorant. And the voices that cry out, 'Behold, the light is with us,' are the heretics and the schismatics each of which say, 'Ours is the correct dogma.' The pillars around which they turn are the originators of error in whom the simple have confidence because they say, 'We are the ones who save; they are the ones who lead astray.' The brothers guiding them are all those who love the

Lord and proceed in the right faith as it is written: 'For you are all one in Christ.' And again he was told that those among the brothers who let go represent the bishops who are in the right faith of Christ, but are in communion with the heretics and lead astray a multitude by what they teach to each of the simple men. And they forsake those who behave well and scandalize the multitudes, as it is written: 'Woe to him through whom scandal comes.' [The small light guiding the brothers is the gospel, divine truth; truly he who is deluded by himself and by his passions is not pure, as it is written, 'Among them God has blinded the hearts of the faithless ones of this age that they might not see the light of the gospel of Christ who is the image of God.']⁴⁴ That is why that light is small. For it is written in the holy gospels about the kingdom of heaven that 'It is like a mustard seed that is small.' And the abundant light above the opening is the word spoken by the apostle: 'Until we all attain to this same idea of the faith and the knowledge of the Son of God, to a perfect man, the measure of the stature of the fullness of Christ Jesus.'"

(RESULTING ACTION) And after our father Pachomius had seen these things, he called the brothers whom he saw let go in the vision, and advised them to struggle in the fear of the Lord so as to live. But when they had left him, they were not vigilant in turning away from their negligence and their contempt, but persevered in their former attitude until they became strangers to the brethren and to the eternal life of the Lord Jesus.

THE FIRST GREEK LIFE OF PACHOMIUS 102

(INTRODUCTION) And one day Abba Pachomius himself told the brothers this, which is a vision:

(VISION) "I once saw a large place with many pillars in it. And there were many men in the place who could not see where they were going. And some of them were circling around the pillars, thinking that they had traveled a great distance toward the light. And a voice [was heard] from all sides: 'Behold, the light is here.' And they turned back in order to find it. And there would be a

---

44. This portion of the text does not appear in *Bo*. It has been supplied from Veilleux's translation (*Pachomian Koinonia*, 1.144), which draws on the Coptic and Arabic parallels. Lefort, *Vies coptes*, 174.

voice again, and they would turn back again. And there was great wretchedness in that place.

"And then I saw a lamp moving before many men. Four of them saw it and all [of the others] were following them, each holding fast to the shoulder of the one near [him] lest he go astray in the dark. And if someone let go of the man in front of him, he would go astray together with those following [him]. And when I recognized two who let go, I shouted to them: 'Hold on, lest you destroy yourselves and others.' And with the lamp leading, those who followed went up through an opening to this light."

(INTERPRETATION) After he had seen these things, he told them to some in private. And after this, we heard from them much later also the following interpretation. "This world is dark on account of the error of each heresy thinking it is on the right path. The lamp is the faith in Christ, which saves those who believe aright and leads to the kingdom of God." [G3 adds: "And the four who were leading [them] to it are the four evangelists."]

THE LETTER OF AMMON 12

(INTRODUCTION) And when Pachomius heard these things from Theodore, he said to him: "As you were able to see and hear, so was it shown to you. For I too was troubled when I took up the solitary life. At one time I was called upon by the followers of Melitius the Lycopolitan, and at another by those of Marcion, to join them and study their teachings. And I learned that there were other groups, each of which claimed to possess the truth. And with many tears, I beseeched God to reveal to me which ones possessed the truth, for I was utterly confused.

(VISION) "And while I was still praying, I became ecstatic and saw everything under heaven as if it were night. And from different regions I heard a voice calling: 'The truth is here.' And I saw many following each voice, being led by one another in darkness. And only in the eastern region of the world did a lamp appear on high, shining like a morning star. And from there I heard a voice say to me: 'Do not be deceived by those who draw [men] into darkness, but follow this light, for the truth is in it.'

(INTERPRETATION) "And immediately a voice arose and said to me:

'This lamp that you see shining like a morning star will shine for you now more than the sun. For it is the proclamation of Christ's gospel, which is proclaimed in his holy church in which you were baptized. The one who is calling is the Christ who is in Alexander, the bishop of the Alexandrian church. The other voices in the darkness are the voices of the heresies. There is a demon in the leader of each heresy who calls and leads many astray.'

"And so, when I saw many in shining garments running toward the lamp, I blessed God.

(RESULTING ACTION) "And disregarding those who would lead me astray, I dwelt with the man of God Palamon, who was an imitator of the saints, until an angel of the Lord appeared to me and said: 'Warm those who come to you with the fire that God has kindled in you.' And guided by him, I established these monasteries through God.

"Know also that Athanasius, the bishop of the Alexandrian church, is full of the Holy Spirit."

PARALIPOMENA 17

(INTRODUCTION) And as the brothers were going to prayers, he also joined with them and finished the prayers. And when they departed to eat, he remained alone in the house in which he was accustomed to perform the prayers of the synaxis. And after he shut the door, he prayed to God, requesting that the state of the brothers after these events [*Para* 15–16] be made known to him and what would befall them in later times. And he continued in prayer from the tenth hour until they gave the brothers the signal for the night service.

(VISION) About midnight, a heavenly apparition suddenly appeared to him, making known to him the perfection of the state of the brothers after these events and that they would live in like manner righteously according to Christ, and that there would be a future expansion of the monasteries.

But he also saw a countless multitude of brothers journeying along an extremely deep and dark valley. And many of them wanted to climb up out of the valley, but did not have the strength. Many, although they encountered one another face to face, did not recognize each other because of the great darkness surrounding them. Many fell from exhaustion, and others cried out in a pitiful voice. But a few from among them with great effort were able to come up out of that valley. And immediately as they came up, they were met by a light. And proceeding to the light, they heartily gave thanks to God.

(INTERPRETATION) Then the blessed man knew what was to befall the brothers in the end, and the negligence that would arise in those times, both the great hardening and error, and the failing of the shepherds that would befall them, and that the most negligent [monks] of today will rule over the good, conquering them by their number.

(RESULTING ACTION) And these things are only an example, the beginning of which we the writers have gone through. For wicked men will rule the brothers, and those without knowledge will control the monasteries and fight for rank. And the good will be persecuted by the wicked, and the good will have no confidence in the monasteries. And, as it is said, divine things will be transformed into human things.

It is clear from a summary reading of the four accounts that the *Paralipomena (Para)* episode is distinct. The remaining three versions record the same vision, though the setting and detail vary considerably. Although the precise relationship between the versions in the Bohairic *Vita (Bo)* and the Greek *Vita prima (G1)* remains obscure, the fact that they both place this episode toward the middle of Pachomius's career is witness to their connection.[45] In the *Letter of Ammon (EpAm)*, on the other hand, the vision is given as a reminiscence of an event that occurred to the newly converted Pachomius. It served as his guide, distinguishing between orthodoxy and heresy and setting him off in his career on the right path. The *EpAm* dates the episode to the reign of the Alexandrian patriarch Alexander (312–28 C.E.). Thus, on the basis of the setting alone, the *EpAm* version is distinguished from that recorded in *Bo* and *G1*.

Festugière, in his comparative analysis of *Bo* and *G1*, concluded that *Bo* preserved the better or more complete version of Pachomius's vision of heresy. *G1* "condense à l'exces" (condenses to excess).[46]

---

45. The parallel episodes are clearly laid out by Festugière, *Moines d'orient*, 8–14.
46. Festugière, *Moines d'orient*, 51–52; cf. 70–71.

While *Bo* does offer a more detailed account, it is not immediately clear whether *G1* has condensed an original *Bo*-type version or *Bo* has expanded a *G1*-type account. Although *G1* is occasionally obscure due to its brevity,[47] *Bo* has difficulty keeping all of the threads straight in its longer version. *Bo* appears to interweave multiple traditions.

Four sections can be distinguished in the episodes: the introduction, the vision, the interpretation, and the resulting action. The four sections occur in *Bo, EpAm,* and *Para. G1* does not offer a resulting action. In the *Bo* version, the vision section has two parts: a general vision of heresy and a particularization of that vision in terms of the Pachomian community. In the first part, the general vision, Pachomius sees the likeness of Amenti. It is dark and oppressive, and a single pillar stands in its middle. Men are seen groping about and hurrying to follow various voices that claim to possess the light. A number of these men are seen to be circling the pillar, thinking that they are making progress, unaware that they are going in a circle.

To this point, the vision is general in nature. In *Bo,* however, it simply sets the stage for the second, particular half of the vision. Pachomius looks again and sees the entire congregation of the community (ϯⲑⲱⲟⲩⲧⲥ ⲧⲏⲣⲥ ⲛ̄ⲧⲉϯⲕⲟⲓⲛⲱⲛⲓⲁ) proceeding in single file through the darkness. Each is holding on to the one in front of him lest he become lost together with those behind him. The entire line is following a small light which only four of the brothers can see. At this point, the particularization increases. Pachomius sees a certain Paniski, a great one among the brothers, let go. A number of others let go with him and are presumably lost. Pachomius responds by crying out to the others to hold firm. They do and proceed to an opening that leads to the great light.

Problems arise in the interpretation of the vision that follows as a result of the attempt to deal with both the general and the particular parts of the vision together. The interpretation of the general part is fairly straightforward. The likeness of Amenti is this world. The oppressive darkness is the futile errors and anxieties in it. The men groping about are the souls of the ignorant, and the voices that claim to possess the light are the heretics and schismatics. The pillars

---

47. *G1* is, in general, very concise.

(*sic*) around which the men turn are the originators of the heresies, the heresiarchs. Beyond the difficulty in moving from the single pillar in the vision to pillars in the interpretation,[48] the equations are fairly clear.

When the interpretation moves on to the second, particular half of the vision, however, a major problem occurs. The interpretation does not follow the particular elements of the vision. It is as though the interpretation has its own particular point to make and will make it regardless of the particular elements in the vision that it is supposed to be interpreting. No mention of Pachomius's monks or monastic community occurs in the interpretation. Rather it moves from the simple ones who are being deceived by the heresiarchs into circling the pillars to the brothers who love the Lord and guide them in the right faith. In the vision, these brothers were not connected with those circling the pillar, but with those leading the entire Pachomian community through the darkness. The ones who let go in the vision (there identified as the high-ranking Pachomian monk, Paniski, among others) are interpreted to represent the bishops, who, although their faith is correct, are in communion with the heretics. Finally, the small light, which in the vision only four of the brothers could see, is identified as the gospel, the divine truth. Thus while the Pachomian community figures prominently in the second half of the vision, it disappears completely in the interpretation.

In the action that follows the interpretation in *Bo*, Pachomius calls upon the monks whom he saw "let go" in the vision to correct their ways. They do not heed his warning and eventually become strangers to the Pachomian community and everlasting life. The resulting action thus connects directly with the particular half of the vision, the half that was ignored in the interpretation. The vision serves in typical fashion[49] to reveal an internal Pachomian problem that needs correction. The resulting action, building on the vision, records Pachomius's effort to effect the needed correction. The interpretation, however, has completely ignored this issue. It would appear that the author/compiler of *Bo* is caught in a process of de-

---

48. Festugière, *Moines d'orient*, 51.
49. The clairvoyant revelation of errant monks to Theodore is frequently encountered in the *Letter of Ammon* (*Epistula Ammonis* 3, 17, 19–20, 22, 24, 25, 26); cf. *Bo* 77, 106; *G1* 89.

velopment from a particular vision dealing with a specific problem in the Pachomian community to a reinterpretation of that vision in terms of a later understanding of heresy. In view of the interpretation's reference to bishops in communion with heretics, the most likely setting for this later understanding is the post-Chalcedonian difficulties between the Monophysite and Melchite communities.[50] A comparison with the other versions of this episode will further delineate the development of this tradition within the Pachomian sources.[51]

The closest parallel to the *Bo* version occurs in *G1*. It reveals a number of interesting variants. It is much more concise. The difficulty between the singular pillar of the vision and the plural pillars of the interpretation in *Bo* does not occur.[52] While in *G1* the plural occurs already in the vision, the pillars do not figure at all in the interpretation. In the *G1* version of the vision section, both parts recognized in *Bo* are present. The second part, however, now remains general. The particular connection to the Pachomian community has disappeared. In *G1*, Pachomius sees a dark place with men circling around the pillars. A voice cries from all sides, "Behold, the light is here." At this point, the second part is joined. Pachomius sees a column of men moving single file behind a lamp. Only four of them actually see the lamp. Each holds on to the one before him lest he go astray together with those following him. Pachomius recognizes two men who let go and calls to them to hold firm. The two are not identified. The vision ends by noting that those who followed the lamp went up through a window to the light. The interpretation is brief. It simply states that the world is dark because of the heresies. The lamp is the faith in Christ which saves the orthodox and leads to God's Kingdom. The third Greek life (*G3*) adds that the four who could see the lamp are the four evangelists. There is no resulting action recorded in *G1*.

In this version, the vision is simply a general statement against

---

50. This divisive split had a direct effect on the Pachomian community (see above, p. 139).

51. One must be careful to distinguish the Pachomian community from the Pachomian sources. Ammon was not physically a member of the community when he recorded his account.

52. A problem may be seen in *G1*'s use of a singular voice which is heard coming from all directions. Festugière, *Moines d'orient*, 51.

heresy. While the particular half of the vision from *Bo* that limited it to the Pachomian community is present, those elements in it that made it particular have faded considerably. The line of men following the lamp are not identified as Pachomian monks. Although Pachomius recognizes two of them who let go, the two are not identified. They need not have been monks at all. While in *Bo* the general half of the vision set the stage for its particularization in the second half in terms of the Pachomian community, in *G1* the general half has drawn the particular half into itself. The particular connection to the Pachomian community has all but disappeared.

In the *EpAm*, this process is taken even further. As noted above, the vision is placed at the beginning of Pachomius's career. It functions as evidence that Pachomius was doctrinally pure from the start, having been steered clear of the Melitians and Marcionites through divine revelation. Here again, Pachomius sees the world as darkness. The pillars, however, are gone. He simply hears voices from various regions claiming that the truth[53] is with them. The second part of the vision in *Bo* and *G1* is merged in at this point and becomes almost indistinguishable. There is no single column of men being led by the lamp. Rather, Pachomius sees many following each voice, being led by one another. The lamp merges with the great light beyond the opening reported in *Bo* and *G1*. Now the lamp shines on high in the east. A voice calls from it, telling Pachomius not to be deceived by the other voices. It claims that the truth is in this light to the east.

The interpretation is given by a voice in the vision.[54] It reverses the order of interpretation found in *Bo* and *G1*. Instead of identifying the heresies and moving from there to the light, it identifies the lamp or light first as Christ's gospel. It in turn is linked with Pachomius's baptism and the Alexandrian bishop, Alexander. Finally, the voices are said to represent the heresies. There is a demon in the leader of each which leads men astray.

After the interpretation, Pachomius sees many in shining garments running toward the lamp and blesses God. The resulting action is Pachomius's decision to take up the monastic life under

---

53. *G1* and *Bo* report that the voices claim to possess the light.

54. *Bo* also places the interpretation within the vision. *G1*, on the other hand, while not specifying when Pachomius received the interpretation, reports two stages in the oral traditions between Pachomius and the author.

Palamon and the eventual establishment of his own monastic community. The section ends with a gloss that links its position on orthodoxy to Athanasius, the current patriarch in Alexandria. Thus the *EpAm* not only removes the particular link to the Pachomian community, it places the vision at a time before the community existed. It is a revelation from God of the general distinction between heresy and orthodoxy that serves as a guide to the newly converted Pachomius. The reader is thus assured that the father of coenobitic monasticism was orthodox from the beginning.

It is evident from this examination of the three versions of Pachomius's vision of heresy that the *Bo* version, apart from the altered interpretation,[55] preserves the most particular account. In *Bo*, the vision and resulting action are linked directly to problems within the Pachomian community. In *G1*, on the other hand, while traces of the particular nature of the original vision remain, it has become throughout a general condemnation of heresy. No specific connection to the Pachomian community is made. In *EpAm*, the development in this direction has gone to the extreme. The vision has become an element at the beginning of Pachomius's Christian career. The particular elements of the vision have receded even further into the background. The vision functions to assure the reader of Pachomius's orthodoxy from the start. There is no question of him slowly finding his way to the "orthodox faith." It was revealed to him before he took up the monastic life!

The development of the traditions seems clear. An original account with particular significance for the Pachomian community was variously altered as its chronological and geographical distance from its original *Sitz im Leben* increased. While *Bo* retained the original particular vision and resulting action, it crudely altered the interpretation to make the episode relevant in the post-Chalcedonian, anti-Melchite debate. The Greek tradition, on the other hand, while showing greater literary care in preserving the linkage between vision and interpretation, has generalized the entire episode. Thus its value for later debates on "orthodoxy versus heresy" is increased. The development may be summarized as follows:

---

55. See above, pp. 149–50. The alteration of the interpretation in *Bo* is a later development, unrelated to the generalization of the entire episode in *G1* and *Epistula Ammonis*.

Original Account
(*Bo* minus altered interpretation)

- Particular vision and interpretation
- Specific Pachomian linkage throughout

G1 Account	Bo Account

G1 Account

- General vision and interpretation

- Specific Pachomian linkage has disappeared

Bo Account

- Particular vision, post-Chalcedonian interpretation

- Specific Pachomian linkage in vision and resulting action

EpAm Account

- General vision and interpretation
- Vision occurs prior to the existence of Pachomius's community

Two lines of development are detectable in the tradition. While it is evident that the altered interpretation in *Bo* grew out of the post-Chalcedonian difficulties, it is difficult to say when and where the process of generalization evident in the Greek versions occurred. That it was a process of generalization seems assured. It would be difficult to understand why a general vision against heresy would become particular. On the other hand, as the original particular *Sitz im Leben* receded into the past both chronologically and geographically, the generalization of the account would be natural. Specifics are lost on a wider audience. Furthermore, the content of this particular episode would naturally lead to its generalization as the Pachomian community became a focal point of Alexandrian interest in its own fight against "heresy." Surely there were various forces and stages involved. Within the Pachomian community itself, varied accounts of the same event arose. Not everyone heard or understood it in precisely the same way. Nor would it have been reported and remembered identically among all of the monks in the various monasteries.[56] Even within a single monastery different elements existed that could be expected to retain different traditions. The younger monks were not told everything that was related to the older brothers.[57] The Greek-speaking house learned of Pachomius's words secondhand through an interpreter. While the Greek sources report that the translator worked on the spot next to Pachomius as he spoke — thus insuring the accuracy of their account — the Coptic *Vitae* report that Pachomius's words were translated only after the event, when the assembly had broken up and the Greek-speaking monks returned together to their house.[58] Some of the divergence and generalization could thus have occurred very early within the community. The impetus toward generalization would not have been strong in this setting, however, unless there was some involvement at that early stage with the distinction between the Coptic and Greek members of the community.

The distinction between the Coptic and Greek elements in Egyptian society certainly played a role in the later stages of Pachomian monasticism. It is clear that the Pachomian community suffered during the difficulties between the Coptic and Melchite elements in Egypt in the fifth and sixth centuries.[59] Its monastery at Canopus in Lower Egypt had definite Melchite leanings, while those in Upper Egypt were clearly Monophysite until Justinian forced the Chalcedonian position upon them.[60] This is significant because it was through Alexandria[61] and Canopus that the Pachomian *Vita* traveled beyond Egypt. It was *G1* or a closely related version that served as the basis of the Latin translation.[62] Likewise, the material used by

---

56. There were nine monasteries and two affiliated houses for women between Panopolis and Latopolis by Pachomius's death. After his death, others even further afield were added, including one, in the time of Archbishop Theophilus, at Canopus in the Delta. Peeters, "Dossier copte," 269.

57. *G1* 99.

58. *Bo* 91; *G1* 95; *Epistula Ammonis* 3–4; cf. *Bo* 194.

59. Van Cauwenbergh, *Étude*, 153–59.

60. Van Cauwenbergh, *Étude*, 153–59; Kuhn, *Panegyric on Apollo*, xiii–xvi; Campagnano, "Monaci egiziani," 239–46.

61. Lefort, *Vies coptes*, 389–90.

62. Views vary as to the precise relationship between *G1* and the Latin translation. Veilleux, *Liturgie*, 28–32; Van Cranenburgh, *Vie latine*, 7–27.

Jerome for his Latin translation of the Pachomian *Rule* was obtained through the Pachomian monastery on Canopus.[63] The Coptic versions, on the other hand, survived in Monophysite communities in Upper and Lower Egypt.[64] Thus while the alteration of the heresy episode in *Bo* served to support the Monophysite community, the Greek *Vita* tradition was already moving via the Melchite faction outside of Egypt.

One can see that the pressure on the Greek tradition to generalize Pachomius's vision of heresy would have been greater. While the Coptic version incorporated a new post-Chalcedonian particularism, the Greek tradition was growing closer to the broader Eastern church. The Alexandrian patriarchs, even before Chalcedon, would have had a decided interest in such a development. The Greek tradition functioned to bring Pachomian monasticism under the umbrella of Alexandrian orthodoxy. Of course, the process was symbiotic. As Pachomian and Alexandrian interests began to coincide, the Pachomians would naturally seek to establish their own orthodoxy early in their communal development. One suspects that there was a decided movement in this direction during the efficient administration of Theodore (351–68 C.E.). He had Alexandrian connections, and the problems that he solved — problems confronting the community after Pachomius's death — highlighted the need for greater institutionalization.[65] We have seen that Ammon, a Pachomian monk under Theodore who later became a bishop, carried the development to the extreme. According to him, Pachomius's Alexandrian "orthodoxy" existed before he established the community. Hence, the community was always "orthodox."

What this means in terms of Pachomian history is that the presentation of that history that has come down to us often represents a *Sitz im Leben* other than that of the original Pachomian community. While edification is already basic to the creation of a *Vita*, the movement from particular event to general statement represents a new and important development. The loss of valuable information about the original community occurs through this development. It is

---

63. *Praefatio Hieronymi* 1, in Boon, *Pachomiana latina*, 3–5.
64. Specifically, in the monasteries of Shenoute and the Wadi Natrun.
65. Chadwick, "Pachomios," 17–19; Goehring, "New Frontiers" (chap. 8 in the present volume).

not a question of the historical event itself, if indeed that event even existed, but of the interpretation of that event. Thus in the present example, the surviving forms of Pachomius's vision against heresy reveal a developmental process. Regardless of the "historical" event, the developments in the *Vitae* make it clear that the presentation in the Greek tradition of a general vision against heresy that includes specific support of Alexandrian orthodoxy is secondary. The original statement involved a corrective vision against an error within the Pachomian community. While as such it was edifying to the Pachomian community, the story's lasting appeal beyond the Pachomian community and eventually outside of Egypt lay in its generalization.

The original error in the Pachomian community that served as the *Sitz im Leben* for this vision has not survived in the accounts. Paniski, mentioned in *Bo*, is not found elsewhere in the sources. *Bo* simply records his failure to improve and his loss to the community.

Amélineau, in his edition of the Bohairic and Arabic *Lives*,[66] suggested that this episode was misplaced. He believed that it referred to the difficulties that arose after Pachomius's death. Pachomius died in the plague that ravished his community in 346 C.E.[67] Earlier difficulties with his supposed successor Theodore led him on his deathbed to appoint a certain Petronios as the new abbot.[68] Petronios died in the same plague. He appointed Horsiesius to succeed him.[69] Horsiesius, a relative newcomer to the community, did not meet with the approval of a number of the Pachomian monks. They sought wealth and fame, and eventually threatened to withdraw a number of monasteries from the system. Horsiesius, recognizing the grave situation, turned the leadership of the community over to Theodore, who succeeded in averting disaster for a time.[70] The importance of these events for the self-understanding of the Pachomians is wit-

---

66. Amélineau, *Monuments au IVᵉ siècle*, 185.

67. Seventh Sahidic Codex: *Life of Pachomius* (S7) (Lefort, *S. Pachomii vitae sahidici scriptae*, 94–98; Veilleux, *Pachomian Koinonia*, 1.178); *G1* 116.

68. S7 (Lefort, *S. Pachomii vitae sahidici scriptae*, 92–93; Veilleux, *Pachomian Koinonia*, 1.176, 177); *G1* 117.

69. S5 (Lefort, *S. Pachomii vitae sahidici scriptae*, 180–81; Veilleux, *Pachomian Koinonia*, 1.187); S6 (Lefort, *S. Pachomii vitae sahidici scriptae*, 265; Veilleux, *Pachomian Koinonia*, 1.179); *G1* 117.

70. S6 (Lefort, *S. Pachomii vitae sahidici scriptae*, 268–71; Veilleux, *Pachomian Koinonia*, 1.195–97); *G1* 127–29.

nessed by the high profile they receive in the *Vitae*. While hardly edifying, the events are faithfully recorded.

These events are also foreboded in the *Vitae* through a vision granted to Pachomius of the difficulties to be faced by the community after his death. This vision is recorded in *Bo* 66, *G1* 71, and *Para* 17. A translation of *Para* 17 was given above. While it is clearly distinct from Pachomius's vision of heresy, a similarity with that part of the *Bo* version that is linked to the Pachomian community is to be noted.[71] While Amélineau does not refer to this specific pericope, it certainly lies behind his claim that the vision of heresy is misplaced.

Difficulties do exist with Amélineau's suggestion. The problem monk identified in the *Bo* version of the vision of heresy, Paniski, plays no role in the difficulties encountered by the community following Pachomius's death. The ringleader of that revolt is Apollonios, the abbot of the Tmoušons monastery. But even more problematic for the equation is that Pachomius himself attempts to resolve the problem revealed in the *Bo* version. As such, it is not an event that was to take place after his death, but one revealed to him that had already occurred and needed correction. He himself acts upon the vision.

The Pachomian sources are fluid enough that one can imagine the transfer of an episode from after Pachomius's death back into his life. Indeed, the vision of the problems that follow Pachomius's death is an *ex eventu* prophecy. In support of such a development behind the vision of heresy, one could argue that the four brothers in the vision who see the lamp correspond to the four general abbots of the community recorded in the *Vitae*, namely, Pachomius, Petronios, Horsiesius, and Theodore. The *Vitae* end with the death of Theodore. Thus those who let go represent those who failed to follow the accepted leadership of the community. Of course, later tradition, in the process of generalization, linked the four who saw the lamp to the four evangelists. However, it would be stretching the evidence to build a case on such conjectures. The fact that the vision of heresy in *Bo* is connected to an event that occurred in Pachomius's lifetime and that it names the offending party are strong arguments against the connection.

---

71. Veilleux, *Pachomian Koinonia*, 1.284.

Amélineau's suggestion should be rejected. The vision of heresy is not a metamorphosed form of Pachomius's *ex eventu* vision concerning the problems that would be faced by his community after his death. Rather, it fits a common pattern of a vision that serves to uncover an internal problem and that leads to its correction. This pattern is preserved to some extent in *Bo*. It has disappeared in the remaining two versions found in *G1* and *EpAm* in which it fell victim to a theological process of generalization.

The trajectories outlined here for Pachomius's vision of heresy suggest that the Pachomian sources often present the community through the eyes of later Pachomian and non-Pachomian monks. Episodes originally preserved to edify the Pachomian monks were generalized as the audience increased. Numerous factors were involved in this process. The passage of time within the Pachomian community necessitated a continuing reevaluation of their past. The glory of the movement at its height in the later years of Pachomius's life is pushed back into the earlier periods. The efforts of the Alexandrian church to enlist the Pachomian movement in its fight against "heresy" played a large role in the molding of the traditions. Use of the material by the church at large required its generalization. No one knew Paniski, but everyone recognized the threat of "heresy." Finally, the division of the Egyptian society between the Melchite or Greek-speaking Egyptians and the Coptic or native Egyptians influenced the development of this material throughout its entire history. Already within the Pachomian community the distinction between Coptic and Greek-speaking monks led to various accounts of the same event. It was the Greek version that made its way to Alexandria and from there to Byzantium and the West. This is the reason that it survived the decline and fall of Pachomian monasticism in the fifth and sixth centuries. The Coptic, on the other hand, survived in the Egyptian monasteries of Shenoute and those of the Wadi Natrun.

Again, this is not to suggest that generalization and later developments epitomize the Greek *Vitae* over against the earlier particularism of the Coptic version. The traditions are much too complex to suggest such a simple relationship. This paper began by suggesting that the individual pericopes must be examined alone in order to understand their own particular development. Although a more general relationship between the Greek and Coptic versions certainly exists, it has eluded scholarly unanimity. Too many stages and influences are involved in the various *Vita* traditions.

In conclusion, the evidence suggested in the present study serves to caution historians as to the value of the Pachomian *Vitae* for reconstructing the earliest Pachomian period. They mirror much more truly the period during which they were composed.[72] Any individual is idealized after his death by those who love him. This fact is only magnified for the founder of a community. The legends that surround George Washington, the father of the United States, serve as a prime example. In his case, however, there is considerable nonlegendary material, e.g., personal letters and English accounts, that serve to distinguish legend from fact. In the case of Pachomius, this nonlegendary material does not exist. Hence, the difficulty in unraveling history from legend greatly increases, or even more to the point, becomes impossible. The quest for the historical Pachomius falters on the same rocks encountered in the quest for the historical Jesus.

This study of Pachomius's vision of heresy serves not so much to uncover the actual history of the early stages of the Pachomian movement as to unmask the preserved accounts of it as idealizations often influenced by non-Pachomian considerations. It has not revealed Pachomius's position on theological heresy, but established that the general pro-Alexandrian position preserved in the Greek account is an anachronism, the product of later pressures and considerations.[73] It is doubtful that Pachomius defined "orthodoxy" so carefully. His emphasis was on an orthodox practice and not on an orthodox theology.[74] The latter emphasis is Alexandrian. Pachomius's actual position on theological matters must remain obscure. But the acknowledgment of that fact is far better than acceptance of the well-defined, later orthodoxy imposed upon him in the *Vitae*. This is not to suggest that Pachomius was a heretic, but that the more

---

72. The impetus to write a *Life of Pachomius* arose after his death (*Bo* 194; *S21* in Lefort, *Vies coptes*, 389; *G1* 99). The problem of interpreting the various *Vitae* is increased by the fact that the most complete forms that survive are all compilations.

73. Robinson, "Introduction," 18. The anti-Origenist statements in the *Vitae* appear to represent such an example. Dechow, *Dogma and Mysticism*, 32–34, 100–105; 190.

74. The *Rule* emphasized an ascetical practice and was probably instituted because of problems experienced in such matters. *S1* (Lefort, *S. Pachomii vitae sahidici scriptae*, 4–6; Veilleux, *Pachomian Koinonia*, 1.431–33); *G1* 8, 38; *Bo* 24, 102, 104.

subtle and rigid Alexandrian definitions of orthodoxy and heresy only gradually became relevant within his community.[75] The earlier stages of the movement were certainly less rigid in such matters than is often portrayed in the later *Vitae*.[76]

---

75. The close association between Athanasius and Pachomius is recorded one-sidedly in the Pachomian sources. Pachomius is not mentioned in the preserved writings of Athanasius apart from those that are attributed to him within the Pachomian sources. In a similar fashion, Athanasius only refers to Antony once (*Historia Arianorum 14*) outside of the *Life of Antony*. One suspects that Athanasius's charismatic appeal had much to do with his popularity in monastic circles. H. Idris Bell, "Athanasius: Chapter in Church History," *CQ* 3 (1925) 175–76; Chadwick, "Pachomios," 18.

76. A less rigid approach would explain the presence of the Nag Hammadi Codices within the Pachomian community. Discussions on this matter are multiplying. Robinson, "Introduction," 16–21; Hedrick, "Gnostic Proclivities"; Wisse, "Gnosticism"; Douglas M. Parrott, "The Nag Hammadi Library and the Pachomian Monasteries," paper delivered at the 1978 International Conference on Gnosticism at Yale University; Barns, "Greek and Coptic Papyri"; Barns, Browne, and Shelton, *Cartonnage*, 1–11.

8

New Frontiers
in Pachomian Studies

From its origins in the first quarter of the fourth century until
its demise in the Chalcedonian controversies of the sixth century,[1]
Pachomian monasticism played a significant role in Egyptian Christianity. Though its influence certainly spread beyond Egypt and
has long outlived the movement's own existence, it is the evidence
of its rise, its success, and its decline that concerns us here. Its
significance beyond its own temporal and geographical boundaries
is important only insofar as these periods and places external to
the movement impressed their own concerns on the Pachomian
sources.[2]

The presentation of the Pachomian movement preserved in the
traditional sources suggests a division of the movement's history
into three periods. The first period covers the lifetime of Pachomius and ends with his death in 346 C.E. A brief transitional period
follows and leads into the second period of the movement under
Theodore and Horsiesius.[3] It is from this period that the majority of

First published in Birger A. Pearson and James E. Goehring, eds., *The Roots of Egyptian
Christianity* (SAC; Philadelphia: Fortress Press, 1986) 236–57.

1. When the movement ended is unclear. Justinian's efforts to force the Chalcedonian position on the Pachomians resulted in the departure of many from the
monasteries. While he did have Chalcedonian abbots installed, the total lack of
sources after this date suggests the movement's rapid demise. See Kuhn, *Panegyric
on Apollo*, xiii–xvi; van Cauwenbergh, *Étude*, 153–59; Goehring, "Pachomius' Vision
of Heresy," 243 (see p. 139 in the present volume); and idem, "Chalcedonian Power
Politics and the Demise of Pachomian Monasticism" (OP 15; Claremont, Calif.: Institute for Antiquity and Christianity, 1989), which appears as chapter 12 in the present
volume.

2. The abridgment of the Pachomian rule for Italian monasteries is a good example. L. Th. Lefort, "Un texte original de la Règle de saint Pachôme," *CRAI* (1919)
341–48.

3. The transitional period belongs neither to the first period under Pachomius nor
to the second period that begins with the leadership of Theodore. It represents the first
unsuccessful attempt to continue the authority of a central abbot after Pachomius's
death.

the sources derive. The final period follows Horsiesius's death and continues through the breakup of the movement during the reign of Justinian I (527–65 C.E.).[4] It must be cautioned that while the division between the first and second periods is clear, the transition between the second and third is less certain. The former represents a historical and sociological division recognized by the movement and preserved in its writings. The latter is at least in part the result of the nature and quantity of the sources preserved.[5]

The vast majority of the written sources date from the middle period under Theodore and Horsiesius. These include the original form or forms of the *Life of Pachomius*, the *Paralipomena*, the *Letter of Ammon*, the Pachomian *Rule*, the letters and instructions of Theodore, the letters and instructions of Horsiesius, the *Regulations* of Horsiesius, and the *Testament* of Horsiesius.[6] The only sources that claim to derive from the lifetime of Pachomius, on the other hand, are the letters of Pachomius and two instructions attributed to him.[7] The authenticity of the letters is beyond dispute, while that of the instructions is debated.[8] As for the last period, the written sources are sparse and more legendary in nature. An account of the dedication of the great fifth-century basilica at Pbow, the central Pachomian monastery, contains some useful information.[9] A few *vitae* and panegyrics deal with later abbots and record events that led to the dissolution of the community in the sixth and seventh centuries.[10]

---

4. Even the date of Horsiesius's death remains unclear. See Bacht, *Vermächtnis*, 27.

5. The death of Horsiesius would certainly have marked a transition for the movement. But the sources do not preserve the history of that transition as they do for that marked by the death of Pachomius. It is the lack of sources for the period after Horsiesius that requires this division.

6. Lefort, *S. Pachomii vita bohairice scripta*; idem, *S. Pachomii vitae sahidice scriptae*; idem, *Vies coptes*; idem, *Oeuvres*; Halkin, *Sancti Pachomii Vitae Graecae*; idem, *Corpus athénien*; idem, "Vie inédite"; Goehring, *Letter of Ammon*; Boon, *Pachomiana latina*; van Cranenburgh, *Vie latine*; Amélineau, *Monuments au IVe siècle*; Veilleux, *Pachomian Koinonia*. See Veilleux's bibliographies.

7. Quecke, *Briefe Pachoms*; E. A. Wallis Budge, *Coptic Apocrypha in the Dialect of Upper Egypt* (London: British Museum, 1913) 146–76, 352–82; Veilleux, *Pachomian Koinonia*, 3.13–89.

8. Veilleux, *Pachomian Koinonia*, 3.2–3; Tito Orlandi, "Coptic Literature," in Pearson and Goehring, *Roots*, 60–63.

9. Van Lantschoot, "Allocution."

10. Van Cauwenbergh, *Étude*, 153–59; Kuhn, *Panegyric on Apollo*, passim; Campagnano, "Monaci egiziani."

PERIOD 1: The lifetime of Pachomius (ca. 323–46)	Letters of Pachomius Instruction of Pachomius
PERIOD 2: The movement under Theodore and Horsiesius (ca. 346–400)	*Vitae* *Paralipomena* *Letter of Ammon* Pachomian *Rule* Letters of Theodore Instructions of Theodore Letters of Horsiesius Instructions of Horsiesius *Regulations* of Horsiesius *Testament* of Horsiesius
PERIOD 3: From the death of Horsiesius through the reign of Justinian I (ca. 400–565)	Speech of Timothy of Alexandria *Life of Abraham* *Life of Manasseh* *Panegyric on Apollo*

Given this division of the sources and their nature, it is clear that the history of the first and third periods is the most difficult to reconstruct accurately. The problem in the final period is straightforward. The sources are few and legendary. They supply no continuous history. Rather the reader catches sight of a few moments in history as these moments reflect off a particular saint. While more work needs to be done with these sources, we cannot expect from them major new revelations about later Pachomian history.[11]

It is with the first period that the most acute problems arise. The difficulty has nothing to do with a lack of sources or the failure of these sources to offer a relatively continuous history of the movement in this period. Rather, the problem centers on the question of the accuracy of the depiction of the first period in sources that date from the second period. No one would deny that the *Vitae* accurately record the growth of the movement, the acquisition and foundation of new monasteries, the devastation by plagues, and the change of abbots through time. There is basic agreement about these events. However, the sources are also in basic agreement about the prac-

---

11. The Corpus dei Manoscritti Copti Letterari, directed by T. Orlandi, has been preparing microfiche copies of certain of these texts. The published microfiche include photographs of the original manuscripts, transcriptions, and translations.

tices and beliefs of the movement throughout its development. The practices and beliefs are presented in the sources as relatively static. The impression given is that these elements, endowed with authority through their institution by Pachomius, remained constant throughout the movement's history.[12] While one expects this in the sources, one must question whether reports of constancy represent a concern for historical accuracy or for an authority that has its basis in a continuity with the past.

The fact that the *Vitae* preserve an accurate account of the movement's external historical events does not guarantee that they represent with equal accuracy the developments and changes in the more internal matters of practice and belief. Insofar as modern presentations of Pachomian history do not take this distinction into account, they perpetuate the hagiographic thrust of their sources.

This problem is particularly acute in matters of belief and its boundaries. In the eyes of the believer, belief is related to ultimate truth. Since the latter cannot change, neither should the former. While the writing of hagiography cannot change the fact that abbots die and are replaced, it can alter earlier belief patterns that no longer fit a current situation.[13] In fact, not only can it change them, it is compelled to change them. If the purpose of writing a *vita* lies in the notion of *imitatio patrum*, it follows that the fathers to be imitated must meet the theological requirements of those who composed the *Vita*.[14]

The one source that assuredly comes from Pachomius's lifetime, namely his own letters, underscores the problem. The mystical alphabet contained in these texts is, in this form, significantly absent in the later sources.[15] The possibility of a Pachomian origin for the Nag Hammadi Codices with their many heterodox texts is another case

---

12. The *Rule* attributed in toto to Pachomius is a prime example. The notion of its angelic origin arose very early. See Palladius, *Historia Lausiaca* 32.1–3.

13. The anti-Origenist sentiments attributed to Pachomius (d. 346 C.E.) are a good example. Dechow, *Dogma and Mysticism*, 183–229.

14. This is not the process of a single author. It is part of the changing self-understanding of the movement after the death of its founder. The *raison d'être* of the composition demands it, whether the author realizes it or not. First Greek *Life of Pachomius* (G1) 17, 98–99; Bohairic *Life of Pachomius* (Bo) 194.

15. Compare the description of such letters in Palladius, *Historia Lausiaca* 32.4; G1 99; Veilleux, *Pachomian Koinonia*, 3.3–5; Quecke, *Briefe Pachoms*, 18–40; Wisse, "Language Mysticism"; idem, "Gnosticism," 438.

in point. Pachomian ownership can no longer be discounted simply because of the "orthodoxy" of the Pachomian sources. It is becoming clear that the sources composed in the period under Theodore and Horsiesius tell us as much about the period of their composition as about the earlier period they purport to describe, if in fact they do not tell us more about the period of their composition.[16]

Given the recognition of this fact, it is little wonder that the desire to unravel the stemmatic relationship of the various *Vitae* is now a thing of the past.[17] While these efforts offered many valuable insights into Pachomian history, it is now clear that the earliest form of the *Vita*, even if it were recoverable, would still not supply an unbiased version of the period under Pachomius. New methods are needed.[18]

THE MOVEMENT IN THE LIFETIME OF ITS FOUNDER:
A SOCIAL-HISTORICAL APPROACH

The death of a movement's founder marks a major turning point in its history. A crisis is averted and the movement survives only if the authority vested in him has a clearly defined new resting place. If the founder was able to share or surrender his authority before his death, the movement's continuity is maintained. Thus Elijah passed his authority on to Elisha before his own departure. Alternatively, if the founder appointed a clear successor or established the path through which the authority was to flow after his death, continuity is maintained. This path may be hereditary, by appointment, or by election. The important point is that it was established by the authority of the founder in his own lifetime.[19] When the founder fails in this matter,

---

16. Rousseau, *Ascetics*, 68; Goehring, "Pachomius' Vision of Heresy" (chap. 7 in the present volume).

17. Various accounts of the history of this debate exist. Rousseau, *Ascetics*, 243–47; Timbie, "Dualism," 23–58; Goehring, *Letter of Ammon*, 3–23; Jozef Vergote, "La valeur des vies grecques et coptes de S. Pakhôme," *OLP* 8 (1977) 175–86.

18. It needs to be stated that these "new" approaches are well under way. The point to underscore is that Pachomian scholarship has moved beyond its desire to rank the *Vitae* in value and instead has begun to ask new critical questions about the movement.

19. Objections or alternatives to the founder's choice are possible. This is particularly true when the founder alters a developing pattern shortly before his death. Such was the case in the Pachomian movement.

a crisis of continuity inevitably follows. The difficulty is heightened when the founder dies unexpectedly.[20]

Social theorists have long recognized this process. Its earliest and clearest interpreter was Max Weber.[21] He understood the process as an evolution from the charismatic authority, through which a movement originated, to the later, more stable forms of authority through which it insured its continuing success. He termed this evolution "the routinization of charisma."[22]

Weber defined charisma as

> a certain quality of an individual personality by virtue of which he is set apart from ordinary men and treated as endowed with supernatural, superhuman, or at least specifically exceptional powers or qualities. These are such that they are not accessible to the ordinary person but are regarded as of divine origin or as exemplary, and on the basis of them the individual is treated as a leader.[23]

The desire to continue the community founded by such an individual after his death demands that his followers give radical attention to this charisma and the authority based upon it. The continuity of the movement depends upon the successful transferral of this authority to a more stable basis. While the particular form of the more stable authority may vary, the nature of the stability over against the charismatic moment remains the same.[24]

When one looks at the events that surround Pachomius's death and the eventual continuity of the community under Theodore, it is remarkable how well the facts fit this abstract theory.[25] Pacho-

---

20. The case of Jesus is notable. In the early Christian movement the transfer of authority followed various patterns, including hereditary (James), apostolic (Peter), and revelatory (Paul).

21. Weber, *Theory,* 358–92; idem, "The Social Psychology of the World Religions," in H. H. Gerth and C. Wright Mills, eds., *From Max Weber: Essays in Sociology* (New York and London: Oxford University Press, 1946) 295–301; Talcott Parsons, *The Structure of Social Action* (New York: McGraw-Hill, 1937) 658–72; Thomas F. O'Dea, *The Sociology of Religion* (Englewood Cliffs, N.J.: Prentice-Hall, 1966) 22–24, 36–39.

22. Weber, *Theory,* 363–73.

23. Weber, *Theory,* 358–59.

24. Weber, *Theory,* 363–66. It is not simply a matter of finding a new charismatic leader. While such a person may solve the immediate problem, he does not offer the more stable basis of authority that will insure the community's existence after *his* death.

25. Rousseau, *Ascetics,* chaps. 1–5. Rousseau describes the changing concept of authority in the relationship between early monasticism and the church. He does not, however, link this account to the abstract theory of the social scientists. One should

mius died unexpectedly in a plague that ravaged his community in 346 C.E.[26] A serious crisis of continuity followed, a crisis that had its origins not only in Pachomius's death but in a series of events that had taken place approximately two years before it. At that time too a serious illness threatened Pachomius's life. On that occasion the community's leaders made premature plans for his replacement. They clearly recognized the problem of continuity. They compelled Theodore, who had entered the community circa 328 C.E. and had since become a confidant and the heir apparent to Pachomius, to agree to succeed Pachomius if he should die.[27] But Pachomius did not die. He recovered and took offense at Theodore's acceptance of the elders' recognition of him as Pachomius's successor. As a result Pachomius removed all authority from him. Theodore spent two years in penance.[28]

While there is some indication that Pachomius's reaction against Theodore softened in the following two years,[29] it is certainly no accident that on his deathbed in 346 C.E. he appointed Petronios as his successor. Petronios was a wealthy landowner and a relatively recent addition to the community.[30] The older brothers who represented support for Theodore were bypassed.[31] Petronios led the community for only two and one-half months. He died in the same plague that killed Pachomius. Before he died he appointed a certain Horsiesius from the monastery of Šeneset (Chenoboskion) to succeed him.[32] Horsiesius too was a relative newcomer to the community.[33]

---

also note Karl Holl, *Enthusiasmus und Bussgewalt beim griechischen Mönchtum* (Leipzig: Hinrichs, 1898; reprint, Hildesheim: Olms, 1969).

26. *G1* 114–17; *Bo* is missing at this point. The material is supplied from various Sahidic versions (*S7, S3, S5*). A number of the community's leaders perished in this plague.

27. *G1* 106; *Bo* 94.

28. *G1* 106–7; *Bo* 94–95.

29. *Bo* 97; *G1* 109; Veilleux, *Pachomian Koinonia*, 1.282, *SBo* 97 n. 3 (*SBo*=Veilleux's Sahidic-Bohairic compilation).

30. *G1* 80; *Bo* 56.

31. Derwas J. Chitty, "A Note on the Chronology of the Pachomian Foundations," *SP* 2 [TU 64] (1957) 384–85; Veilleux, *Pachomian Koinonia*, 1.420; *G1* 129 n. 1.

32. *G1* 117–18; *S5* 130–31.

33. In *G1*, Horsiesius is first mentioned in section 114, shortly before Pachomius's death in section 116 and Horsiesius's appointment as general abbot in section 117. The earliest reference in the Coptic sources (*Bo* 91) is a reference to his latter period as general abbot. Apart from this reference, he first appears in the account of Pachomius's appointment of Petronios (*S5* 121).

Horsiesius appears to have maintained control for little more than a year.[34] His own weakness and the desire among many of the brothers to be led by Theodore worked against him.[35] Before long a major revolt broke out in the monasteries. Led by Apollonios, the abbot of the monastery of Tmoušons, the breakdown of authority threatened the very existence of the movement. Apollonios's monastery seceded, and others allied themselves with him.[36] Cries such as "We no longer belong to the community of the brothers" and "We will have nothing to do with Horsiesius nor will we have anything to do with the rules which he lays down" were heard.[37] It is clear that a stable form of authority had not yet evolved to replace the charismatic authority enjoyed by Pachomius.

Horsiesius recognized the serious nature of the problem and his own inability to deal with it. He summoned Theodore and turned the authority of the community over to him.[38] It is at this juncture that the routinization of Pachomius's charismatic authority occurs. The brief reigns of Petronios and Horsiesius represent an interruption in this process, an interruption caused by an event that occurred two years before Pachomius's death and that set aside the path of authority that had been evolving prior to it. Theodore represented the established power base of the older brothers. Petronios and Horsiesius were newcomers imposed upon the brothers by Pachomius because of the older brothers' earlier indiscretion in championing Theodore.[39] While the choice of Petronios had Pachomius's authority behind it, it represented an aberration from his longer sharing of authority with Theodore prior to the latter's indiscretion. Theodore's acceptance of the leadership role from Horsiesius signals a return of authority to the natural course that had evolved during Pachomius's lifetime.

Theodore quelled the revolt and restored unity to the system with relative ease.[40] In the eyes of the brothers he was the repository of

---

34. *G1* 118–30; *S5* 125–32 (*SBo* 131–38).

35. Theodore's succession had been short-circuited only two years before. *G1* 106–7; *Bo* 94–95.

36. *S6* (*SBo* 139); *G1* 127–28; *Bo* 204; Theodore, *Instruction* 3.46.

37. *S6* (*SBo* 139); *G1* 127. I have used Veilleux's translations.

38. *G1* 129–30; *S6* (*SBo* 139–40).

39. See above, p. 167–168.

40. *G1* 131; *S6*; *S5*; *Bo* (*SBo* 141–44).

Pachomius's authority. The recent events underscored, however, the need to stabilize this authority in institutions and not individuals if the movement was to survive. Thus to avoid a similar revolt in the future, a revolt dependent upon a single abbot's power base within his own monastery, Theodore instituted the practice of shuffling the various abbots among the various monasteries twice each year.[41] But Theodore did not institute a system for selecting his own successor. He apparently expected, as Pachomius had before him, to appoint his successor prior to his death.[42]

While Theodore did not solve the problem of continuity through an institutionalized basis of succession,[43] he did further stabilize the authority recognized in the community by more fully joining it with the ecclesiastical authority centered in Alexandria. Pachomius's charismatic authority was institutionalized not only in the internal regulations of the community, but also through the community's closer identification of its own internal authority with the ecclesiastical authority and institutions representing the Athanasian party.[44]

It is no accident that Theodore moved in this direction. Throughout the *Vitae* it is clear that he is more closely tied to the Alexandrian hierarchy and Athanasius than was Pachomius. His closer association may well be the result of his social status. He was born into a wealthy Christian family that had ready access to the bishop.[45]

---

41. *S6* (*SBo* 144). This practice is not recorded in the First Greek *Life of Pachomius* (*G1*). A subsequent letter of Horsiesius suggests that the practice was not easily accepted and caused discord after Theodore's death. The letter, unpublished in the original, has been translated by Veilleux (*Pachomian Koinonia*, 3:161–65). For a discussion of this letter, see chapter 11 in the present volume.

42. *Bo* 204–9; *G1* 145–49. One should note the juristic method of designating an abbot's replacement during his absence recorded in *P. Lond.* 1913. Pageus, the abbot of the Melitian monastery at Hathor, had been summoned by Constantine to attend the Synod of Caesarea. The document records an agreement between himself and the priors of the monastery that his brother Gerontios shall take his place and discharge his function during his absence (Bell, *Jews and Christians in Egypt*, 45–53). It must be pointed out that this was an interim agreement and not a matter of succession. Nothing similar is known from the Pachomian milieu.

43. The lack of sources after Theodore's death makes the question of succession and the means of deciding upon it unclear. It seems that Horsiesius faced renewed difficulties when he succeeded Theodore upon the latter's death. See above, n. 41; Bacht, *Vermächtnis*, 24.

44. Rousseau, *Ascetics*, chaps. 1–5; Ruppert, *Das pachomianische Mönchtum*, 428–43; Goehring, "Pachomius' Vision of Heresy."

45. *G1* 33, 37; *Bo* 31, 37. Theodore's Greek Christian name is noteworthy. On the in-

Pachomius was a pagan. It is no accident that whereas Pachomius hid from Athanasius to avoid ordination when the latter journeyed upriver, Theodore on a similar occasion after Pachomius's death marched out with the leaders of the community to greet him.[46] It is no accident that Pachomius controlled his community from his own base of authority. He did not venture out to meet Antony or to visit Alexandria. Theodore did.[47] It is no accident that the source that most clearly strives to link the Pachomian movement with Athanasian orthodoxy, the *Letter of Ammon*, was authored by an individual who knew the movement only as it existed under Theodore and who held Theodore as his hero.[48] In this context it should also be noted that there is an apparent shift away from the authority and power of vision, as one moves from Pachomius to Theodore. Although both Pachomius and Theodore were visionaries, the evidence of Pachomius's ecstatic trances and the charges against him at Latopolis are in stark contrast to Theodore's milder approach to the subject.[49]

In this same period when the community was redefining its concept of authority, it was also emphasizing the need to emulate the idealized period under Pachomius. While the community's authority structure was routinized in a combination of monastic and ecclesiastical institutions, support for this new structure of authority was sought in the concept of *imitatio patrum*. This means that the community's writings during the era under Theodore and Horsiesius were under the influence of this newly developed structure of authority. In

---

creasing use of Christian names in Egypt, see Roger S. Bagnall, "Religious Conversion and Onomastic Change in Early Byzantine Egypt," *BASP* 19 (1982) 105–24.

46. *G1* 30, 143–44; *Bo* 28, 200–203. It is significant that in the two accounts of Pachomius's hiding from Athanasius, the Bohairic has Athanasius marvel at Pachomius while *G1* would have its readers believe that Pachomius was in awe of the archbishop from his place of concealment.

47. *G1* 109, 113, 120; *S5* (*SBo* 126–29); *Epistula Ammonis* 28–29; Chadwick, "Pachomios," 17–19.

48. Goehring, *Letter of Ammon*, 103–22.

49. *Bo* 33–34, 66, 87–88, 103; *S2*; *G1* 71, 96, 135; *Epistula Ammonis* 12. Pachomius is made to play down the importance of visions in *G1* 48–49. Neither these sections nor *G1* 135 have a clear parallel in the Coptic material. This, coupled with the fact that *G1* alone records the Council of Latopolis, where Pachomius was charged with being a clairvoyant, makes one wonder about the intent of the First Greek *Life of Pachomius* (*G1*). Veilleux (*Pachomian Koinonia*, 1.412; *G1* 48 n. 1) suggests that *G1* 48–50 stems from a lost collection of Pachomius's instructions. I would argue that it represents a later position on vision important to the circle behind *G1*, a position that was written back into the lifetime of Pachomius. See Ruppert, *Das pachomianische Mönchtum*, 431–34.

fact, the writings functioned to support this new authority.[50] While this development insured the survival of the movement, it renders questionable the reliability of the writings in presenting the nature of the movement prior to the institution of this newer structure of authority. Since the movement at the time of composition had institutionalized its authority in part by closely associating itself with the Athanasian party, and since support of this new authority was sought through the principle of *imitatio*, it was necessary that the writings describe a movement in the early ideal period that is in close accord with the new institutionalized authority. Evidence that exists within these sources to the contrary represents survival of earlier material. Such evidence is of particular importance for reconstructing the earlier period before the composition of the sources.[51] Evidence that aligns the early period with the new institutionally based authority must remain suspect.[52]

This does not mean that the movement under Pachomius was heretical nor that Pachomius opposed Athanasius. Rather, in the early period the movement simply did not understand authority in these terms. Our understanding of church history depends in large part on the writings of the great theologians (Greek and Latin) for whom doctrinal issues and definitions were of vital significance. It is doubtful that the Copt Pachomius felt the same need for systematic theology. Henry Chadwick has observed that "it is not inherently probable that Pachomius was interested in the niceties of orthodox doctrine or a theological system...; it is reasonable to think the early Pachomian tradition largely indifferent where dogma is con-

---

50. Rousseau, *Ascetics*, 68. It may well be that the sources showed an even stronger movement in this direction under Horsiesius. Horsiesius completed what Theodore had begun.

51. The problem confronted by Pachomius at the Council of Latopolis, preserved in *G1* 112 alone, is a good example. So too the recording of Pachomius's first failure when he attempted to organize a monastic community, recorded in *S1*. Likewise the call for the removal of apocryphal books would suggest that they were used in the community at an earlier date (*Bo* 189; *S3b*; Lefort, *Vies coptes*, 371).

52. On the matter of Pachomius's opposition to Origen see above, n. 13. The reference to the bishops in communion with the heretics that has found its way into Pachomius's vision of heresy in *Bo* 103 suggests a period after Chalcedon (cf. *G1* 102; *Epistula Ammonis* 12; Goehring, "Pachomius' Vision of Heresy," 252–53 [see pp. 150–51 in the present volume]). Sometimes it is the stylized form that suggests a late date, as with the styled liturgical prayer attributed to Pachomius in *S1* 16.

cerned, content to make use of a diversity of gifts so long as they all encouraged renunciation of the world."[53]

The recognition of the process that routinized Pachomius's charismatic authority after his death makes the movement's acquisition and use of the documents discovered near Nag Hammadi more understandable. The "orthodoxy" of the movement portrayed in the sources can no longer be accepted as an accurate representation of the facts. Again, the alternative to this "orthodox" movement is not a heretical movement, but a movement that did not yet define its being in these either/or terms. As difficult as it may be for us to fathom in this modern age of reason, it was not impossible for one to support Athanasius and to read the Nag Hammadi texts.

The prevalence of this either-orthodoxy-or-heresy attitude among many historians accounts for the early denial of a Pachomian origin of the Nag Hammadi Codices. Doresse simply stated that "already the contents of these Gnostic collections had led us to suppose that whoever may have possessed them, they cannot have been monks."[54] Others have followed him in this conclusion.[55] The number of scholars who argue for a Pachomian origin of the texts, however, is growing. While the evidence currently in hand cannot firmly establish the Pachomian origin of the Nag Hammadi texts, the circumstantial evidence is mounting for such a relationship. Refer-

---

53. Chadwick, "Pachomios," 18; idem, "Domestication of Gnosis." The dating of the cartonnage suggests that at least some of the Nag Hammadi Codices were copied during the leadership period of Theodore. I do not consider this a problem for the theory of Theodore's routinization of Pachomius's charismatic authority. Routinization is not a rapid process. Theodore certainly emphasized closer ties with the Alexandrian hierarchy. Witness his reading of Athanasius's festal letter concerning apocryphal books in 367 C.E. (*Bo* 189). This does not mean, however, that he succeeded in converting the entire movement to his position overnight. Indeed, in his later years he bemoaned the growing wealth of the brothers (*Bo* 197–98; *G1* 146). Theodore, in a sense, functions as an intermediate stage. He shares in Pachomius's charisma (*Bo* 34; *Epistula Ammonis* 14). Hence he rules with charismatic authority while at the same time institutionalizing that authority. The charismatic factor fades much further into the background with Horsiesius, who composed his own series of regulations. He undoubtedly carried the ecclesiastically based authority to its conclusion; the removal of the Nag Hammadi Codices ensued.

54. Jean Doresse, *The Secret Books of the Egyptian Gnostics: An Introduction to the Gnostic Coptic Manuscripts Discovered at Chenoboskeia* (trans. Philip Mairet; New York: Viking Press, 1960) 135.

55. Krause, "Erlassbrief," 230; Shelton, "Introduction"; Adalbert de Vogüé, "Foreword," in Veilleux, *Pachomian Koinonia,* 1.xix; Rousseau, *Pachomius,* 26–28. Timbie ("Dualism," 230–33) is very cautious.

ences in the Pachomian sources to the removal of apocryphal works and against the idea that Cain was conceived by the devil, which were earlier taken as evidence of the system's opposition to the Nag Hammadi texts, are now seen to support the existence of such texts in the movement during its initial stages.[56] Wisse has supplied data on the diversity of monasticism in Upper Egypt and the congruity of ideas shared between the Nag Hammadi texts and monasticism.[57] Hedrick, who worked with the first Greek *Life of Pachomius* (*Vita prima*) alone, has suggested the existence in the movement's early stage of a vision-oriented group. He argues that this group, which was played down in the later periods, offers the most obvious link to the Nag Hammadi texts.[58] Parrott has suggested that concern with heresy in Pachomius's day centered on the Melitians and the Arians. In this scenario, the Gnostic controversies were a thing of the past, and hence their literature was once again usable.[59] I have elsewhere noted a tendency in the sources to generalize the movement's opposition to heresy and to write this more general opposition back into the lifetime of Pachomius.[60] Finally, Dechow has argued that the texts were removed from the monastery as a result of the fourth- and fifth-century Origenist controversy that raged in Egypt.[61]

The most intriguing but uncertain bit of evidence that has come to bear on this question is that preserved in the cartonnage of the Nag Hammadi Codices. In his preliminary report on this material, Barns noted a significant correspondence between the proper names preserved in the cartonnage and those found in the Pachomian sources.[62] One letter in particular seemed almost to offer the

---

56. See above, n. 51; Doresse, *Secret Books,* 135; Robinson, "Introduction," 19.

57. Wisse, "Language Mysticism"; idem, "Gnosticism"; idem, "The Nag Hammadi Library and the Heresiologists," *VC* 25 (1971) 205–23; Chadwick, "Pachomios," 17–19.

58. Hedrick, "Gnostic Proclivities."

59. Douglas Parrott, "The Nag Hammadi Library and the Pachomian Monasteries," paper delivered at the 1978 International Conference on Gnosticism at Yale University.

60. Goehring, "Pachomius' Vision of Heresy" (chap. 7 in the present volume).

61. Dechow, *Dogma and Mysticism,* 183–230. This later date for the removal of the codices from the monastery is acceptable. I do not think that the institutionalization process under Theodore was completed during his lifetime (see above, n. 53). Various others have supported a Pachomian origin for the Nag Hammadi texts (see Chadwick, "Pachomios," 17–19; idem, "Domestication of Gnosis," 14–16; R. van den Broek, "The Present State of Gnostic Studies," *VC* 37 [1983] 47–48).

62. Barns, "Greek and Coptic Papyri."

"smoking gun" that would link the texts to the movement. It was from a certain Papnoute to Pachom. While the precise identity of the two is not given in the letter, Barns pointed out that the chief economic officer for the community during Pachomius's lifetime was a certain Papnoute.

It is now clear that Barns overstated the case. A significant number of proper names are shared in the two sets of sources. But this in and of itself proves nothing. Shelton, who studied the cartonnage in depth for his production of the critical edition, concluded that "there are no certain traces of classical Pachomian monasticism in the cartonnage."[63] The cartonnage sources include, after all, accounts that mention large amounts of wine, wheat, and barley, and they include tax lists, imperial ordinances, contracts for shipping goods, contracts for weavers' goods, private letters, monastic letters, and bits of scripture. Shelton argued that "it is hard to think of a satisfactory single source for such a variety of documents except a town rubbish heap."[64]

Shelton's conclusions are acceptable in the sense (contra Barns) that the cartonnage offers no indisputable evidence of the codices' manufacture by the Pachomian monks. It is wrong, however, to move beyond that position and suggest that the cartonnage and hence the codices could not have come from a Pachomian monastery. Shelton himself has suggested that the monks may have gathered materials from the town rubbish heap for use in the manufacturing of their books.[65] Dechow has argued more recently that the economic life of the Pachomian community could indeed account for many of the documents preserved in the cartonnage.[66]

While the connection of certain texts in the cartonnage to the Pachomians is difficult to understand,[67] Dechow's position is well

---

63. Shelton, "Introduction," 11.

64. Shelton, "Introduction," 11.

65. Shelton, "Introduction," 11. A similar unprovable suggestion was offered by Robinson ("Introduction," 16–17). He suggested that uninscribed codices might have been produced and sold by the Pachomians.

66. Jon Dechow, "The Nag Hammadi Milieu: An Assessment in the Light of the Origenist Controversies," paper delivered at the 1982 annual meeting of the Western Region of the American Academy of Religion.

67. This is particularly true for the agreement of the oil-workers guild in Codex I (Barns, Browne, and Shelton, *Cartonnage*, 15–17).

taken. The fact that the various documents do not mention specific Pachomian connections is not proof that they did not belong
to the Pachomians. Certainly the monastic letters and bits of scripture could come from the Pachomian monastery. In fact, a monastery
might seem the more likely place of origin. The other private letters
could equally be found in a monastic setting. Letters from outside
the community undoubtedly came in to the monks.[68] There is no reason that these would always use monastic titles. Indeed, an outsider
may well have been unfamiliar with them.[69]

When one turns to tax lists, contracts, shipping papers, etc., many
of which were certainly drawn up in government offices, we must
not be too quick to assume that they have no connection with the
Pachomian system. One should not automatically extend the division
between the spiritual and secular world in Pachomian monasticism
into the economic realm as well. While the movement divided itself
from the world by a wall, it must be remembered that it built its
monasteries in the greenbelt of the Nile. The monks practiced various crafts, gathered their own materials for weaving and building,
retained their own boats for travel up and down the Nile, conducted business outside the monastery, and farmed.[70] It is certainly
improbable that the Byzantine government in Egypt granted the
movement a tax-exempt status. Indeed, a document has come to light
that reports on tax paid by a monk for the Pachomian monastery
of Tabennese.[71] Likewise, imperial ordinances and guild contracts,
while more difficult to explain, do not exclude a Pachomian origin. If
the movement had grown large and influential in Upper Egypt and
had begun to play a significant role in the economy of the region, it

---

68. Theodore's mother had letters from the bishop sent in to Pachomius (*Bo* 37;
G1 37). *Regula: Praecepta* 51–54 reports on the role of the gatekeeper to insure the
separation from the world. Yet food from relatives, while not allowed for the individual, was received for the monastery. General communication concerning farming,
business, and governmental requirements should be expected as well.

69. The earliest preserved reference to a μοναχός dates to 324 C.E. Judge, "Earliest
Use"; idem, "Fourth-Century Monasticism."

70. Palladius, *Historia Lausiaca* 32.9–10; *Regulations* of Horsiesius 55–58, 62; Dechow, "Nag Hammadi Milieu," 6–11. The sources seem to indicate that farming and
self-sufficiency were not practiced during Pachomius's lifetime but developed after his
death, particularly under Horsiesius's influence. Wipszycka, "Terres," 625–36.

71. Wipszycka, "Terres"; Stephan Schiwietz, *Das morganländische Mönchtum* (3 vols.;
Mainz: Kirchheim, 1904–39) 1.347. The document dates to 367–68 C.E.

is not improbable that local government offices would send copies of such matters to the monastery.[72]

While these observations do not prove the Pachomian origin of the Nag Hammadi Codices, they show that the cartonnage documents themselves do not clearly refute it. In this connection it is interesting to consider the type of documents found at the late monastic settlement of Deir el-Bala'izah.[73] The 1914 excavation of this site, some twelve miles south of Assiut, produced fragments of some three thousand texts. A large number of these are nonliterary documents, and most fall into the Arabic period (675–775 C.E.). Although this is admittedly late, it is important to note that these documents include tax receipts, letters from Arab governors, accounts relating to taxation, deeds of sale, repayments of debts, private letters, various article lists, lists of names, and even a marriage contract.[74] The site is non-Pachomian, but the makeup of this collection stemming from the Bala'izah monastery would suggest that the various documents preserved in the cartonnage of the Nag Hammadi Codices could indeed have come from a monastery.

An additional point of parallel needs to be drawn from the Bala'izah case. Among the Bala'izah texts were a large number of biblical fragments, lives of the saints, homilies, and other literary pieces. This is to be expected in the remains of the monastery.[75] The vast majority of these texts fit the standard depiction of Coptic orthodoxy. They include a story about Athanasius and Antony, and a sermon by Athanasius. Now one might suspect that such an interest in Athanasius would keep such a monastery from dabbling with more heterodox materials. Such is often the assumption about the Pachomian movement. However, the Bala'izah literary documents also contain magical texts, a possible amulet and horoscope, and what is most interesting, a Gnostic treatise. The treatise dates from the fourth century and is very fragmentary. The text is a revelation to John. Even though it does not correspond to any other known Gnos-

---

72. *Paralipomena* 21 records the purchase of wheat from the city of Hermonthis.

73. Kahle, *Bala'izah*.

74. Kahle, *Bala'izah*, 1.xi–xvii, the table of contents, lists the variety.

75. Such documents, apart from some biblical fragments, were not in the cartonnage from Nag Hammadi because of the early date of the codices. The hagiographic material was coming into existence at this time and hence would not yet be worn enough for the scrap heap.

tic text to date, it is replete with the usual Gnostic terminology. It belongs to the type of document represented by the *Apocryphon of John*, which offers a Gnostic reinterpretation of the events recorded in Genesis.[76]

What I want to underscore is not the precise nature of the text but the mere fact of its existence in a monastic library that also contained works connected with Athanasius. The fact that it was preserved to such a late date is also striking. While we do not know the nature of the monasticism practiced at Bala'izah, this evidence at least allows the possibility of the use of Gnostic and Athanasian literature in the same movement![77]

In conclusion, the Pachomian sources, when viewed in light of the social theory of authority and its routinization, betray their own participation in this routinization process. They support adherence to authority in its new routinized form by demanding that monks imitate the heroes of the past. These two facts can work together only if the heroes of the past are portrayed as supportive of the new institutionalized form of authority. This being the case, the historicity of the sources in such matters is highly questionable.

This brief analysis has also demonstrated that certain presuppositions about Pachomian monasticism do not warrant support on closer examination. The notion that monastic withdrawal includes a strict division between the spiritual matters of the monastery and the economic concerns of the state is not always correct. The Pachomian sources themselves do not support it, nor does it gain support from other monastic sites where our documentation is more complete.[78]

The same problem has been shown to exist with the idea that one could not read works of Athanasius and express support of him, and yet read a Gnostic text. Rationalism has taught us to appreciate a systematic theology. But to write these expectations back into the early stages of Pachomian monasticism is simply to continue

---

76. Kahle, *Bala'izah*, 1.473–77; Walter E. Crum, "Coptic Anecdota," *JTS* 44 (1943) 176–79.

77. One should note the monk Annarichus in Gaza as another example. See E. A. Wallis Budge, *Miscellaneous Coptic Texts in the Dialect of Upper Egypt* (London: British Museum, 1915) 58–60, 63–38; van den Broek, "Present State," 47–48.

78. Shenoute spoke to secular leaders and dealt harshly with the pagan elements in his area. See Leipoldt, *Schenute von Atripe*, 162–66, 175–82.

the hagiographic process already begun in the *Vitae* in the time of Theodore.

THE MOVEMENT AFTER HORSIESIUS: ARCHAEOLOGICAL EVIDENCE

The other period of Pachomian monasticism of which we know very little is that from the death of Horsiesius (ca. 400 C.E.) through the movement's disintegration in the Chalcedonian controversy of the sixth and seventh centuries. The problem in this case arises not so much from a distortion in the sources that deal with the movement of this period as from the simple lack of sources themselves.

The creative period of the movement occurred in the lifetime of Pachomius. The second period under Theodore and Horsiesius represents a period of institutionalization and written preservation. The final period after Horsiesius's death represents a stage of literary stagnation. While the movement did apparently grow and did build the great fifth-century basilica at Pbow,[79] its own identity was tied to the past. The past was now available in written documents that bore their own authority.

Though we have a highly imaginative account of the dedication of the great basilica and a few later lives and panegyrics, they preserve relatively little historical information on the period. It is true, however, that more work needs to be done with this later material, including the production of critical texts and translations.[80]

A second source of data on the later period of the Pachomian movement has received only minor attention, namely, the archaeological evidence. Lefort did conduct a surface survey in 1939 in an attempt to identify the sites of the various Pachomian establishments,[81] but the only site that has been clearly identified by archaeological evidence is that of the central monastery of Pbow.[82] This site has never been lost because of the pillars of the large fifth-century basilica that are strewn about the surface.

---

79. Van Lantschoot, "Allocution"; B. T. A. Evetts, *The Churches and Monasteries of Egypt and Some Neighboring Countries Attributed to Abu Salih, the Armenian* (Oxford: Clarendon Press, 1895).

80. See above, n. 11.

81. Lefort, "Premiers monastères."

82. Lefort, "Premiers monastères," 387–93.

The site was visited in the early twentieth century,[83] but it received its first actual excavation in 1968 under the direction of Fernand Debono of L'Institut français d'archéologie orientale.[84] Debono's analysis of the surface remains suggested to him evidence for two basilicas. The large fifth-century structure that was recognized by all was built with brick walls and used rose granite columns in its interior. A number of architectural blocks gathered at the southeast edge of the site, however, were identified by Debono on the basis of the construction material and different proportions as remnants of a second church. He tentatively suggested that this second church was the modest chapel described in the Pachomian *Vitae*, a chapel that was demolished to make way for the later basilica.[85] It was apparently this identification that led Debono to excavate beside these remains of the second church.

Debono's excavation uncovered the ruins of several brick buildings and a rather sophisticated channel for running water. The objects unearthed included a large amount of pottery (mostly shards), a few pieces of metal, several coins, and animal bones. The coins identified by Debono date from Constantius II (337–61 C.E.) through Theodosius (379–95 C.E.).[86]

Debono's efforts represent but a start. His report is unfortunately preliminary, and we can no longer expect a final report on his work. While the structures he unearthed cannot be clearly identified, his efforts did establish the existence of the monastery to the west of the basilica.[87] Debono did not return to the field.

Between 1975 and 1980, the Institute for Antiquity and Christianity conducted four excavation seasons and one survey in the Nag Hammadi area.[88] The caves of the Jabal al-Tarif, the site of the discovery of the Nag Hammadi Codices, were thoroughly explored.

---

83. Michel Jullien, "Quelques anciens couvents de l'Égypt," *MisCath* 35 (1903) 283–84; M. Louis Massignon, "Seconde note sur l'état d'avancement des études archéologiques arabes en Égypte, hors du Caire," *BIFAO* 9 (1911) 88–90; Lefort, "Premiers monastères," 387–93.

84. Debono, "Basilique."

85. Debono, "Basilique," 205–7.

86. Debono, "Basilique," 218.

87. Efforts by the Institute for Antiquity and Christianity to locate accurately Debono's squares failed, though their approximate position is clear.

88. Robinson and van Elderen, "First Season"; idem, "Second Season"; van Elderen, "Nag Hammadi Excavation"; Grossmann, "Basilica"; Lease, "Fourth Season";

Evidence of the use of the Sixth Dynasty tombs in this cliff by Byzantine monks is plentiful. Red painted crosses and a Coptic psalm
inscription are to be noted.[89] Excavations also unearthed pottery
from this period and Byzantine coins from the reign of Anastasius I
(491–518 C.E.) through Heraclius (610–41 C.E.).[90]

Excavations at the monastery of Pbow began in the second season (November 22–December 29, 1976). Two further seasons have
been undertaken, and we are hopeful of future work. The excavations
centered on the basilica itself and have been successful in delineat-
ing the architectural structure of this great fifth-century church. The
basilica was indeed massive, measuring approximately 36 meters
in width by 72 meters in length. It retained the usual architectural features of a Coptic basilica. The five aisles of the interior
were separated by rose granite columns, and the floor was paved
with limestone slabs of uneven size.[91] The outside walls were brick.
That they were large is evidenced by the massive foundation walls
that remain.[92] The apse has not been excavated. It lies below an
existing house.

Excavations below this fifth-century basilica have also revealed a
fourth-century basilica of similarly large dimensions. Its width is 30
meters and its length at least 35 meters. The excavations have not
yet located the western wall. The size of this lower basilica underscores the early success of the movement. It is doubtful, however,
whether this building should be identified with the small chapel in
the Pachomian sources, built by Pachomius.[93]

Meyer, "Wadi Sheikh Ali"; Marvin W. Meyer and H. Keith Beebe, "Literary and
Archeological Survey of Al-Qasr," *NARCE* 121 (1983) 25–29.

89. M. Paul Bucher, "Les commencements des psaumes LI a XCIII: Inscription
d'une tombe de Kasr es Saijad," *Kemi* 4 (1931) 157–60. Graffiti to Sarapis are also
present in one cave (Robinson, "Discovery," 213; pp. 202 and 228 of the same
issue offer photographs of the psalms inscription). See van Elderen, "Nag Hammadi
Excavation," 226.

90. James E. Goehring, "Byzantine Coins from the Jabal al-Tarif in Upper Egypt,"
BSAC 26 (1984) 31–41; idem, "Two New Examples of the Byzantine 'Eagle' Countermark," *NumC*, ser. 7, 23 (1983) 218–20; idem, "A Byzantine Hoard from Upper Egypt,"
NFAQJ 26 (1983) 9–10. It is interesting to note that the coins identified by Debono were
late Roman. The earliest from the cave hoard is Byzantine.

91. Van Elderen, "Nag Hammadi Excavation," 229; Lease, "Fourth Season," 79.

92. Grossmann, "Basilica," 233–34. Many of the foundation walls have been
plundered for the stone.

93. Grossmann, "Basilica," 234–35; Lease, "Fourth Season," 80; *G1* 54; *Bo* 49; *Par-*

Other structures have been located below this fourth-century basilica, though their precise dimensions and functions are unclear. One, at least, contained a series of large storage jars sheared off to level the site for the fourth-century basilica.[94]

To date, these excavations have identified two basilicas (the largest and the oldest in Egypt). It is possible, though doubtful, that they correspond to Debono's two basilicas.[95] It would be my view that the earlier basilica dates to the very last years of Pachomius's life or even more probably to the years under Theodore and Horsiesius. Its size is to be interpreted not in terms of the number of monks at Pbow itself, but in terms of the two annual gatherings of the entire community at Pbow held each Easter and in August.[96]

In addition to the work at the basilica and Jabal al-Tarif, the institute's team has also learned of other sites in the area that are of importance for our understanding of the milieu of Pachomian monasticism. A government project to dig a large canal some 750 meters to the north of the basilica site unexpectedly turned up large quantities of early Roman pottery.[97] An inspection of the trenching operation further revealed large limestone blocks at one point in the newly dug canal. The heavy machinery had clearly cut through a sizable early Roman wall. While this discovery was accidental and no scientific effort has yet been undertaken on it, it raises some interesting questions about the nature of the "deserted village" that Pachomius chose for his central monastery.[98]

A second intriguing site was learned of through James Robinson's inquiries about manuscript discoveries in the area. It lies in a desert wadi that proceeds in a northeasterly direction from the northeast corner of the Dishna plain. It is called the Wadi Sheikh Ali.[99] Sev-

---

alipomena 32. The size of the lower basilica is too large to fit the *Vita* description. The dating of the lower basilica is not precise. Pottery analysis has pointed only to the fourth century. Pachomius died in 346 C.E. Thus it could well date after this point. The *Vita* accounts are all situated early in Pachomius's career.

94. Van Elderen, "Nag Hammadi Excavations," 229, photograph on 232.

95. Debono, "Basilique," 201–7; Grossmann, "Basilica," 233–35; Lease, "Fourth Season," 80.

96. *G1* 83; *Bo* 71; Bacht, *Vermächtnis*, 23 n. 74; Veilleux, *Pachomian Koinonia*, 1.278; *SBo* 71 nn. 2, 3.

97. Van Elderen, "Nag Hammadi Excavations," 230–31.

98. *Bo* 49; *G1* 54.

99. Meyer, "Wadi Sheikh Ali."

eral kilometers back into the wadi there exists a pilgrimage site. Large rock overhangs at the site allowed respite from the sun. The site was used very early. It preserves numerous incised graffiti of animals and ships and a crude cartouche of Menkaure of the Old Kingdom. More significant for our period are the large number of monastic inscriptions. They are mostly painted on the rock overhang in typical red paint or occasionally scratched into the surface of the rock. The inscriptions ask for the usual remembrance in prayer or love, and frequently include a statement identifying the writer as a sinner. Thus, for example, "I am Chael the sinner. Please pray for me." A piece of rock found at the site and used in the fashion of an ostracon preserved the words "I am Archeleos. Remember me please." One particular monk, John, even drew his likeness on the wall in the orant position.[100] Roman bricks and potsherds from the early Roman through the Byzantine periods were also found. Further work needs to be done to record this site. While the Pachomian use of the site cannot be established, it is further evidence of the widespread monastic presence in this area.

Finally, brief mention must be made of a survey of the town of al-Qasr carried out by the Institute for Antiquity and Christianity in December 1980.[101] The village, ancient Chenoboskion, was a fairly significant Roman station in Pachomian times. Nearby stands the existing monastery of Apa Palamon, the possible site of the Pachomian monastery of Šeneset. The village also borders the inner desert.[102] The survey produced considerable evidence of the Roman presence. Excavation would, however, be difficult because of the modern village situated over the site.

Further field work awaits. While another season can surely complete the effort to delineate the dimensions of the lower basilica at Pbow and possibly excavate the apse, much more work awaits in the monastery itself.[103] It is here that one might hope to gather significant information that can be related to the description of the monastery

---

100. Meyer, "Wadi Sheikh Ali," 24.

101. Meyer and Beebe, "Literary and Archeological Survey."

102. Lefort, "Premiers monastères," 6. A NASA satellite photograph of this area that I obtained recently offers a vivid view of the inner desert.

103. The Institute for Antiquity and Christianity is hopeful of returning to the field in the near future.

complex in the *Vitae*. It is indeed unfortunate that the effort has not received greater support. Pbow is the only authentically Pachomian site so far identified and offers a chance to uncover the remains of this center of coenobitic origins. Though the significance may be magnified for the Pachomian scholar, the importance of the movement for monastic origins in general should broaden the site's appeal.

ADDENDUM

Since the publication of this article in 1986, two further excavation seasons have been conducted at the site of the Pachomian basilica at Faw Qibli under the direction of Peter Grossmann. The fifth season, conducted in the early months of 1986, was undertaken to clarify the relationship between the great fifth-century basilica and the earlier basilica that had been identified beneath it in the previous excavation seasons. The earlier basilica had been tentatively dated to the middle of the fourth century and identified with the church constructed in Pachomius's lifetime, though I questioned that connection in the above article.[104] The 1986 excavations[105] established the dimensions of the lower basilica at about 56 meters in length and 30 meters in width. It was further concluded that the previously suspected mid-fourth-century date for this earlier basilica was incorrect. It is now believed to date to the end of the fourth or early fifth century.[106] It can thus not have been the church, mentioned in the *Life of Pachomius*, constructed in Pachomius's lifetime.

The 1986 season also found evidence of yet an earlier building beneath the lower basilica. The sixth season (1989) was conducted with a skeleton crew to further establish the size and nature of this earlier

---

104. Grossmann, "Basilica," 234; Lease, "Fourth Season," 80; Goehring, "New Frontiers," 255 (see p. 181 in the present volume).

105. For a brief communication on the season, see Peter Grossmann, "Report on the Excavation in Faw-Qibli–Season 1986," in the International Association of Coptic Studies *Newsletter* 20 (1987) 5–8. Results of the season were also incorporated in Grossmann, "Pbow"; Grossmann and Lease, "Faw Qibli: 1989 Excavation Report"; and Lease, "Traces." The latter two publications include references to forthcoming articles on the 1986 season, but they have not yet appeared in print to the best of my knowledge.

106. Grossmann and Lease, "Faw Qibli: 1989 Excavation Report," 11; Lease, "Traces," 7; Grossmann, "Pbow," 6.1928.

structure.[107] Excavations revealed that this earlier building was also a church of smaller proportions (approximately 41 by 24 meters) dating to the middle of the fourth century. Like the later two basilicas built on top of it, it too contained five aisles and an apse, though the apse was apparently a later addition to the original building. This building now seems the most likely candidate for the smaller church constructed in Pachomius's lifetime and mentioned in the *Life of Pachomius*.

The tentative identification of this lowest basilica with the church used in Pachomius's lifetime gains additional support from a story preserved in section 32 of the Greek *Paralipomena*.[108] According to this account, Pachomius built an oratory with porticoes and pillars of brick. The building was so beautiful that he found himself admiring it, a distraction that he interpreted as the work of a devil. Lest the beauty lead the monks away from their proper contemplation of the divine, Pachomius had the monks tie ropes to the pillars and pull and bend them out of alignment. Derwas Chitty had recognized that "this sounds like an attempt to explain the actual crookedness of a church the writer knew, due, in fact, to inadequate foundations, faulty material, or inexpert building."[109] What is amazing about this story and Chitty's insight is the fact that the archaeological evidence now in hand for the earliest basilica at Pbow reveals that its northern wall was indeed not straight.[110] As one moves from the rear of the basilica toward the apse, at about two-thirds of the way the wall bends outward, forcing the eastern wall and apse to be slightly out of square with the major portion of the basilica. While Chitty seems to associate the oratory mentioned in this story with the monastery of Tabennese, the text does not, in fact, locate the building in a particular monastery. The connection of the archaeological evidence with the story seems too close to be mere coincidence.[111]

---

107. Grossmann and Lease, "Faw Qibli: 1989 Excavation Report"; Lease, "Traces."

108. Halkin, *Sancti Pachomii Vitae Graecae*, 157–58; Veilleux, *Pachomian Koinonia*, 2.55–56. I have not found any reference to this story in the analysis of the archaeological evidence.

109. Chitty, *Desert a City*, 22.

110. For archaeological plans of the basilica, see Grossmann, "Pbow," 6.1928; Grossmann and Lease, "Faw Qibli: 1989 Excavation Report," figs. 1–2; Lease, "Traces," fig. 7.

111. Of course, this does not establish that the basilica was built in Pachomius's

The excavations at Faw Qibli have thus revealed three phases in the construction history of the Pachomian basilicas. The first church (Phase I) was built ca. 330–46 in the lifetime of Pachomius. An apse was added at some point to the original construction. Toward the end of the fourth or at the beginning of the fifth century, the early church was razed to make way for a larger five-aisle basilica (Phase II), which in turn was replaced by the Great Basilica (also with five aisles) completed in 459 (Phase III).[112]

The excavations of the Pachomian basilicas at Faw Qibli found no evidence supporting the violent destruction of the great fifth-century basilica. Destruction of the basilica during the period of Persian control (620s) or during the Arab invasion (640s) is thus difficult to maintain. The legend attributing the site's destruction to al-Hakim (996–1021 C.E.) is likewise to be rejected.[113] Grossmann suggests that "if there is a historical core to this note, it is more likely to be that al-Hakim plundered a building that was already in a ruined state."[114] From the archaeological evidence, it appears that the Pachomian monastery of Pbow, which reached its zenith in the fifth century, began to decline in the aftermath of the Council of Chalcedon.[115] The process continued until the site was abandoned toward the end of the sixth century.

---

lifetime. The legend may have ascribed its building to that period, though the archaeological evidence for its date makes its construction prior to Pachomius's death the most likely scenario.

112. Lease, "Traces," 7 and fig. 7; Grossmann, "Pbow," 6.1928; Grossmann and Lease, "Faw Qibli: 1989 Excavation Report," 9–10 and figs. 1–2.

113. Grossmann and Lease, "Faw Qibli: 1989 Excavation Report," 12; Lease, "Traces," 8–9; Grossmann, "Pbow," 6.1928–29.

114. Grossmann, "Pbow," 6.1929.

115. James E. Goehring, "Chalcedonian Power Politics and the Demise of Pachomian Monasticism" (OP 15; Claremont, Calif.: Institute for Antiquity and Christianity, 1989). See chap. 12 in the present volume.

9

Melitian Monastic Organization:
A Challenge to Pachomian Originality

An accurate picture of early monastic development in Egypt, so far as it is available to us, requires not only a careful study of the facts preserved in the sources that survive, but also serious consideration of the varied nature of the sources themselves. Evidence of the early Pachomian movement, for example, derives almost exclusively from literary sources[1] composed and/or compiled at a date later than the periods they purport to describe. They are in various ways anachronistic with respect to their presentation of the Pachomian movement's early development,[2] and furthermore, because of their subsequent widespread success as literary texts both in Egypt and beyond, they tend to distort the early history of communal monasticism in Egypt in general as "primarily" Pachomian.

Evidence of monks of Melitian persuasion, on the other hand, comes almost exclusively from documentary sources. While such texts are not anachronistic in that they, when dated, offer precise evidence of the movement at a particular point in its history, their impact on the subsequent literary history of Egyptian monasticism has been, at best, minimal. The failure of Melitian monks to survive in a positive way in the later literature of Egyptian monasticism[3] leads to the understanding of their ascetic communities as either a brief experiment overshadowed as a result of Pacho-

---

First published in *Studia Patristica* 25 (1993) 388–95=Elizabeth A. Livingstone, ed., *Papers Presented at the Eleventh International Conference on Patristic Studies Held in Oxford 1991: Biblica et Apocrypha, Orientalia, Ascetica* (Leuven: Peeters Press, 1993). Primary research for this article was conducted at the Akademie der Wissenschaften in Göttingen, West Germany, in 1989–90 under the auspices of the Alexander von Humboldt Stiftung.

1. I distinguish literary sources as those with a textual history within and/or beyond the community from documentary sources which exist in autograph.

2. Goehring, "New Frontiers" (chap. 8 in the present volume).

3. For a list of literary references to Melitian monks, refer to Goehring, *Letter of Ammon*, 230–31.

mius's superior organizational ability,[4] or a by-product developing from[5] or in reaction to[6] the earlier and more dominant "orthodox" Pachomian model.

I want to argue briefly here that any division between Pachomian and Melitian monasticism is in fact a by-product of the tendency, ancient and modern, to define early Christian movements in terms of theological issues rather than organization and lifestyle. Looked at solely in terms of the latter elements, while details may vary, there is really very little that clearly distinguishes an "orthodox" from a "schismatic" monk. To argue for the priority of one monastic community over another when the two groups are divided in the literature on the basis of their theology rather than their ascetic practice forces a division in the development of asceticism in Egypt that was probably not apparent in antiquity. Once so divided, the further notion is fostered that one form of ascetic practice must have been original and others copied or deviated from it. Against the theological background of "orthodoxy" and "heresy," it is the link to the ultimately victorious party that equates with success and *literary* survival, which in turn translates anachronistically as primacy. I would argue that just as the model of "orthodoxy" and "heresy" has been rethought on the theological level so as to transcend the understanding of an earlier period in terms of later labels, so too must we now rethink on the organizational or sociological level earlier models of monastic development that present it simplistically in terms of the successful patterns preserved in the surviving literary texts of a later era.

Evidence of Melitian monasticism may be much more widespread in the papyri than is normally assumed since one is limited in describing Melitian monasticism to those texts that explicitly mention it.[7] Given the latter criterion, the Melitian papyri published by Bell in 1924 remain our most certain evidence of a significant monastic

---

4. Heussi, *Ursprung,* 129–31.

5. Holl, "Bedeutung," 30–31.

6. Ghedini, "Luci nuove," 277–78; cf. idem, review of *Jews and Christians in Egypt.*

7. The correspondence of Papnouthios (*P. Lond.* 1923–29), for example, could as easily be Melitian as not (Bell, *Jews and Christians in Egypt,* 100–120). Bell holds that "Paphnutius, as far as we can tell, was an orthodox Catholic" (102), but his arguments are hardly convincing. Cf. Kramer and Shelton, *Archiv des Nepheros,* 21.

movement among the Melitians early in the fourth century.[8] These texts may be cautiously supplemented by the important archive of Nepheros, which appears to come from the same Melitian community at a slightly later date in the same century.[9] The only other documents referring specifically to Melitian monasticism come from the area of Antinoë in the sixth century and report the sale of cells within the Melitian monastery of Labla by a monk who has left the community to join a nearby orthodox establishment (*SB* I 5174–5175).[10]

The London papyri (*P. Lond.* 1913–22) shed considerable light on the internal organization of individual Melitian monastic communities. This evidence has been detailed in numerous studies and need not be repeated here.[11] I would only mention, in agreement with Heussi, that shared terminology and limited hierarchical patterns are insufficient evidence to establish a connection between the Melitian communities and those of Pachomius.[12] What has not been studied in any detail in these texts, however, is the evidence for an organizational connection among distinct Melitian communities, a connection that, if established, would parallel at approximately the same date the Pachomian *koinonia* or "community of monasteries" and thus challenge the usual assumption of such a system as a Pachomian innovation.

A number of distinct Melitian communities are mentioned in the London papyri. The monastery of Hathor in the Upper Kynopo-

---

8. Bell, *Jews and Christians in Egypt,* 38–99.

9. Kramer and Shelton, *Archiv des Nepheros.*

10. Sayce, "Deux contrats grecs." Evidence indicates that Melitian ascetics continued to seek "converts" as late as the eighth century (Bell, *Jews and Christians in Egypt,* 42–43).

11. Bell, *Jews and Christians in Egypt,* 44–45; Hengstenberg, review of *Jews and Christians in Egypt;* idem, "Bemerkungen," 357–58; Holl, "Bedeutung," 26–31; Ghedini, "Luci nuove"; idem, review of *Jews and Christians in Egypt,* 275–77; Wilhelm Schubart, review of *Jews and Christians in Egypt,* by H. Idris Bell, *Gnomon* 1 (1925) 34–37; Steinwenter, "Rechtsstellung," 20–21; Heussi, *Ursprung,* 129–31; Judge, "Earliest Use," 84–85.

12. Heussi, *Ursprung,* 129–31; Ghedini ("Luci nuove," 271) reads the Melitian texts through the filter of the Pachomian evidence. His suggestion that Patabaeis (Patabeit), who appears in *P. Lond.* 1913 and 1914 with Pageus (Paieous), might be seen as the latter's "second," paralleling the Pachomian office, is unwarranted. The title "second" is nowhere used in the papyri, and when Pageus turns over control of his community during his absence (*P. Lond.* 1913), he turns it over to his full brother Gerontios, not to Patabaeis as one would expect.

lite nome, the apparent source of the collection,[13] is named twice (1913.3; 1920.2).[14] Additional sites mentioned include a community on the island of Memphis (1917.9), one located in the Upper Country (1917.18), probably meaning the Thebaid, and a μονή (hostel, cell, monastery?) to which the Melitians have access in Alexandria (1914.16).[15] Some scholars have suggested that the letter from the wayward monk (*P. Lond.* 1917), who left the community on the island of Memphis, to Paieous, the head of the community at Hathor, in which he pleads to the latter to intercede with the monks on the island on his behalf, indicates that Paieous was a sort of superior general of Melitian monasticism.[16] The letter, however, indicates nothing more than Paieous's renown. There is, in fact, no clear evidence in these texts to indicate an official link among the four Melitian sites mentioned above.

More relevant to the question of an official intercommunity connection is the relationship between *P. Lond.* 1913 and the remaining texts of the archive. This document is a contract for the appointment of a temporary replacement to serve as head of a Melitian monastic community during the absence of its regular leader. The document was drawn up by the community's regular leader, the priest Pageus, son of Horus, of the village of Hipponon in the Herakleopolite nome (Παγεῦς Ὥρου ἀπὸ κώμης Ἱππώνων τοῦ Ἡρακλεοπολίτου νομοῦ πρεσβύτερος), and submitted by him to "the priors of the monastery of monks called Hathor (τοῖς προεστῶσ[ι] μονῆς μονοχῶν [καλ]ουμένης Ἄθορ) situated in the eastern desert of the Upper Kynopolite nome." The occasion for the contract was the ex-

---

13. Although the London papyri were not acquired together, their relationship to each other, with the possible exception of *P. Lond.* 1923, has never been doubted (Bell, *Jews and Christians in Egypt*, 43).

14. The archive of Nepheros likewise derives from a monastery of Hathor, though it is said to be located in the Herakleopolite nome (*P. Neph.* 48), a fact which the editors effectively overcome in their suggested connection of the two collections (Kramer and Shelton, *Archiv des Nepheros*, 11–14).

15. In addition, the Melitian monastery of Labla mentioned in sixth-century papyri is situated near Antinoë (above, p. 189). There is no indication of the date of its foundation, though it could easily have existed already in the fourth century. The archive of Nepheros, if it is Melitian, also preserves evidence suggesting the existence of other Melitian communities, as do various literary sources (Bell, *Jews and Christians in Egypt*, 42–43; Goehring, *Letter of Ammon*, 230–31). The discussion to follow, however, deals only with the evidence in *P. Lond.* 1913–23.

16. Holl, "Bedeutung," 29; Ghedini, "Luci nuove," 270–71.

pected absence of Pageus from his community as a result of his summons to the Synod of Caesarea in 334 C.E. He reports in the text that he gathered together "the monks of our monastery" (τοὺς μονοχοὺς τῆς ἡμετέρας μονῆς) and various important persons from the village of Hipponon[17] and that they together approved the appointment of his natural brother Gerontios to serve in his stead.[18] The contract was signed by Pageus and by others present at this meeting before it was sent to the priors of the monastery of Hathor. The letter includes a list of duties expected of the appointed replacement and thereby supplies our clearest evidence for the internal organization of a specific Melitian ascetic community.

Early discussions of this document centered on this evidence of the community's internal organization and on the figure of Pageus and his relationship to Paieous, the recognized leader of the monastery of Hathor in the remaining texts in the archive. Bell originally distinguished Pageus from Paieous, though he later accepted the growing scholarly consensus that the two names represented alternate spellings and referred to the same person.[19] During the initial debate, no one questioned the assumption that a single monastery, the monastery of Hathor, was involved. The quick identification of the two figures seems to have assured the identification of Pageus's reference to the origin of the contract at the hands of "the monks

---

17. It is clear from the Melitian evidence that a close connection existed between the monastic communities and the village social and ecclesiastical order. The early Pachomian communities also had close ties with the nearby villages. Goehring, "World Engaged," 139–41 (see pp. 46–48 in the present volume).

18. The appointment of a natural brother suggests an establishment founded and/or owned by Pageus and/or his family. Hengstenberg, review of *Jews and Christians in Egypt*, 140–41; idem, "Bemerkungen," 357; Steinwenter, "Rechtsstellung," 21; Krause, "Apa-Apollon-Kloster," 197.

19. Bell, *Jews and Christians in Egypt*, 51 n. 2; idem, "Bibliography: Graeco-Roman Egypt, A. Papyri (1923–1924)," *JEA* 11 (1925) 95–96 n. 2. Identification of Pageus with Paieous is accepted by Ulrich Wilcken, review of *Jews and Christians in Egypt, APVG* 7 (1924) 310–11; Steinwenter, "Rechtsstellung," 20 n. 4; Hengstenberg, review of *Jews and Christians in Egypt*, 139; idem, "Bemerkungen," 357; Holl, "Bedeutung," 28; Ghedini, review of *Jews and Christians in Egypt*, 275–76; idem, "Luci nuove," 261; Hans Hauben, "On the Melitians in *P. London* VI (*P. Jews*) 1914: The Problem of Papas Heraiscus," in Roger S. Bagnall et al., eds., *Proceedings of the Sixteenth International Congress of Papyrology, New York, 24–31 July 1980* (AmSP 23; Chico, Calif.: Scholars Press, 1981) 447 n. 6. Schubart (review of *Jews and Christians in Egypt*, 35) refuses to declare himself on the question, and Judge ("Earliest Use," 84) simply notes the question; cf. E. A. Judge and S. R. Pickering, "Papyrus Documentation of Church and Community in Egypt to the Mid–Fourth Century," *JAC* 20 (1977) 57.

of our monastery" with his identification of the addressees as "the priors of the monastery of monks called Hathor." The question of Pageus's identification as a person "from Hipponon in the Herakleopolite nome" was solved by seeing it as a reference to his place of birth[20] or by concluding that while he headed the monastery of Hathor, he did so as a resident of the village of Hipponon.[21] While both interpretations are possible, they beg the question of why Pageus refers to the gathering together of "the monks of our monastery" in the village of Hipponon in the Herakleopolite nome to confirm his decision, and sends a contractual statement of it to the monastery of Hathor in the eastern desert of the Upper Kynopolite nome.[22]

The use of these two phrases is more easily reconciled with the assumption that the author is referring to two distinct communities, one in Hipponon and the other in the eastern desert of the Upper Kynopolite nome. This conclusion was first suggested by Judge in 1977, though he does not explore the implications of it. His conclusion does force him to reopen the question of the identity of Pageus and Paieous, though he notes that their identity does not affect his argument for the existence of two communities rather than one.[23] I would agree strongly with the latter point, since it seems probable that Pageus, following his selection as a representative to the Synod of Caesarea, became on his return more rather than less influential in the Melitian asectic community and might easily have been transferred to the leadership of the central establishment at Hathor.[24]

---

20. Hengstenberg, review of *Jews and Christians in Egypt*, 139; Steinwenter, "Rechtsstellung," 20.

21. Holl, "Bedeutung," 27; Hengstenberg, "Bemerkungen," 358; Krause, "Apa-Apollon-Kloster," 197; contra Steinwenter ("Rechtsstellung," 20) and Ghedini ("Luci nuove," 274–75) who prefer to place Pageus in the monastery of Hathor.

22. So Judge, "Earliest Use," 84 n. 34.

23. Judge, "Earliest Use," 84–85.

24. Such a move, coupled to the clearly close relationship between the Hipponon foundation and Hathor, more easily solves the rather clear placement of Pageus in *P. Lond.* 1913 in Hipponon with that of Paieous in Hathor in *P. Lond.* 1920 (cf. Steinwenter, "Rechtsstellung," 20 n. 4). The overlap of various names between certain letters, the number of which is relatively few, can be explained in various ways. First, one must note that the common nature of the names makes certain identification problematic in most cases. The most significant overlap occurs between *P. Lond.* 1913 and 1914. In this case, it is possible that the author of *P. Lond.* 1914, an important communication coming from outside the local Melitian community, addressed his letter

If we accept Judge's suggestion, then we have in this contract evidence of a Melitian "community of monasteries" answerable in some form to a central monastery. It may be that the community on the island of Memphis (*P. Lond.* 1917) belongs also to this group. In any case, Paieous, rather than being understood as the superior general of Melitian monasticism in Egypt as some have argued in the past,[25] is better seen simply as the head of an important community of affiliated Melitian monasteries. If such is the case, then we have here a Melitian organization which parallels closely the Pachomian *koinonia.* Additional limited support may be found in the Nepheros archive, where, according to the editors, certain texts appear to indicate the existence of affiliate communities.[26]

This conclusion naturally invites one to speculate over a possible borrowing between the two groups, speculation which I would argue simply leads one astray since any answer lies beyond the evidence at hand. The Melitian evidence indicates an intercommunity connection between two (or more) Melitian monasteries by 334 C.E. The Pachomian sources report that Pachomius formed his first successful community at Tabennese at some point after 323 C.E.[27] In 329 C.E., he founded a second community at Pbow, which served as his headquarters and under which Tabennese was affiliated. Other monasteries were founded by him or joined his system so that by about 340 a total of nine monasteries and two women's communities belonged to his organization.

While the dates alone may favor Pachomian priority, a careful look at the distinct nature of the two systems of affiliation demands greater caution. According to the Pachomian dossier, in Pachomius's lifetime it was his authority alone that held the community together. He appointed the heads of the individual monasteries with the exception of those that joined the system with a leader already in place. There is no indication of a contractual agreement to assure commu-

---

and sent greetings to individuals in different, closely affiliated monasteries, whom he knew and to whom he assumed the contents of the letter would be related.

25. Holl, "Bedeutung," 29; Ghedini, "Luci nuove," 271.

26. Kramer and Shelton, *Archiv des Nepheros,* 13, 33–34.

27. His initial efforts at Tabennese ca. 323 C.E. proved futile. Armand Veilleux, "Pachomius," in Atiya, *Coptic Encyclopedia,* 6.1859–60. The story of the initial difficulties is preserved in the Coptic tradition. Lefort, *S. Pachomii vitae sahidice scriptae,* 3–7, 116–19; English translation in Veilleux, *Pachomian Koinonia,* 1.430–40.

nal acceptance of a replacement or successor. In fact, the near collapse of the *koinonia* in the years immediately following Pachomius's death indicates the lack of such guidelines. It was Theodore who instituted a firmer policy to control the affiliate monasteries by controlling the assignment of leaders to the individual communities.[28] He assumed control of the *koinonia* circa 350 C.E., some sixteen years after the Melitian contract.

The Melitian evidence, on the other hand, indicates that already by 334 C.E. a carefully defined system of leadership control was in place, a system in which changes were contractually confirmed and communicated to a central monastery. One must assume a certain period for such a system to have materialized, and thus the five years between Pachomius's founding of his second monastery at Pbow, which necessitated some form of affiliation, and the Melitian contract seems insignificant. To assume that the Pachomian system, five years after its initial inception, had gained such renown so as to influence the Melitian organization stretches the imagination.

One might argue as easily the reverse, namely, that the Melitian pattern influenced Pachomius.[29] The reference in the *Letter of Ammon* to Melitians who sought to attract Pachomius when he first took up the solitary life could preserve a kernel of truth.[30] While Pachomius may have rejected their ecclesiastical stance, he could have taken notes on their organization. But such speculation too goes beyond the evidence.

It is better to avoid the temptation to assign priority to one community or the other. Given the appearance of these two parallel

---

28. Goehring, "New Frontiers," 240–52 (see pp. 166–79 in the present volume).

29. One might wonder in this regard about the link between monasticism and ecclesiastical politics. It is clear from the Melitian evidence that the Melitian ascetic communities were actively involved in ecclesiastical politics; Pageus attended the Synod of Caesarea. One wonders if Athanasius's efforts to harness other ascetic forces for his side, both real and literary, gained impetus if not an initial push from the influence of Melitian ascetics and their effective network in Egypt. If such is the case, the process thus begun and then preserved in the later literary sources of Egyptian monasticism may indicate an ecclesiastical interest within the so-called orthodox ascetic communities that did not exist in the communities' earlier stages. Cf. Robert C. Gregg and Dennis E. Groh, *Early Arianism: A View of Salvation* (Philadelphia: Fortress Press, 1981), esp. chap. 4.

30. *Epistula Ammonis* 12; Goehring, *Letter of Ammon*, 132 (text), 165 (translation); in the notes to this passage (230–31) I suggested that the evidence was too slight to suggest a Melitian influence on Pachomius.

systems at approximately the same period in the fourth century, it is more appropriate to ask what forces in the development of Egyptian asceticism led at this time to the creation of such multicommunity systems. I suspect that the answer lies simply in a combination of the growing number of monks and the practical advantages that the affiliated systems offered. Just as it was easier for a group of monks to live in a community, or at least in close proximity to one another, than it was to live in complete isolation,[31] so it proved easier on occasion for a group of monasteries to join together than for each to survive alone. Rather than the result of the spread of a single innovative act, such multicommunity organizations arose as a natural product of monastic expansion. Success of a single monastery might naturally lead to the foundation of a second nearby community and result in the affiliation of the two. Less successful communities might naturally affiliate with more successful ones.[32] Whatever the cause, the result was advantageous politically and economically, both in terms of the welfare of the individual communities within the system as well as in terms of the greater influence that they, as a larger group, could wield beyond their walls.

---

31. Growing numbers alone often precluded isolation and thereby necessitated some form of cooperation or communal organization.

32. Both factors were involved, for example, in the formation and growth of the Pachomian *koinonia*.

10

Monastic Diversity
and Ideological Boundaries
in Fourth-Century Christian Egypt

A simple history of the origins and development of Egyptian monasticism is no longer possible. The received tradition, the standard source of that history, has been challenged on two fronts. First, analysis of the traditional literary sources has increasingly called into question their value as descriptive documents of actual historical events. While the degree and nature of the history preserved in these sources remains a subject of debate, there can be little doubt that the authors and compilers of this literature were fashioning their subjects as saints. The literature has rhetorical and ideological purpose. It preserves the figures of monastic origins as ascetic trailblazers who opened up new paths for Christians to follow. The texts are in fact guidebooks for a practice of *imitatio patrum,* and as such they present the ascetic fathers in terms of the ideals that the authors and compilers of the texts wanted their readers to imitate. The degree to which the author's ideals were those of the monk whose story he tells is, at best, difficult to know. It is the recognition of this fact that complicates the use of the literary sources in the reconstruction of monastic history. The saints of monastic origins have receded from the historian's grasp in the same way as the figure of Jesus. The unlettered, anti-Arian Antony of the *Life of Antony* represents the religious ide-

First published in *JECS* 5 (1997) 61–84. This paper was first presented to The Society for the Culture and Religion of the Ancient Mediterranean at the Virginia Polytechnic Institute and State University in Blacksburg, Virginia, on October 15, 1994, and again in a revised form at the Joint Manichaean-Gnosticism section of the American Academy of Religion and Society of Biblical Literature Annual Meeting in Chicago on November 19, 1994. The current form has benefited from comments made by numerous individuals on both occasions as well as from a critical reading by Richard Valantasis and suggestions offered by the anonymous readers for the *Journal of Early Christian Studies.* I thank them all.

ology of the *Vita*'s author, Athanasius;[1] the lives and teachings of the monks of the *Apophthegmata* have been problematized by an increasing awareness of the complexity of the sources and their origin;[2] and the originality and orthodoxy of Pachomius and his communities appears increasingly anachronistic.[3] While the sources surely contain history, efforts to unravel history from its literary embodiment are proving increasingly difficult.

In addition to the difficulties imposed on the interpretation of the traditional literary sources, manuscript and documentary papyrus discoveries have added a wealth of new evidence revealing the controlled perspective of the literary sources and suggesting a diversity and complexity within ascetic development hitherto unimagined. Documentary papyri have indicated the significance of women in the initial stages of the ascetic movement,[4] underscored its early urban setting,[5] and supplied unique evidence of the strength of so-called Melitian ascetics in fourth-century Egypt.[6] The discovery of Manichaean manuscripts has shed light on their considerable presence in Egypt,[7] and the papyri evidence coming now from the Dakhleh Oasis promises more exciting information on their social location.[8] The

1. Rubenson, *Letters of St. Antony*; Brakke, *Athanasius*; Dörries, "Die Vita Antonii."

2. Rubenson, *Letters of St. Antony*, 145–62; Jean-Claude Guy, *Recherches sur la tradition grecque des Apophthegmata Patrum*, 2e Édition avec des compléments (Brussels: Société des Bollandistes, 1984). Graham Gould (*The Desert Fathers on Monastic Community* [OECS; Oxford: Clarendon Press, 1993] 1–25) is less skeptical on the historical value of the text. See idem, "Recent Work on Monastic Origins: A Consideration of the Questions Raised by Samuel Rubenson's *The Letter of St. Antony*," *SP* 25 (1993) 405–16.

3. Chadwick, "Domestication of Gnosis"; idem, "Pachomios," 18; Goehring, "New Frontiers" (chap. 8 in the present volume).

4. Emmett, "Female Ascetics"; idem, "An Early Fourth-Century Female Monastic Community in Egypt?" in Ann Moffitt, ed., *Maistor: Classical, Byzantine, and Renaissance Studies for Robert Browning* (ByzA 5; Canberra: The Australian Association for Byzantine Studies, 1984) 77–83; Judge, "Earliest Use," 85.

5. Judge, "Earliest Use"; Goehring, "Encroaching Desert" (chap. 4 in the present volume).

6. Bell, *Jews and Christians In Egypt*; Kramer and Shelton, *Archiv des Nepheros*; Bagnall, *Egypt in Late Antiquity*, 306–9; Goehring, "Melitian Monastic Organization" (chap. 9 in the present volume); Alberto Camplani, "In Margine alla Storia dei Meliziani," *Aug* 30 (1990) 313–51.

7. Koenen, "Manichäische Mission." A later presence of Manichaeans who hid themselves within "orthodox" monasteries is suggested by G. Stroumsa, "Monachisme et marranisme chez les manicheens d'Égypte," *Numen* 29 (1982) 184–201; idem, "Manichaean Challenge," 308–9.

8. Iain Gardner, "A Manichaean Liturgical Codex Found at Kellis," *Or* 62 (1993) 30–59; idem, "The Manichaean Community at Kellis: Progress Report," *Manichaean*

Nag Hammadi and Dishna manuscript discoveries[9] have added further challenges for the study of early Pachomian history and led to serious reevaluation of the sources.[10]

The evidence increasingly indicates the diversity of ascetic paths available in early Christian Egypt and suggests that interaction across such paths was more common than previously thought. Manichaeans have been credited, for example, not only with influencing the formative stages of coenobitic monasticism, but also with surviving into the later centuries hidden within mainstream monastic communities.[11] Such contact appears to be at odds with the general picture offered by the received tradition, and that fact alone argues for a more careful and critical examination of that tradition. Historical forces preserved the literary works of those authors whose religious ideologies conformed with and furthered an emerging ecclesiastical orthodoxy. Manuscript discoveries have yielded literary texts representing views expunged from the record by the same historical forces, and documentary evidence, preserved by chance, offers additional data. Together, they allow for a fuller, if still unfocused, picture of monastic development in Egypt.

The increased awareness of the diversity of ascetic practitioners in Egypt raises interesting questions about the scope and nature of interaction between monks of different ideological persuasions. There is, of course, no single or simple answer to this question. The degree and nature of the ideological difference, as well as the personalities of the individuals and groups in question and those of their patrons,

Studies Newsletter (1993) 18–26; idem, "Personal Letters from the Manichaean Community at Kellis," paper presented at the Third International Conference of Manichaean Studies, Calabria, Italy, September 1993; idem, "The Manichaean Community at Kellis: Directions and Possibilities for Research," paper presented at the Dakhleh Oasis Project Conference, University of Durham, 1994; Colin A. Hope et al., "Dakhleh Oasis Project: Ismant el-Kharab, 1991–92," *JSSEA* 19 (1989) 1–26.

9. For the Nag Hammadi Codices, see Robinson, "Discovery"; idem, "From the Cliffs to Cairo: The Story of the Discoverers and Middlemen of the Nag Hammadi Codices," in Bernard Barc, ed., *Colloque international sur les textes de Nag Hammadi (Québec, 22–25 août 1978)* (BCNH 1; Québec: L'Université Laval, 1981) 21–59; idem, "Introduction." For the Dishna Papers, see Robinson, "Pachomian Monastic Library."

10. See above, n. 3.

11. Koenen, "Manichäische Mission"; Stroumsa, "Monachisme"; idem, "Manichaean Challenge." One wonders to whom the Manichaeans appeared hidden. It is hard to imagine that they remained completely unnoted as such in the monastic communities themselves.

necessarily impacted the degree and nature of the interaction. Nonetheless, there is increasing evidence that interaction among ascetics occurred across ideological lines that more often sharply separate individuals and groups in the preserved literary sources. The rigorous ideological boundaries drawn by certain authors and furthered by the preservation process cannot be taken as indicative of the Egyptian social and ecclesiastical landscape at large. Rhetoric of value in the politics of Alexandria should not be taken to reflect the actual situation in Egypt. It was rather local ascetic practice, politics, and patronage that determined the degree of ideological openness and interaction in monastic circles in Egypt.

In the pages that follow, I would like to offer two examples that illustrate this problem. The first, the case of Melitian and non-Melitian ascetics in the vicinity of Arsinoë, illustrates the impact of documentary sources on the interpretation of the received tradition. The issues of the Melitian debate were political rather than theological. This is reflected in the harsh antagonism of Athanasius, whose claim to ecclesiastical power was threatened by the Melitian movement. As seen in the writings of Athanasius, the Melitians become dangerous schismatics. Rejection rather than communication is expected. Outside of their immediate political threat to the episcopal throne, however, there is little evidence of an active campaign against Melitians elsewhere in Egypt. While they eventually became associated with heresy, the process was slow and uneven. A careful review of the literary and documentary sources suggests that so-called Melitian and non-Melitian ascetics interacted regularly well into the sixth century.

The second example I wish to explore concerns the question of Origenism, Pachomian monasticism, and the Nag Hammadi Codices. It is my contention that the received Pachomian tradition, impacted by later conceptions of orthodoxy and heresy, fosters the impression of a community bound by a more rigorous theological ideology than actually existed. I do not mean to suggest that the Pachomians rejected orthodox teaching, but only that their orthodoxy was not initially rigorous in its rejection of diverse texts and traditions. The early Pachomians came together as ascetics, not as theologians. This does not mean that they were not interested in theology, but only that the ascetic ideology was the dominant ideology in the movement. As such, it embraced the use of ascetic texts of diverse theological persuasion precisely because of these texts' ascetic orientation. The subsequent rise of a more rigorous orthodoxy within the Pachomian *koinonia* is reflected in the sources which anachronistically impose the later situation on the earlier period. Written as ascetic manuals for later monks, the sources portray an early community, the imitation of which generates orthodoxy in the current community. The more open ascetic ideology of the earlier period had become problematic.

MELITIANS AND NON-MELITIANS IN ARSINOË:
ECCLESIASTICAL POLITICS AND ASCETIC COMMUNITY IN CONFLICT

In the latter years of his life, probably toward the end of the fourth century, the accomplished ascetic Abba Sisoes[12] left his remote abode on Antony's mountain and moved to the outer mountain of the Thebaid near Arsinoë. Word of the arrival of the renowned holy man spread among the local people,[13] and some wished to visit him. As they planned their visit, however, they were put off by the knowledge that there were Melitians on the mountain in the monastery of Kalamon. They knew that the Melitians could not harm the old ascetic, but they feared that by going to the mountain they might fall into the temptation of the heretics. As a result, they did not visit Abba Sisoes.

There is much of interest in this brief story found among the sayings in the alphabetical collection of the *Apophthegmata Patrum*.[14] It is significant that of all the apophthegms in the collection, it alone preserves a reference to Melitians. The narrative voice behind the story speaks from the non-Melitian camp. The desire of the local people

---

12. Uncertainty remains over the number of individuals named Sisoes whose sayings are set forth in the *Apophthegmata Patrum*. The collection refers to a Sisoes of Scetis, Sisoes the Theban, and a Sisoes of Petra. Lucien Regnault, "Sisoes," in Atiya, *Coptic Encyclopedia*, 7.2141.

13. The precise nature of these people (τινές in Greek) is not clear. While they could be ascetics from the surrounding area, it seems more likely that they are general members of the local population (laity).

14. Sisoes 48 (*PG* 65.405); Benedicta Ward, *The Sayings of the Desert Fathers* (London: A. R. Mowbray; Kalamazoo, Mich.: Cistercian Publications, 1975) 185; Lucien Regnault, *Les sentences des pères du désert: Collection alphabétique* (Sablé-sur-Sarthe: Abbaye Saint-Pierre de Solesmes, 1981) 294.

to visit Sisoes coupled with their opposition to the Melitians makes it clear that Sisoes is considered non-Melitian. Sisoes, however, has moved to an ascetic location that includes both Melitian and non-Melitian ascetics.[15] There does not appear to be any difficulty in this arrangement from his point of view. The local people, on the other hand, while they accept his decision to reside on the mountain, have divided the ascetics there more exclusively into the categories of Melitian and non-Melitian. They will only visit the non-Melitian Sisoes in a situation in which he is clearly separated from the schismatics. Mixed communities, acceptable in the ascetic culture, are shown as unacceptable outside of it in the Arsenoite nome.

This story is unique to my knowledge among the literary accounts of the Melitians in central Egypt. The more common pattern preserved in the received monastic tradition is to emphasize the schismatic nature of the Melitians and to preach their avoidance.[16] It is, however, the Sisoes story that finds support in the new documentary sources. They too indicate an interactive and complex relation between ascetics of the two persuasions. In the earlier sources, the Melitians appear every bit as connected with the surrounding community as any non-Melitian faction, and in later materials they reside together with non-Melitian monks in the same monastic community.

The archive of Paieous (mid-330s C.E.),[17] best known for the letter reporting Athanasius's heavy-handed tactics against the Melitians (*P. Lond.* VI 1914), reveals as a whole an active community sympathetic to the Melitians in the Herakleopolite and Upper Kynopolite

---

15. The text is unclear as to whether he has actually moved into the monastery of Kalamon that houses the Melitians or simply resides nearby.

16. *Epistula Ammonis* 12 (Goehring, *Letter of Ammon,* 132, 165) reports that Pachomius rejected the solicitations of the Melitians to join them when he first entered the monastic life, and a Sahidic *Life of Pachomius* (S5 129; Lefort, *S. Pachomii vitae sahidice scriptae,* 179–80; Veilleux [*Pachomian Koinonia,* 1.186]) reports that visitors to the Pachomian monasteries were first questioned as to whether or not they were Melitian. The *Panegyric on Apollo* (Kuhn, *Panegyric on Apollo,* CSCO 394,19–20, CSCO 395,15) reports that the saint, when he fled the Pachomian monastery of Pbow in the emperor Justinian's purge of the non-Chalcedonian elements, had trouble with Melitians in the community in which he sought to settle near Herakleopolis. Melitians are likewise condemned in the *Life of Pamin* (E. Amélineau, *Monuments pour servir à l'histoire de l'Égypte chrétienne aux IVᵉ, Vᵉ, VIᵉ, et VIIᵉ siècle* [Mémoires 4; Paris: Ernest Leroux, 1888] 740; Wipszycka, "Monachisme égyptien," 31-32).

17. *P. Lond.* VI 1913–22; Bell, *Jews and Christians in Egypt,* 38–99.

nomes, centered in the monastery of Hathor, and involved both in ecclesiastical politics and in the more common affairs of the surrounding social world. In fact, it is the integration of the ascetic community within the social fabric of the wider community that dominates the evidence in the texts. Ecclesiastical concerns appear only when outside pressures necessitate a response.[18] *P. Lond.* VI 1913, which records the appointment by Aurelius Pageus[19] of his full brother, Gerontios, to oversee his monastery while he is away at the Synod of Caesarea, indicates a close connection between the Melitian ascetic community[20] and the ecclesiastical structure of the villages. The appointment of Gerontios is approved by "Patabaeis, priest of Hipponon, and Paphnutius, the deacon of Paminpesla and Prôous, former monk, and many others."[21] Among the remaining documents, one finds a request for aid for a brother whose children have been carried off by creditors (*P. Lond.* VI 1915–16); a record of shipment of foodstuffs to the community from a certain Charisios (1918); a request/order for a cloak and a pair of shoes placed with Paieous and his community (1920); a record of items sent to the community (1921); and a report on a series of commercial dealings, including the shipment of a cloak and napkins (1922; the connection of this text to the archive is less certain).

---

18. *P. Lond.* VI 1913 reports Paieous's plans for an interim replacement for himself as head of the community while he is away at the Synod of Caesarea, to which he has been summoned. *P. Lond.* 1914 reports on the problems caused elsewhere by the adherents of Athanasius. It is not surprising that the majority of these texts do not address theological issues, since the reflection of such diversity is rare, by nature, in the documentary papyri (Bagnall, *Egypt in Late Antiquity,* 305–6).

19. Although Bell (*Jews and Christians in Egypt,* 51 n. 2) concluded that Pageus and Paieous, the more common name in the archive, represented two distinct persons, a scholarly consensus grew rapidly to identify the two names as alternate spellings that refer to the same individual. Ulrich Wilcken, review of *Jews and Christians in Egypt, APVG* 7 (1924) 310–11; Steinwenter, "Rechtsstellung," 20 n.4; Hengstenberg, "Review of *Jews and Christians in Egypt,* 139; idem, "Bemerkungen," 357; Holl, "Bedeutung," 26–31; Ghedini, review of *Jews and Christians in Egypt,* 275–77; idem, "Luci nuove," 269–80; Hans Hauben, "On the Melitians in *P. London* VI (*P. Jews*) 1914: The Problem of Papas Heraiscus," in Roger S. Bagnall et al., eds., *Proceedings of the Sixteenth International Congress of Papyrology, New York, 24–31 July 1980* (AmSP 23; Chico, Calif.: Scholars Press, 1981) 447 n. 6. Bell ("Bibliography: Graeco-Roman Egypt, A. Papyri [1923–1924]," *JEA* 11 [1925] 95–96 n. 2) quickly agreed with the growing consensus.

20. Or communities. See Goehring, "Melitian Monastic Organization" (chap. 9 in the present volume).

21. Bell, *Jews and Christians in Egypt,* 50. The association of monks and deacons in a village setting recalls *P. Coll. Youtie* 77. Judge, "Earliest Use."

The later archives of Papnouthios (ca. 340s C.E.) and Nepheros (350s C.E.), which derive from the same community,[22] confirm this picture. The Papnouthios archive consists of seven letters addressed to the anchorite requesting remembrance in prayer, deliverance from difficulties, and healing for beloved ones who are ill.[23] The Nepheros archive, connected with the monastery of Hathor, offers the most complete picture of the community's dealings.[24] Roger Bagnall, summarizing the archive's contents, notes that it "sheds far clearer light on the monks' involvement with the world than on the monastery itself. Letters and contracts show an endless flow of goods in and out of the monastery, journeys by monks, prayers and requests for prayers of lay supporters, the borrowing of commodities, the buying and selling of real property, and the involvement of the clergy in the affairs of the neighboring villages."[25] The archive's editors, in fact, concluded from the material that "the world not only appears to be fully Christianized, but the Melitians openly consider themselves as entirely normal Christians."[26]

The evidence indicates that the Melitians in mid-fourth-century middle Egypt fit quite naturally into their local social landscape. While they undoubtedly had opponents, they conducted their affairs openly in society, many members of which not only accepted them, but supported them financially and sought them out for advice and aid (medical, spiritual, and financial). In all likelihood, their identity as Melitian had little impact on the local population.[27] Their primary social identity was that of monk, and it was as monks that they related to the local community. While they surely understood

22. The Papnouthios archive (*P. Lond.* VI 1923–29) is found in Bell, *Jews and Christians in Egypt,* 100–120. The Nepheros archive (*P. Neph.*) has been published by Kramer and Shelton, *Archiv des Nepheros.* Neither archive contains the certain evidence of Melitian origin offered by the *P. Lond.* VI 1913–22 collection. The editors' careful analysis of the Nepheros texts, however, has established its linkage to the same Melitian community at a slightly later date (pp. 20–21). The same editors also show that the Papnouthios letters, in all probability, have the same Melitian provenance. Bagnall (*Egypt in Late Antiquity,* 308) simply assumes their Melitian provenance.

23. *P. Lond.* VI 1923–29; Bell, *Jews and Christians in Egypt,* 100–120.

24. The archive includes twenty letters (plus six letter fragments) and twelve documents (plus four fragments).

25. Bagnall, *Egypt in Late Antiquity,* 308.

26. Kramer and Shelton, *Archiv des Nepheros,* 5; translated in Bagnall, *Egypt in Late Antiquity,* 308.

27. Bagnall, *Egypt in Late Antiquity,* 305–6.

themselves as Melitians and their allegiance as such was recognized, it appears to have made no difference to their lives as monks.

At the beginning of the sixth century, the peaceful coexistence of Melitian and non-Melitian ascetics is confirmed by three documents concerning the possession, occupancy, and sale of a cell in the monastery of Labla in the district of Arsinoë.[28] In the earliest agreement (*Trinity College Dublin Pap.* D 5), the monk Aioulios wills his cell to his cellmate, the Melitian monk Eulogios, retaining the right to reside in the cell until his death. One of the most intriguing elements in this document is the list of witnesses to the agreement. It is witnessed by "Apa Hol and Tourbos most reverent Melitian priests of the holy catholic church in the monastery of Labla, and Elias deacon of the same nome (?); and we Anoup and Pamoutios and Sambas most reverent orthodox priests in the monastery of Labla."[29] The two later agreements (*SB* I 5174–75) concern the sale of the same cell by Eulogios, who has since become orthodox and moved to the monastery of Mikrou Psuon.

Until the publication of the Trinity College Dublin text in 1990, a common assumption drawn from the two other agreements (first published in 1890) was that Eulogios sold his cell to Melitian monks upon his shift to orthodoxy, a shift that also necessitated his move from the Melitian monastery of Labla to the orthodox monastery of Mikrou Psuon. The new document, however, bears witness to the fact that both "most reverent Melitian priests" and "most reverent orthodox priests" not only resided in the monastery of Labla, but worked together in some fashion in the running of the community. While the precise nature of the monastic settlements around Arsinoë remains unclear,[30] the texts appear to preclude the identification of at least one of the communities, the Labla monastery, as either Melitian or orthodox.

While these contracts, in contrast to the fourth-century archives, offer little information on the interaction of the community with the

---

28. *Trinity College Dublin Papyrus* D 5 (the will) and *SB* I 5174 and 5175 (the sales agreements). The most recent and best discussion of this material is that of McGing ("Melitian Monks"). Earlier studies include Sayce, "Deux contrats grecs"; Krause, "Apa-Apollon-Kloster," 136–74.

29. Translation from McGing, "Melitian Monks," 89–90.

30. McGing, "Melitian Monks," 67–71.

local population, they raise intriguing questions about the relationship of Melitian and non-Melitian monks within a monastic setting. The fact that the witnesses in the initial contract identified themselves as Melitian or orthodox priests indicates that the members of the community divided themselves along these lines. Eulogius's shift to orthodoxy further establishes that the two persuasions competed in some fashion within the community, as might also his eventual move to the nearby ascetic community of Mikrou Psuon.[31] But whatever form the competition took, it was not so divisive as to sunder the community along party lines. Melitian priests and orthodox priests continued to reside in the monastery of Labla. Membership in the Labla monastery was determined on ascetic rather than on schismatic grounds.[32] The monks' political differences did not take precedence over their shared ascetic lives.

A similar situation apparently existed in Scetis until the end of the sixth century. The Arabic *History of the Patriarchs of the Coptic Church of Alexandria* reports that when Damian, a deacon and monk from the Wadi Habib (Scetis), ascended the patriarchal throne in 569 C.E., he banished the Melitians from the monasteries of Scetis.[33] The Melitians, who shared the eucharistic cup many times during the night before they went to the church, apparently had been living freely within ascetic communities that included non-Melitian members (e.g., Damian). That some members within the community opposed them seems clear from the fact that Damian, once he had the outside ecclesiastical authority to do so, banned them from the monasteries.[34] That he could not accomplish it before his election as patriarch, however, suggests that his was a minority view within the community. It thus seems clear that the peaceful coexistence of monks of the two persuasions within a single ascetic community, as

31. The reason behind his move is not clarified.

32. This does not mean that there were no repercussions from the schism within the monastery. It does mean that the schism had not yet impacted the community in such a way as to define membership in terms of the schism.

33. B. Evetts, ed., *History of the Patriarchs of the Coptic Church of Alexandria*, vol. 2: *Peter I to Benjamin I (661)* (PO 1, 4; Paris: Didot, 1948) 473–74. For a general discussion of the sources, see White, *Monasteries of the Wadi 'n Natrun*, 248–49. For even later references see Bell, *Jews and Christians in Egypt*, 42–43.

34. The reason for his opposition is not clear, though mention of ritual deviation in the celebration of the eucharist reflects substantive issues of disagreement. It appears that in the viewpoint of some the Melitians remained a potential ideological threat.

evidenced in the Labla contracts, had remained possible well into the sixth century.

Given the later evidence for cohabitation within a single monastery, one might wonder with respect to the earlier evidence whether the ascetics in question would have applied the episcopal labels to themselves. Would Papnouthios have identified himself as a Melitian, or simply as a monk? Would he have been concerned whether or not those with whom he interacted, both monastics and laity, were Melitian? Or do we, by identifying the three archives of Paieous, Papnouthios, and Nepheros as Melitian, foster a bipolar construction of ascetic history in terms of a debate that is not inherently ascetic? By defining the interpretive parameters in terms of party affiliation, the ascetics who appear in the texts are automatically located in their "proper" pigeonhole as Melitian. The monastery of Hathor, the source of much of the material, is identified as a Melitian monastery. But the question remains whether such Melitian identification and dominance belongs properly to the ascetic community as such or rather to the ecclesiastical structure of the cities and villages with which the ascetic community was economically and socially linked. The documentary evidence suggests that ascetic communities functioned as social institutions within the regional economy. It may well be that the association of certain communities with the Melitian or the non-Melitian party did not occur initially as a phenomenon internal to the ascetic community, but arose only insofar as the ascetic community was economically and ecclesiastically linked to the broader community whose other elements were more directly controlled and defined by the episcopal hierarchy. If such is the case, then the identification of the Hathor monastery as Melitian has primarily to do with the location of the ascetic community in an area dominated ecclesiastically by the Melitian party. This is not to suggest that the monks did not consider themselves Melitian. It is only to argue that they considered themselves monks first. One suspects that there is little if anything that would distinguish them from monks in a non-Melitian monastery. What in fact distinguishes them and makes them Melitian is the location of their community.

The documentary evidence on the social location of Melitian ascetics in the fourth through the sixth centuries supplies the necessary information to make sense of the story of Sisoes in the *Apophthegmata Patrum*. Sisoes had moved from the mountain of Antony to the outer mountain of the Thebaid. The new location included Melitian ascetics among its inhabitants. Some locals, who wanted to visit the famous anchorite, chose not to because of their fear of personal contamination by the Melitian monks. As noted above, the inherent problem in the story is the conflict between the apparent acceptance of the Melitians within an ascetic community that included non-Melitian monks (e.g., Sisoes) and their feared rejection by those outside of the community. The documentary evidence makes it clear, however, that well into the sixth century, Melitian and non-Melitian monks freely cohabited within the same ascetic community. Sisoes's decision to move to an ascetic community that included Melitian monks makes perfect historical sense.

While the evidence is less clear with respect to the view of those outside of the monastery toward the Melitian monks within it, one suspects that through the centuries they had been increasingly turned against them by the non-Melitian episcopal party as it gained the upper hand. The episcopacy sought validation through the establishment of ecclesiastical unity in Egypt. The initial struggles within the episcopal hierarchy, of course, had their lay and monastic[35] components, and they certainly produced their fair share of casualties. But the evidence indicates that the reach of the non-Melitian party could only be extended gradually through all of the elements of Christian society. The Melitian evidence further suggests what should perhaps be obvious, namely, that the efforts of the episcopal party were initially most effective among the laity whose religious lives they oversaw most directly. The ascetic world, on the other hand, offered a haven for those whom the empowered episcopal party opposed, precisely because within the ascetic world, validation and hence communal unity was not based on the same desire for ecclesiastical unity. Within the monastery, differences of opinion on ecclesiastical issues found greater toleration. In the end, of course, the episcopal form of validation prevailed. Melitians were

---

35. One wonders if the initial connection occurred between the episcopacy and the urban ascetics. Badger, "New Man," pt. 3; see also Brakke, *Athanasius*.

banished from Scetis, and Melitian became another synonym for heresy.[36]

ANTI-ORIGENISM, PACHOMIAN MONASTICISM, AND THE NAG HAMMADI CODICES: THE LITERARY ENACTMENT OF ORTHODOXY

The outcome of the Origenist controversy in Egypt clearly impacted the literary record of asceticism. The received tradition became an anti-Origenist tradition. In the *Apophthegmata Patrum*, the natural focus on ascetic practice coupled with the inclusion of anti-Origenist sayings in the final compilation creates the impression of doctrinal unity on this issue.[37] The sayings and stories preserved in the various collections are the primary source for the ideal of anchoritic spirituality espoused in the communities of Nitria and Scetis.[38] They offer, however, little direct information on the doctrinal and ecclesiastical disputes raging elsewhere in the church. What unites the apophthegms in the collections is rather their common interest in the ascetic life.[39] They answer for the most part questions of practical and psychological concern: how to practice obedience, to master the senses, and to avoid the sin of pride. When the issue of doctrine does emerge directly, it is the orthodox point of view that is espoused. In the case of the Origenist controversy, the only direct doctrinal statements to occur are anti-Origenist.

The collection does, however, include sayings attributed to various of the allegedly Origenist monks who were banished from the

---

36. The Melitians with whom Sisoes resided on the outer mountain of the Thebaid are labeled heretics. *Apophthegmata Patrum*, Sisoes 48 (*PG* 65.405). Cf. n. 15 above.

37. Read together with other texts in the broader context of ecclesiastical history, of course, the ideological differences are apparent. The point I wish to score is that in a purely ascetic context, read for ascetic purposes, the sayings appear more ideologically uniform.

38. Good recent studies of the spirituality portrayed in the *Apophthegmata Patrum* are Gould, *Desert Fathers*, and Douglas Burton-Christie, *The Word in the Desert: Scripture and the Quest for Holiness in Early Christian Monasticism* (Oxford: Oxford University Press, 1993). Both authors are rather accepting of the sources as fairly accurate portrayals of early monasticism in Egypt. For a more cautious approach, see Rubenson, *Letters of St. Antony*, 145–62.

39. The *Apophthegmata Patrum*, of course, are diverse in their accounts and their ascetic prescriptions. They are united, however, in their focus on ascetic issues rather than on the issues of doctrine and ecclesiology.

communities. Though exiled because of their teaching, they could not be forgotten because of their ascesis. Too many of them were simply too important within the ascetic culture. The new "orthodox" tradition retained them by purging them of their theological beliefs. Literarily shorn of their theology, they became "orthodox" monks, ascetic heroes renowned for their ascetic teachings. Thus within the alphabetical collection, one can find both a specifically anti-Origenist saying attributed to Abba Lot[40] and three sayings assigned to Dioscoros, one of the four Tall Brothers. One discovers sayings attributed to Evagrius Ponticus, a major influence in the developing Origenism of fourth-century Egypt,[41] alongside others associated with Epiphanius of Salamis, a major opponent of the movement. The sayings of the Origenist figures that are preserved are, of course, ascetical and not theological sayings. While the later compiler, in an anti-Origenist climate, included only direct anti-Origenist statements, he found nothing wrong with the practice of preserving ascetical sayings attributed to those who had been rejected by the church because of doctrinal errors.[42] The ascesis which had unified the monks historically within the same community, now unified them literarily as well. In the literature, however, the anti-Origenist orientation of the later compilation expands the monks' ascetic unity into an apparent doctrinal unity.

The effect of the Origenist debate on the ascetic literature was more overt in the Pachomian dossier. The *Vita prima*, the earliest form of the Greek *Life of Pachomius*, includes a story that strongly affirms Pachomius's opposition to Origen and his teachings. It reports that Pachomius "hated the man called Origen...because he recognized him as a blasphemer," and further states that he "emphatically ordered the brothers not only not to dare to read that man's writings but not even to listen to his sayings." After reporting the saint's destruction of a book by Origen (he threw it in water, since he could

---

40. It is reported that Lot, a solitary living near Arsinoë, became anxious upon hearing words of Origen being quoted and said, "The Fathers must not think that we are like that" (Lot 1; *PG* 65.253–56).

41. Clark, *Origenist Controversy*, chap. 2.

42. Compare the case of Evagrian tradition in the Greek world. Antoine Guillaumont, *Les "Kephalaia Gnostica" d'Evagre le Pontique et l'histoire de l'Origénisme chez les Grecs et chez les Syriens* (PatrS 5; Paris: Editions du Seuil, 1962) 166–70; Clark, *Origenist Controversy*, 249.

not burn it as the Lord's name appeared in it), the text continues by affirming that "the Holy Man [Pachomius] gave to the orthodox bishops and successors of the apostles and of Christ himself the heed of one who sees the Lord ever presiding upon the episcopal throne in the church and teaching from it."[43] The portrayal is of a monk whose primary allegiance is to the orthodox episcopacy in Alexandria.

When one turns to the parallel section of the Bohairic *Life of Pachomius,* however, the story is lacking. The account that precedes it, which is paralleled in the Greek *Vita,* reports that when Athanasius came south to the Thebaid, Pachomius went into hiding to avoid being ordained by the archbishop.[44] His effort to avoid ordination indicates his fear of losing personal control over his spiritual life to the bishop. As such, it calls into question the degree of episcopal allegiance suggested in the Greek anti-Origenist story. Furthermore, while in the Bohairic version Athanasius praises Pachomius to the monks, there is no report of Pachomius's view of Athanasius. The account simply concludes that "after the archbishop had gone away our Father Pachomius came out of the place where he had been hiding."[45] The parallel *Vita prima* account (*G1* 30), on the other hand, reports Pachomius's thoughts and actions from his hiding place. "He gazed," it says, "at [Athanasius] on the boat, and recognized him as a holy servant of God, all the more as he heard of the trials which Athanasius had endured for the sake of the Gospel and of his right faith (τὴν ὀρθήν) for the sake of which he was going to suffer later on."[46] It is precisely here, immediately after this statement, that the Greek *Life* adds the anti-Origen story. While the Greek account does retain Pachomius's fear of ordination, it clearly separates that fear from any challenge to episcopal authority in matters of teaching (doctrine).[47]

---

43. *Vita prima* 31; translations from Veilleux, *Pachomian Koinonia,* 1.317–18. Halkin, *Sancti Pachomii Vitae Graecae,* 20; idem, *Corpus athénien,* 21; Tim Vivian, *St. Peter of Alexandria: Bishop and Martyr* (SAC; Philadelphia: Fortress Press, 1988) 4–6.

44. Bohairic *Life of Pachomius (Bo)* 28; Lefort, *S. Pachomii vita bohairice scripta,* 28–30; Veilleux, *Pachomian Koinonia,* 1.51–52.

45. Translation from Veilleux, *Pachomian Koinonia,* 1.52.

46. *Vita prima* 30 (Halkin, *Sancti Pachomii Vitae Graecae,* 19–20); translation from Veilleux, *Pachomian Koinonia,* 1.317.

47. The problems that Pachomius confronted at the Council of Latopolis, an account of which is preserved only in the Greek tradition (*Vita prima* 112; Halkin, *Sancti Pachomii Vitae Graecae,* 72–73), hints of differences and difficulties between the Pachomians and the local ecclesiastical hierarchy.

Given the evidence of these texts, it is hard to avoid the conclusion that the Greek version, both through its revisions and additions, has posthumously aligned Pachomius with the Alexandrian episcopacy and the anti-Origenist faction. It is interesting to note, in fact, that the only other independent[48] anti-Origenist account in the Pachomian dossier appears in the *Paralipomena* (sec. 7), a Greek source that evidences Lower Egyptian influence.[49] One thus further suspects that the ecclesiastical alignment of Pachomius with the Alexandrian hierarchy was fostered first and foremost within the Greek tradition, probably in Lower Egypt.[50] The interest in the Pachomian movement in Alexandria is apparent in the letter attributed to the archbishop Theophilus in which he requests a copy of the *Life of Pachomius and Theodore* from the Pachomian abbot Horsiesius.[51] If the present form of the Greek texts had their origin in an anti-Origenist climate in Lower Egypt, it is little wonder that they became vehicles to espouse the anti-Origenist cause among the ascetics. If Pachomius, who had come to be seen as the author of the coenobitic enterprise, could be shown to have hated Origen, so might the present-day coenobites be rallied against his latter-day followers. The result of the process, however, is the anachronistic portrayal of Pachomius and his early community as finding their validation as much in doctrine as in ascesis. It is a similar literary process to that which we saw at work in the *Apophthegmata Patrum* that claimed the Nitrian fathers, as a whole, for the anti-Origenist cause. In both cases the result is the rejection of the possibility that an ascetic community could find unity in shared ascetic practice apart from conformity to a particular teaching defined by the episcopacy.

---

48. Later editions of the Greek *vita* have preserved the anti-Origenist account. The editor of *G3*, in fact, elaborates on the pro-Athanasian material. Vivian, *St. Peter of Alexandria*, 6; Veilleux, *Pachomian Koinonia*, 1.411.

49. Veilleux, *Liturgie*, 21–24.

50. Chadwick, "Pachomios," 15–17.

51. Crum, *Papyruscodex*, 12–17, 65–72; Lefort, *Vies coptes*, 389–95. The authenticity of the letter has been challenged by W. Hengstenberg ("Pachomiana mit einem Anhang über die Liturgie von Alexandrien," in A. M. Koeniger, ed., *Beiträge zur Geschichte des christlichen Altertums und der byzantinischen Literatur: Festgabe Albert Ehrhard* [Bonn: Kurt Schroeder Verlag, 1922] 238–52). Whether or not the letter is authentic, its claim indicates that a linkage was being affirmed. Goehring, *Letter of Ammon*, 118–19.

Samuel Rubenson's recent analysis of the Antonian traditions[52] suggests an even more systematic revision of the figure of Antony both to fit and to shape later ascetic ideals. Rubenson, who builds his case on the authenticity of the *Letters* of Antony, argues that the unlettered monk described in the *Life of Antony* is a purposeful creation designed to separate monasticism from its historic origins in the philosophically oriented world of dissatisfied intellectuals. While Antony was not a systematic teacher or philosopher, the letters indicate that he developed a Christian gnosis under the influence of Origenist theology and within what was to him a self-evident Platonic framework. The *Life of Antony*, on the other hand, presents Antony and his teachings as a product of a "native and naive Coptic Biblicism unaffected by Greek thought."[53] The *Life of Antony* is, in Rubenson's words,

> a political text; it has the express purpose to present *the* model for Christian living. While the author of the letters exhorts his disciples to strive toward a deeper understanding of his words, the author of the *Vita* exhorts them to emulate the ideal presented. The letters show that the purpose of the *Vita* was neither to "humanize" a charismatic teacher nor to "elevate" a simple monk, but to use the influence of Antony to depict the victory of Orthodoxy over pagans and heretics, the victory of the cross over demons, of *gnosis* by faith over *gnosis* by education, of the "man taught by God," the *theodidaktos*, over the philosophers.[54]

The long-treasured and influential picture of a simple, unlettered Copt, whose wisdom came from God and whose orthodoxy was beyond reproach, has more to do with Athanasian ideology than with an identifiably historical Antony. While details of the historic

---

52. Rubenson, *Letters of St. Antony*. The impact of Athanasius's theology on the depiction of Antony in the *Vita* has long been recognized (see above, n. 2).

53. Rubenson, *Letters of St. Antony*, 186. Rubenson supports his argument for the philosophical background of monasticism's origins by noting that "in Egypt in the late third century, a country where new leaders and new social structures were in high demand and traditional religion was in decline, new religious movements such as monasticism were not the products of people on the margin of society, but of intellectuals dissatisfied with what tradition had to offer" (187). It may in fact have been precisely such an academic setting that allowed for diverse points of view in early ascetic communities. *Gnosis* by faith is often less tolerant than *gnosis* by education. As the propaganda literature carried the day for the former, the proponents of the latter, who by nature were more tolerant of the former, were themselves no longer tolerated. Cf. Brakke, "Canon Formation."

54. Rubenson, *Letters of St. Antony*, 187.

Antony lie beyond our grasp, Rubenson's analysis underscores the impact of the episcopal program on the received tradition of ascetic history.

The ascetic tradition represented in the *Life of Antony*, the *Apophthegmata Patrum*, and the Pachomian dossier has become, in a sense, a mythic history. It places the origins of Christian asceticism in an orthodox mythic past, made ever present through imitation, yet always beyond the imitator's grasp.[55] The authors/compilers of the texts have fashioned acceptable literary icons. Conscious or otherwise, they created a powerful, self-perpetuating ideology. By rewriting ascetic history in terms of more rigidly defined doctrinal and ecclesiological boundaries, the famed ascetics of the past became sanctioned saints, and their imitation swelled the ranks of the ascetic movement as so defined. Those who did not conform to the picture were either re-created as "orthodox" monks, or they were marginalized as heretics. Orthodoxy and ecclesiastical conformity became defining elements of authentic ascetic formation.

The impact of this received tradition occurs not only through its vocal presentation of orthodoxy, but also through its chosen silence concerning diversity. The marginalized heretics, as in the case of the Origenist visitor to Pachomius, come from without the authentic ascetic community. The sacred time of ascetic origins is fashioned pure. If Rubenson is correct in his revolutionary study of the Antonian tradition, one must suspect that the process he uncovered there impacted the ascetic tradition more broadly and systematically. Its visible influence on the Pachomian dossier, as described above, occurred through the anachronistic inclusion of anti-Origenist stories in the Greek tradition. Less visibly, it impacted the tradition through the deletion of evidence that contrasted with it. If the naive, unlettered, and orthodox Copt portrayed in the *Life of Antony* was in reality a literate figure whose asceticism was influenced by Origenist theology and Platonist thought, it is equally arguable that the simple and naively orthodox Coptic community of the Pachomians portrayed in the literature, in reality, drew from similar heterodox

---

55. One suspects that the common monastic complaint that present-day ascetics are pale copies of the heroic past has as much to do with the elevation of the past as with the decline of the present.

traditions.[56] Pachomius's use of a secret alphabet in his own letters as well as his trial before the Council of Latopolis offer suggestive examples from within the Pachomian dossier itself.[57] The influence of the Manichaean ascetic movement on the emergence of Christian coenobitic monasticism offers an example from outside of the received tradition.[58] While it does not mean that the Pachomians included Manichaeans among their original numbers, or that they showed interest in Manichaean theology, it does suggest that the ascetic impulse interacted and borrowed across ideological lines.

Even more suggestive is the possibility that both the Nag Hammadi Codices and the Dishna Papers[59] derived from Pachomian monasteries. While the available evidence does not permit certainty with respect to the origin of these manuscript collections,[60] both the circumstantial evidence[61] and the refined theoretical argu-

---

56. Note, for example, Pachomius's own use of a mysterious alphabet in his letters. Quecke, *Briefe Pachoms*; cf. Wisse, "Language Mysticism," 101–20.

57. *Vita prima* 112 (Halkin, *Sancti Pachomii Vitae Graecae*, 72–73).

58. Koenen, "Manichäische Mission"; Goehring, "Origins of Monasticism," 245–46 (see pp. 29–30 in the present volume); see also, for a Melitian parallel, idem, "Melitian Monastic Organization" (chap. 9 in the present volume).

59. The Dishna discovery, which includes many of the Bodmer and Chester Beatty papyri, may perhaps more easily be offered as part of a Pachomian monastic library, since it includes no clearly heterodox texts and, if James Robinson is correct, does include copies of the letters of Pachomius. In addition to the Pachomian letters and an expected sizable number of canonical and apocryphal Christian texts, the collection includes manuscripts containing portions of Homer (5 mss.), works of Menander (1), Thucydides (1), Cicero (1), and Achilleus Tatios (1). In addition, one finds a satyr play, scholia to *Odyssey* 1, mathematical exercises, a Greek grammar, tax receipts from Panopolis, and a piece of ethnography or a philosophical treatise. The classical texts may well have come into the monastery, if indeed it is a monastic library, with persons entering the community. But it still raises the issue of the diversity allowed within the community. The received Pachomian tradition leaves little room for the existence of such diversity within the community's library. Robinson, "Pachomian Monastic Library."

60. The issue has spawned a considerable bibliography. See especially Säve-Söderbergh, "Holy Scriptures or Apologetic Documentations?"; Barns, "Greek and Coptic Papyri"; Robinson, "Introduction"; Wisse, "Gnosticism"; Hedrick, "Gnostic Proclivities"; Chadwick, "Domestication of Gnosis"; idem, "Pachomios"; Shelton, "Introduction"; Rousseau, *Pachomius*, 26–28; Armand Veilleux, "Monachisme et gnose," *LTP* 40 (1984) 275–94 and 41 (1985) 3–24; idem, "Monasticism and Gnosis"; Goehring, "New Frontiers" (chap. 8 in the present volume); Scholten, "Die Nag-Hammadi-Texte als Buchbesitz."

61. The proximity of the discovery to the central Pachomian monastery of Pbow first raised the issue of a possible connection. On the location of the discovery, see Robinson, "Discovery"; idem, "From the Cliffs." The caves in the cliffs offer clear evidence of monastic usage. Van Elderen, "Nag Hammadi Excavation"; Torgny Säve-

ments[62] make the case for Pachomian provenance convincing. The extent and manner of the influence of Origenist theology and Platonic thought in the formative stage of Egyptian monasticism suggested by Rubenson[63] adds weight to the argument for the Pachomian origin of the codices. The interest in such material gains credence. There seems no reason, given the nature of the received tradition, to reject the gathering and use of such texts by elements within an ascetic community not yet defined in terms of the rigorous orthodoxy of the Alexandrian episcopacy.[64]

This is not to suggest that all Pachomian monks read such texts,[65] or that those who did believed all that they read.[66] It is only to

---

Söderbergh, *The Old Kingdom Cemetery at Hamra Dom (El-Qasr wa es Saiyad)* (Stockholm: Royal Academy of Letters, History and Antiquities, 1994), 17–18. The quality of the codices indicates their nature as sacred texts rather than heresiological reference books; contra Säve-Söderbergh, "Holy Scriptures or Apologetic Documentations?" The texts preserved in the cartonnage are consistent with a monastic provenance (Barns, "Greek and Coptic Papyri"; Goehring, "New Frontiers," 248–50 [see pp. 174–77 in the present volume]; Scholten, "Die Nag-Hammadi-Texte als Buchbesitz," 157–59; contra Shelton, "Introduction"). Colophons and a scribal note (II.145.20–23; VI.65.8–14; VII.127.28–32) likewise fit a monastic provenance. Archaeological excavations at the central Pachomian monastery of Pbow unearthed a fourth-century bowl remarkably similar to the one used to seal the jar in which the codices were buried. The bowl is housed at the Institute for Antiquity and Christianity in Claremont, California. The lid of the jar is in the collection of the Norwegian bibliophile, Martin Schøyen. Recent study of the orthographic variations in the editions of the *Apocryphon of John* preserved in the codices suggest evidence of "the beginning of the Sahidic standardization process," which is best understood as occurring within a monastic setting. Frederik Wisse, "Redaction and the Apocryphon of John," paper delivered at the 1993 annual meeting of the Society of Biblical Literature in Washington, D.C.

62. The early theories of Säve-Söderbergh ("Holy Scriptures or Apologetic Documentations?"), who saw the texts as heresiological sourcebooks, and Hedrick ("Gnostic Proclivities"), who explored the first Greek *Life of Pachomius* for evidence of Gnostic leanings, find little support today. More recent efforts focus on reexamining the nature of early monasticism, questioning the interest and abilities of early monks in matters of theology, and viewing the application of the categories of orthodoxy and heresy to the early movement as anachronistic. See especially Chadwick, "Domestication of Gnosis"; Wisse, "Gnosticism"; Goehring, "New Frontiers" (chap. 8 in the present volume); Scholten, "Die Nag-Hammadi-Texte als Buchbesitz."

63. Rubenson (*Letters of St. Antony*, 185) notes that "although Antony presents no systematic teaching, it is evident that his theology must be understood against the background of contemporary Platonic traditions."

64. The success of the episcopal culture in bringing the Pachomian movement more directly under its control appears to have occurred during the period of Theodore's leadership. Goehring, "New Frontiers."

65. Chadwick ("Domestication of Gnosis," 15) notes that "the hypothesis of a gnostic sympathizer among Pachomius's monks is not ridiculous."

66. Chadwick ("Pachomios") held that "it is not inherently probable that Pa-

argue that a community that did not yet define itself in terms of doctrine did not yet banish books from its library over issues of doctrine. As Theodore moved the movement more closely into harmony with the Alexandrian patriarchy after Pachomius's death,[67] the library was purged along episcopal guidelines. It was under Theodore's leadership that Athanasius's festal letter of 368 C.E., which defined scripture and called for the rejection of apocryphal texts, was read in the monasteries.[68] One suspects that he was instrumental in the community's early deacquisition process.[69]

CONCLUSIONS

The two examples presented here illustrate situations in which the boundaries between ecclesiastically or doctrinally distinct individuals, groups or literatures appear remarkably fluid. The Melitians and non-Melitians in the Labla monastery certainly recognized each other as such, and yet that recognition did not preclude their interaction in some form. When the impact of the anti-Origenist movement on ascetic literature is taken into account, the ideological exclusivity portrayed in the literature becomes suspect, and the bases for denying the use of heterodox texts fade away. While one cannot

chomios was interested in the niceties of orthodox doctrine as a theological system" (18). Links to the episcopal hierarchy were initially few and weak, and interest in doctrine grew in step with the development of those links. "This is not," he notes, "a matter of naively setting out to 'discover' Pachomios to have been a heretical ascetic subsequently covered in orthodox plasterwork, but rather of asking to what extent it is reasonable to think the early Pachomian tradition largely indifferent where dogma is concerned, content to make use of a diversity of gifts so long as they encourage renunciation of the world" (18). On the other hand, I have no doubt that various of the monks understood what they read and were capable of using the material discriminatingly. The point is that they initially discriminated in how they read a text (and possibly who could read it) and only later in terms of which texts they, as a community, were allowed to possess.

67. Goehring, "New Frontiers," 236–52 (see pp. 162–79 in the present volume); Chadwick, "Pachomios," 21–24.

68. Bohairic *Life of Pachomius* 189. Lefort, *S. Pachomii vita bohairice scripta,* 175–78; Veilleux, *Pachomian Koinonia,* 1.230–32.

69. If one assumes that both the Nag Hammadi Codices and the Dishna Papers belonged to the Pachomians, then the archbishop's letter was not understood to cover all noncanonical literature. The Nag Hammadi Codices contained Christian apocryphal texts of particularly suspicious nature. The Dishna Papers (see above, n. 59), which survived longer in the Pachomian community, included other apocryphal texts as well as classical texts, some of which might be considered questionable in an ascetic library.

finally prove that Pachomian monks produced and read the Nag Hammadi Codices, no longer can one deny it on the basis of the texts' heterodoxy alone.

More broadly speaking, the examples suggest a need to rethink the varied use and impact of ecclesiastical and doctrinal categories in discussions of the social world of early Christianity in general and of ascetic communities in particular. The employment of dualistic categories to establish boundaries between divergent ideologies does not necessarily translate into impervious social divisions. Melitian and orthodox priests worked together at Labla, so-called Origenist and anti-Origenist ascetics lived together in Scetis prior to the conflicts caused by Theophilus's festal letter of 399 C.E.,[70] and Pachomians most likely read heterodox texts.

The social enforcement of ecclesiastical or doctrinal boundaries through public condemnation and expulsion represents a rigorous application of ideology. The cases presented here suggest, however, that it was not party difference (*haeresis*) alone that forced rigorous social division. The equation of doctrinal division with social separation arises among those elements that find self-validation in doctrinal unity and control. It is perhaps easiest to associate the episcopacy, driven by the nature and needs of ecclesiastical hierarchy, with this position. Ascetic communities, on the other hand, with their independent basis of authority and their focus on shared ascesis as the source of self-validation and unity, appear in many cases to have been less threatened by interaction across the same ecclesiastical and/or doctrinal boundaries. But the situation was certainly more complex. Not all bishops were equally rigorous, and not all abbots were equally open to diversity.[71] I would hold, nonetheless, that

---

70. A later example is the comparatively peaceful coexistence of Chalcedonian and non-Chalcedonian elements at Scetis, each with their own church. *Apophthegmata Patrum* (Alphabetical Collection), Phocus 1–2 (*PG* 65.431-34); Chitty, *Desert a City,* 148–49.

71. The enforcement of "orthodoxy" varied over time and space, both for ascetic practitioners and for members of the episcopacy. A rigorous abbot meant less diversity in the monastery, and a more lenient bishop allowed for greater diversity within his see. Shenoute supplies an example of the more rigorous abbot (Tito Orlandi, *Shenute contra origenistas* [Rome: C.I.M., 1985]; idem, "A Catechesis against Apocryphal Texts by Shenute and the Gnostic Texts of Nag Hammadi," *HTR* 75 [1982] 85–95). The Egyptian bishops who harbored members of a Gnostic sect in their church until they were pointed out by Epiphanius illustrates the less rigorous bishop (Epiphanius, *Pa-*

the differences in primary focus and in the nature of authority between the two institutions did in general orient their representatives
differently — the bishop toward ecclesiastical and doctrinal rigor, the
monk toward ascetic rigor.

The implementation of a more rigorous and exclusive ecclesiastical and doctrinal ideology within the ascetic movement did take
place on a case-by-case basis over time both historically and literarily. The success of the more rigorous proponents in enforcing
their exclusive view within the ascetic movement was, in each case,
made retroactive and permanent by filtering the received tradition
through the newly defined categories of orthodoxy and heresy. Such
filtering formed the ascetic heroes of the past as literary icons. The
early monks became idealized saints; their lives became textbooks
for imitation. It is, in fact, precisely through the creation of this
iconography that the category of orthodoxy, used rigorously and exclusively, became a constituent element in the definition of early
Christian asceticism. The true ascetic becomes the one who practices orthodoxy; the heterodox monk's ascesis is ultimately labeled
docetic.[72]

---

narion 26.17.9; Karl Holl, ed., *Epiphanius [Anachoretus und Panarion]* [GCS; Leipzig: J. C.
Hinrichs, 1915] 1.98; Williams, *Panarion I*, 98).

72. This is the argument of Epiphanius of Cyprus in his *Panarion*. He notes, for
example, that the elderly man Peter, with whom the origin of the Archontics is associated, "appeared to be a hermit (ἀναχωρητὴς γὰρ ἐδόκει εἶναι) because he would sit
in a certain cave" (*Panarion* 40.1.4; Holl and Dummer, *Epiphanius II*, 81; Williams, *Panarion I*, 262). In a similar vein, he describes the Origenist ascetics as persons who
appear to have adopted the ascetic life (δοκοῦσι τὸν μονήρη βίον) by withdrawing to
the desert (*Panarion* 64.4.1; Holl and Dummer, *Epiphanius II*, 409; Williams, *Panarion II
and III*, 134).

PART THREE

PACHOMIAN STUDIES:
THE LATER YEARS

11

The Fourth Letter of Horsiesius and the Situation in the Pachomian Community following the Death of Theodore

Three previously unknown Coptic letters attributed to two of Pachomius's immediate successors were discovered in codices of the Chester Beatty Library in Dublin in the mid-1970s. They include a letter of Theodore, a critical edition of which was published by Hans Quecke in 1975,[1] and two letters of Horsiesius, the critical edition of which has yet to appear. A second copy of the new letter of Theodore preserved in a small private German collection was published by Martin Krause in 1981.[2] In addition to the translations of the letter of Theodore that appeared with the critical editions of the two copies, translations of all three new letters of Theodore and Horsiesius have been published by Adalbert de Vogüé and Armand Veilleux.[3] Little interpretation or discussion of these letters and their import for our understanding of the Pachomian movement after Pachomius's death, however, has occurred.

Prior to the discovery of these three texts, the Pachomian corpus included fourteen letters attributed to Pachomius, Theodore, or Horsiesius.[4] Twelve of these were long known from the collection of

---

This paper is published here for the first time. It was originally written in 1980 following research conducted in Rome through a grant from the Corpus dei Manoscritti Copti Letterari. The paper was to be included in the publication of the critical edition of the letters by Tito Orlandi, Hans Quecke, and Adalbert de Vogüé. The critical edition has yet to appear. Minor revisions of the 1980 form of the paper have been made in preparation for its inclusion in this volume.

1. Hans Quecke, "Ein Brief von einem Nachfolger Pachoms (Chester Beatty Library Ms. Ac. 1486)," *Or* 44 (1975) 426–33.

2. Krause, "Erlassbrief."

3. Vogüé, "Épîtres"; Veilleux, *Pachomian Koinonia*, 3.127–29, 157–65.

4. The fourteen represent texts that survive independently as letters. An additional letter attributed to Theodore appears in *Epistula Ammonis* 32. It is presented as a letter sent by Theodore to the monks in Nitria, assuring them of God's mercy and

Pachomian materials translated by Jerome.[5] Eleven of these twelve letters are attributed to Pachomius himself, while the twelfth is ascribed to Theodore.[6] Eight of the eleven letters of Pachomius also survive in Greek and/or Coptic.[7] In addition to these twelve letters, two letters of Horsiesius were also previously known (Epistles 1 and 2). They both survive in a single Coptic manuscript published by Lefort in 1956.[8] The three new letters likewise exist only in the original Coptic. The two new letters attributed to Horsiesius are referred to here as Epistles 3 and 4.[9]

The three new letters, whose authenticity is beyond dispute, supply valuable evidence of the Coptic epistolary style of Pachomius's two main successors. The letters, produced by the abbots themselves, offer direct access to the period of the movement from which they derive. They do not participate in the anachronistic developments discernible in other Pachomian sources. Theodore and Horsiesius speak for themselves in their original language, free from the hagiographic *Sitz im Leben* of the *Vitae* or the layering effect of the Pachomian *Rule*. Their individual character and spirituality shine through. In the various versions of the *Life of Pachomius*, on the other hand, they are seen through the eyes of the religious community that they led; a community that, in defining its existence through them, necessarily sanctified them. While the *Vitae*, by their very nature, offer more chronological history, their representation of the abbots reveals as much, if not more, about the spirituality of the community at the time of the individual *Vita*'s composition than about that of the individual abbots.[10]

---

predicting the further advance of the Arian persecution. It was written, according to Ammon's chronology, in 356 C.E.

5. Boon, *Pachomiana latina*, 77–106.

6. Boon, *Pachomiana latina*, 105–6; Steidle, "Osterbrief."

7. Quecke, *Briefe Pachoms*; idem, "Ein neues Fragment der Pachombriefe in koptischer Sprache," *Or* 43 (1974) 66–79; idem, "Briefe Pachoms in koptischer Sprache: Neue deutsche Übersetzung," in *Zetesis Album amicorum aangeboden aan Dr. E. de Strycker* (Antwerp: De Nederlandsche Boekhandel, 1973) 655–63.

8. Lefort, *Oeuvres*, 63–66; Georg Zoega, *Catalogus codicum copticorum manuscriptorum qui in Museo Borgiano Velitris adservantur* (Rome, 1810; reprint, Leipzig: Hinrichs, 1903) clxxviii.

9. They are so numbered by Veilleux (*Pachomian Koinonia*, 3.157–65), who translates all of the letters. Vogüé ("Épîtres"), who translates only the new letters, labels them Epistles 1 and 2.

10. Although Pachomius's use of an alphabetical code is noted in the first Greek

Beyond the importance of all seventeen Pachomian letters in this regard, some also contain important information about the history of the community. At least four of the letters were sent out to the various monasteries in the system (*koinonia*) to call the monks together at the central monastery of Pbow for the biannual gatherings that took place each Easter and in August.[11] Pachomius's fifth letter and the letter of Theodore translated by Jerome were sent out in connection with the annual Easter celebration. As such, they represent a borrowing of the festal letter genre that emanated from Alexandria.[12] Pachomius's seventh letter and the new letter of Theodore represent the appropriation of this genre for the calling of the monks together for the August reckoning.[13] The second new letter of Horsiesius may also represent a call to the annual Easter celebration, though the connection is less certain since the opening of the letter has been destroyed. It must be noted, however, that in these cases the historical situation is determined by the genre. The letters are tied only in a general way to the annual assemblages at Pbow. Furthermore, beyond the assignment of each letter to the period during which its author was functioning as general abbot, more precise dating is impossible. There is no "festal index" for the Pachomian corpus.

In the case of the letters translated by Jerome, a sort of index does occur in the form of secondary titles attached to the letters. These titles name the addressee and supply some detail in terms of the original *Sitz im Leben* of the epistles. Presumably such information passed on orally with the letters at first, perhaps added in the margin with the passage of time. Its survival, especially once

---

Life of Pachomius (*G1* 99), the nature and extent of its use becomes apparent only in the letters. It is to the letters that Jerome refers in mentioning the *lingua mystica* (*Praefatio Hieronymi* 9; Boon, *Pachomian latina*, 8–9). Palladius does attempt an explanation of the code (*Historia Lausiaca* 32.4), which seems to be related to the reference in Horsiesius's *Testament* 7. It has been suggested, however, that the latter is an interpolation (Basilius Steidle and Otmar Schuler, "Der 'Obern-Spiegel' im 'Testament' des Abtes Horsiesi," *EA* 43 [1967] 30). It is clear that the use of the *lingua mystica* in the letters is considerably more difficult to interpret than one would gather from Palladius's account alone. Quecke, *Briefe Pachoms*, 28–29.

11. Bohairic *Life of Pachomius* (*Bo*) 71; Fourth Sahidic *Life of Pachomius* (*S4*) 71; First Greek *Life of Pachomius* (*G1*) 83; Veilleux, *Liturgie*, 249–61, 366–70; Steidle, "Osterbrief."

12. Veilleux, *Liturgie*, 136.

13. Goehring, "World Engaged," 141 (see p. 48 in the in the present volume); Veilleux, *Liturgie*, 366–70; Ruppert, *Das pachomianische Mönchtum*, 323–26; Steidle, "Osterbrief," 106–10.

the letters left their original setting, depended on its becoming part
of the written tradition, added at some point in the scribal transmission.[14] The information contained in the Latin titles is, however,
often of limited value in interpreting the letters themselves. Beyond
the three reunion letters contained in the collection, it is difficult to
surmise their original historical setting from the internal evidence
alone. There are few references capable of precise historical connection, and Pachomius's use of his enigmatic alphabetical code often
makes interpretation of the letters problematic at best. It must be remembered that the letters were addressed to Pachomian monks who
knew the community and the current situation. There was no need
to spell such factors out. In a sense, it is the very lack of precise
historical data that allowed the *Sitz im Leben* of the moment of composition to metamorphose into one of general edification, warranting
the continued transmission of the letters both within the community
and beyond.

In spite of the lack of specific concrete historical references in
the individual letters, the original *Sitz im Leben* for all of the letters
of Pachomius and Theodore is discernible in some form. Both letters of Theodore are reunion letters and although the information
contained in the titles to the Pachomian epistles is limited and secondary, there is nothing in the letters themselves to challenge its
veracity. In the case of the four letters of Horsiesius, however, other
criteria must be sought. The opening survives for only one letter,
and although the title preserved there identifies the addressee as
Theodore, the occasion of the letter is not specified.[15] None of the
letters offers clear internal evidence that can be linked to the *Vitae*
tradition. Furthermore, Horsiesius's reliance on biblical quotation in
place of narrative proves almost as enigmatic in this regard as Pachomius's secret alphabetical code. Horsiesius's letters read much like a
florilegium.

The importance of scripture in the Pachomian community has

---

14. Alternatively, one must also question the Pachomian origin of the titles. The
extent of Jerome's effort in the production of the titles is not clear. Non-Pachomian
influences on these letters is also possible. Rousseau, *Pachomius*, 38.

15. Lefort, *Oeuvres*, 65. Admittedly many of the titles for the Pachomian letters
offer little information beyond the name of the addressee. It is clear that the letter
addressed to Theodore was written before his death, while Epistle 4 was written after
Theodore's death (see below, n. 37).

long been recognized.[16] The prophetic understanding of scripture as addressed to the community itself was underscored through the equation of the community with Israel. Although this equation had already been made by Pachomius,[17] it gained special prominence in the writings of Theodore and Horsiesius, not least through the identification of Pachomius with Moses.[18] A result of this equation, or rather an indivisible part of it, was the continual contact with scripture experienced within the community. The monks had to know and live scripture. It addressed them directly. Memorization was required,[19] and frequent periods of scriptural instruction and interpretation occurred.[20] All of this made the language of scripture extremely well known, obscuring the dividing line between actual quotation and the simple use of biblical language.

Although this factor is evident throughout the Pachomian literature,[21] it is particularly apparent in the writings of Horsiesius.[22] His letters and *Testament* are replete with quotations understood as first-person references to the community. In fact, the dependence is so great that one is left with the impression that Horsiesius is using the quotations less as proof texts than as a "scriptural" language in and of itself, through which he is expressing his own ideas.[23] At the end of Epistle 3, for example, he writes, "[We are] writing to you, therefore, my dear brothers, so that you may *comfort the weak* [1 Thess. 5:14], *if we are not near you in body, we are however with you in spirit* [1 Cor. 5:3], and, moreover, remember the word which is written, *If you love one another, everyone will know by this that you are truly my dis-*

---

16. Corbinian Gindele, "Die Schriftlesung im Pachomiuskloster," *EA* 41 (1965) 114–22; Ruppert, *Das pachomianische Mönchtum*, 128–58; Bacht, *Vermächtnis*, 191–212; Veilleux, *Liturgie*, 262–75.

17. *Epistle* 8; Pius Tamburrino, "Koinonia: Die Beziehung 'Monasterium' — 'Kirche' im frühen pachomianischen Mönchtum," *EA* 43 (1967) 5–21.

18. Theodore, *Epistle 1*, in Boon, *Pachomiana latina*, 105–6; *Liber Horsiesii* 10, 46, 47; *Bo* 178; *G1* 17, etc.

19. *Regula Praecepta* 49, 139, 140; *Liber Horsiesii* 51; *G1* 58, 61, 88.

20. *Epistula Ammonis* 3, 16; *G1* 34, 56, 88, 99, 122, 140–42, etc.

21. Theodore's letters also make considerable use of biblical quotation, as do all of the catecheses that survive. That such usage was associated with the Pachomian monks is clear. Gennadius, *De viris illustribus* 7–9; L. Th. Lefort, "S. Athanase écrivain copte," *Mus* 46 (1933) 4–5.

22. It is interesting in this regard to note Horsiesius's humble complaint that he was destitute of the perfect knowledge of scripture possessed by Pachomius (*G1* 118).

23. Ruppert, *Das pachomianische Mönchtum*, 131–32.

ciples [John 13:35]."[24] While Horsiesius can, of course, acknowledge the citation as scripture as he does here in the case of John 13:35, what he writes as his own words is also most often composed of scriptural passages only marginally altered to fit an immediate context; note the use of 1 Thessalonians 5:14 and 1 Corinthians 5:3.[25] He has integrated the scriptural language so completely into his thinking that he simply expresses his ideas through it. In the case of the Pauline passages in the above citation, for example, it is in a sense no longer Paul that is speaking, but Horsiesius himself.[26] Another good example occurs in Horsiesius's *Testament* 36.

> Let us keep watch and be on our guard. *If he did not spare the natural branch, neither will he spare you* [Rom. 11:21]. I am not talking about everybody but about the negligent. This lament can rightly be applied to them, *Woe to those who have strayed from me* [Hos. 7:13]. It has been made manifest that they have acted impiously against me: *They have abandoned me, the fountain of living water, and have dug for themselves broken cisterns that cannot hold water* [Jer. 2:13].[27]

Unintroduced as such, the biblical citations function as part of Horsiesius's speech. They are woven together with his own words in his thinking and writing. As such, they have become direct references to the monastic community and Horsiesius's own situation in it.

With this understanding of Horsiesius's use of scriptural language, it is possible to read the biblical passages in his letters as direct references to the situation that he is confronting instead of as general calls to righteousness. Even then, however, the historical situation is not greatly illumined. It is impossible to move from the general nature of the biblical quotations to a precise historical setting without some previous nonbiblical connection. Unfortunately, we are rather poorly informed concerning the history of the Pachomian community after Theodore's death, the cutoff date for most of

---

24. Epistle 3.5 (3.5–9); translations from Veilleux, *Pachomian Koinonia*, 3.160. Citations of the letters are given according to Veilleux's letter and section numbers (3.5=letter 3, section 5). The numbers which follow in the parentheses list the column and line numbers of the Coptic text which Tito Orlandi kindly shared with me.

25. It is not a question of passing off biblical citations as one's own words. Rather, the biblical passages have become a language in and of themselves. One suspects that Horsiesius recognized the power inherent in the use of his "scriptural" language. To argue against it was to argue against scripture.

26. Cf. Epistle 4.2 (1.36–39) and 4.5 (3.32–38).

27. Boon, *Pachomiana latina*, 133; translation from Veilleux, *Pachomian Koinonia*, 3.198.

the *Vitae*. Furthermore, the nonbiblical passages within the letters themselves are extremely sparse. For the most part, the biblical citations are connected by brief introductory formulas, e.g., "as David said," "as it is written," "and again" (ⲁⲩⲱ ⲟⲛ), etc. The common exception is found in the prescript, the salutation, and the postscript of the letters, when they exist. Among the letters of Horsiesius, however, the opening survives intact only for the letter to Theodore (Epistle 2).[28] The new Epistle 3 supports the nonbiblical nature of the opening, though it is too fragmentary to be of much value. The postscript survives for all of the letters except the letter to Theodore. In the case of this material, however, Horsiesius is simply complying with standard epistolary form. As a result, little precise information concerning the original function of the letters occurs.

When one moves beyond these sections, the narrative material shrinks to a minimum. The two letters published by Lefort offer no further historical allusions. In the first of these two letters, the only extended nonbiblical passage is a sentence interpreting 1 Corinthians 15:31 in terms of bearing the cross of Christ.[29] In the letter to Theodore, apart from the brief introductory formulas, no nonbiblical passage occurs after the salutation. The first new letter (Epistle 3) is a little better in this regard. Beyond an intriguing call in the opening not to let disorder arise (ⲛ̄ⲧⲙ̄ⲧⲉϣⲧⲁⲣⲧⲣ̄ ϣⲱⲡⲉ),[30] the few nonbiblical passages that occur are too general to allow any definite historical connection to be made.[31] It is only with the second new letter (Epistle 4) that one is able to note a real improvement. It is to the interpretation of this letter that the present essay now turns.

Apart from a brief nonbiblical reference to purity within the community,[32] two extended narrative passages occur in Epistle 4.[33] The first begins at the end of column three, following an unidentified quotation that picks up on the idea of Exodus 3:5 (also quoted), asserting that the place in which they (the monks) stand is holy

---

28. Lefort, *Oeuvres*, 65.22f.
29. Lefort, *Oeuvres*, 64.29–31.
30. Epistle 3.1 (1.8).
31. Epistle 3.2 (1.33–35 and 2.1–3), 3.5 (3.5–7).
32. Epistle 4.2 (1.37).
33. Both sections are interrupted internally by biblical quotations. There are two further mutilated sections that may have contained narrative material (Epistle 4.2.28–31 and 4.3.14–24).

ground. In this regard, Horsiesius calls upon the monks to remember
Pachomius, who gathered them together through God. He describes
Pachomius as just and pleasing to God. He is the one who taught
the monks about the God they did not know and how they should
live together.[34] After quoting Proverbs 11:7 in support, he continues
the narrative, calling on the brothers to remember the rules and the
laws (ΜΑⲓⲢ̄Ⲡ̄Ⲣ̄ ⲠⲘⲉⲉⲨⲉ ⲚⲚⲉⲞ̄ⲈⲚⲦⲞⲖⲎ ⲘⲚ̄ ⲓⲚⲉⲓⲞ̄ⲓⲚⲞⲓⲘⲞⲤ) that Pachomius
had established for them. Likewise, they should remember Petronios, who passed a brief time with them, and Theodore, who wrote
something (lacuna) for them.[35] At this point, Horsiesius returns to
the biblical quotations.

The second narrative section picks up at the end of column four.
After a call upon the brothers to aid one another and three biblical
passages in support of this stance, the most interesting passage in
terms of the historical situation occurs. It is necessary to quote it
here in full.

> *The man who wants to separate companions seeks some pretext; such a man*
> *will always be prone to quarrels* [Prov. 18:1]. Let no one say, therefore, "I
> want to remain in this place" (†ⲟⲓⲨⲉⲱ 6ⲱ Ⲙ̄ⲠⲉⲓⲘⲀ), or else say "I want
> to go into that community" (†ⲟⲨⲉⲱ ⲓⲂⲓⲰⲔ ⲉⲦⲉⲉⲓⲤⲟⲟⲨⲌ̄Ⲥ̄); but let us all
> remain in what is established and commanded. May no one, therefore,
> stretch... [18 lines mutilated]... assembly which has been fixed for us
> by our righteous father, so that the God of our fathers may make us
> worthy also of the assembly which will take place in the age to come.
> And this will happen to us if we correct and admonish each other for
> our salvation, as it is written,...[36]

Here it is clear that Horsiesius is confronting a problem of certain monks who want to make their own decision concerning the
particular monastery within the Pachomian system of monasteries
(*koinonia*) in which they should dwell. He calls upon them all to "remain in what is established and commanded" (ⲘⲀⲢⲟⲓⲨⲓⲱⲱⲠⲉ ⲦⲎⲢⲞⲨ
Ⲍ̄Ⲛ̄ ⲟⲨⲦⲱⲱ ⲘⲚ̄ ⲟⲨⲉⲌⲤⲀⲌ̄ⲓⲚⲓⲉ). It is unfortunate that the first eighteen
lines of column five are damaged. They would have further clarified the problem, for when the text picks up, a relative clause refers
to the "assembly which has been fixed for us by our righteous father." Presumably it too represents a call to adhere to the rule, for

---

34. Epistle 4.5 (3.35–38).
35. Epistle 4.5 (3.40–44).
36. Epistle 4.7 (4.35–5.24); translation from Veilleux, *Pachomian Koinonia*, 3.164–65.

the stated result is God's acceptance of those in question as worthy of the gathering in the world to come.

The question naturally arises as to whether or not this particular problem is identifiable in the various *Vitae* traditions. This particular letter, however, dates after Theodore's death,[37] a period for which the *Vitae* supply very little information. The first Greek *Life of Pachomius* (G1 149) notes only that Horsiesius carried on the leadership to the best of his ability. The Bohairic *Life of Pachomius* (Bo 208) supplies some additional information in the form of a speech given by Horsiesius to the brothers three days after the death of Theodore. He consoles them over their loss and calls upon them to remember Theodore and to walk according to the directives that he had given them (ⲉϣⲱⲡ ⲁⲛϣⲁⲛⲙⲟϣⲓ ⲕⲁⲧⲁⲛⲏ ⲉⲧⲁϥϩⲟⲛϩⲉⲛ ⲙ̄ⲙⲱⲟⲩ). If they do this, Horsiesius assures them, Theodore will act as an advocate for them before God and Pachomius.[38] After a pair of biblical quotations in support of this position, he again calls on the brothers to remember Pachomius, Petronios, and Theodore. This then passes into a call on the abbots of the various monasteries to "guard the rules that our fathers imposed upon us and the precepts that they have given us to practice" (ⲙⲁⲣⲉⲛⲁⲣⲉϩ ⲉⲛⲓⲛⲟⲙⲟⲥ ⲉⲧⲁⲩⲭⲁⲩ ⲛⲁⲛ ⲉϩⲣⲏⲓ ⲛ̄ϫⲉⲛⲉⲛⲓⲟⲧ̇ ⲛⲉⲙⲛⲓⲉⲛⲧⲟⲗⲏ ⲉⲧⲁⲩⲧⲏⲓⲧⲟⲩ ⲉⲧⲟⲧⲉⲛ ⲉⲑⲣⲉⲛⲁⲓⲧⲟⲩ).[39] Again he assures them that if they follow this advice, it will be recognized when they die, and they will inherit eternal life with the fathers.[40] After a few further statements to the same effect, it is reported that the speech spread great joy among the assembled abbots and monks. Each returned to his monastery in peace and was in turn often visited by Horsiesius, who "made them firm in the law of the Lord and the precepts of our father" (ⲉϥⲧⲁⲭⲣⲟ ⲙ̄ⲙⲱⲟⲩ ϧⲉⲛⲫⲛⲟⲙⲟⲥ ⲙ̄ⲡⲭ̄ⲥ̄ ⲛⲉⲙⲛⲓⲉⲛⲧⲟⲗⲏ ⲛ̄ⲧⲉⲡⲉⲛⲓⲱⲧ).[41]

The call upon the memory of the fathers is to be expected in this period, as is the emphasis on adherence to the rules. The loss of Pachomius's charismatic leadership required it. Theodore's catecheses

---

37. The letter calls upon the brothers to remember Theodore, placing him in the same category with Pachomius and Petronios (Epistle 3.43–4.2).
38. Lefort, *S. Pachomii vita bohairice scripta*, 211.13–16.
39. Lefort, *S. Pachomii vita bohairice scripta*, 212.4–6.
40. Lefort, *S. Pachomii vita bohairice scripta*, 212.10–15.
41. Lefort, *S. Pachomii vita bohairice scripta*, 213.13–14.

repeatedly make the same call. One is to act in accordance with the law that he established, both with respect to the minor and the major precepts (ⲭⲉⲉⲛⲉⲓⲣⲉ ⲕⲁⲧⲁ ⲡⲛⲟⲙⲟⲥ ⲉⲛⲧⲁⲁⲡⲁ ⲧⲁⲁϥ. ⲭⲓⲛⲟⲩⲕⲟⲩⲓ ⲛ̄ⲉⲛ-ⲧⲟⲗⲏ ⲱⲁⲟⲩⲛⲟ6).[42] In the first Greek *Life of Pachomius*, it is recorded that Horsiesius nurtured the brothers, commanding them to obey the rules of the community set down by Pachomius.[43] It is nonetheless interesting to note the parallel emphases in the Bohairic account of Horsiesius's speech and Horsiesius's fourth letter. Both call upon the memory of all three preceding general abbots: Pachomius, Petronios, and Theodore.[44] Both emphasize adherence to the rules of the fathers and the salvation that will result from it. Finally, the reference in the Bohairic *Vita* to the directives set down by Theodore recalls the statement in Horsiesius's letter referring to something (lacuna) that Theodore had written for the brothers.[45] The parallels are general. While they may point only to the two sources' shared connection with Horsiesius, one wonders whether the letter may have served as the source from which the author of the *Vita* fashioned Horsiesius's speech.

Heinrich Bacht has suggested that Horsiesius's emphasis on adherence to the rules of the fathers, in his speech before the abbots after Theodore's death, points to the fact that the problem between the various abbots and Horsiesius, which had been quelled by Theodore at an earlier date, reemerged after the latter's death.[46] It is recalled that when Horsiesius succeeded Petronios, a schism broke out within the community. Certain monasteries, led by Apollonios, abbot of Tmoušons, threatened to withdraw from the system. The schism was avoided and order restored by Theodore, who, because of the problem, had been made coadjutor by Horsiesius. If Bacht is correct, then the problems noted in Horsiesius's fourth letter could well represent a stage in the reemergence of this crisis. It is unfortunate that the sources have so little to say for the period after Theodore's

---

42. Lefort, *Oeuvres*, 50.17–18.

43. *G1* 122.

44. This list, of course, occurs elsewhere (*S5* 128; *S3b*=Lefort, *S. Pachomii vitae sahidice scriptae*, 299.6–10). However, Petronios's short leadership period (*S5* 118–21; *G1* 111–17) limited his influence (cf. Theodore, *Catechesis* 3).

45. *Bo* 208; Lefort, *S. Pachomii vita bohairice scripta*, 211.13–14; Horsiesius, Epistle 4.5 (4.1–2).

46. Bacht, *Vermächtnis*, 24.

death. No clear reference to the post-Theodoran crisis of authority appears in the *Vitae.* It is clear from Horsiesius's subsequent fame, however, that he did succeed in retaining authority and holding the community together.[47]

Some information can be gleaned through a comparison of the problems presented in the letter with the earlier crisis following Petronios's death, as it is found in Lefort's sixth Sahidic codex of the *Life of Pachomius* (*S6*).[48] The Coptic *Vita* reports that certain monasteries began to break away from Horsiesius's leadership. Led by the abbot of Tmoušons, Apollonios, they asserted that they had nothing to do with Horsiesius and his rules (ⲉⲩϫⲱ ⲙ̄ⲙⲟⲥ ϫⲉⲙⲛ̄ⲧⲁⲛ ϩⲱⲃ ⲙⲛ̄ ϩⲱⲣⲥⲓⲏⲥⲉ· ⲟⲩⲇⲉ ⲛ̄ⲕⲉⲧⲱϣ ⲛ̄ⲧⲁϥⲧⲟϣⲟⲩ ⲙⲛ̄ⲧⲁⲛ ϩⲱⲃ ⲛⲙ̄ⲙⲁⲩ).[49] Horsiesius, recognizing his weakness, prays for guidance. He is instructed by Pachomius, who appears to him in a vision, to make Theodore coadjutor. In a speech before the assembled brothers at Pbow he announces the Lord's decision and then returns himself to the Šeneset monastery. When Theodore, who was not present for the speech, is found, he is reluctant to accept his new appointment. At this point, a break in the text occurs. It picks up again with Theodore's return to Pbow and his speech to the brothers in support of Horsiesius. He laments the negligence that has arisen so shortly after the death of Pachomius and the neglect of his rules (ⲁⲛϫⲱⲱⲣⲉ ⲉⲃⲟⲗ ⲛ̄ⲛⲉϥⲛⲟⲙⲟⲥ).[50] His speech moves the brothers to tears.

After the speech, it is reported that the news of Theodore's appointment was relayed to the abbots of the various monasteries. They rejoice and journey to Pbow to visit him, expecting to be well received. When they appear before Theodore, however, he is seized with anger. In a speech to the abbots, he defends "our beloved holy father, Apa Horsiesius" and condemns their revolt against him. Their act is an act against the decision of the Lord. He calls for their repentance, remembering Pachomius's vision of the problems that would arise after his death. After another break in the text, the account picks up with Theodore still on the subject of repentance. He

47. There is, of course, always the possibility that certain monks or even whole monasteries left the *koinonia.*

48. Lefort, *S. Pachomii vitae sahidice scriptae,* 268–80.

49. Lefort, *S. Pachomii vitae sahidice scriptae,* 268.9–16.

50. Lefort, *S. Pachomii vitae sahidice scriptae,* 272.17–18.

complains of the twisted words in their mouths, and quotes their statements: "This monastery is mine," and "this object is mine" (ϩⲟⲓⲛⲉ ⲙⲉⲛ ϫⲉⲧⲱⲓⲧⲉ ϯϩⲉⲛⲉⲉⲧⲉ· ϩⲉⲛⲕⲟⲟⲩⲉ ϫⲉⲡⲱⲓⲡⲉ ⲡⲉⲓⲉⲓⲧⲱⲥ).[51] He demands that they change their attitude. They must renounce their positions as abbots of the various monasteries and submit to him in all matters. They agree to his demands and call upon him to hasten in reestablishing the rules of their righteous father (ⲥⲡⲟⲩⲇⲁⲍⲉ ⲉⲧⲁϩⲟ ⲉⲣⲁⲧⲟⲩ ⲛ̄ⲛⲕⲁⲛⲟⲛ ⲙ̄ⲡⲉⲛⲉⲓⲱⲧ ⲛ̄ⲇⲓⲕⲁⲓⲟⲥ).[52] They acknowledge that they are prepared to submit to the yoke of the congregation, whereupon Theodore leaves them weaving mats like the rest of the brothers and proceeds to visit the other monasteries, strengthening them in the word of God and the rules of their father. Upon his return to Pbow, the former abbots go out to meet him in great humility.

The *Vita* goes on to report that Theodore prayed to the Lord for guidance concerning these men. He falls into ecstasy, and Pachomius appears to him. Pachomius proceeds to name each former abbot and to appoint him to a particular monastery as its abbot. He makes sure, however, that none are appointed to the same monastery that they led during the revolt against Horsiesius.[53] After the vision, Theodore calls the abbots together and discloses the new appointments. It is further stated that he has instituted a revolving system of leadership, clearly designed to control the individual monasteries and to keep them integrally dependent upon the larger Pachomian community. Under this new system, the abbots were shuffled among the various monasteries twice a year, on the occasions of the biannual gatherings at Pbow for Easter and the August reckoning.[54] After the new assignments were made, Theodore called upon the abbots to accept them willingly, recognizing them as the will of God working toward their salvation and that of the brothers. He tells them that they should not complain about the appointment to a difficult monastery or rejoice over the assignment to an easier one. Rather, they should accept whatever assignment they receive humbly as the will of God.

Returning to Horsiesius's fourth letter, the problem he was con-

51. Lefort, *S. Pachomii vitae sahidice scriptae*, 277.20–21.
52. Lefort, *S. Pachomii vitae sahidice scriptae*, 277.29–30.
53. Lefort, *S. Pachomii vitae sahidice scriptae*, 279.9–14.
54. Lefort, *S. Pachomii vitae sahidice scriptae*, 279.21–28.

fronting included monks who made the statements, "I want to remain in this place," or "I want to go into that community."[55] If these monks are the various abbots, then Horsiesius's problem clearly reflects a revolt against Theodore's new regulations. Although it is not specifically stated that they were the abbots of the various monasteries, the connection is so close as to warrant that interpretation. The only parallel to these statements found in the letter is that noted from S6, where it clearly refers to the abbots. Such complaints from the average monks, though easily understandable and possible, are never recorded in the sources. Furthermore, it should be noted that the letters were addressed to the abbots. Thus, Theodore's reunion letter, translated by Jerome, closes with the postscript: "We and all the brothers who are with us wholeheartedly greet you with all the brothers who are in your monasteries."[56] The salute is to the abbots. The brothers are addressed through them. The same letter is addressed to "us who are seen to be the masters of the brothers"[57] and "us, the elders of the sons of Israel."[58] The one letter of Horsiesius that is addressed was sent to Theodore. Epistle 4 is unclear as to the addressee, while Epistle 3, in its postscript, greets you (the abbots) and all those with you. Of course, such letters would naturally be sent to the abbots of the various monasteries. The chain of command was well organized in the Pachomian system. One would expect the material in the letters, if not the letters themselves, to be related to the brothers.[59] Nonetheless, every indication seems to argue that the statements noted by Horsiesius were being made by the abbots.

Theodore's system of rotating abbot assignments and his cautioning of the abbots humbly to accept their biannual appointments

---

55. Epistle 4.7 (4.39–41).

56. Boon, *Pachomiana latina*, 106.19–20; translation from Veilleux, *Pachomian Koinonia*, 3.125.

57. Theodore, *Epistle* 1.4; translation from Veilleux, *Pachomian Koinonia*, 3.124. Cf. Boon, *Pachomiana latina*, 105.19–20 (*Nos quoque qui uidemur praepositi esse fratibus*).

58. Theodore, *Epistle* 1.5; translation from Veilleux, *Pachomian Koinonia*, 3.124. Cf. Boon, *Pachomiana latina*, 106.5 (*Omnes nos, senatus filiorum Israel*).

59. In *Epistula Ammonis* 29, a letter from Antony is first shown to Theodore, who then has it read to the monks. In section 32 of the same work, Ammon receives a letter from Theodore at Nitria. He shows it to the elders first and obtains their permission to read it to the brothers.

clearly set the stage for the type of complaints registered by Horsiesius. In the crisis of Horsiesius's first leadership period, the abbots had welcomed Theodore as their chosen successor to Pachomius. They recognized and welcomed his authority in their desire to replace Horsiesius. His innovations were accepted. With his death, however, the authority behind his innovative biannual shuffling of the abbots among the various monasteries was removed. The *Vita* account itself had supported the innovation by attributing it to Pachomius through a vision granted to Theodore.[60] The account of the vision is secondary, an attempt to link Theodore's innovation to the community's founder and thus to give it equal status with the rest of the *Rule*. It could no longer be undercut as something unknown to Pachomius. This development, in and of itself, suggests the need to undergird the innovation. It would be precisely the undercutting of the innovation on Theodore's death, witnessed in Horsiesius's letter, that would require the undergirding noted in the *Vita*. The fact that the Coptic tradition alone mentions the biannual shuffling of the abbots suggests that even after Horsiesius this particular rule was not readily accepted.[61]

The notion that Horsiesius understood his letter in these terms is further supported by his use of two biblical quotations in this fourth epistle, which appear elsewhere in the Pachomian dossier only in Theodore's speech to the revolting abbots. Ecclesiastes 10:8, quoted by Horsiesius in column three of the letter, appears elsewhere only in the *S6* account.[62] Matthew 13:27 is found outside of Horsiesius's letter again only in the *S6* account and its parallel from *S5*.[63] All of this data places Horsiesius's fourth letter in the context of a reemergence of the crises of authority that he had experienced earlier during his first period as general abbot. With this background in mind and remembering Horsiesius's technique of using biblical quo-

---

60. It is to be noted that the vision proper only has Pachomius appointing the abbots to the various monasteries. The biannual shuffling introduced by Theodore is not actually a part of the vision. However, one may assume that the vision was used to undergird the entire practice.

61. Only *S6* records the biannual shuffling of the abbots.

62. Epistle 4.4 (3.26–27); *S6* (Lefort, *S. Pachomii vitae sahidice scriptae*, 272.23–28).

63. Epistle 4.4 (3.3–4); *S6* (Lefort, *S. Pachomii vitae sahidice scriptae*, 275.17–18); *S5* (Lefort, *S. Pachomii vitae sahidice scriptae*, 188.28–29).

tations as a language in themselves, it is possible to reread the letter, understanding the citations as more direct references to the sort of negligence he was confronting.

In the first two columns of the epistle, Horsiesius works upon the equation of the community with Israel.[64] In this connection, a number of biblical passages are cited that refer to going up to Jerusalem for the feast of Passover.[65] These passages, coupled to the identification of the community with Israel, suggest a reference to the gathering of the community for the Easter feast at Pbow. This is supported by Theodore's paschal letter. It too begins with a number of quotations referring to the Israelite feast of Passover. The same notion of going up to Jerusalem occurs.[66] Thus, it seems most likely that Horsiesius's fourth epistle represents a third example of the reunion-letter genre used for calling the monks together for the annual Easter festivities at Pbow. In this connection, it is to be remembered that the Easter gathering was one of the two annual occasions on which the reshuffling of the various abbots occurred. It was also, by its very nature, an occasion that recognized the centralized authority of the system and conversely played down the individuality and decentralized authority of the various monasteries. As a result, it was a time at which complaints about such matters could be expected to be at a height. Horsiesius's confrontation of them in a pre-Easter letter would be aimed at silencing the debate before it arose. Theodore's paschal letter likewise emphasizes adherence to the rules.[67]

Returning to Horsiesius's letter, one finds that many of the biblical passages cited confront various forms of negligence arising within the community. Toward the end of column two, after the monks have been called upon to renounce the things of this world, they are instructed to avoid judging one another.[68] Rather, they should consider the weaker brothers and act accordingly.[69] They should not con-

---

64. Especially Epistle 4.2 (1.39–42)=Bar. 4:4–5.
65. Epistle 4.2 (1.35–36)=John 11:55; Epistle 4.3 (2.14–15)=Zech. 14:18 or 19; Epistle 4.3 (2.16–17)=John 7:8; Epistle 4.3 (2.17–20)=John 7:37–38.
66. Boon, *Pachomiana latina*, 105–6.
67. Boon, *Pachomiana latina*, 105.14–17; 106.1–2, 10–11.
68. Epistle 4.3 (2.32–33)=Rom. 14:13.
69. Epistle 4.3 (2.33–35)=Rom. 14:15.

sider themselves wise,[70] since uncorrected learning deceives.[71] They should strive to improve themselves and not worry about reproaching others or finding fault with them.[72] Problems have arisen within the monastery. The good seed that was sown by Pachomius has been infiltrated with weeds.[73] The good vine that he planted and fruited in truth has been turned by some into bitterness and has become a strange vine.[74] Psalm 109 (108):17–18 is quoted as a reference to those who have chosen the wrong path. What follows is too fragmentary to be precisely understood. It does, however, clearly represent a call upon the monks to be prepared, like the servants who had their lamps lit when the Lord returned.[75]

After a mutilated section, the biblical citations pick up again, this time suggesting that those who instigate the wrong action will suffer as a result.[76] Against such action, Horsiesius calls upon the monks to recognize that God's word addressed to Moses is also meant for them. "The place in which you stand is holy ground."[77] It has its foundation in purity, peace, and faith. It is at this point that the first large narrative section occurs. The idea implied is that this holy ground or pure foundation is to be identified with the fathers, Pachomius, Petronios, and Theodore, and the rules that they set down.[78] This is again supported by further quotations. As Moses sent Joshua as a servant of the Lord, so should the monks understand that Pachomius sent Theodore.[79] They should rejoice in their words[80] and love the Lord's name and avoid scandal.[81]

After a few mutilated lines, quotations in the same vein follow. The light has arisen in the darkness and is there to illumine their

---

70. Epistle 4.3 (2.35–37)=Isa. 5:21.
71. Epistle 4.3 (2.37)=Prov. 10:17.
72. Epistle 4.3 (2.37–43)=Prov. 18:9; 9:7; 12:8, 23; 11:6; Matt. 7:4; Prov. 4:25.
73. Epistle 4.4 (3.3–4)=Matt. 13:27.
74. Epistle 4.4 (3.5–6)=Jer. 2:21.
75. Epistle 4.4 (3.15f)=Luke 12:35–36; cf. Horsiesius, Epistle 3.1 (1.16–19); *Testament* 19–20; *Regulations* 3.
76. Epistle 4.4 (3.24–32)=Prov. 26:27; Eccl. 10:8–9; Dan. 3:47–50; Prov. 19:6; 29:24; 28:17.
77. Epistle 4.5 (3.32–33)=Exod. 3:5.
78. Epistle 4.5 (3.35–4.4.2).
79. Epistle 4.5 (4.3–5)=Josh.14:7.
80. Epistle 4.5 (4.5–8)=Ps. 119 (118):162.
81. Epistle 4.5 (4.11–12)=Ps. 119 (118):165.

way.[82] The upright will rejoice over this, and the lawless will remain silent. The monks should be wise and good toward one another, Horsiesius asserts, avoiding hate and anger and pretexts for instigating trouble.[83] At this point, the second narrative section occurs. A specific example of such "pretexts" appears, namely, those who complain about the monastery to which they have been assigned.[84] Instead, they should abide by the rules and thereby be deemed worthy of the gathering in heaven,[85] perhaps a play on the call to the annual earthly gathering at Pbow for Easter. Finally, Horsiesius notes that the correction of one another is both useful and necessary, so long as it is done humbly. If it is carried out for the proper reasons and openly, the monks will become true disciples of the Lord.[86]

It must be admitted that the biblical citations used by Horsiesius can be understood as general calls for monastic virtue and the avoidance of the various pitfalls of the human predicament. Such usage is common and appears throughout the sources. However, the situation confronted by the letter that emerged through the study of the non-biblical passages supports an understanding of the biblical citations in relationship to it. The letter, sent to the various monasteries calling the monks together for the annual Easter gathering, confronted a growing negligence and questioning of authority that followed Theodore's death. How soon after his death is difficult to say.[87] Theodore himself had been disturbed in his last years by the growing negligence.[88] It was the loss of Theodore's recognized authority with his death that naturally led this negligence to find expression in the renewed questioning of Horsiesius's leadership.

The same questioning had occurred following Pachomius's death. On that occasion, it was the loss of the centripetal force of his lead-

---

82. Epistle 4.5 (4.18–25)=Pss. 112 (111):4; 18 (17):29; 139 (138):2.
83. Epistle 4.6 (4.29–38)=Prov. 10:12; 15:18; 18:1.
84. Epistle 4.7 (4.38–40).
85. Epistle 4.7 (4.41–5.22)
86. Epistle 4.7–8 (5.27–32)=Prov. 27:5–6; John 13:35.
87. Theodore died shortly after Easter 368 C.E. (G1 148). If, as seems probable, the present epistle represents an Easter letter, then the earliest possible date for it would be shortly before Easter 369 C.E.
88. Basilius Steidle, "Der heilige Abt Theodor von Tabennesi: Zur 1600. Wiederkehr des Todesjahres (368–1968)," EA 44 (1968) 97–98.

ership that gave rise to the centrifugal forces of decentralization and independence. With no clear line of succession (the connection between Pachomius and Horsiesius was broken by the short reign of Petronios), the struggle for authority led to schism. Without Theodore's intervention it probably would have meant the end of the Pachomian movement. Theodore's recognized authority and close relationship to Pachomius, however, allowed him to hold the community together. His new regulations regarding the appointment and biannual shuffling of the various abbots effectively broke the forces toward independence that had arisen in some of the monasteries. With his death, however, the authority behind these innovations was removed. The questioning of their validity and that of the whole structure of authority once again threatened to divide the community. The reappearance of Horsiesius as the sole figure at the helm of the system naturally raised questions. The memory of the earlier problems led to a questioning of his leadership. It is apparently this renewed questioning that lies behind Horsiesius's fourth epistle — a questioning that found expression also in increased negligence within the community. The specifics of this post-Theodoran negligence are not clear. Our sources on this period are too sparse. The letter suggests that self-interest had replaced humility as the driving force among certain monks.[89] Arguments among the brothers, complaints over particular monastery assignments, laxity with respect to the rules, pride, and self-confidence are all suggested. Of course, such negligence was not limited to this period in the history of Pachomian monasticism. It had existed already from the start. The letter, however, clearly reveals a renewed challenging of Horsiesius's authority and a questioning of the innovative regulations instituted by Theodore.

The occurrence of such a crisis on both occasions when the office of general abbot fell to Horsiesius suggests his unpopularity among certain elements within the community.[90] It also suggests that the centripetal force that originally drew the monasteries together[91] was

---

89. Cf. *G1* 126.

90. Derwas Chitty, "A Note on the Chronology of the Pachomian Foundations," *SP* 2 [TU 64] (1957) 384–85.

91. It is to be recalled that not all of the monasteries were founded by Pachomius. Some already had a history of their own when they joined. *G1* 54, 83; *Bo* 50–51.

bound to the charismatic figure of Pachomius, the man of God. With his death, an equivalent authority had to be found if the unity of the system was to be maintained. Apparently the traditions, rules, and memory of Pachomius were not yet sufficiently authoritative.[92] It is clear that Horsiesius also failed in this calling. The authority to hold the community together was found in Theodore. In reality, the monks had always recognized that fact.[93] It had always been assumed that he would succeed Pachomius until his premature acceptance of that fact altered things and resulted in Pachomius, on his deathbed, naming Petronios as his successor. This unexpected passing over of Theodore certainly lay behind the original schism that arose during Horsiesius's first period as general abbot. When Theodore did take over, he was able to quell the uprising. The rapidity of his success alone argues that his authority was widely recognized among the monks. It is clear that he recognized the problems inherent in defining the community's unity in terms of the authoritative man of God alone. His regulations aimed at undergirding the centralizing authority. He strove to institutionalize that authority, playing down visions and firming up contact with Alexandria. Emphasis on the memory of the fathers and the rule increased. They came to enjoy almost scriptural authority. Nonetheless, the fact that similar problems arose after his death argues that Theodore was not totally successful. The forces of independence were strong. Theodore had, however, begun the process that allowed Horsiesius to deal with the problem effectively the second time around.

These factors make it clear that the original unity of the Pachomian system was less a unity under a single rule and with a single uniform goal than a clustering around a recognized man of God. The independence of the various monks within each monastery and of the various monasteries within the system was greater than the later sources, stemming from the post-Pachomian period, reveal. This is not to argue that the monasteries did not have a common rule and

---

92. Or at least the proper interpretation of them was not yet established, i.e., the interpretation that survives in the sources.

93. Horsieisus's question to the monks in *S6* (Lefort, *S. Pachomii vitae sahidice scriptae* 270.30ff.) concerning whom they want to replace him is interesting in this regard. This *Vita* reports that the monks had no one in mind. They claim to know no one except Horsiesius. This is difficult to imagine in view of the joy that arose on their learning of Theodore's appointment.

a common goal in the ascetic life. It is only to point out that while the latter united all monks, the former was a secondary result of becoming part of the community. The choice of becoming part of the community, however, did not rest so much on the rule as on the charismatic authority of the founder.

12

Chalcedonian Power Politics and the Demise of Pachomian Monasticism

The study of Pachomian monasticism has experienced a renaissance in the last decade and a half. New texts have come to light,[1] new editions have appeared,[2] and new translations have made the sources widely available.[3] The quantity of secondary literature has likewise increased as these sources have received a new and often more critical inspection.[4] In addition, efforts undertaken at the community's central monastery of Pbow have added important archaeological data.[5]

This renewed activity is due in part, though not exclusively,[6] to the manuscript discoveries that occurred in the 1940s in close

---

First published as Occasional Paper 15 (Claremont, Calif.: Institute for Antiquity and Christianity, 1989).

1. Hans Quecke, "Eine Handvoll pachomianischer Texte," *ZDMG*, Supp. 3, 1 (1977) 221–29; Tito Orlandi, "Nuovi Testi copti pachomiani," in J. Gribomont, ed., *Commandements du Seigneur et libération évangelique: Études monastiques proposées et discutés à St. Anselme, 15–17 Février 1976* (StAns 70; Rome: Herder, 1977) 241–43; Spanel, "Toronto Sahidic Addition"; Halkin, "Vie inédite"; Campagnano, "Monaci egiziani."

2. Quecke, *Briefe Pachoms*; idem, "Ein Brief von einem Nachfolger Pachoms," *Or* 44 (1975) 426–33; Krause, "Erlassbrief"; Spanel, "Toronto Sahidic Addition"; Halkin, "Vie inédite"; idem, *Corpus athénien*; Goehring, *Letter of Ammon*; Kuhn, *Panegyric on Apollo*.

3. This is especially true of the three-volume English edition of the major documents of the Pachomian dossier prepared by Veilleux (*Pachomian Koinonia*). One should also note Bacht (*Vermächtnis*); Vogüé, "Épîtres"; Hans Quecke, "Briefe Pachoms in koptischer Sprache: Neue deutsche Übersetzung," in *Zetesis Album amicorum: Aangeboden aan Dr. E. de Strycker* (Antwerp: De Nederlandische Boekhandel, 1973) 655–63; Apostolos A. Athanassakis, *The Life of Pachomius (Vita Prima Graeca)* (Missoula, Mont.: Scholars Press, 1975); Halkin, *Corpus athénien* (translation by A. J. Festugière); Goehring, *Letter of Ammon*; and Kuhn, *Panegyric on Apollo*.

4. Book-length studies alone include Bacht, *Vermächtnis*; Goehring, *Letter of Ammon*; Quecke, *Briefe Pachoms*; Ruppert, *Das pachomianische Mönchtum*; Timbie, "Dualism"; and Rousseau, *Pachomius*.

5. Debono, "Basilique"; Robinson and van Elderen, "First Season"; idem, "Second Season"; van Elderen, "Nag Hammadi Excavation"; Grossmann, "Basilica"; Lease, "Fourth Season."

6. The intensity of the debate between Lefort and Chitty over the priority of the Coptic or Greek *Vita* stilled Pachomian scholarship for a time in the mid-1950s.

proximity to the central Pachomian monastery of Pbow. The Gnostic-oriented collection of tractates unearthed near Nag Hammadi has raised the question of its possible relationship to the Pachomian movement and the significance of such a relationship for our understanding of the movement's early years.[7] The more recent identification of the Dishna Papers or Bodmer papyri as a portion of a Pachomian library is just beginning to influence Pachomian scholarship.[8]

The more recent Pachomian studies have, like those of the past, centered on the movement's early years. This is due in large part to the fact that the literary remains of Pachomian monasticism are limited for the most part to the first sixty-five years of the community's existence.[9] With the death of the movement's fourth general abbot, Apa Horsiesius (ca. 387 C.E.), the sources diminish drastically in both quantity and quality.[10] As a result, the last 160 years of the movement's existence are shrouded in uncertainty.[11]

Rousseau, *Ascetics*, 243–47; Goehring, *Letter of Ammon*, 3–23. With time, the scars healed and interest in the subject renewed.

7. The discussion and debate are growing. Robinson, "Introduction," 16–21; Hedrick, "Gnostic Proclivities"; Wisse, "Gnosticism"; Barns, "Greek and Coptic Papyri"; Shelton, "Introduction"; Robert A. Kraft and Janet A. Timbie, review of *The Nag Hammadi Library in English*, by James M. Robinson, *RSR* 8 (1982) 36; Chadwick, "Pachomios," 17–19; Goehring, "New Frontiers" (chap. 8 in the present volume); Veilleux, "Monasticism and Gnosis."

8. James M. Robinson, "The Story of the Bodmer Papyri: The First Christian Monastic Library" (manuscript); idem, "Introduction," in William Brashear et al., eds., *Chester Beatty Library Acc. 1390: Mathematical School Exercises in Greek and John 10:17–13:38 in Subachmimic* (Chester Beatty Monographs 13; Leuven and Paris: Peeters, 1990) 3–32; idem, "Pachomian Monastic Library."

9. Included among these remains are the letters and instructions attributed to Pachomius, Theodore, and Horsiesius, the various forms of the *Life of Pachomius*, the *Paralipomena*, the *Letter of Ammon*, the *Rule* of Pachomius, and the *Regulations* and *Testament* of Horsiesius. English translations of those sources may be found in Veilleux, *Pachomian Koinonia*. Veilleux also supplies the bibliographic data for the critical texts. The temporal distribution of the Pachomian sources is discussed in greater detail in Goehring, "New Frontiers," 236–38 (see pp. 162–64 in the present volume).

10. These include the allocution of Timothy of Alexandria (van Lantschoot, "Allocution"; van Cauwenbergh, *Étude*, 153–54), the *Vitae* and *encomia* of Abraham and Manasseh (Campagnano, "Monaci egiziani"; van Cauwenbergh, *Étude*, 154–58), and the *Panegyric on Apollo* (Kuhn, *Panegyric on Apollo*; van Cauwenbergh, *Étude*, 158–59).

11. Little has been written about the fate of the movement after Horsiesius's death. Often the later years are ignored. Thus Derwas J. Chitty, in his *The Desert a City*, closes his discussion of the movement with the death of Horsiesius and the establishment of the monastery of Metanoia on Canopus in Lower Egypt. Cf. van Cauwenbergh, *Étude*, 153–59.

It is the goal of this essay to explore these latter days of the Pachomian movement in general and to focus, in particular, on the movement's fateful involvement in the struggle between the Chalcedonian and non-Chalcedonian forces of the empire during the middle years of the reign of Justinian I (527–65 C.E.).[12] This struggle, which effectively removed the movement from the plane of history,[13] cannot be fully understood apart from the development of the Pachomians' own self-understanding of their religio-political affiliation and influence and the perception of this development by those outside of the movement. What follows will thus seek not only to reconstruct the external events of the conflict, but to explore as well the causes which led to it.

The basic facts and outcome of the confrontation between Justinian I and the Pachomian movement represented in the person of the abbot of their central monastery of Pbow, Apa Abraham, are relatively clear. The details and precise chronology, however, remain confused in the sources. This is due in part to the fragmentary nature of the *Vita* and two *encomia* of Abraham that survive,[14] and to the summary fashion in which they are treated in the *Alexandrian*

---

12. The difficulties inherent in the terminology of the opposing forces following the Council of Chalcedon in 451 C.E. are well known. Frend, *Rise of the Monophysite Movement*, xiii; David W. Johnson, "Anti-Chalcedonian Polemics in Fifth- to Seventh-Century Coptic Texts," in Pearson and Goehring, *Roots*, 218–20. I do not wish in this essay to explore the various differences within the non-Chalcedonian camp in Egypt, but use the terms non-Chalcedonian and Monophysite to refer to the Christian majority in Egypt which, in Johnson's words, "rejected the decrees of Chalcedon and gave allegiance to the non-Melkite succession of patriarchs of Alexandria." I want by these terms simply to distinguish the ecclesiastical-political forces represented by the Emperor Justinian I and the Pachomian Apa Abraham.

13. While remnants of the movement did survive, the nature of the solution imposed by Justinian I, coupled to the fact that Egypt remained non-Chalcedonian, meant that neither side had an interest in preserving the movement's subsequent history.

14. E. Amélineau, *Monuments pour servir à l'histoire de l'Égypte chrétienne aux IVe, V^e, VIe, VIIe siècles* (Mémoires 4; Paris: Leroux, 1888) 511–14, 742–53; Campagnano, "Monaci egiziani," 229–33, 239–43. The texts come from two White Monastery codices, the leaves of which were earlier separated and scattered among various libraries and museums. The reconstruction of the White Monastery codices has been undertaken by Tito Orlandi, director of the Corpus dei Manoscritti Copti Leterari in Rome. The codices which contain the Abraham material are labeled GB and GC in Orlandi's system. I am indebted to Professor Orlandi for the photographs of these texts, which he supplied. I have cited the texts according to the pagination of his reconstructed codices.

Synaxarium[15] and the *Panegyric on Apollo Archimandrite of the Monastery of Isaac, by Stephen, the bishop of Herakleopolis magna.*[16]

The *Life of Abraham* reports that Justinian initiated the contact with Abraham. It states that "he (Justinian) wrote a letter to the whole land of Egypt, to the bishops everywhere and to the leaders of the monasteries, [informing them] that they should come to him in the royal city [Constantinople]." It then narrows the focus and reports that "he wrote to the holy Apa Abraham, who was leader of Pbow at that time, [informing him] that he should come to the court and meet him."[17] Upon receiving the letter, Abraham departed with a number of brothers for Constantinople.[18]

When they arrived in the imperial city, they were summoned (apparently together with other monastic leaders)[19] to appear before the emperor. Upon their arrival at the court, Justinian addressed them and said, "It was on account of a vital matter that I sent for your holiness, so that you might understand our faith and unite with us, so that I might give you glory and much honor in my kingdom." The *Vita* reports simply that Abraham "did not put his trust in the glory which will perish, but chose for himself the glory which will endure forever." The point is clearly that Abraham rejected Jus-

---

15. Basset, *Synaxairë arabe-jacobite*, 11.684–88 (24 Toubeh); I. Forget, *Synaxarion Alexandrinum* (CSCO 78; Louvain: Durbecq, 1953) 401–5.

16. Kuhn, *Panegyric on Apollo.*

17. Codex GC f. 4v; my translation. According to the *encomium* of Abraham contained in Codex GB, Justinian had Abraham arrested by the duke of Antinoë. Campagnano, "Monaci egiziani," 242.

18. The *Vita* mentions four brothers, who apparently in the end succumbed to the imperial propaganda (Codex GC f. 4v; cf. van Cauwenbergh, *Étude,* 155). The author of the *Vita* also accompanied Abraham to Constantinople (Codex GC f. 5r).

19. The *Vita* does not clarify the relationship between the emperor's confrontation with Abraham (the aim of the account) and his summons "to the bishops everywhere." Justinian did invite bishops and monastic leaders in Constantinople on a number of occasions between 554 and 563 C.E. (van Cauwenbergh, *Étude,* 155; Frend, *Rise of the Monophysite Movement*, 275). These took place after, however, the death of Theodora (548 C.E.), who figures prominently in the present account. Thus the summons of Abraham does not appear to fit into these major monastic concourses. The other leaders brought before the emperor Justinian may have been additional Pachomian functionaries who accompanied Abraham from Egypt. The *Vita* simply reads (my translation): "And when he [Abraham] saw the king's letter, he took four brothers with him; would that he had not taken them with him! He arose and went to the king at the court. When they were announced to the king, he ordered them to be brought before him. He spoke with leaders and said ... "

tinian's invitation to enter into communion with the Chalcedonian forces.[20]

The sequence of events and the nature of the verbal exchange which follows in the *Vita* are not always clear. This is due not only to the poor state of preservation of the text but also to the fact that the exchange involves a play on the use of such terms as *faith, orthodoxy, bishop,* and *archbishop* by the Chalcedonian and non-Chalcedonian opponents in the account.[21]

After the initial meeting, Justinian sent his referee to the Pachomians to request that Abraham go to the archbishop and hold fast to him in accordance with the custom of their fathers. Justinian, of course, meant the archbishop of Constantinople. The Pachomians, however, went on the emperor's advice to the Alexandrian archbishop Theodosius, who had been summoned from Alexandria to Constantinople in December 536 C.E.[22] Theodosius, on learning of the confrontation between Justinian and Abraham, wrote to the queen (Theodora), a non-Chalcedonian sympathizer, and instructed her to order the bishop (of Constantinople)[23] not to dispute with the old monk.

This set the stage for a second meeting between Abraham and Justinian, who on this occasion had the (arch)bishop (of Constantinople) by his side. The author of the *Vita* uses this encounter to underscore Justinian's misunderstanding of the "custom of the fathers." The emperor began the meeting by asking Abraham why he had refused to go and prostrate himself before the archbishop (of Constantinople). Abraham does not answer the question but instead simply asserts that he now has the opportunity to meet the bishop at this second meeting with the emperor. In response, Justinian repeats the question, this time linking it to the "custom of the fathers." He asks, "Why did you not go in accordance with the

---

20. Codex GC f. 4v, my translation.

21. Abraham understands Theodosius of Alexandria to be the archbishop and representative of the orthodox non-Chalcedonian faith. Justinian I means by *archbishop* the Archbishop of Constantinople, and the orthodox faith is for him that of the Council of Chalcedon. Cf. Johnson, "Anti-Chalcedonian Polemics," 216–34.

22. Frend, *Rise of the Monophysite Movement,* 274.

23. The title *bishop* is used here by the author of the *Vita* to refer to the archbishop of Constantinople. The loftier title of *archbishop* is reserved in most instances for Theodosius, the archbishop of Alexandria.

custom of your fathers?" Here it is clear that the emperor, as portrayed in the *Vita*, understands the custom of the fathers in terms of
their acceptance of the archbishop as the "legal" representative of ecclesiastical authority and hence of the faith. The authority is in the
office. Hence Abraham should have gone to the archbishop as his fathers went to the archbishop, because the archbishop was the "legal"
representative of the faith.

Abraham's response offers a different interpretation. "The custom of the fathers" is connected for him to the archbishop's faith
rather than to his office. "The savior," he asserts, "did not say that
faith is changed from the time of our fathers." When Justinian asks
in response if Abraham's faith is then the same as that of all men,
Abraham avoids the question and suggests that he ask the orthodox bishop.[24] He notes that he himself is but an uneducated peasant.
Nonetheless, he goes on to explain that Athanasius had entrusted
the faith to Pachomius[25] and that the present-day Pachomians still act
in accordance with the canons which Athanasius had entrusted (to
them).[26] For Abraham, the custom of the fathers is their adherence to
the faith entrusted to them by Athanasius. It is not their adherence
to the archbishop himself.

We are here in the midst of a play on the theological conflict by
the author of the *Vita*. Both Justinian and Abraham understand the
word *faith* in reference to their own theological positions. Both likewise are seen to accept the continuity of their position with the past.
Thus when Abraham asserts that faith has not changed from the time

---

24. This must be Theodosius the archbishop of Alexandria. The author of the *Vita*
has cleverly constructed this entire exchange so that Abraham, while he avoids a clear
statement implicating himself with the non-Chalcedonian cause, nonetheless remains
firm to the faith and makes the emperor appear as the fool. The Monophysite readers
would certainly have enjoyed the story.

25. While the Pachomian *Vitae* stress the close relationship between their community and Athanasius, it is a fact that the archbishop never met Pachomius (Bohairic
Life of Pachomius supplemented by the Sahidic and Arabic versions [cited henceforth as
SBo] 28; cf. Veilleux, *Pachomian Koinonia*, 1.1–4 and the parallel in the First Greek *Life
of Pachomius* [*G1*] 30). Athanasius does not mention Pachomius in his writings. The
association of the movement with the archbishop was underscored during the period
when Theodore was general abbot (350–68 c.e.; cf. *SBo* 96, 134, 185, 189, 202, 210; *G1*
120, 136–38, 143–44, 150; *Epistula Ammonis* 34). Cf. Goehring, "New Frontiers" (chap. 8
in the present volume).

26. The author here aligns the canons of Athanasius with the customs of the
(Pachomian) fathers. Basset, *Synaxaire arabe-jacobite*, 11.684–88.

of the fathers, by which he of course means that it has remained as it was understood by the majority in Egypt prior to Chalcedon, Justinian understands him to be in support of Chalcedon, since he equates the faith of the fathers with the Chalcedonian position.

Unfortunately, the *Vita* breaks off at this point. It does not resume until after the confrontation in Constantinople is over. The denouement of the incident is thus lost. The report in subsequent sections that Abraham founded his own monastery near his native village of Tberčot (Farshut), however, confirms his return to Egypt.

The *Alexandrian Synaxarium*,[27] which does not report Abraham's summons to Constantinople, offers a brief though complete account of the results of his refusal to accede to the emperor's demands. It begins by reporting that Abraham wrote a letter to his monks from Constantinople informing them of Justinian's efforts to compel his acceptance of Chalcedon. The emperor had informed Abraham that if he would accept Chalcedon, he would be permitted to return to Egypt as abbot of Pbow. If he refused, he would not be allowed to return to Egypt. According to the *Synaxarium*, Abraham acted first and renounced his role as abbot and quit the monastery. As a result, Justinian sent Pankaras with soldiers to enforce the Chalcedonian position in the monastery.[28] Those monks who resisted were expelled. Many dispersed into the deserts and mountains.[29] Abraham, whose return to Egypt is not mentioned in the *Synaxarium*, is nonetheless reported to have found refuge first in the monastery of Shenoute at Atripe. At a later point he founded his own monastery at Farshut.

The *encomia* of Abraham offer additional information, although at certain points they are in conflict with the other sources.[30] According to the better preserved of the two *encomia*,[31] Abraham was accused by certain persons toward the beginning of Justinian's reign. The emperor decided to arrest him and sent a letter to the duke of Antinoë and ordered him to send Abraham to Constantinople.[32] The duke

---

27. Forget, *Synaxarion Alexandrinum*, 401–5.
28. Cf. Campagnano, "Monaci egiziani," 242.
29. *Panegyric on Apollo* 10.
30. Campagnano, "Monaci egiziani," 242.
31. Codex GB. Campagnano, "Monaci egiziani," 242–43.
32. The *Life of Abraham* reports that Abraham went to Constantinople at the invitation of Justinian (Codex GC f. 4v).

carried out the order with the aid of his troops. The text breaks off at this point due to lost folios.

The account picks up again at the conclusion of the confrontation between Justinian and Abraham in Constantinople. As in the *Synaxarium*, the emperor threatened to replace Abraham as archimandrite of Pbow if he refused to accept Chalcedon. He so refused and was removed as abbot. At this point, the *encomium* offers some new information that may shed light on how Abraham was able to return to Egypt. It reports that the empress Theodora attempted to intercede with Justinian on Abraham's behalf. When Justinian remained firm in his decision, Theodora sent two eunuchs by night to summon Abraham. Unfortunately the text is interrupted again at this point through the loss of additional folios. One nonetheless suspects that Theodora played a role in Abraham's eventual return to Egypt. When the text resumes, it reports that Abraham wrote to the brothers from exile[33] and exhorted them to maintain the orthodox (non-Chalcedonian) faith. The *encomium* then reports the arrival of Pankaris at Pbow to enforce the emperor's decision.[34]

The last text which records this incident, the *Panegyric on Apollo*,[35] reports the confrontation between Justinian and Abraham as background for the story of Apollo, who was one of the monks who left Pbow after Abraham's removal as abbot. We do learn from this text the important fact that the monastery of Pbow together with most of Egypt had opposed the results of the Council of Chalcedon from the beginning.[36] It also reports that after Abraham was removed as abbot, the emperor sent a Chalcedonian replacement to Pbow. The continuation of the monastery as a Chalcedonian establishment is thus suggested, although the length of its survival as such remains unclear.[37]

While numerous inconsistencies among these accounts make an ac-

---

33. The letter was written from Constantinople according to the *Synaxarium* (Basset, *Synaxaire arabe-jacobite*, 11.684; cf. Campagnano, "Monazi egiziani," 243).

34. Campagnano, "Monazi egiziani," 243. Unfortunately the pages of the *Vita* which would have reported this incident are lacking.

35. This has been admirably edited and translated by Kuhn, *Panegyric on Apollo*; cf. van Cauwenbergh, *Étude*, 158–59.

36. *Panegyric on Apollo* 10 (CSCO 394.16.11–12); contra van Cauwenbergh, *Étude*, 159.

37. *Panegyric on Apollo* 10 (CSCO 394.17.24–27).

curate chronology of this confrontation impossible, various facts can be determined with relative accuracy. The date of the episode must be placed between the arrival of the Alexandrian archbishop Theodosius in Constantinople in December 536 C.E. and his death in 566 C.E.[38] The involvement of Theodora reported in both the *Vita* and the *encomia* moves the *terminus ante quem* to 548 C.E., the year of her death.[39] The confrontation can thus be dated between 537 and 548 C.E.[40]

It is clear from the sources that the Pachomian movement as represented by Abraham of Pbow had been opposed to Chalcedon from the beginning.[41] Justinian, in his desire to restore Chalcedonian obedience to Egypt,[42] sought to establish a Chalcedonian presence in Upper Egypt at the Pachomian monastery of Pbow. It remains unclear whether Justinian effected Abraham's trip to Constantinople through his invitation to the monk (so the *Vita*) or by means of his arrest (so the *encomium*). Once Abraham was in the royal city, however, the emperor sought to gain his support for the Chalcedonian position first through persuasion and then by force.[43] It is at this point that the empress Theodora interceded on Abraham's behalf. It may have been through her efforts that he was able to return to Egypt. He did, at some point after the confrontation, write a letter to the monks at Pbow in which he encouraged their opposition to Chalcedon and reported his own removal as abbot of their monastery.[44]

---

38. Frend, *Rise of the Monophysite Movement*, 274–76.

39. Frend, *Rise of the Monophysite Movement*, 281. This precludes the association of this incident with the various monastic concourses held between 554 and 563 C.E. (Frend, *Rise of the Monophysite Movement*, 275; van Cauwenbergh, *Étude*, 155).

40. The second *encomium* (Codex GB) suggests that accusations against Abraham began early in Justinian's reign. Cf. Campagnano, "Monazi egiziani," 242.

41. One must be careful, of course, from reading later anti-Chalcedonian propaganda as historical fact. While this is not the place for a detailed discussion of the developments in Egypt after the Council of Chalcedon (451 C.E.) and the place of the Pachomian movement in those developments, it is fair to say from the evidence (contra van Cauwenbergh, *Étude*, 159) that the Pachomians were in early opposition to the council's decrees.

42. Frend, *Rise of the Monophysite Movement*, 273f.

43. The second *encomium* (Codex GB) suggests that Justinian applied force from the beginning, since he effected Abraham's trip to Constantinople through his arrest (Campagnano, "Monazi egiziani," 242). The *Life of Abraham*, however, reports that Abraham proceeded to Constantinople on the invitation of the emperor. Both the *Life* and the *Synaxarium* report that at their meeting in Constantinople, the emperor sought first to persuade Abraham to accept Chalcedon. While his offer was in reality an ultimatum, it was nonetheless made before the emperor acted against the monk.

44. Cf. above, n. 33.

Justinian followed up his removal of Abraham as abbot by sending a military force to Pbow to compel the monks to accept his solution.[45] A Chalcedonian abbot was installed, and the members of the community who refused to accept the change were dispersed from the monastery. While the *Panegyric on Apollo* suggests the continued existence of Pbow as a Chalcedonian stronghold for some time,[46] we hear nothing of its activities or abbots after this point. For all practical purposes it has disappeared from the plane of history, a Chalcedonian island swallowed up in an non-Chalcedonian sea. At the same time, Abraham, who did return to Egypt, went first to the monastery of Shenoute at Atripe, where he copied the Pachomian rules. He eventually established his own community at Tberčot (Farshut) in Upper Egypt.

It appears from these accounts that Justinian's efforts were confined in Upper Egypt to the Pachomian movement in general and to their central monastery of Pbow in particular. Apart from this conclusion it is difficult to reconcile Justinian's use of troops to enforce his decision at Pbow with Abraham's freedom to move to the large and well-known monastery of Shenoute at Atripe, and the eventual establishment of his own monastery at Tberčot, which is located close to Pbow in the heart of the Pachomian system.[47] Given such a focused effort on Justinian's part in Upper Egypt, one is compelled to inquire into the internal forces that lay behind his decision. It is in the answer to this deeper question that the ultimate roots of the demise of the Pachomian movement are laid bare.

---

45. Basset, *Synaxaire arabe-jacobite*, 11.684; cf. Campagnano, "Monazi egiziani," 242 (Codex GB); van Cauwenbergh, *Étude*, 155. Justinian's use of troops against the Pachomians may also be reflected in a legend that Professor James M. Robinson learned from Riyad Girgis Fam of Dishna in Upper Egypt. It records that the ruler in the period when the monastery at Faw Qibli had many monks was an idolater. He instructed his son to take soldiers and destroy the monastery. However, the son did not carry out the order because he, like his mother, was a Christian. The Christian wife of the idolatrous ruler may be the legend's reflection of Theodora's Monophysite orientation. The fact that Justinian and Theodora had no son is best explained as legendary enhancement of the story, through the transformation of the Egyptian duke into the royal family. The full legend will be published by Robinson in his forthcoming book on the Bodmer papyri.

46. See above, n. 37.

47. Tberčot, modern Farshut, is located approximately five miles west of Nag Hammadi. While it is on the other side of the river from Faw Qibli (the site of the monastery of Pbow), it is certainly within the territory covered by the Pachomian community represented in the *Life of Pachomius*.

To begin with, in the fifth and sixth centuries, the sheer size of the Pachomian monastery of Pbow would have made it an obvious target for Justinian's efforts in Upper Egypt. Beyond its own impressive size, Pbow also served as the central monastery of a system of monasteries extending throughout Upper Egypt.[48] Already by the early 350s, some 2,000 monks from the various Pachomian monasteries gathered at Pbow for the annual Easter celebration.[49] Palladius reports (ca. 420 C.E.) a total of 1,300 to 1,400 monks at Pbow and 200 to 300 at each of the other Pachomian foundations.[50] Jerome, who translated the Pachomian *Rule* into Latin, exaggerated when he listed their total number as 50,000.[51] His figure nonetheless underscores the perception of the movement's size at this time. While similar estimates do not exist for the fifth and sixth centuries, there is little reason to assume a major decline. Certainly the great basilica of Pbow completed in the reign of Emperor Leo I (457–74 C.E.) argues for a continuing sizable population in the Pachomian system.[52] This great fifth-century basilica was reported by the Armenian Abu Salih to have been 150 cubits in length and 75 cubits in width.[53] He reports that its pillars were marble and that it contained pictures composed of tesserae of glass, gilded and colored. The structure was destroyed by the Khalif al-Hakim in the eleventh century.

Excavations conducted at Faw Qibli by the Institute for Antiquity and Christianity have confirmed the size and beauty of this basilica.[54] The 75 meter x 37–meter structure had massive exterior walls. The interior was divided into five aisles with a return aisle at the west end. Four rows, each consisting of eighteen rose-granite

---

48. At the time of Pachomius's death (346 C.E.), the system included nine monasteries, which ranged from Panopolis (*G1* 83=*SBo* 53) to Latopolis (*G1* 83=*SBo* 58). Theodore (d. 368 C.E.) added two monasteries further downriver near Hermopolis (*G1* 135; *SBo* 202). How many of these were still a functional part of the Pachomian system in the sixth century is unknown.

49. *Epistula Ammonis* 21.

50. Palladius, *Historia Lausiaca* 32.8–9.

51. *Regula Pachomii, Praefatio Hieronymi* 7.

52. The size of the basilica at Pbow was necessitated in part by the two annual assemblages of the monks from the various Pachomian monasteries at their central monastery for Easter, and the annual reckoning in August (*Epistula Ammonis* 21; *SBo* 71; *G1* 83).

53. B. T. A. Evetts, *The Churches and Monasteries of Egypt and Some Neighboring Countries Attributed to Abu Salih, the Armenian* (Oxford: Clarendon, 1895) 281–82.

54. Cf. above, n. 5; especially Grossmann, "Basilica."

columns of Roman and Byzantine origin,[55] separated the five aisles. The basilica floor was composed of uneven limestone pavers of approximately 25 to 30 centimeters square. Although the destruction of the basilica was thorough, several examples of decorated stone have surfaced, which add to the impression one gains of the beauty of this church and the wealth that lay behind it. There has been, however, no confirmation of the pictures of tesserae mentioned by Abu Salih.[56] In addition to the evidence of the great fifth-century basilica, the excavations have also uncovered an earlier fourth-century basilica beneath it.[57] This earlier structure was equally immense for its age (56 meters x 30 meters). The basilica, like its successor, contained five aisles. Since it was razed for the construction of the fifth-century basilica, however, the type of the columns that composed the interior stylobate walls remains uncertain.[58]

The existence of these two great basilicas at Pbow underscores the size and importance of the community in Upper Egypt. A late Arabic manuscript which preserves the text of an allocution spoken at the dedication of the later fifth-century basilica (ca. 459 C.E.) supplies further evidence of a rather intimate relationship between the Pachomians of this period and the ecclesiastical and political authorities in Alexandria and Constantinople.[59] The homily, attributed to Timothy, the archbishop of Alexandria, contains valuable information on the events that led to the construction of the basilica.[60]

Considerable discussion has arisen over the identification of the Timothy to whom this allocution is attributed. Van Cauwenbergh

---

55. Grossmann, "Basilica," 233. The source of these columns remains a mystery. The accidental exposure of a significant first-century C.E. Roman site some 750 meters north of the basilica (van Elderen, "Nag Hammadi Excavation," 230–31), however, suggests a possible hitherto unsuspected source. Cf. Lease, "Fourth Season," 81; Goehring, "New Frontiers," 256 (see p. 182 in the present volume).

56. Even with the thorough nature of the basilica's destruction, one would expect evidence of such tesserae. None was found. If they were limited to the apse, however, they may yet be found. The apse has not been excavated as it is situated beneath a modern home.

57. Grossmann, "Basilica," 234–35; van Elderen, "Nag Hammadi Excavations," 229; Lease, "Fourth Season," 77–81.

58. The Roman and Byzantine columns used in the fifth-century basilica may also have served the fourth-century basilica. There is no way to know for certain.

59. Van Lantschoot, "Allocution" (above, n. 10); van Cauwenbergh, *Étude,* 153–54.

60. Van Lantschoot, "Allocution"; van Cauwenbergh, *Étude,* 153–54; cf. Leipoldt, *Schenute von Atripe,* 20.

believed that he was to be identified with Timothy II Salofaciolus, the Chalcedonian Tabennesiote monk from the Canopus monastery who had been made the archbishop of Alexandria upon
the forced removal of the non-Chalcedonian archbishop Timothy II
Aelurus in January 460 C.E. He used this evidence to argue for a
pro-Chalcedonian orientation of the Pachomian movement in this
period.[61] Van Lantschoot, however, who supplied an edited version
of the text with a translation in 1934, dated the dedication of the
basilica to 459 C.E. The Timothy in question was thus in his view
Timothy II Aelurus, who was not exiled until the following year.[62]

The allocution itself begins by recounting the journey of Apa Victor, the archimandrite of Pbow; Apa Shenoute of Atripe; and the
Alexandrian archbishop Cyril to Constantinople to meet with Emperor Theodosius II (408–51 C.E.) concerning Nestorius.[63] Victor is
portrayed as playing an influential role in the meeting with the emperor, a fact which leads to their joint decision to build the great
basilica at Pbow. The involvement of the emperor is made very
clear.[64]

The project was interrupted, however, by the death of Theodosius II, and little was accomplished during the reign of his successor
Marcian (451–57 C.E.). With the accession to the throne of Leo I in
457 C.E., however, construction was renewed and rapidly brought to
completion. Apa Martyrius, who was at that time archimandrite of
Pbow, proceeded to Alexandria to announce the completion of the
basilica. From there he went to Constantinople and reported to the
emperor that

> l'église, dont on commença la construction sur l'ordre de l'empereur
> Théodose et du saint Apa Victor, supérieur des moines, nous l'avons
> achevée sur l'ordre de Dieu et grâce à votre puissance. Que notre
> seigneur l'empereur nous commande donc de la consacrer au nom de
> notre père le prophète Apa Pachôme.[65]

---

61. Van Cauwenbergh, *Étude*, 153–54, 159.

62. Van Lantschoot, "Allocution," 16–22.

63. Cf. *Sinuthii Vita* 17; Johannes Leipoldt, *Sinuthii vita bohairice* (CSCO 41; Paris: E
typographeo reipublicae, 1906) 15–16.

64. Van Lantschoot, "Allocution," 42–44.

65. "…the basilica, the construction of which was begun by the order of the emperor Theodosius and the holy Apa Victor, superior of the monks, we have completed
by the order of God and the grace of your eminence; which our lord, the emperor,

The emperor instructed Martyrius to return to Pbow and prepare for the dedication. He himself promised to dispatch the four patriarchs of Antioch, Jerusalem, Alexandria, and Rome to Pbow for the consecration.

This text clearly emphasizes the close affiliation of the Upper Egyptian Pachomian movement with the ecclesiastical and imperial authorities in Alexandria and Constantinople in the middle of the fifth century. It is possible that the closeness of the relationship was exaggerated by the allocution's author, the Archbishop of Alexandria. No evidence exists, however, which refutes the relationship.[66] It is clear in any event that the perception of the Pachomian movement in the mid–fifth century in Alexandria and Constantinople was one of its close affiliation with the church and the state.[67]

This affiliation had actually begun quite early in the movement's history and gained impetus from the support given to it in the Pachomian *Vitae*. It is clear from the *Vitae* that Theodore, Pachomius's eventual successor as general abbot,[68] fostered close relations with the Alexandrian patriarch Athanasius. Theodore came from a

---

therefore commands us to consecrate in the name of our father, the prophet, Apa Pachomius" (Van Lantschoot, "Allocution," 46).

66. We do have evidence that the Alexandrian archbishop Theophilus (d. 412 C.E.) worked to effect close ties with the Pachomians. A sixth- to seventh-century text contains a letter of Theophilus to Apa Horsiesius in which the archbishop requests that the monk come to Alexandria and bring a copy of the *Life of Pachomius and Theodore* with him. Lefort, *Vies coptes*, 389–99; Crum, *Papyruscodex*, 12–21 (text), 65–75 (trans.). Theophilus is also reported to have brought Pachomian monks from Upper Egypt to Canopus to found a monastery there after the destruction of the pagan sanctuaries located there. Tito Orlandi, ed., *Storia della Chiesa di Alessandria* (2 vols.; TDSA 17 and 31; Milan: Cisalpino, 1968–70) 2.12–14 (text), 61–62 (trans.).

67. The view of the Pachomians gained from their own literature, most of which had been composed long before the Council of Chalcedon, was one of the movement's "orthodoxy" and close affiliation with the Alexandrian hierarchy. While the division between those who supported and those who rejected Chalcedon was growing, it had not yet impinged upon the written sources through which those outside of Upper Egypt knew the Pachomians.

68. Although Pachomius on his deathbed named Petronios as his successor (*S7*; Lefort, *S. Pachomii vitae sahidice scriptae*, 93; *G1* 114), who in turn a short time later named Horsiesius to succeed him (*SBo* 123; *G1* 117), it is Theodore who ultimately succeeds to this post and insures the system's survival (*SBo* 139–40; *G1* 127–30). The *Vitae*, which serve as an apology for Theodore, present him from the start as Pachomius's favorite (*SBo* 30; *G1* 35–36; *Epistula Ammonis* 9). He was passed over by Pachomius because he had promised the brothers before Pachomius died to serve as their leader after Pachomius's death, an act that Pachomius interpreted as evidence of Theodore's arrogance and pride (*SBo* 94; *G1* 106–7).

wealthy family which had access to the local bishops.[69] He made trips to Alexandria and certainly knew Athanasius personally.[70] When Athanasius journeyed to the Thebaid in 363 C.E., Theodore took a number of monks with him and proceeded downriver to meet the archbishop. According to the Bohairic version, Athanasius had actually sent to Pbow requesting that Theodore come and meet him.[71] This affiliation is underscored by Theodore in the *Vita* when he attributes the following words to Pachomius himself:[72]

> In our generation in Egypt I see three important things that increase by God's grace for the benefit of all those who have understanding: the bishop Athanasius, the athlete of Christ contending for the faith unto death; the holy Abba Antony, the perfect model of anchoritic life; and this *koinonia,* which is a model for all those who wish to assemble souls in God, to succor them until they be made perfect.

The two principal *Vitae,* which may be seen as apologies for Theodore,[73] close after Theodore's death with a letter from Athanasius to Apa Horsiesius, in which the archbishop consoles and encourages the monks. Its very existence and placement at the end of these texts indicates the Pachomians' own self-understanding of their intimate relationship with the archbishop at this point in their history.[74]

It is not clear, however, that this close affiliation with ecclesiastical authority and organization is representative of the Pachomian movement in the time of Pachomius himself.[75] Such a presentation of Pachomius represents at least in part an anachronistic depiction of the early years in terms of the situation as it actually existed at the time of the composition of the *Vitae.*[76] The advances in this direc-

---

69. *SBo* 31, 37; *G1* 33, 37.

70. *SBo* 96; *G1* 109, 113.

71. *SBo* 201–3; *G1* 143–44.

72. *G1* 136 (translation by Veilleux, *Pachomian Koinonia,* 1.395); cf. *SBo* 134.

73. M. M. van Molle, "Confrontation entre les règles et la littérature Pachômienne postérieure," *SVS* 21 (1968) 394–424, esp. 415f.

74. *SBo* 210; *G1* 150. The fact that both the Alexandrian Theodore (*Epistula Ammonis* 4; cf. *Bo* 89; *G1* 94) and Ammon (*Epistula Ammonis* 2) came to the Pachomian *koinonia* from the Alexandrian church of Pierius also reveals the close connection. Ammon was steered to the community by Paul, the priest at Pierius (Goehring, *Letter of Ammon,* 191–92).

75. Goehring, "New Frontiers," 240–52 (see pp. 166–79 in the present volume).

76. Goehring, "New Frontiers," 240–52 (see pp. 166–79 in the present volume); Robinson, "Introduction," 18.

tion under Theodore (351–68 C.E.) and Horsiesius (368–87 C.E.) are presupposed in the *Vitae*.

This is not meant to suggest that Pachomius was opposed to Athanasius, but merely that he did not link closely the authority of his monastic enterprise with the ecclesiastical authority centered in Alexandria.[77] It is clear from the *Vitae*, in spite of their anachronistic presentation, that the successs of the Pachomian movement lay in Pachomius's own charismatic authority. He never met Athanasius. On one occasion, when the opportunity did present itself, the *Vitae* report that he hid from the archbishop in order to avoid ordination.[78] Ordination, of course, made one subject to the bishop. Toward the end of his life, Pachomius was even called before a council at Latopolis to answer charges that he was a visionary.[79]

It must be stressed that this understanding of Pachomius is not meant to call his theology into question. It is rather to underline the fact that what was primary to Pachomius was his understanding of the charismatic authority inherent in the monastic enterprise and the distinction of this authority from that of the church.[80] It is this understanding that clearly shifts during the leadership period of Theodore (351–68 C.E.). The authority which holds the movement together becomes much more closely identified with the ecclesiastical authority emanating from Alexandria.

This new understanding continued to develop under Theodore's successor, Horsiesius. He is reported to have met with Archbishop Theophilus in Alexandria and to have brought to him a copy of a *Life of Pachomius and Theodore*.[81] It is this period also that produced the important Pachomian text, the *Letter of Ammon* (written ca. 400 C.E.). While it reports on Ammon's three-year sojourn as a young monk at Pbow between 352–55 C.E., it is written from his later position as a bishop of the church. As such it functions more than any other document in the Pachomian dossier to underscore the movement's close

---

77. Robinson, "Introduction," 18; Chadwick, "Pachomios," 18.

78. *SBo* 28; *G1* 30; cf. *G1* 143–44.

79. *G1* 112.

80. Two excellent studies of the dichotomy between monastic and ecclesiastical authority are Karl Holl, *Enthusiasmus und Bussgewalt beim griechischen Mönchtum: Eine Studie zu Symeon dem neuen Theologen* (Leipzig: Hinrichs, 1898; reprint, Hildesheim: Olms, 1969), and Rousseau, *Ascetics*.

81. Above, n. 66.

association with the anti-Arian ecclesiastical authorities in Alexandria.[82] It is surely from sources such as these, written in Greek, that the Pachomian movement gained recognition outside of Egypt.[83]

The close affiliation of the Pachomian movement in the fifth century with the ecclesiastical and political authorities in Alexandria and Constantinople can thus be seen as but the continuation of a process begun by Theodore. While his affiliation of Pachomian monastic authority with ecclesiastical authority within Egypt helped to see the movement through the crisis of leadership that followed Pachomius's death,[84] it made the movement vulnerable in the long run to the pressure of ecclesiastical authority outside of Egypt. It was just such pressure, applied by Justinian I in the middle of the sixth century, which led directly, as we have seen, to the demise of the Pachomian movement.

Justinian's efforts can thus be explained in terms of his perception of the movement's size and significance in Upper Egypt and its apparent willingness to accept outside authority. Given these two factors alone, however, one might still wonder how the emperor could hope to succeed in view of the strength of the non-Chalcedonian elements in Egypt and the popularity there of the archbishop Theodosius whom he had just detained in Constantinople. Surely his advisers would have recognized that the gulf opened by Chalcedon had altered the equation. One could not simply assume that the close affiliation of the Pachomians with church and state would automatically bridge this new divide.[85]

It is here that we must look more closely at the significance of the Tabennesiote monastery at Canopus in Lower Egypt and the role that it played in the perception of the Pachomian movement to those outside of Egypt. The monastery was established ca. 391 C.E. by the archbishop Theophilus after the suppression of the pagan sanctuar-

---

82. Goehring, *Letter of Ammon,* 107, 251–52.

83. The various Greek *Lives of Pachomius* all survive in manuscripts preserved outside of Egypt. It was the emergence of the Greek and Latin versions of the Pachomian literature that insured its lasting influence beyond Egypt. Shenoute, on the other hand, in spite of the fact that he is said to have accompanied the Alexandrian archbishop Cyril to the Council of Ephesus (above, n. 63), was quickly forgotten outside of Egypt because his *Vita* and his writings were not translated out of the Coptic vernacular.

84. Above, n. 68.

85. The dedication of the large basilica at Pbow in 459 C.E. suggests that the extent of the gulf between the two parties became fully apparent only with time.

ies located at the site. According to the Coptic *History of the Church of Alexandria*,[86] Theophilus first brought monks from Jerusalem to occupy the monastery. When the local Egyptian demons proved too much for them, he sent to Upper Egypt, to the monasteries of Apa Pachomius, for monks able to control the evil powers and establish the monastery. These Pachomian monks were successful. Their monastery of Metanoia was the source of the copy of the *Rule* which Jerome translated into Latin.[87] One may wonder as well whether it was the avenue through which the first Greek *Life of Pachomius* (*Vita prima* or *G1*) left Egypt.[88]

It is necessary to note at this juncture that the term *Tabennesiote* had come to be used by this period of any monastery that used the Pachomian *Rule*. The use of the *Rule*, however, did not necessarily mean that the monastery belonged to the Pachomian *koinonia* or system centered at the Upper Egyptian monastery of Pbow. Shenoute's White Monastery at Atripe thus made use of the *Rule* but certainly did not belong to the Pachomian system headquartered at Pbow.[89] The monastery of the Tabennesiotes led by Ammon, mentioned in the *Historia Monachorum in Aegypto*, should be likewise so identified.[90] It is probable that the monastery of Metanoia at Canopus falls into this category, though the reference noted above to Theophilus's acquisition of monks from the monasteries of Pachomius in Upper Egypt to found this monastery suggests a closer connection.[91] It does appear from other sources that Archbishop Theophilus had a keen interest in the Pachomian movement.[92] However, even if this monastery was not a member of the Upper Egyptian Pachomian system, one suspects that the perception of the Upper Egyptian

---

86. Orlandi, *Storia*, 2.12–14 (text), 61–62 (trans.).

87. *Reguli Pachomii, Praefatio Hieronymi* 1.

88. The earliest external reference to a *Life of Pachomius* occurs in a text that reports a request made to Apa Horsiesius by the Alexandrian archbishop Theophilus to bring a copy of the *Life of Pachomius and Theodore* (above, n. 66) to him. One might assume, if indeed Theophilus established Pachomian monks at Canopus, that the monastery would have had a *Life of Pachomius* as well as the *Regula*.

89. Leipoldt, *Schenute von Atripe*, 36.

90. *Historia Monachorum in Aegypto* 3.

91. Above, n. 86.

92. Above, n. 66. The *Letter of Ammon*, if indeed it was written to the archbishop Theophilus (Goehring, *Letter of Ammon*, 183–84), offers additional evidence for this connection.

movement outside of Egypt was colored by the perception of this "Tabennesiote" community. This would be particularly true if the Pachomian sources at their disposal were known to come from this monastery. Jerome made this connection explicit in the case of the *Rule*.[93]

When one examines the references to this monastery in the fifth and sixth centuries, its involvement in the ecclesiastical politics in Alexandria is clear. It is furthermore clear that this Tabennesiote monastery was decidedly in the Chalcedonian camp. When the Emperor Leo I acted in 460 C.E. to arrest and exile the Alexandrian archbishop Timothy II Aelurus, who had refused to accept the hated *Tome* of Leo and the decrees of Chalcedon, he turned to the Tabennesiote monks at Canopus for a replacement. One of their number, Timothy II Salofaciolus, was consecrated patriarch in the spring of 460 C.E.[94] When this Timothy died in February 482 C.E., he was succeeded as Chalcedonian patriarch of Alexandria by his fellow Tabennesiote monk, John Talaia. His reign was short-lived, however, as Peter III Mongus arrived in the capital in the same year, overcame the schism between Alexandria and Constantinople, and gained the support of the emperor Acacius, which brought with it his restoration as patriarch of Alexandria.[95]

A third Chalcedonian patriarch was named from among the Tabennesiote monks at Canopus in 537 C.E. This was Paul the Tabennesiote. He proved, however, to be an unfortunate choice (he was implicated in a charge of murder) and was replaced in 540 C.E. by Zoilos (540–51 C.E.).[96] It is nonetheless clear that the Chalcedonian orientation of the Tabennesiote monastery of Metanoia at Canopus had continued from the middle of the fifth century to the middle of the sixth century.

This Chalcedonian orientation of the Tabennesiotes at Canopus is in direct opposition to the non-Chalcedonian stance of the Upper Egyptian Pachomians at Pbow.[97] If the authorities in Alexandria

---

93. Above, n. 87.

94. Frend, *Rise of the Monophysite Movement*, 163.

95. Frend, *Rise of the Monophysite Movement*, 177–80.

96. Frend, *Rise of the Monophysite Movement*, 274–75.

97. It should be pointed out that the extent of the Pachomian "system" at this time is unknown. While the Pachomian sources report the foundation of nine monasteries by Pachomius and an additional three or four by Theodore, one hears nothing of the

and Constantinople knew the movement chiefly through the nearby Canopus monastery, however, they would have perceived it in general, throughout Egypt, as in fundamental agreement with the Chalcedonian position. A major basilica, after all, had been dedicated at Pbow in the early years of Leo I with the emperor's approval. Even if the authorities suspected different attitudes among the Pachomians in Upper Egypt, they undoubtedly believed that the Upper Egyptian abbots could be persuaded to unite with their colleagues from the North. While this view of the Upper Egyptian Pachomians proved incorrect, it was nonetheless the view on which Justinian and his advisers acted when they summoned Abraham of Pbow to Constantinople.

In conclusion, the demise of the Pachomian movement in the sixth century must be viewed first of all against the success of the movement after Pachomius's death. The authority and influence of the movement in Upper Egypt led to its close affiliation with the ecclesiastical authority in Alexandria. The compilation of the movement's history in the period when this affiliation was more secure led to the presentation of the movement from its very beginning as closely associated with the Alexandrian church. It was through these sources that the movement was known outside of Egypt. There were mutual advantages to the close affiliation of the movement with the church prior to Chalcedon. With the theological rift that followed, however, this affiliation, interpreted by the ecclesiastical and political authorities in terms of their own authority over the movement, set the stage for Justinian's attempt to compel the Pachomians' acceptance of Chalcedon.

The importance of gaining the Pachomians as allies in his efforts to force Chalcedonian obedience in Egypt would have been clear to Justinian. The size and influence of their central monastery at Pbow alone would have made it an obvious target. Add to this the fact that it served as the central monastery of a system of monasteries

----

fate of these individual monasteries in the fifth and sixth centuries. The Pachomian "system" in these latter centuries is seen only through its central monastery of Pbow. While the size of the fifth-century basilica at Pbow may suggest the continuation of the system of monasteries (above, n. 52), it gives no indication of which monasteries belonged to it or even how many it included.

throughout Upper Egypt, and the importance of this effort becomes even clearer.

Finally, the Chalcedonian persuasion of the Tabennesiote monastery at Canopus suggested that the chances of success were high. Since the Greek East knew the Pachomian movement through this monastery, Justinian and his advisers would have had every reason to believe that they could persuade Abraham of Pbow to join with them in their call for unity. Justinian was no doubt surprised when Abraham, once in Constantinople, aligned himself so firmly with Theodosius, the deposed non-Chalcedonian archbishop of Alexandria.

The demise of the Pachomian movement at the hands of Justinian I was thus the result of policies based upon certain perceptions and misperceptions of the Upper Egyptian movement centered at Pbow. The emperor correctly perceived the movement's widespread influence in the Thebaid and recognized from this the significance of gaining the movement as an ally for his Chalcedonian efforts in Egypt. He perceived incorrectly, however, that the movement had Chalcedonian leanings and thus might be expected to join his cause. This misperception resulted from equating the stance of the Tabennesiote monastery at Canopus with that of the Upper Egyptian Pachomians centered at Pbow.

Justinian's subsequent efforts to enforce his position through the use of troops represent simply his response to his failed diplomacy. While his use of force enabled him to turn his misperception into reality by making Pbow Chalcedonian, it destroyed the movement's influence in Egypt and with it the reason for the effort in the first place. While Justinian had won the battle, he had lost the war. In the process, he effectively removed the latter stages of the Pachomian movement from history. Forgotten in the Byzantine empire when Egypt remained non-Chalcedonian, it was ostracized from Coptic history as a result of its (forced) adherence to Chalcedon.

Bibliography of Cited Works

Achelis, Hans. Review of *Pachomius und das älteste Klosterleben,* by Georg Grützmacher. *ThLZ* 9 (1896) 240–44.

Amélineau, E. *La géographie de l'égypte à l'epoche copte.* Paris: Imprimerie nationale, 1893. Reprint, Osnabrück: Otto Zeller, 1973.

————. *Monuments pour servir à l'histoire de l'Égypte chrétienne au IVe siècle: Histoire de saint Pachôme et de ses communautés.* AnMG 17. Paris: Leroux, 1889.

————. *Monuments pour servir à l'histoire de l'Égypte chrétienne aux IVe, V^e, VIe, et VIIe siècle.* Mémoires 4. Paris: Ernest Leroux, 1888.

Amidon, Philip R. *The Panarion of St. Epiphanius, Bishop of Salamis: Selected Passages.* New York and Oxford: Oxford University Press, 1990.

Anson, John. "The Female Transvestite in Early Monasticism: The Origins and Development of a Motif." *Viator* 5 (1974) 1–32.

Athanassakis, Apostolos A. *The Life of Pachomius (Vita Prima Graeca).* Missoula, Mont.: Scholars Press, 1975.

Atiya, Aziz S., ed. *The Coptic Encyclopedia.* 8 vols. New York: Macmillan, 1991.

Bacht, Heinrich. *Das Vermächtnis des Ursprungs.* STGL 5. Würzburg: Echter, 1972.

Badger, Carlton Mills. "The New Man Created in God: Christology, Congregation, and Asceticism in Athanasius of Alexandria." Ph.D. diss., Duke University, 1990.

Bagnall, Roger S. *Egypt in Late Antiquity.* Princeton: Princeton University Press, 1993.

————. "Religious Conversion and Onomastic Change in Early Byzantine Egypt." *BASP* 19 (1982) 105–24.

Bagnall, Roger S., and Naphtali Lewis. *Columbia Papyri VII: Fourth-Century Documents from Karanis.* AmSP 20. Missoula, Mont.: Scholars Press, 1979.

Bainton, Roland H. *Christendom: A Short History of Christianity and Its Impact on Western Civilization.* 2 vols. New York: Harper & Row, 1964.

Barison, P. "Ricerche sui monasteri dell'Egitto bizantino ed arabo secondo i documenti dei papiri greci." *Aeg* 18 (1938) 29–148.

Barnes, Timothy D. "Angel of Light or Mystic Initiate? The Problem of the *Life of Antony.*" *JTS* 37 (1986) 353–68.

————. *Constantine and Eusebius.* Cambridge and London: Harvard University Press, 1981.

Barns, J. W. B. "Greek and Coptic Papyri from the Covers of the Nag Hammadi Texts." In Martin Krause, ed., *Essays on the Nag Hammadi Codices in Honour of Pahor Labib.* NHS 6. Leiden: E. J. Brill, 1975, 9–18.

Barns, J. W. B., G. M. Browne, and J. C. Shelton. *Nag Hammadi Codices: Greek and Coptic Papyri from the Cartonnage of the Covers*. NHS 16. Leiden: E. J. Brill, 1981.

Barraclough, Geoffrey, ed. *The Christian World: A Social and Cultural History*. New York: Abrams, 1981.

Bartelink, G. J. M. *Athanase d'Alexandrie: Vie d'Antoine*. SC 400. Paris: Éditions du Cerf, 1994.

Basset, René Marie Josef. *Le synaxaire arabe-jacobite (rédaction copte)*. PO 1, 3, 11, 16, 17, 20. Paris: Didot, 1904–29.

Bauer, Walter. *Orthodoxy and Heresy in Earliest Christianity*. Translated by Robert A. Kraft et al. Philadelphia: Fortress Press, 1971.

Bell, H. Idris. "Athanasius: Chapter in Church History." *CQ* 3 (1925) 158–76.

———. "Bibliography: Graeco-Roman Egypt, A. Papyri (1923–1924)." *JEA* 11 (1925) 84–106.

———. *Jews and Christians in Egypt: The Jewish Troubles in Alexandria and the Athanasian Controversies*. London: The British Museum, 1924. Reprint, Westport, Conn.: Greenwood Press, 1972.

———. "Two Official Letters of the Arab Period." *JEA* 12 (1926) 265–81.

Blaise, Albert. *Dictionnaire latin-français des auteurs chrétiens*. Turnhout: Éditions Brepols, 1954.

Boak, Arthur E. R. "An Egyptian Farmer of the Age of Diocletian and Constantine." *ByzM* 1 (1946) 39–53.

Boak, Arthur E. R., and Herbert C. Youtie. "Flight and Oppression in Fourth-Century Egypt." In Edoardo Arslan, ed., *Studi in onore di Aristide Calderini e Roberto Paribeni*. 2 vols. Milan: Casa editrice Ceschina, 1956–57, 2.325–37.

Boon, Amand. *Pachomiana latina: Règle et épîtres de s. Pachôme, épître de s. Théodore et "liber" de s. Orsiesius: Texte latin de s. Jerome*. BRHE 7. Louvain: Bureaux de la revue, 1932.

Bousset, Wilhelm. *Apophthegmata: Textüberlieferung und Charakter der Apophthegmata Patrum. Zur Überlieferung der Vita Pachomii. Euagrios-Studien*. Tübingen: Mohr, 1923.

Bowman, Alan K. *Egypt after the Pharaohs*. Berkeley: University of California Press, 1986.

Brakke, David. *Athanasius and the Politics of Asceticism*. Oxford Early Christian Studies. Oxford: Clarendon Press, 1995.

———. "The Authenticity of the Ascetic Athanasiana." *Or* 63 (1994) 17–56.

———. "Canon Formation and Social Conflict in Fourth-Century Egypt: Athanasius of Alexandria's Thirty-ninth *Festal Letter*." *HTR* 87 (1994) 395–419.

———. "St. Athanasius and Ascetic Christians in Egypt." Ph.D. diss., Yale University, 1992.

Brock, Sebastian. "Early Syrian Asceticism." *Numen* 20 (1973) 1–19.

Brock, Sebastian, and Susan Ashbrook Harvey. *Holy Women of the Syrian Orient*. TCH 13. Berkeley: University of California Press, 1987.

Brown, Peter. *The Body and Society: Men, Women, and Sexual Renunciation in Early Christianity*. New York: Columbia University Press, 1988.

————. *The Cult of the Saints: Its Rise and Function in Latin Christianity.* Chicago: University of Chicago Press, 1981.

————. "The Rise and Function of the Holy Man in Late Antiquity." *JRomS* 61 (1971) 80–101.

Bucher, M. Paul. "Les commencements des psaumes LI a XCIII: Inscription d'une tombe de Kasr es Saijad." *Kemi* 4 (1931) 157–60.

Budge, E. A. Wallis. *The Book of Governors: The "Historia Monastica" of Thomas Bishop of Marga A.D. 840.* London: Kegan Paul, Trench, Trübner & Co., 1893.

————. *The Book of the Saints of the Ethiopian Church: A Translation of the Ethiopic Synaxarium Made from the Manuscripts Oriental 660 and 661 in the British Museum.* Cambridge: Cambridge University Press, 1928.

————. *Coptic Apocrypha in the Dialect of Upper Egypt.* London: British Museum, 1913.

————. *Miscellaneous Coptic Texts in the Dialect of Upper Egypt.* London: British Museum, 1915.

Bunge, Gabriel, and Adalbert de Vogüé. *Quatre eremites égyptiens d'après les fragments coptes de l'Histoire Lausiaque.* Spiritualité orientale 60. Bégrolles-en-Mauges: Abbaye de Bellefontaine, 1994.

Burton-Christie, Douglas. *The Word in the Desert: Scripture and the Quest for Holiness in Early Christian Monasticism.* Oxford: Oxford University Press, 1993.

Butler, Cuthbert. *The Lausiac History of Palladius I/II.* Cambridge: Cambridge University Press, 1898. Reprint, Hildesheim: Georg Olms, 1967.

Cadell, H., and R. Rémondon. "Sens et emplois de τὸ ὄρος dans les documents papyrologiques." *REG* 80 (1967) 343–49.

Campagnano, Antonella. "Monaci egiziani fra V e VI secolo." *VetChr* 15 (1978) 223–46.

Camplani, Alberto. "In Margine alla Storia dei Meliziani." *Aug* 30 (1990) 313–51.

Canivet, P., and A. Leroy-Molinghen, eds. *Théodoret de Cyr: Histoire des moines de syrie.* SC 234, 257. Paris: Éditions du Cerf, 1977–79.

Chadwick, Henry. "The Domestication of Gnosis." In Bentley Layton, ed., *The Rediscovery of Gnosis: Proceedings of the Conference at Yale, March 1978.* 2 vols. Leiden: E. J. Brill, 1980, 1.3–16.

————. "Pachomios and the Idea of Sanctity." In S. Hackel, ed., *The Byzantine Saint: University of Birmingham Fourteenth Spring Symposium of Byzantine Studies.* London: Fellowship of St. Alban and St. Sergius, 1981, 11–24.

Chaîne, M. "La double recension de l'Histoire Lausiaque dans la version copte." *RevOC* 3–4 (1925–26) 232–75.

Chitty, Derwas J. *The Desert a City: An Introduction to the Study of Egyptian and Palestinian Monasticism under the Christian Empire.* Oxford: Blackwell, 1966.

————. "A Note on the Chronology of the Pachomian Foundations." *SP* 2 [TU 64] (1957) 379–85.

————. "Pachomian Sources Reconsidered." *JEH* 5 (1954) 38-77.

Clark, Elizabeth A. *The Origenist Controversy: The Cultural Construction of an Early Christian Debate.* Princeton: Princeton University Press, 1992.

Cohn, Leopold, and Paul Wendland. *Philonis opera quae supersunt.* 7 vols. in 8. Berlin: Georg Reimer, 1896–1930.

Colson, F. H. *Philo.* 10 vols. LCL. Cambridge: Harvard University Press, 1967.

Coquin, René-Georges. "Akhmim." In Aziz S. Atiya, ed., *The Coptic Encyclopedia.* 8 vols. New York: Macmillan, 1991, 1.78.

———. "Tabennese." In Aziz S. Atiya, ed., *The Coptic Encyclopedia.* 8 vols. New York: Macmillan, 1991, 7.2197.

Coquin, René-Georges, and Maurice Martin. "Anba Palaemon." In Aziz S. Atiya, ed., *The Coptic Encyclopedia.* 8 vols. New York: Macmillan, 1991, 3.757.

———. "Bawit: History." In Aziz S. Atiya, ed., *The Coptic Encyclopedia.* 8 vols. New York: Macmillan, 1991, 2.362–63.

———. "Dayr Anba Bidaba." In Aziz S. Atiya, *The Coptic Encyclopedia.* 8 vols. New York: Macmillan, 1991, 3.731–32.

———. "Dayr Anba Shinudah: History." In Aziz S. Atiya, ed., *The Coptic Encyclopedia.* 8 vols. New York: Macmillan, 1991, 3.761–66.

Crook, J. A. *Legal Advocacy in the Roman World.* Ithaca, N.Y.: Cornell University Press, 1995.

Crum, Walter E. "Coptic Anecdota." *JTS* 44 (1943) 176–82.

———. *A Coptic Dictionary.* Oxford: Clarendon Press, 1939.

———. "Inscriptions from Shenoute's Monastery." *JTS* 5 (1904) 552–69.

———. *Der Papyruscodex saec. VI–VII der Phillippsbibliothek in Cheltenham: Koptische theologische Schriften.* Strasbourg: Trübner, 1915.

———. *Varia Coptica: Texts, Translations, Indexes.* Aberdeen: University Press, 1939.

Debono, Fernand. "La basilique et le monastère de St. Pacôme (Fouilles de l'Institut Pontifical d'Archéologie Chrétienne, a Faou-el-Qibli, Haute-Égypte, Janvier 1968)." *BIFAO* 70 (1971) 191–220.

Dechow, Jon F. *Dogma and Mysticism in Early Christianity: Epiphanius of Cyprus and the Legacy of Origen.* NAPSMS 13. Macon, Ga.: Mercer University Press, 1988.

———. "The Nag Hammadi Milieu: An Assessment in the Light of the Origenist Controversies." Paper delivered at the 1982 annual meeting of the Western Region of the American Academy of Religion.

Doresse, Jean. *The Secret Books of the Egyptian Gnostics: An Introduction to the Gnostic Coptic Manuscripts Discovered at Chenoboskeia.* Translated by Philip Mairet. New York: Viking Press, 1960.

Dörries, Hermann. "Die Vita Antonii als Geschichtsquelle." NAWG 14. Göttingen: Vandenhoeck & Ruprecht, 1949, 357–410; reprinted in idem, *Wort und Stunde: Gesammelte Studien zur Kirchengeschichte des vierten Jahrhunderts.* 3 vols. Göttingen: Vandenhoeck & Ruprecht, 1966, 1.145–224.

Eliade, Mircea. "The Quest for the 'Origins' of Religion." *HR* 4 (1964) 154–69. Reprinted in idem, *The Quest: History and Meaning in Religion.* Chicago and London: University of Chicago Press, 1969, 37–53.

Elm, Susanna. "The Organization and Institutions of Female Asceticism in Fourth-Century Cappadocia and Egypt." Ph.D. diss., Oxford University, 1986.

——. *Virgins of God: The Making of Asceticism in Late Antiquity.* OCM. Oxford: Clarendon Press, 1994.

Emmett, Alanna. "An Early Fourth-Century Female Monastic Community in Egypt?" In Ann Moffitt, ed., *Maistor: Classical, Byzantine, and Renaissance Studies for Robert Brown.* ByzA 5. Canberra: The Australian Association for Byzantine Studies, 1984, 77–83.

——. "Female Ascetics in the Greek Papyri." In Wolfram Hörander et al., eds., *XVI Internationaler Byzantinistenkongress Wien, 4.-9. Oktober 1981.* JÖB 23, 2. Wien: Der österreichischen Akademie der Wissenschaften, 1982, 507–15.

——. "The Nuns and the Ostrich Egg." Lecture.

Evans, J. A. S. *A Social and Economic History of an Egyptian Temple in the Greco-Roman Period.* YCS 17. New Haven: Yale University Press, 1961.

Evetts, B., ed. *History of the Patriarchs of the Coptic Church of Alexandria.* Vol. 2: *Peter I to Benjamin I (661).* PO 1, 4. Paris: Didot, 1948.

Evetts, B. T. A. *The Churches and Monasteries of Egypt and Some Neighboring Countries Attributed to Abu Salih, the Armenian.* Oxford: Clarendon Press, 1895.

Festugière, A.-J. *Historia Monachorum in Aegypto.* SH 53. Brussels: Société des Bollandistes, 1961.

——. *Les moines d'orient.* Tome IV/2. *La première vie grecque de saint Pachôme.* Paris: Éditions du Cerf, 1965.

Forget, I. *Synaxarion Alexandrinum.* CSCO 47–49, 67, 78, 90. Louvain: Durbecq, 1953–54.

Frank, K. Suso. *ΑΓΓΕΛΙΚΟΣ ΒΙΟΣ: Begriffsanalytische und begriffsgeschichtliche Untersuchung zum "Engelgleichen Leben" im frühen Mönchtum.* BGAMB 26. Münster: Aschendorff, 1964.

Frazer, Ruth F. "The Morphology of Desert Wisdom in the *Apophthegmata Patrum.*" Ph.D. diss., University of Chicago, 1977.

Frend, W. H. C. *The Rise of Christianity.* Philadelphia: Fortress Press, 1984.

——. *The Rise of the Monophysite Movement: Chapters in the History of the Church in the Fifth and Sixth Centuries.* Cambridge: Cambridge University Press, 1972.

Gardner, Iain. "The Manichaean Community at Kellis: Directions and Possibilities for Research." Paper presented at the Dakhleh Oasis Project Conference, University of Durham, 1994.

——. "The Manichaean Community at Kellis: Progress Report." *Manichaean Studies Newsletter* (1993) 18–26.

——. "A Manichaean Liturgical Codex Found at Kellis." *Or* 62 (1993) 30–59.

——. "Personal Letters from the Manichaean Community at Kellis." Paper presented at the Third International Conference of Manichaean Studies, Calabria, Italy, September 1993.

Gauthier, Henri. "Notes géographiques sur le nome Panopolite." *BIFAO* 4 (1904) 39–101.

———. "Nouvelles notes géographiques sur le nome Panopolite." *BIFAO* 10 (1912) 89–130.

Ghedini, Giuseppi. "Luci nuove dai papiri sullo scisma meleziano e il monachismo in Egitto." *La Scuola Cattolica* 53 (1925) 261–80.

———. Review of *Jews and Christians in Egypt*, by H. Idris Bell. *Aeg* 6 (1925) 273–77.

Gindele, Corbinian. "Die Schriftlesung im Pachomiuskloster." *EA* 41 (1965) 114–22.

Goehring, James E. "Byzantine Coins from the Jabal al-Tarif in Upper Egypt." *BSAC* 26 (1984) 31–41.

———. "A Byzantine Hoard from Upper Egypt." *NFAQJ* 26 (1983) 9–10.

———. "Chalcedonian Power Politics and the Demise of Pachomian Monasticism." OP 15. Claremont, Calif.: Institute for Antiquity and Christianity, 1989. Appears as chapter 12 in the present volume.

———. "The Encroaching Desert: Literary Production and Ascetic Space in Early Christian Egypt." *JECS* 1 (1993) 281–96. Appears as chapter 4 in the present volume.

———. "The Letter of Ammon and Pachomian Monasticism." Ph.D. diss., Claremont Graduate School, 1981.

———. *The Letter of Ammon and Pachomian Monasticism.* PTS 27. Berlin: Walter de Gruyter, 1986.

———. "Melitian Monastic Organization: A Challenge to Pachomian Originality." In Elizabeth A. Livingstone, ed., *Papers Presented at the Eleventh International Conference on Patristic Studies Held in Oxford 1991: Biblica et Apocrypha, Orientalia, Ascetica.* Leuven: Peeters Press, 1993.=*SP* 25 (1993) 388–95. Appears as chapter 9 in the present volume.

———. "Monastic Diversity and Ideological Bundaries in Fourth-Century Christian Egypt." *JECS* 5 (1997) 61–84. Appears as chapter 10 in the present volume.

———. "New Frontiers in Pachomian Studies." In Birger A. Pearson and James E. Goehring, eds., *The Roots of Egyptian Christianity.* SAC. Philadelphia: Fortress Press, 1986, 236–57. Appears as chapter 8 in the present volume.

———. "The Origins of Monasticism." In Harold W. Attridge and Gohei Hata, eds., *Eusebius, Christianity, and Judaism.* Detroit: Wayne State University Press, 1992, 235–55. Appears as chapter 1 in the present volume.

———. "Pachomius' Vision of Heresy: The Development of a Pachomian Tradition." *Mus* 95 (1982) 241–62. Appears as chapter 7 in the present volume.

———. "Theodore's Entry into the Pachomian Movement (Selections from the *Life of Pachomius*)." In Vincent L. Wimbush, ed., *Ascetic Behavior in Greco-Roman Antiquity: A Sourcebook.* SAC. Minneapolis: Fortress Press, 1990, 349–56.

———. "Through a Glass Darkly: Diverse Images of the *Apotaktikoi(ai)* of Early Egyptian Monasticism." In Vincent L. Wimbush, ed., *Discursive Formations, Ascetic Piety, and the Interpretation of Early Christian Literature.* Pt. 2. *Semeia* 58 (1992) 25–45. Appears as chapter 3 in the present volume.

———. "Two New Examples of the Byzantine 'Eagle' Countermark." *NumC,* ser. 7, 23 (1983) 218–20.

———. "Withdrawing from the Desert: Pachomius and the Development of Village Monasticism in Upper Egypt." *HTR* 89 (1996) 267–85. Appears as chapter 5 in the present volume.

———. "The World Engaged: The Social and Economic World of Early Egyptian Monasticism." In James E. Goehring et al., eds., *Gnosticism and the Early Christian World: In Honor of James M. Robinson.* Sonoma, Calif.: Polebridge Press, 1990, 134–44. Appears as chapter 2 in the present volume.

Gould, Graham. *The Desert Fathers on Monastic Community.* OECS. Oxford: Clarendon Press, 1933.

———. "Recent Work on Monastic Origins: A Consideration of the Questions Raised by Samuel Rubenson's *The Letters of Antony.*" *SP* 25 (1993) 405–16.

Grant, Robert M. *Eusebius as Church Historian.* Oxford: Clarendon Press, 1980.

Gregg, Robert C. *Athanasius: The Life of Antony and the Letter to Marcellinus.* CWS. New York: Paulist Press, 1980.

Gregg, Robert C., and Dennis E. Groh. *Early Arianism: A View of Salvation.* Philadelphia: Fortress Press, 1981.

Gribomont, J., ed. *Commandements du Seigneur et libération évangelique: Études monastiques proposées et discutés à St. Anselme, 15–17 Février 1976.* StAns 70. Rome: Herder, 1977.

Grossmann, Peter. "The Basilica of St. Pachomius." *BA* 42 (1979) 232–36.

———. "Pbow: Archeology." In Aziz S. Atiya, ed., *The Coptic Encyclopedia.* 8 vols. New York: Macmillan, 1991, 6.1927–29.

———. "Report on the Excavation in Faw-Qibli-Season 1986." *Newsletter* (International Association of Coptic Studies) 20 (1987) 5–8.

———. "Die Unterkunftsbauten des Koinobitenklosters 'Dair al-Balayza' im Vergleich mit dem Eremitagen der Mönche von Kellia." In *Le site monastique copte des Kellia: Sources historiques et explorations archéologiques. Actes du Colloque de Genève, 13 au 15 août 1984.* Geneva: Mission suisse d'archéologie copte de l'Université de Genève, 1986, 33–39.

Grossmann, Peter, and Gary Lease. "Faw Qibli: 1989 Excavation Report." *GöM* 114 (1990) 9–12, and figs. 1–6.

Guillaumont, Antoine. "La conception du désert chez les moines d'Égyptes." *RHR* 188 (1975) 3–21; reprinted in idem, *Aux origines du monachisme chrétien: Pour une phénoménologie du monachisme.* SpO 30. Bégrolles en Mauges, France: Abbaye de Bellefontaine, 1979, 69–87.

———. "Hieracas of Leontopolis." In Aziz S. Atiya, ed., *The Coptic Encyclopedia.* 8 vols. New York: Macmillan, 1991, 4.1228–29.

————. *Les "Kephalaia Gnostica" d'Evagre le Pontique et l'histoire de l'Origénisme chez les Grecs et chez les Syriens*. PatrS 5. Paris: Editions du Seuil, 1962.

Guy, Jean-Claude. *Recherches sur la tradition grecque des Apophthegmata Patrum*. SH 36. Brussels: Société des Bollandistes, 1962; 2e Édition avec des compléments, Brussels: Société des Bollandistes, 1984.

Hagedorn, Dieter. "Sklavenfreilassung." In Bärbel Kramer et al., eds., *Kölner Papyri (P. Köln)*. PCol 7. Opladen: Westdeutscher Verlag, 1980.

Halkin, François. *Le corpus athénien de saint Pachôme*. COr 2. Geneva: Patrick Cramer, 1982.

————. Review of *La liturgie dans le cénobitisme pachômien*, by Armand Veilleux. *AB* 88 (1970) 337.

————. *Sancti Pachomii Vitae Graecae*. SH 19. Brussels: Société des Bollandistes, 1932.

————. "Une vie inédite de saint Pachôme: BHG 1401a." *AB* 97 (1979) 5–55, 241–87.

Hardy, Edward Rochie. *Christian Egypt: Church and People, Christianity and Nationalism in the Patriarchate of Alexandria*. New York: Oxford University Press, 1952.

Harnack, Adolf. "Hierakas und die Hierakiten." *RE* 8 (1900) 38–39.

Harpham, Geoffrey Galt. *The Ascetic Imperative in Culture and Criticism*. Chicago: University of Chicago Press, 1987.

————. "Old Water in New Bottles: The Contemporary Prospects for the Study of Asceticism." In Vincent L. Wimbush, ed., *Discursive Formations, Ascetic Piety, and the Interpretation of Early Christian Literature*. Pt. 2. *Semeia* 58 (1992) 135–48.

Harvey, Susan Ashbrook. *Asceticism and Society in Crisis: John of Ephesus and the "Lives of the Eastern Saints."* TCH 18. Berkeley: University of California Press, 1990.

————. "The Sense of a Stylite: Perspectives on Simeon the Elder." *VC* 42 (1988) 376–94.

Haslam, M. W. "3203. Lease of Exedra and Cellar." In A. K. Bowman et al., eds., *The Oxyrhynchus Papyri*. Vol. 44. London: Egypt Exploration Society, 1976, 182–84.

Hauben, Hans. "On the Melitians in *P. London* VI (*P. Jews*) 1914: The Problem of Papas Heraiscus." In Roger S. Bagnall et al., eds., *Proceedings of the Sixteenth International Congress of Papyrology. New York, 24–31 July 1980*. AmSP 23. Chico, Calif.: Scholars Press, 1981, 447–56.

Hedrick, Charles W. "Gnostic Proclivities in the Greek *Life of Pachomius* and the *Sitz im Leben* of the Nag Hammadi Library." *NovT* 22 (1980) 78–94.

Hengstenberg, Wilhelm. "Bemerkungen zur Entwicklungsgeschichte des ägyptischen Mönchtums." *BIAB* 9 (1935) 355–62=*Actes du IVe congrès international des études byzantines*. Ed. Bogdan D. Filou. Sofia: Imprimerie de la Cour, 1935, 355–62.

————. "Pachomiana mit einem Anhang über die Liturgie von Alexandrien." In A. M. Koeniger, ed., *Beiträge zur Geschichte des christlichen Altertums und der byzantinischen Literatur: Festgabe Albert Ehrhard*. Bonn: Kurt Schroeder Verlag, 1922, 228–52.

———. Review of *Jews and Christians in Egypt*, by H. Idris Bell. *ByzZ* 27 (1927) 138–45.

Heussi, Karl. *Der Ursprung des Mönchtums*. Tübingen: J. C. B. Mohr, 1936. Reprint, Aalen: Scientia, 1981.

Hobson, Deborah. "Agricultural Land and Economic Life in Soknopaiou Nesos." *BASP* 21 (1984) 89–109.

———. "House and Household in Roman Egypt." In Naphtali Lewis, ed., *Papyrology*. YCS 28. Cambridge and New York: Cambridge University Press, 1985, 211–29.

Holl, Karl. "Die Bedeutung der neuveröffentlichten melitianischen Urkunden für die Kirchengeschichte." SPAW (1925) 18–31.

———. *Enthusiasmus und Bussgewalt beim griechischen Mönchtum: Eine Studie zu Symeon dem neuen Theologen*. Leipzig: Hinrichs, 1898. Reprint, Hildesheim: Olms, 1969.

———. *Epiphanius (Anachoretus und Panarion)*. GCS. Leipzig: J. C. Hinrichs, 1915.

Holl, Karl, and Jürgen Dummer, eds. *Epiphanius II: Panarion haer. 34–64*. 2d rev. ed. GCS. Berlin: Akademie Verlag, 1980.

———. *Epiphanius III: Panarion haer. 65–80, de fide*. 2d rev. ed. GCS. Berlin: Akademie Verlag, 1985.

Hope, Colin A., et al. "Dakhleh Oasis Project: Ismant el-Kharab, 1991–92." *JSSEA* 19 (1989) 1–26.

Horn, Jürgen. "Tria sunt in Aegypto genera monachorum: Die ägyptischen Bezeichnungen für die 'dritte Art' des Mönchtums bei Hieronymus und Johannes Cassianus." In Heike Behlmer, ed., *Festgabe für Wolfhart Westendorf zu seinem 70. Geburtstag*. Göttingen: Seminar für Ägyptologie und Koptologie, 1994, 63–82.

Joest, Christoph. "Ein Versuch zur Chronologie Pachoms und Theodoros." *ZNW* 85 (1994) 132–44.

Johnson, Allan Chester. *Roman Egypt to the Reign of Diocletian*. Vol. 2 of Tenney Frank, ed., *An Economic Survey of Ancient Rome*. Paterson, N.J.: Pageant Books, 1959.

Johnson, David W. "Anti-Chalcedonian Polemics in Fifth- to Seventh-Century Coptic Texts." In Birger A. Pearson and James E. Goehring, eds., *The Roots of Egyptian Christianity*. SAC. Philadelphia: Fortress Press, 1986, 216–34.

Judge, E. A. "The Earliest Use of Monachos for 'Monk' (*P. Coll. Youtie* 77) and the Origins of Monasticism." *JAC* 10 (1977) 72–89.

———. "Fourth-Century Monasticism in the Papyri." In Roger S. Bagnall et al., eds., *Proceedings of the Sixteenth International Congress of Papyrology, New York, 24–31 July 1990*. AmSP 23. Chico, Calif.: Scholars Press, 1981, 613–20.

Judge, E. A., and S. R. Pickering. "Papyrus Documentation of Church and Community in Egypt to the Mid–Fourth Century." *JAC* 20 (1977) 47–71.

Jullien, Michel. "A la recherche de Tabenne et des autres monastères fondés par saint Pachôme." *Études* 89 (1901) 238–58.

———. "Quelques anciens couvents de l'Égypt." *MisCath* 35 (1903) 283–84.

Kahle, Paul E. *Bala'izah: Coptic Texts from Deir el-Bala'izah in Upper Egypt.* 2 vols. London: Oxford University Press, 1954.

Kannengiesser, Charles. "St. Athanasius of Alexandria Rediscovered: His Political and Pastoral Achievement." *CCR* 9 (1988) 68–74.

Kasser, Rodolphe. *Le site monastique des Kellia (Basse-Égypte): Recherches des années 1981–83.* Mission suisse d'archéologie copte de l'Université de Genève. Louvain: Peeters, 1984.

Kees, Hermann. "Leontopolis." *PW* 13.2053–57

Koenen, Ludwig. "Manichäische Mission und Klöster in Ägypten." In Günter Grimm et al., eds., *Das römisch-byzantinische Ägypten: Acten des internationalen Symposions, 26.-30. September 1978 in Trier.* AegT 2. Mainz: Philipp von Zabern, 1983, 93–108.

Kraemer, Casper J., and Naphtali Lewis. "A Referee's Hearing on Ownership." *TAPA* 68 (1937) 357–87.

Kraft, Robert A., and Janet A. Timbie. Review of *The Nag Hammadi Library in English*, by James M. Robinson. *RSR* 8 (1982) 32–52.

Kramer, Bärbel, and John C. Shelton. *Das Archiv des Nepheros und verwandte Texte.* AegT 4. Mainz: Philipp von Zabern, 1987.

Krause, Martin. "Das Apa-Apollon-Kloster zu Bawit: Untersuchungen unveröffentlichter Urkunden als Beitrag zur Geschichte des ägyptischen Mönchtums." Ph.D. diss., Karl-Marx-Universität, 1958.

———. "Bawit." In Klaus Wessel, ed., *Reallexikon zur byzantinischen Kunst.* Vol. 1. Stuttgart: Hiersemann, 1966, 568–83.

———. "Der Erlassbrief Theodors." In Dwight W. Young, ed., *Studies Presented to Hans Jacob Polotsky.* East Gloucester, Mass.: Pirtle & Polson, 1981, 220–38.

———. "Zur Möglichkeit von Besitz im apotaktischen Mönchtums Ägyptens." In Tito Orlandi and Frederik Wisse, eds., *Acts of the Second International Congress of Coptic Studies, Rome, 22–26 September 1980.* Rome: CIM, 1985, 121–33.

Krüger, Julien. *Oxyrhynchus in der Kaizerzeit: Studien zur Topographie und Literaturrezeption.* EH 441. Frankfurt: Peter Lang, 1990.

Kuhn, K. H. *A Panegyric on Apollo Archimandrite of the Monastery of Isaac, by Stephen Bishop of Heracleopolis Magna.* CSCO 394 (text) and 395 (trans.). Louvain: Secrétariat du CSCO, 1978.

Lake, Kirsopp, J. E. L. Oulton, and H. J. Lawlor. *Eusebius: The Ecclesiastical History.* 2 vols. LCL. Cambridge: Harvard University Press, 1926–32.

Lambert, A. "Apotactites et Apotaxamènes." In R. P. dom Fernand Cabrol, ed., *Dictionnaire d'archéologie chrétienne et de liturgie.* Vol. 1. Paris: Letouzey et Ané, 1907, cols. 2604–26.

Lampe, G. W. H. *A Patristic Greek Lexicon.* Oxford: Clarendon Press, 1961.

Lassus, Jean. *Sanctuaires chrétiens de Syrie: Essai sur la genèse, la form et l'usage liturgie des édifices du culte chrétien en Syrie, du IIIe siècle à la conquête musulmane.* Paris: Geuthner, 1947.

Lease, Gary. "The Fourth Season of the Nag Hammadi Excavation, 21 December 1979–15 January 1980." *GöM* 41 (1980) 75–85.

———. "Traces of Early Egyptian Monasticism: The Faw Qibli Excavations." OP 22. Claremont, Calif.: Institute for Antiquity and Christianity, 1991.

Lebon, J. "Athanasiana Syriaca II: Une lettre attribuée à saint Athanase d'Alexandrie." *Mus* 41 (1928) 169–216.

Lefort, L. Th. *Oeuvres de S. Pachôme et de ses disciples.* CSCO 159 (text) and 160 (trans). Louvain: L. Durbecq, 1956.

———. "Les premiers monastères pachômiens: Exploration topographique." *Mus* 52 (1939) 379–407.

———. "La règle de S. Pachôme (étude d'approche)." *Mus* 34 (1921) 61–70.

———. "S. Athanase écrivain copte." *Mus* 46 (1933) 1–33.

———. *S. Athanase: Lettres festales et pastorales en copte.* CSCO 150–51. Louvain: L. Dubercq, 1955.

———. *S. Pachomii vita bohairice scripta.* CSCO 89. Paris: E typographeo reipublicae, 1925. Reprint, Louvain: Secrétariat du CSCO, 1965.

———. *S. Pachomii vitae sahidice scriptae.* CSCO 99/100. Paris: E typographeo reipublicae, 1933. Reprint, Louvain: Secrétariat du CSCO, 1965.

———. "Les sources coptes pachômiennes." *Mus* 67 (1954) 217–29.

———. "Un texte original de la Règle de saint Pachôme." *CRAI* (1919) 341–48.

———. *Les vies coptes de saint Pachôme et de ses premiers successeurs.* BMus 16. Louvain: Bureaux du Muséon, 1943.

Leipoldt, Johannes. *Schenute von Atripe und die Entstehung des national ägyptischen Christentums.* Leipzig: Hinrichs, 1933.

———. *Sinuthii vita bohairice.* CSCO 41. Paris: E typographeo reipublicae, 1906.

Lesko, Leonard. "Monasticism in Egypt." In Florence D. Friedman, ed., *Beyond the Pharaohs: Egypt and the Copts in the 2nd to 7th Centuries A.D.* Providence, R.I.: Museum of Art, Rhode Island School of Design, 1989, 45–47.

Lewis, Naphtali. *Life in Egypt under Roman Rule.* Oxford: Clarendon Press, 1983.

Lucius, Ernst. *Die Therapeuten und ihre Stellung in der Geschichte der Askese: Eine kritische Untersuchung der Schrift "De vita contemplativa."* Strasbourg: Schmidt, 1879.

MacCoull, Leslie S. B. "A Coptic Session of Land by Dioscorus of Aphrodito: Alexandria Meets Cairo." In Tito Orlandi and Frederik Wisse, eds., *Acts of the Second International Congress of Coptic Studies, Rome, 22–26 September 1980.* Rome: CIM, 1985, 159–66.

———. *Dioscorus of Aphrodito: His Works and His World.* TCH 16. Berkeley: University of California Press, 1988.

Maraval, Pierre. *Égérie: Journal de voyage (Itinéraire).* SC 296. Paris: Éditions du Cerf, 1982.

Massignon, M. Louis. "Seconde note sur l'état d'avancement des études archéologiques arabes en Égypte, hors du Caire." *BIFAO* 9 (1911) 84–98.

Mauser, Ulrich. *Christ in the Wilderness: The Wilderness Theme in the Second Gospel and Its Basis in the Biblical Tradition.* SBT 39. Chatham, Great Britain: W. & J. Mackay, 1963.

McGing, Brian C. "Melitian Monks at Labla." *Tyche* 5 (1990) 67–94.

Meinardus, Otto. "Dayr Anba Antuniyus: History." In Aziz S. Atiya, *The Coptic Encyclopedia.* 8 vols. New York: Macmillan, 1991, 3.719–21.

Meyer, Marvin W. "Wadi Sheikh Ali Survey." *NARCE* 117 (1982) 22–24, and *GöM* 64 (1983) 77–82.

Meyer, Marvin W., and H. Keith Beebe. "Literary and Archeological Survey of Al-Qasr." *NARCE* 121 (1983) 25–29.

Meyer, Robert T. *Palladius: The Lausiac History.* ACW. New York: Newman Press, 1964.

———. *St. Athanasius: The Life of Saint Antony.* ACW. New York: Newman, 1950.

Mission suisse d'archéologie copte de l'Université de Genève sous la direction de Rodolphe Kasser, *Le site monastique des Kellia (Basse-Égypte): Recherches des années 1981–83.* Louvain: Peeters, 1984.

Murray, R. "The Characteristics of Earliest Syriac Christianity." In N. Garsoian, T. Mathews, and R. Thomson, eds., *East of Byzantium: Syria and Armenia in the Formative Period.* Washington, D.C.: Dumbarton Oaks, 1982, 3–16.

O'Dea, Thomas F. *The Sociology of Religion.* Englewood Cliffs, N.J.: Prentice-Hall, 1966.

O'Neil, Edward N. "The Chreia and History." Paper delivered at the 1981 annual meeting of the Society of Biblical Literature in San Francisco.

Orlandi, Tito. "A Catechesis against Apocryphal Texts by Shenute and the Gnostic Texts of Nag Hammadi." *HTR* 75 (1982) 85–95.

———. "Commento letterario." Chap. 6 in Orlandi et al., "Pachomiana Coptica," manuscript.

———. "Coptic Literature." In Birger A. Pearson and James E. Goehring, eds., *The Roots of Egyptian Christianity.* SAC. Philadelphia: Fortress Press, 1986.

———. "Nuovi Testi copti pachomiani." In J. Gribomont, ed., *Commandements du Seigneur et libération évangelique: Études monastiques proposées et discutés à St. Anselme, 15–17 Février 1976.* StAns 70. Rome: Herder, 1977, 241–43.

———. *Shenute contra origenistas.* Rome: C.I.M., 1985.

———. *Storia della Chiesa di Alessandria.* 2 vols. TDSA 17 and 31. Milan: Cisalpino, 1968–70.

Parrott, Douglas M. "The Nag Hammadi Library and the Pachomian Monasteries." Paper delivered at the 1978 International Conference on Gnosticism at Yale University.

Parsons, Talcott. *The Structure of Social Action.* New York: McGraw-Hill, 1937.

Pearson, Birger A. "Earliest Christianity in Egypt: Some Observations." In Birger A. Pearson and James E. Goehring, eds., *The Roots of Egyptian Christianity.* SAC. Philadelphia: Fortress Press, 1986, 132–59.

———. "The Figure of Melchizedek in Gnostic Literature." In Birger A. Pearson, ed., *Gnosticism, Judaism, and Egyptian Christianity.* SAC. Minneapolis: Fortress Press, 1990, 108–23.

Pearson, Birger A., and James E. Goehring, eds. *The Roots of Egyptian Christianity*. SAC. Philadelphia: Fortress Press, 1986.

Peeters, Paul. "Le dossier copte de S. Pachôme et ses rapports avec la tradition grecque." *AB* 64 (1946) 258–77.

Pelikan, Jaroslav. *Jesus through the Centuries: His Place in the History of Culture.* New Haven and London: Yale University Press, 1985.

Perry, Ben Edwin, ed. *Babrius and Phaedrus.* LCL. Cambridge: Harvard University Press, 1975.

Pokorny, Petr. "Strategies of Social Formation in the Gospel of Luke." In James E. Goehring et al., eds., *Gospel Origins and Christian Beginnings: In Honor of James M. Robinson.* Sonoma, Calif.: Polebridge Press, 1990, 106–18.

Preuschen, Erwin. *Palladius und Rufinus: Ein Beitrag zur Quellenkunde des ältesten Mönchtums.* Giessen: J. Rickershe Buchhandlung, 1897.

Price, R. M. *A History of the Monks of Syria by Theodoret of Cyrrhus.* CistStud 88. Kalamazoo, Mich.: Cistercian Publications, 1985.

Quecke, Hans. "Ein Brief von einem Nachfolger Pachoms (Chester Beatty Library Ms. Ac. 1486)." *Or* 44 (1975) 426–33.

———. *Die Briefe Pachoms: Griechischer Text der Handschrift W. 145 der Chester Beatty Library.* TPL 11. Regensburg: Pustet, 1975.

———. "Briefe Pachoms in koptischer Sprache: Neue deutsche Übersetzung." In *Zetesis Album amicorum: Aangeboden aan Dr. E. de Strycker.* Antwerp: De Nederlandische Boekhandel, 1973, 655–63.

———. "Eine Handvoll pachomianischer Texte." *ZDMG*, Supp. 3, 1 (1977) 221–29.

———. "Ein neues Fragment der Pachombriefe in koptischer Sprache." *Or* 43 (1974) 66–79.

———. "Ein Pachomiuszitat bei Schenute." In Peter Nagel, ed., *Probleme der koptischen Literatur.* Halle-Wittenberg: Martin Luther Universität, 1968, 155–71.

Rapp, Claudia. "Epiphanius of Salamis: The Church Father as Saint." In *"The Sweet Land of Cyprus": Papers Given at the Twenty-fifth Jubilee Spring Symposium of Byzantine Studies, Birmingham, England, March 1991.* Birmingham, England: University of Birmingham; Nicosia: Cyprus Research Centre, 1993, 169–87.

———. "Der heilige Epiphanius im Kampf mit dem Dämon des Origenes: Kritische Erstausgabe des Wunders BHG 601i." In Frederike Berger et al., eds., *Symbolae Berlinensis für Dieter Harlfinger.* Amsterdam: Adolf M. Hakkert, 1993, 249–69.

———. "The *Vita* of Epiphanius of Salamis: An Historical and Literary Study." D.Phil. diss., Worcester College, 1991.

Rea, J. R. *The Oxyrhynchus Papyri.* Vol. 46. London: Egypt Exploration Society, 1978.

Regnault, Lucien. *Les sentences des pères du désert: Collection alphabétique.* Sablé-sur-Sarthe: Abbaye Saint-Pierre de Solesmes, 1981.

———. *Les sentences des pères du désert: Troisième recueil & tables.* Sablé-sur-Sarthe: Abbaye Saint-Pierre de Solesmes, 1976.

———. "Sisoes." In Aziz S. Atiya, ed., *The Coptic Encyclopedia*. 8 vols. New York: Macmillan, 1991, 7.2141.

Rémondon, Roger. "Le monastère alexandrin de la metanoia était-il beneficiaire du fisc ou à son service?" In *Studi in Onore de Edoardo Volterra*. Milan: Giuffre, 1971, 5.769–81.

Robinson, James M. "The Discovery of the Nag Hammadi Codices." *BA* 42 (1979) 206–24.

———. "From the Cliffs to Cairo: The Story of the Discoverers and Middlemen of the Nag Hammadi Codices." In Bernard Barc, ed., *Colloque international sur les textes de Nag Hammadi (Québec, 22–25 août 1978)*. BCNH 1. Québec: L'Université Laval, 1981, 21–59.

———. "Introduction." In James M. Robinson, ed., *The Nag Hammadi Library in English*. New York: Harper & Row, 1977, 1–25.

———. "Introduction." In William Brashear et al., eds., *Chester Beatty Library Acc. 1390: Mathematical School Exercises in Greek and John 10:17–13:38 in Subachmimic*. Chester Beatty Monographs 13. Leuven and Paris: Peeters, 1990, 3–32.

———. "The Pachomian Monastic Library at the Chester Beatty Library and the Bibliothèque Bodmer." OP 19. Claremont, Calif.: Institute for Antiquity and Christianity, 1990.

———. "Reconstructing the First Christian Monastic Library." Paper presented at the Smithsonian Institution Libraries, Washington, D.C., September 15, 1986.

———. "The Story of the Bodmer Papyri: The First Christian Monastery Library." Manuscript.

———., ed. *The Nag Hammadi Library in English*. San Francisco: Harper & Row, 1977; 2d ed., 1981; 3d ed., 1988.

Robinson, James M., and Bastiaan van Elderen. "The First Season of the Nag Hammadi Excavation, 27 November–19 December 1975." *NARCE* 96 (1976) 18–24, and *GöM* 22 (1976) 71–79.

———. "The Second Season of the Nag Hammadi Excavation, 22 November–29 December 1976." *NARCE* 99/100 (1977) 36–54, and *GöM* 24 (1977) 57–71.

Rostovtzeff, M. *The Social and Economic History of the Roman Empire*. 2d. ed. Oxford: Clarendon Press, 1957.

Rothenhaeusler, M., and P. Oppenheim. "Apotaxis." *RAC* 1 (1950) 558–64.

Rousseau, Philip. *Ascetics, Authority, and the Church in the Age of Jerome and Cassian*. Oxford: Oxford University Press, 1978.

———. *Pachomius: The Making of a Community in Fourth-Century Egypt*. TCH 6. Berkeley: University of California Press, 1985.

Rubenson, Samuel. *The Letters of St. Antony: Origenist Theology, Monastic Tradition, and the Making of a Saint*. BHEL 24. Lund: Lund University Press, 1990. Reprinted with an English translation of the *Letters of Antony* as *The Letters of St. Antony: Monasticism and the Making of a Saint*. SAC. Minneapolis: Fortress Press, 1995.

Ruppert, Fidelis. *Das pachomianische Mönchtum und die Anfänge klösterlichen Gehorsams*. MünSt 20. Münsterschwarzach: Vier-Türme, 1971.

Russell, Norman, and Benedicta Ward. *The Lives of the Desert Fathers: Historia monachorum in Aegypto.* London and Oxford: Mowbray; Kalamazoo, Mich.: Cistercian Publications, 1981.

Säve-Söderbergh, Torgny. "Holy Scriptures or Apologetic Documentations? The 'Sitz im Leben' of the Nag Hammadi Library." In Jacques-E. Ménard, ed., *Les Textes de Nag Hammadi.* NHS 7. Leiden: E. J. Brill, 1975, 3–14.

———. *The Old Kingdom Cemetery at Hamra Dom (El-Qasr wa es Saiyad).* Stockholm: Royal Academy of Letters, History and Antiquities, 1994.

Sayce, A. H. "Deux contrats grecs du fayoum." *REG* 3 (1890) 131–44.

Scalinger, Joseph Juste. *De emendatione temporum.* Francofurti: I. Wechelum, 1593.

Schiller, A. Arthur. *Ten Coptic Legal Texts.* New York: Metropolitan Museum of Art, 1932.

Schiwietz, Stephan. *Das morganländische Mönchtum.* 3 vols. Mainz: Kirchheim, 1904–39.

Scholten, Clemens. "Die Nag-Hammadi-Texte als Buchbesitz der Pachomianer." *JAC* 31 (1988) 144–72.

Schubart, Wilhelm. Review of *Jews and Christians in Egypt,* by H. Idris Bell. *Gnomon* 1 (1925) 23–37.

Schulz-Flügel, Eva. *Tyrannius Rufinus: Historia Monachorum sive De Vita Sanctorum Patrum.* PTS 34. Berlin and New York: Walter de Gruyter, 1990.

Shaw, Teresa M. *The Burden of the Flesh: Fasting and Sexuality in Early Christianity.* Minneapolis: Fortress Press, 1998.

Shelton, J. C. "Introduction." In J. W. B. Barns, G. W. Browne, and J. C. Shelton, eds., *Nag Hammadi Codices: Greek and Coptic Papyri from the Cartonnage of the Covers.* NHS 16. Leiden: E. J. Brill, 1981, 1–11.

Sheridan, Mark. "Review of Bunge and de Vogüé." *ColCist* 57 (1995) 548–52.

Smith, R. Payne. *Thesaurus Syriacus.* Oxford: Clarendon Press, 1901.

Spanel, Donald. "A Toronto Sahidic Addition to the Pakhom Dossier (*Fischer A1,* ff. 1–2)." *The Ancient World* 6 (1983) 115–25.

Steidle, Basilius. "Der heilige Abt Theodor von Tabennesi: Zur 1600. Wiederkehr des Todesjahres (368–1968)." *EA* 44 (1968) 91–103.

———. "Der Osterbrief unseres Vaters Theodor an alle Klöster." *EA* 44 (1968) 104–19.

Steidle, Basilius, and Otmar Schuler. "Der 'Obern-Spiegel' im 'Testament' des Abtes Horsiesi." *EA* 43 (1967) 22–38.

Steinwenter, Artur. "Aus dem kirchlichen Vermögensrechte der Papyri." *ZSavR* 44 (1958) 1–34.

———. "Die Rechtsstellung der Kirchen und Klöster nach der Papyri." *ZSavR* 19 (1930) 1–50.

Stroumsa, Gedaliahu G. "The Manichaean Challenge to Egyptian Christianity." In Birger A. Pearson and James E. Goehring, eds., *The Roots of Egyptian Christianity.* SAC. Philadelphia: Fortress Press, 1986, 307–19.

———. "Monachisme et marranisme chez les manicheens d'Égypte." *Numen* 29 (1982) 184–201.

Tamburrino, Pius. "Koinonia: Die Beziehung 'Monasterium' — 'Kirche' im frühen pachomianischen Mönchtum." *EA* 43 (1967) 5–21.

Tchalenko, G. *Villages antiques de la Syrie du Nord: Le massif du Bélus à l'époque romaine.* 3 vols. Paris: Geuthner, 1953–59.

Tetz, Martin. "Athanasius und die Vita Antonii: Literarische und theologische Relationen." *ZNW* 73 (1982) 1–30.

Timbie, Janet Ann. "Dualism and the Concept of Orthodoxy in the Thought of the Monks of Upper Egypt." Ph.D. diss., University of Pennsylvania, 1979.

Timm, Stefan. *Das christlich-koptische Ägypten in arabischer Zeit.* Beihefte zum Tübinger Atlas des vorderen Orients. B, 41/3. Wiesbaden: Ludwig Reichert, 1985.

Torp, Hjalmar. "Le monastère copte de Baouit: Quelques notes d'introduction." In Torp et al., eds., *Acta ad archaeologiam et artium historiam pertinentia.* MC 9. Rome: Giorgio Bretschneider, 1981, 1–8.

Valantasis, Richard. *Spiritual Guides of the Third Century: A Semiotic Study of the Guide-Disciple Relationship in Christianity, Neoplatonism, Hermetism, and Gnosticism.* HDR 27. Minneapolis: Fortress Press, 1991.

van Cauwenbergh, Paul. *Étude sur les moines d'Égypte depuis le Concile de Chalcédoine (451) jusqu'à l'invasion arabe (640).* Paris: Imprimerie nationale, 1914.

van Cranenburgh, H. *La vie latine de S. Pachôme traduite du grec par Denys le Petit.* SH 46. Brussels: Société des Bollandistes, 1969.

van den Broek, R. "The Present State of Gnostic Studies." *VC* 37 (1983) 41–71.

van Elderen, Bastiaan. "The Nag Hammadi Excavation." *BA* 42 (1979) 225–31.

van Lantschoot, Arn. "Allocution de Timothée d'Alexandrie prononcée à l'occasion de la dédicace de l'église de Pachôme à Pboou." *Mus* 47 (1934) 13–56.

———. "Lettre de saint Athanase au sujet de l'amour et de la tempérance." *Mus* 40 (1927) 265–92.

van Minnen, Peter. "Deserted Villages: Two Late Antique Town Sites in Egypt." *BASP* 32 (1995) 41–55.

———. "House-to-House Enquiries: An Interdisciplinary Approach to Roman Karanis." *ZPE* 100 (1994) 227–51.

———. "The Roots of Egyptian Christianity." *APVG* 40 (1994) 71–85.

van Molle, M. M. "Confrontation entre les règles et la littérature Pachômienne postérieure." *SVS* 21 (1968) 394–424.

Veilleux, Armand. *La liturgie dans le cénobitisme pachômien au quatrième siècle.* StAns 57. Rome: Herder, 1986.

———. "Monachisme et gnose." *LTP* 40 (1984) 275–294 and 41 (1985) 3–24.

———. "Monasticism and Gnosis in Egypt." In Birger A. Pearson and James E. Goehring, eds., *The Roots of Egyptian Christianity.* SAC. Philadelphia: Fortress Press, 1986, 271–306.

———. *Pachomian Koinonia.* 3 vols. CistStud 45–47. Kalamazoo, Mich.: Cistercian Press, 1980–82.

———. "Pachomius." In Aziz S. Atiya, ed., *The Coptic Encyclopedia.* 8 vols. New York: Macmillan, 1991, 6.1859–60.

———. "Le problème des Vies de saint Pachôme." *RAM* 42 (1966) 287–305.

Vergote, Jozef. "La valeur des vies grecques et coptes de S. Pakhôme." *OLP* 8 (1977) 175–86.

Vivian, Tim. *Histories of the Monks of Upper Egypt and the Life of Onnophrius by Paphnutius.* CistStud 140. Kalamazoo, Mich.: Cistercian Publications, 1993.

———. "The Life of Onnophrius: A New Translation." *CCR* 12 (1991) 99–111.

———. *St. Peter of Alexandria: Bishop and Martyr.* SAC. Philadelphia: Fortress Press, 1988.

Vogüé, Adalbert de. "Épîtres inédites d'Horsièse et de Théodore." In J. Gribomont, ed., *Commandements du Seigneur et libération évangelique: Études monastiques proposées et discutés à St. Anselme, 15–17 Février 1976.* StAns 70. Rome: Herder, 1977, 244–57.

———. "Foreword." In Armand Veilleux, *Pachomian Koinonia.* 3 vols. CistStud 45–47. Kalamazoo, Mich.: Cistercian Press, 1980–82, 1.vii–xxiii.

———. "Saint Pachôme et son oeuvre d'après plusieurs études récentes." *RHE* 69 (1974) 425–53.

———. "La vie arabe de saint Pachôme et ses deux sources présumées." *AB* 91 (1973) 379–90.

Vööbus, A. *A History of Asceticism in the Syrian Orient: A Contribution to the History of Culture in the Near East.* 2 vols. CSCO 184, 197. Louvain: Secrétariat du CSCO, 1958–60.

Waddell, Helen. *The Desert Fathers.* Ann Arbor: University of Michigan Press, 1957.

Ward, Benedicta. *The Sayings of the Desert Fathers.* London: A. R. Mowbray; Kalamazoo, Mich.: Cistercian Publications, 1975.

Weber, Max. "The Social Psychology of the World Religions." In H. H. Gerth and C. Wright Mills, eds., *From Max Weber: Essays in Sociology.* New York and London: Oxford University Press, 1946.

———. *The Theory of Social and Economic Organization.* Translated by A. M. Henderson and Talcott Parsons. New York and London: Oxford University Press, 1947.

Weingarten, Hermann. "Der Ursprung des Mönchtums im nachconstantinischen Zeitalter." *ZKG* 1 (1877) 1–35, 545–74.

White, Hugh G. Evelyn. *The Monasteries of the Wadi 'n Natrun.* Pt. 2: *The History of the Monasteries of Nitria and of Scetis.* New York: Metropolitan Museum of Art, 1932. Reprint, New York: Arno Press, 1973.

Wilcken, Ulrich. Review of *Jews and Christians in Egypt,* by H. Idris Bell. *APVG* 7 (1924) 308–11.

Williams, Frank. *The Panarion of Epiphanius of Salamis: Book I (Sects. 1–46).* NHS 35. Leiden, New York, Copenhagen, and Cologne: E. J. Brill, 1987.

———. *The Panarion of Epiphanius of Salamis: Books II and III (Sects. 47–80, de Fide).* NHMS 35. Leiden, New York, and Cologne: E. J. Brill, 1994.

Williams, Rowan. *Arius: Heresy and Tradition.* London: Darton, Longman, & Todd, 1987.

Wimbush, Vincent L., ed. *Discursive Formations, Ascetic Piety, and the Interpretation of Early Christian Literature.* Pt. 2. Atlanta: Scholars Press, 1992=*Semeia* 58.

Winlock, H. E., and W. E. Crum. *The Monastery of Epiphanius at Thebes.* 2 vols. New York: Metropolitan Museum of Art, 1926. Reprint, New York: Arno Press, 1973.

Wipszycka, Ewa. "Le monachisme égyptien et les villes." *Travaux et mémoires* 12 (1994) 1–44. Reprinted in idem, ed., *Études sur le christianisme dans l'Égypte de l'antiquité tardive.* SEA 52. Rome: Institutum Patristicum Augustinianum, 1996, 282–336.

———. "Les terres de la congrégation pachômienne dans une liste de payments pour les apora." In J. Bingen et al., eds., *Le monde grec: Pensée, littérature, histoire, documents. Hommages à Claire Préaux.* Brussels: L'Université Bruxelles, 1975, 625–36.

Wisse, Frederik. "Gnosticism and Early Monasticism in Egypt." In Barbara Aland, ed., *Gnosis: Festschrift für Hans Jonas.* Göttingen: Vandenhoeck & Ruprecht, 1978, 431–40.

———. "Language Mysticism in the Nag Hammadi Texts and in Early Coptic Monasticism I: Cryptography." *Enchoria* 9 (1979) 101–20.

———. "The Nag Hammadi Library and the Heresiologists." *VC* 25 (1971) 205–23.

———. "Redaction and the Apocryphon of John." Paper delivered at the 1993 annual meeting of the Society of Biblical Literature in Washington, D.C.

Wright, F. A. *Select Letters of St. Jerome.* LCL. Cambridge: Harvard University Press, 1933.

Young, Dwight Wayne. *Coptic Manuscripts from the White Monastery: Works of Shenute.* MPER 22. Wien: Brüder Hollinek, 1993.

Zoega, Georg. *Catalogus codicum copticorum manuscriptorum qui in Museo Borgiano Velitris adservantur.* Rome, 1810. Reprint, Leipzig: Hinrichs, 1903.

Index